D0713177

IN SEARCH OF HUMANITY

John Macquarrie

IN SEARCH OF
HUMANITY

A Theological and Philosophical
Approach

CROSSROAD · NEW YORK

1983
The Crossroad Publishing Company
575 Lexington Avenue, New York, N.Y. 10022

© John Macquarrie 1982

Printed in the United States of America

Library of Congress Cataloging in Publication Data

Macquarrie, John.
In search of humanity.

Includes bibliographical references and index.
1. Philosophical anthropology—Addresses, essays,
lectures. 2. Man (Christian theology)—Addresses,
essays, lectures. I. Title.
BD450.M2525   1983   128   82-22077
ISBN 0-8245-0564-6

Contents

Preface

I have long believed that the best approach to many of the problems of theology and philosophy is through the study of our own humanity. This book is meant to make a small contribution to some aspects of that impossibly large but supremely important subject. No doubt one learns about humanity chiefly from meeting human beings and living oneself in the human condition. Beyond that, my treatment reflects two major influences: on the one hand, Christian theology, and on the other, a variety of philosophies, mainly continental, which from Kant to the present day have reflected on human nature and human destiny. But while I have worked mainly within this tradition, I have also tried to learn what I could from biologists, psychologists, sociologists and others.

The book has been composed over several years, and most of the chapters were given their first airing as lectures in various colleges and universities: The University of North Carolina, Charlotte; The University of Stirling (Hope Lectures); St John's College, Hong Kong (Shann Lectures); The University of Sheffield (Stephenson Lectures); The University of East Anglia (Mackintosh Lecture); Kenyon College, Ohio (Larwill Lecture); The International Christian University, Tokyo; The Yale Divinity School, New Haven (Cheney Lecture); Tulane University, New Orleans; Trinity College, Toronto; The Virginia Theological Seminary, Alexandria (Zabriskie Lectures); King's College, Halifax, NS. I wish to thank these institutions for inviting me and to acknowledge that the questions and criticisms raised by my audiences have contributed much to the finished text. I wish also to thank for their valued comments several friends, including Dr Paul Kent, Professor Eugene Long and Professor Steven Rockefeller. My many other debts are reflected in the footnotes.

Christic Church,   John Macquarrie

I

BECOMING

What is a human being? What is human nature? These are among the most difficult questions that can be asked, yet they are also among the most important. 'The proper study of mankind is man,' wrote Alexander Pope.[1] It could be argued, however, that we have been much more diligent – and much more successful – in studying the non-human environment than in studying ourselves. Self-knowledge has been rightly considered to be the most difficult knowledge of all. At the very outset, we must take note of some of the peculiar problems that attend any attempt to grapple with the problem of what it means to be a human being.

There is, first of all, an ambiguity in the very word 'human'. This ambiguity is brought out very well in an expression which runs almost like a refrain through certain writings of a former colleague of mine, the ethicist Paul Lehmann.[2] The expression is: 'Making and keeping human life human.' This expression is not meant to be a mere tautology, though it is somewhat rhetorical in form. It is not an empty form of words, such as 'making and keeping feline life feline' would presumably be. But the expression can be given sense and rescued from mere rhetoric only if a serious attempt is made to explore the meaning of 'human' in both of the senses in which Lehmann uses it, for it obviously bears two distinct senses. On the first occasion of its use, the word 'human' is descriptive: 'human life' is the life of all those who are biologically classifiable as human beings, as belonging to the species *Homo sapiens*. But on the second occasion of its use, the word 'human' has taken on an evaluating sense; it now means something like 'truly human' or 'authentically human' or 'fully human'.

Moreover, the use of the verbs 'making' and 'keeping' would seem to suggest that 'human life' (in the descriptive sense) is a variable or perhaps unfinished project which may or may not become 'human' (in the sense of 'truly human') and therefore must be *made* so, or, if it has already become 'truly human', then it is in danger of becoming something else, and therefore must be *kept* so. Of course, this also implies that a person using such language must have in mind some criterion for judging what a 'truly human' life is.

I have cited Lehmann as one who has deliberately exploited the ambiguity of the word 'human', but the same ambiguity may be found in our everyday unsophisticated usage. We may say of some cruel dictator or murderer that he is an 'inhuman scoundrel'. We would not be meaning that he is not a member of the human race, but that his conduct does not measure up to what we would expect of a truly human being. Paradoxically, we would only call him 'inhuman' because he is in fact human and ought to behave differently. As Gerhard Ebeling has neatly expressed it: 'Only a human being can be inhuman. And even the one who is inhuman has a claim to be treated as human.'[3] That second sentence indicates that however far one may fall below human standards, it is impossible utterly to renounce one's humanity. Theologians have said of baptism and ordination that they are 'indelible', and the same is true in an even more fundamental sense of humanity itself.

Perhaps one should speak not of a 'human being' but of a 'human becoming', awkward though this usage would be. We could say that we are all *becoming* human, in the sense that we are discovering and, it may be hoped, realizing what the potentials of a human existence are. Yet, it is true that we already *are* human, because these potentialities already belong to us. This holds in the case even of someone who is *slipping back* from an existence worthy to be called human, for even he has not lost the poten- tialities. The point is that our humanity is not simply a natural endowment (as felinity is to a cat) but has to be discoverd and realized. The first obvious complexity in the study of the human, and a major source of elusiveness, is that we have to concern ourselves with the possibilities as well as the actuality. This justifies the choice of the word 'becoming' as the title of this opening chapter. 'Becoming' suggests process, transition, incompleteness, movement from non-existence into existence (or the reverse). That which is becoming is compounded of act and potency, fact and possibility.

If we talk of 'human nature', it would appear that the word 'nature' is just as ambiguous as we have seen 'human' and 'humanity' to be. 'Nature' is often taken to mean the set of distinguishing properties that mark off one class of objects from another. It has often been supposed that human beings have a fixed psychological nature and that this will manifest itself in spite of the accidents of individual and cultural diversity. But many modern writers would deny that there is a human nature in the sense of a universal essence of humanity, or, if they were willing to use the expression 'human nature', they would insist that this is a changing nature.[4] They consider that the doctrine of an invariable human nature does justice neither to the diversity of human beings nor to the dynamic and autonomous character of human existence. Clearly, of course, all human beings share some common characteristics, mental and spiritual as well as physical. But these are more like 'family resemblances', in Wittgenstein's expression, than like a fixed nature or essence.

If we are to speak of human 'nature' at all, then we should have to understand the word in a much more fluid way, going back to something like its root meaning. 'Nature' is derived from *naturus*, the future participle of the Latin verb *nasci*, 'arise', 'be born'. *Natura* is that which is arising or coming to birth and the nature of the human being is the as yet unfinished humanity which is emerging and taking shape in the history of the race and in the existence of each individual. If we have seen from our consideration of the word 'human' that the study of human nature is a study of possibility as much as of actuality, we now see from our consideration of the word 'nature' that this study is concerned with something that is fluid, coming to be and always on the move.

A further point about the kind of study we have in mind is that it cannot be simply empirical. It is not therefore psychology. It is more akin to philosophical anthropology and to the branch of theology known as the doctrine of man. We shall in fact draw heavily both on the Christian doctrine of man and on the various types of philosophical anthropology – Thomist, Marxist, existentialist and so on. Psychology, as an empirical science, describes the human condition as it is. The philosophical and theological anthropologies, however, criticize the actual human condition. In order to do so, they must have accepted, either implicitly or explicity, some norms or criteria of what it means to be a human person. They must therefore have also concerned themselves with exploring the possibilities of the human condition. They are concerned not simply with describing human nature as something given, but with the realization of human nature as an emerging reality.

I should say, however, that I hold no brief for either theologians or philosophers who despise empirical studies of the human. Perhaps the Marxists have been the worst offenders in this matter. Ernst Bloch, for instance, talks about 'crawling empiricism'. Presumably, it is said to be 'crawling' because it describes humanity as it is rather than saying what it ought to be, that is to say, it pays homage to the actual rather than to some ideal. But while I would agree with Bloch that the study of the human must go beyond the empirically given, it cannot afford to neglect this, unless it is going to get lost in utopianism, as does in fact happen in Bloch's own case. Empirical studies reveal the raw materials, so to speak, out of which humanity must be constructed, and it is important to know about these. Marx may have been right in saying that the philosopher's business is not just to describe the world but to change it, but it would be reckless and unrealistic to try to change the world without previously listening to those who have made a careful attempt to describe things as they actually are.

Now we must notice another peculiarity in the study of the human reality. If the proper study of mankind is man, that means that the investigating subject and the investigated object are one and the same. This surely differentiates this study from any other inquiry whatever. The human inquirer is usually studying something other than himself, and in most cases what he is studying remains unaffected by his study. In astronomy, for instance, men and women study such phenomena as the movements of the planets round the sun or the distribution of stars and galaxies, but these phenomena are in no way altered by the fact that intelligent beings on earth are investigating them. But when they study humanity itself, the results of the inquiry enter into the being of the inquirers, and since they are also the object of the inquiry, then the very inquiry has altered that into which it is inquiring. We could put this differently by saying that every theory of the human becomes itself part of the human reality and so helps to determine the character of that reality. If, for instance, I come to the conclusion that human beings are fundamentally aggressive and agree with Hobbes that 'the state of nature is a state of war', then, if I were a politician, I would favour large armed forces and would probably lean towards totalitarian rule. But if, like Locke, I came to believe that the 'state of nature' is men and women living together according to reason, then I would be less concerned with military strength and more inclined to increase civic freedoms. It would be going much too far to say that people become what they believe themselves to be, but it cannot be denied that, to some extent, theories of the human tend to realize themselves among the people who accept them. This would seem to be a form of feedback, though, I believe, of a peculiar kind. Not only information is involved, but values, goals, attitudes and eventually policies of action. Just as in politics some predictions tend to be self-fulfilling, so in philosophical anthropology theories of the human disseminate self-fulfilling models.

When one considers these intimate but obscure relations linking theory, practice and character, one has also to ask what kind of truth (if any) is attainable in such matters. Certainly, there could scarcely be an entirely objective 'value-free' study of the human reality; this ideal will be criticized later, but it seems to be ruled out already just by the fact that here we have no subject facing an alien object, but the subject and the object are identical. Yet it does not follow that a theory of the human must therefore be merely an ideology, a product of interest or subjective preference. Perhaps there are some guidelines given with human nature itself – not indeed rigid laws or detailed blueprints, but, shall we say, directions which the emerging humanity must follow if it is to realize its possibilities, while if it seeks to go in other directions, it experiences retrogression and diminution. It is at this point that empirical information about human beings is important, even if one cannot be content to remain on the level of the empirical. Indeed, if one were to strive consciously to remain within the limits of the empirical, this would itself be an ideology, and one that is so far from being 'value-free' that it is rather the product of a most inadequate value system.

There is still another problem attendant on the study of humanity. Every property or quality or possibility that we discover in the human being seems to be accompanied by its opposite, so that humanity appears to be a self-contradiction. To return for a moment to Alexander Pope, we remember that man is 'in doubt to deem himself a god, or beast':

> Created half to rise, and half to fall;
> Great lord of all things, yet a prey to all;
> Sole judge of truth, in endless error hurled:
> The glory, jest and riddle of the world!

If we glance through the chapter titles of this book, we note such words as 'freedom', 'transcendence', 'alienation' and so on. But these titles might just as well have been 'bondage', 'retrogression', 'belonging', etc. Or perhaps I should have written 'freedom and bondage', 'transcendence and retrogression', 'alienation and belonging'. That would have been cumbrous, and I have in fact put down what seemed to me to be the more fundamental or the more interesting member of the pair. I have not even tried to be consistent in putting down what might seem to be the more affirmative term. Certainly, 'freedom' seems more affirmative than 'bondage', while 'alienation' seems negative in comparison with 'belonging'. But perhaps they only seem so – we shall discover that freedom has to be understood largely in a negative way, while alienation has some affirmative characteristics.

In any case, there are in the human being these extraordinary juxtapositions of opposites, an apparently chaotic mingling of positives and negatives, though it is not even easy to distinguish which is which. And are not decay and death the final contradiction of the whole complex edifice?

> Last scene of all,
> That ends this strange eventful history,
> Is second childishness and mere oblivion,
> Sans teeth, sans eyes, sans taste, sans everything.[5]

Yet, the contradictions run so deeply that even death is not something merely negative.

'The glory, jest and riddle of the world.' Which is he, or could he even be all three at once? Modern writers are as far from agreement as ever on this question. Some seem to have opted for glory. Berdyaev, for instance, declares that 'man is not a fragmentary part of the world but contains the whole riddle of the universe and the solution of it'.[6] To others, humanity appears as an accident, an absurdity, even a cancer in the universe. So Monod writes: 'Our number came up in the Monte Carlo game . . . man at last knows he is alone in the unfeeling immensity of the universe, out of which he emerged only by chance.'[7] These are extreme points of view, and we would do better to listen to the more modest claim of Arthur Peacocke: 'Far from man's presence in the universe being a curious and inexplicable surd, we find we are remarkably and intimately related to it on the basis of contemporary scientific evidence, which is indicative of a far greater degree of man's total involvement with the universe than ever before envisaged.'[8] But when we consider these conflicting theories about man, we realize again that the theories become a part of the human reality and themselves have a share in shaping it. Are we glory, jest or riddle? How we answer the question or whether indeed we try not to answer it, is bound to have its effect on how we live and what we become. I think we can at least say, however, that the presence of apparent contradictions in the human being do not imply that he is either an accident or an unfortunate jest. These very tensions and polarities may provide the only conditions that would make possible the becoming or emerging of the distinctively human.

We have now seen some of the peculiarities and problems which attend any philosophical or theological study of humanity. In sum, such a study concerns itself with possibility as well as actuality. Its subject-matter is an emerging 'nature' in which there is a dialectical interplay of opposites. While it is interested in empirical facts, its own human character as a human study of the human takes it beyond description to criticism and construction. But the theories which it constructs, by a kind of feedback mechanism, influence the reality which it studies.

The next obvious question is: Where does one begin? How does one lay hold on the vastly complex reality that we call a human being? What property or power or quality of life differentiates the human being from other beings?

The question seems to invite us to name one distinguishing characteristic, and is probably therefore misleading, since there is a whole range of characteristics that mark off the human from the non-human. It is true that from ancient times man has often been defined as the 'rational animal'. Rationality is certainly a very important characteristic, though we must remember that alongside it goes its opposite, irrationality. Still, it might be too narrow a way of indicating the distinctively human. The tendency to exalt rationality and to see it in abstraction from its setting in the totality of human life can lead to a one-sided and eventually impoverished view.

Even at the biological level, there is an entire constellation of character-istics that differentiate the human being from even the higher animals.

Most obviously there is his large, complex, highly developed brain. But there is also his erect posture, his speech organs, his stereoscopic vision, his hands that can grasp objects and use them as tools, thus liberating him from the narrowly specialized modes of life for which most animals are adapted.

It could be argued, of course, that the various points I have mentioned are simply modifications of animal life, however striking, and that the human being is in the last resort to be understood as a highly complex animal himself. Admittedly, human beings are descended from animal ancestors and still resemble animals in many ways. According to J. Z. Young, even such higher capacities as choice, 'originally attributed uniquely to man, are to be found in some degree throughout the living world'.[9] Again, light can be thrown on some aspects of human behaviour through studying the behaviour of animals. Yet there are limits to these comparisons, and they do not obscure the fact that in human life something qualitatively different has appeared. To quote some witty remarks of J. Bronowski: 'The wonderful work on animal behaviour by Konrad Lorenz naturally makes us seek for likeness between the duck and the tiger and man; or B. F. Skinner's psychological work on pigeons and rats. They tell us something about man. But they cannot tell us everything. There must be something unique about man because otherwise, evidently, the ducks would be lecturing abour Konrad Lorenz and the rats would be writing papers about B. F. Skinner.'[10]

Let me give just two examples of biological phenomena in the human being which, on the surface, seem hardly distinguishable from the corresponding phenomena in animals, yet seem to have been transformed into phenomena of a different order. I refer to sexuality and death.

Sexuality is found throughout the animal kingdom, and in terms of biology and physiology, human sexual activity may seem not very different from that of other mammals. But there are in fact important differences. Whereas in other animals sexual activity is seasonal, controlled by the oestral cycle, in the human being it is constant, so making possible a new kind of relationship between the sexual partners. Furthermore, in animal intercourse the male enters the female from behind, whereas human beings copulate normally face to face. The human face is incomparably expressive, and to face another human being is to establish much more than a physical relationship. The human sexual act is certainly biological and physiological, but is more – it is a personal relation. And of course this 'more' is not just quantitative, or the personal aspect something merely added on as an extra component. It is the total relationship that receives a new quality. On the other hand, when the human sexual relationship fails to achieve its distinctively human character, when it is 'inhuman,' as in rape or prostitution, it does not revert to a simple animal relationship, but is a corrupt or perverted human relation. We remember that 'only a human being can be inhuman'.

A similar point can be made about death. Outwardly, it might seem that the death of an animal and the death of a human being are the same. In each case, disease or injury or old age has so disabled the organism that life comes to an end. But there is this important difference – the human being knows that he is going to die and lives in the face of death. Theodosius Dobzhansky calls this knowledge 'death-awareness' and claims that it is one of the basic characteristics of mankind as a biological species.[11] The animal lives from moment to moment, but the human being who is aware of death becomes also aware of his life as a whole, as a stretch of time that runs from birth to death. This delivers him from the preoccupation of the moment and establishes a quite different relation to time. Patterns and policies of life and action, impossible for animal, become part of what it means to live as a human being. But this happens only because death has entered his field of awareness. So even the seemingly negative phenomenon of death acquires a distinctively human significance. Heidegger was so impressed by the difference between the end of an animal's life and the end of a human life that he proposed that different words should be used. The end of an animal is 'perishing' (Verenden), while death, strictly speaking, comes only to the human being.[12] Of course, just as sexuality can lose (or never attain) its human quality, so can death. But death-awareness in the human being prevents death from ever reverting to the mere perishing of an animal.

I have used the word 'personal' to describe the new quality of life that appears with the human being and that transforms such features of his existence as sexuality and death. The emergence of personal life from the merely animal life which preceded it must be accounted just as great a leap in the evolutionary process as the much earlier emergence of the living from the non-living. It is this personal quality of life that is distinctive in the human being, and since personality includes rationality, then to define man as 'the living being that is personal' is more adequate than the traditional 'living being that has reason' or 'rational animal' (zōon logon echon). The word 'personal' denotes what I called 'the whole range of characteristics that mark off the human from the non-human'.

But does the introduction of the word 'personal' help us at all? Is it not just as difficult to understand as the word 'human'? There may, of course, be some personal beings that are not human beings. There may be such in other parts of the universe; traditionally angels have been considered persons, while God, if not actually a person, has been believed to have personal characteristics. But the only personal beings with whom we are directly acquainted are human beings, so that any elucidation of the personal must be to a large extent an elucidation of the human, and *vice versa*.

What then is a personal human being? There is no quick inclusive answer, and we shall have to consider a great many aspects, one after the other. But perhaps the first and most obvious point is to say that such a being is a centre of freedom. Kierkegaard poses the question, 'But what then is this self of mine?' He replies: 'If I were required to define this, my first answer would be: It is the most abstract of all things, and yet at the same time it is the most concrete – it is freedom.'[13] Broadly speaking, I would agree with this approach to the problem of a human self, but we should note the qualification in Kierkegaard's answer – he says that it is his *first* answer, and the implication is that much more remains to be said after one has opened the question of freedom, itself paradoxically described as at once the most abstract and the most concrete reality. So it is to the topic of freedom that we must address ourselves as the first step in our quest for a better understanding of humanity.

II

FREEDOM

What do we mean by 'freedom'? The word is often on people's lips, poets have sung about it for centuries, politicians have preached it, men and women have died for it. It is a word that can arouse a great deal of emotion, but as soon as we begin to ask what it means, we find that an answer is very elusive. It is of the essence of freedom not to be pinned down or imprisoned, so how can we grasp it, even in thought? When we try to do so, it seems to escape us on every side. Perhaps then it should be left to poetry, rhetoric and the emotions. Yet if freedom is as precious as most people think it is, we cannot avoid the task of trying to understand it. The better we understand it, the more we shall be in a position to protect and enhance it; and if freedom is, as we are assuming, essential to becoming a human person, then in protecting and enhancing freedom one is at the same time protecting and enhancing humanity.

We may begin by noting the wide variety of contexts in which we speak of freedom. There is political freedom, or liberty, the state of affairs in which people are not subject to some despotic or external government, but have a share in shaping the body politic to which they belong. There is religious freedom, the freedom to practise without external constraint the religion of one's choice, and usually also the freedom to propagate it; and, on the other hand, the freedom not to practise any religion at all, if that is one's choice. There are also freedom of speech and freedom to write, the freedom to express and disseminate opinions, even if these are unpopular. One could go on and enumerate many other kinds of freedom – economic freedom, or the freedom that comes with literacy and education, or the freedom to choose a career or a marriage partner, and so on. Most of these freedoms have been won only slowly and painfully, and even today are enjoyed by only a minority of human beings.

But underlying all these manifestations of freedom and making them-

possible is the fundamental freedom of the autonomous human person as a being who is rational, conscientious, discriminating, responsible, capable of choice, decision and creativity. It is this fundamental freedom that is so elusive when we try to reflect on it. We could call it personal freedom or inner freedom or even metaphysical freedom. It is personal freedom because it distinguishes a person and his actions from a merely natural phenomenon and its behaviour. It is inner freedom because it is never quite extinguished by external constraints. We admire the man or woman whose spirit, as we say, remains unbroken by oppression, poverty or even cruel mistreatment. Yet while we may well admire the inner freedom of an unbroken spirit, we would also have to say that a merely inner freedom remains a frustrated freedom, and that all freedom is directed towards some outward realization. Finally, it is metaphysical freedom – and I offer no apology for using this adjective – because the breach between persons and nature occasioned by the emergence of freedom has introduced something which is not empirically observable but is none the less real.

This brings us back to the elusiveness of freedom and the difficulty in forming a concept of it. The difficulty becomes apparent when we take note of the fact that when we try to define freedom, we usually do so in a negative way. Most things we describe in terms of their affirmative properties. We would describe a metal – copper, let us say – by mentioning its reddish colour, its specific gravity, its chemical affinities and the like. A plant – a rose bush, shall we say – is described in terms of its structure, habits, foliage, blooms and so on. Even a human emotion, such as joy, we would describe by trying to say what it feels like to be joyful and by mentioning any organic changes that may accompany the emotion. But freedom seems to have no characteristics like any of those mentioned. When we say that an animal is free, we mean that it is *not* enclosed in a pen or a cage or a zoo, it is *not* restricted in its movements, it is *not* the property of a human master. When we say that the citizens are free, we mean that in certain matters they are *not* restricted by regulations or pressures, they are *not* acting under compulsion, their behaviour has *not* been prescribed by some external authority. Freedom is not a thing with describable properties; it is not even like a human emotion or state of mind. In a very real sense, freedom is nothing at all. It is the absence of constraints, it is an open space not yet filled up, it is an empty horizon where nothing blocks the way.

Of course, it may seem very odd to say that something so precious as freedom is really nothing at all. Clearly, there must be more to it than that – there certainly is more, and we shall come to it in due course. But perhaps the first thing we do have to understand about freedom is its negative character. Maybe it has been failure to do this that has led to many of the philosophical difficulties over freedom. I do not simply mean that freedom is not like a thing or an objectifiable phenomenon, for this, I believe, would be equally true of love, joy and other ingredients of human and personal life. I mean that even within the realm of the human and the personal, freedom is peculiarly negative. But if freedom is peculiarly negative, and if freedom is also fundamental to a human person, does this mean then that negativity is in some sense of the essence of human and personal life?

A modern philosopher who has not hesitated to draw this conclusion is Sartre, and he too links negativity with indefinability. 'If man,' he declares, 'is not definable, it is because to begin with he is nothing. He will not be anything until later, and then he will be what he makes of himself.'[1] On this view, a human being is almost like a hole or a breach in the *plenum* of the world of things. But this metaphorical hole has an opposite function from that of the black holes of which cosmologists tell us. A black hole is an area of destruction, whereas the empty space of freedom which I have called the metaphorical hole is a centre of creativity. We could put this in a somewhat different way by saying that the distinctively human mode of existence arises from an act of negation, in the sense that humanity has distanced itself from nature or the world of things. It is this distancing, however it may have come about, that has created the breach and so made possible human freedom and human transcendence. Man has stepped out of that closely interwoven texture of forces that we call nature, and is no longer entirely governed by nature's laws. I advisedly insert the word 'entirely', for Sartre so exaggerates human freedom and the breach between man and nature that he ends up in a metaphysical dualism. The fact remains, however, that humanity does not and cannot entirely separate itself from nature, and remains a part of nature in many ways. Yet, with man something new has appeared on the scene, a being who is *not* entirely subject to nature's compulsion, who is in fact increasingly asserting his independence from nature. All other living things survive by adapting themselves to the natural environment. Human beings have stood that evolutionary law on its head, so to speak, for they now survive by adapting the environment to themselves. This is part of the meaning of freedom on the biological level.

Incidentally, although I did mention earlier the freedom of the wild animal which is not restrained by captivity or domestication, it now becomes clear to us that the freedom of the human being is of a different order from the freedom of the animal – indeed, one can scarcely use the word 'freedom' in respect of animals. The lion that is born free and stays free is not subject to any artificial or humanly contrived restraints, but of course it is never for one moment delivered from the constraints of nature. Human freedom is far more fundamental. It is the negation of nature itself, a distancing from nature, a kind of declaration of human independence. Still, the point should not be exaggerated. Human beings do not and cannot entirely free themselves from nature's constraints, and part of the tragedy of the human condition is that man is both free and determined, in some respects transcendent over nature, in other respects subject to nature's laws. Everyone knows that at the present time man's relation to nature has become very fragile. His domination over nature is threatening to turn against him, and a *modus vivendi* must be worked out. The experiment of a nature that has brought forth a child that has transcended nature and then turned against it may possibly end in disaster. But, for better or worse, this is the human condition. An act of negation has taken place, a breach has been made in the order of nature, a finite being has transcended nature. This is the beginning of freedom, of existence and of spirit.

Freedom begins as an act of negation. It is fundamentally nothing. It has no empirical characteristics that can be observed and described. There is a sense then in which freedom remains a mystery – and by a 'mystery' I do not mean something totally incomprehensible, but something that can never be fully taken in by understanding or experience. Berdyaev talks of freedom as an abyss, and applies to it the adjective 'meontic', that is to say, a nothing rather than a something, a potentiality rather than an actuality. 'Freedom is not created by God . . . it is part of the nothing out of which God created the world.'[2] Berdyaev's language, taken over from the mystical tradition, is admittedly obscure, but what he is saying is obviously close to the reflections of the preceding pages. Freedom is the empty space, the room that is still left for manoeuvre and has not yet been filled up and determined. It cannot therefore be grasped by rational thought; it cannot be observed. We only know it through our own exercise of freedom. We are aware of the depth of freedom only in moments of creativity or, again, in moments of difficult decision. At such times we bring out of the abyss of freedom some definite act or policy or idea or intention. The fluid, abyssal, plastic nothingness that was freedom is given a definite shape, and something new enters the world and the stream of happening. Then the moment of freedom is past, and what it has produced becomes part of history and cannot be revoked.

This mysterious experience of freedom can perhaps only be compared with what we could dimly imagine of the divine act of creation. Christian theologians speak of a creation out of nothing. In the beginning, they believe, by the creative *fiat* or 'let there be' of the divine Word, there came forth from the chaos of nothingness a world capable of evolving under ordered laws. It is something like this mystery that human persons know on the finite level through the exercise of their freedom. Out of the nothing that is not yet determined, they bring forth something to which they have given a definite shape. In doing this, they are themselves experiencing creativity. They are at their most godlike, for in a dimly analogous way they are participating in the divine experience of creating out of nothing. It is often thought that freedom to choose between alternative courses of action is the fundamental form of freedom – 'freedom of the will', as it is usually called. But it seems to me that this is too restrictive. The fundamental freedom is creativity, especially the human freedom to shape humanity itself.

Near the beginning of this discussion of freedom, I said that although I would stress the negative character of freedom, there is obviously more to it than that. Now that the term 'creativity' has been introduced, and the thought of human self-creativity, it is time to ask what more there is to freedom other than the empty space or nothing. Freedom is not just randomness. It has direction. It is associated with such aspects of our being as cognition, conscience, purpose. Paul Verghese writes: 'Only when the *hegemonikon*, or the ruling element within ourselves, is in full control of our minds and bodies, do we genuinely taste freedom.'[3] I find his use of the term *hegemonikon* very illuminating at this point. It is derived from the Greek verb *hegeisthai*, 'to lead', and was used by Stoic philosophers and some Christian fathers for what might be called the 'leading edge' of a person, the conscious, rational, unifying and discriminating element that leads us in one direction rather than another. It is the *mot juste* for elucidating the experience of creative freedom.[4]

I said that the fundamental human freedom is to create humanity itself. We remind ourselves of Sartre's claim that to begin with man is nothing, that only later will he become something, and that he himself has to decide what he will become. This is the doctrine that existence precedes essence. But I have already suggested that Sartre exaggerates in apparently claiming for the human being a total freedom. Surely man does not begin as a sheer nothing. There is something given. There is an initial directedness, a *hegemonikon*. In some ways a better account was given five hundred years before Sartre by the Renaissance scholar, Pico della Mirandola. He imagines man as a sculptor, standing before an as yet uncarved block of marble. Under his hands, it can yield many possibilities. These include not only the beautiful but the monstrous. The marble represents potentiality, yet it is not just nothing. Presumably the marble has a grain, so that there are some ways it can be sculpted into something of beauty but other ways in which it will crumble. The analogy is not quite adequate, for the uncarved block before which the human being stands is not something other than himself – it is himself, the raw material out of which he has to form a person. Other creatures are formed by the external forces of nature, but man has to shape himself. Let us hear Pico's words. God has finished the other works of creation, but he leaves man unfinished. And to him he says: 'A limited nature in other creatures is confined within laws laid down by me. In accordance with your free judgment, to which I have entrusted you, you are confined by no bounds and you will fix the limits of your nature for yourself . . . You, appointed like a judge for being honourable, are the moulder and maker of yourself; you may sculpt yourself into whatsoever shape you prefer.'[5]

Does that mean then that man is co-creator with God? To ask this question is to raise a problem that will recur several times in later parts of this book. The problem is whether human freedom is compatible with the existence of God. Sartre's insistence that existence precedes essence, that man begins as nothing, that freedom is total and there is no hidden programme, implies the denial of God, for it seems to him that if God has already laid down what humanity is to become, then freedom is an illusion. But whether one has to choose between God and freedom is by no means clear, nor is it clear that freedom must be all or nothing.

At least, the human being has a share in creating a human essence. Humanity is not a finished product. The human race is coming to be, living in history, seeking a goal which would be a fuller being, both for individuals and for the whole race. At least within limits, this goal can be chosen and humanity can determine what it is to become.

We notice too that not only does man shape himself, he shapes his world. Alongside the old world of nature, he creates a new world, or perhaps a whole series of worlds. More and more, the frontiers of the natural world are pushed back, and a humanized world takes its place. The oldest layer of this is the world of agriculture, and as one flies across England, the pattern of the fields attests the labour of centuries. Then there are newer worlds – worlds of industry, of technology, of transport and communications. There are worlds of science and intellectual achievement, of the arts, of sport and recreation, of political institutions and economic enterprises and so on almost indefinitely. From one point of view, human history could be regarded as the steady absorption and transformation of the natural world and the things of the natural world into this new world (or series of worlds) that has been constructed according to human ideals and ambitions. This is how the human being is sculpting both himself and his environment.

I have been claiming that a creative freedom is at the very heart of our humanity and that this freedom not only differentiates us from the animals but is a breach in the order of nature itself and a mystery that escapes empirical investigation. Before going any further, I should offer some justification for these assertions.

This means that we have to touch on the ancient dispute between the upholders of free will and the upholders of determinism. It is well known that many attempts have been made to prove the freedom of the will, and just as many to disprove it and to show that all human actions are determined in the same way that natural events are, or in comparable ways. Frankly, I do not believe there is any way in which one could either prove or disprove the reality of freedom. The reason for this is not that up till now no one has been clever enough to think out a convincing proof on one side or the other, but that, in the very nature of the case, a proof is in principle impossible. This follows from the considerations that have brought us to this point in our discussion of freedom, for if one were to prove the existence of freedom, one would need to turn it into an object, and this is precisely what it is impossible to do. There are innumerable things, objects, properties in the world, and these are accessible to empirical investigation, but freedom is not one of them. When we search among them, we do not find freedom. From the objective point of view, freedom is nothing, and that is why some people come to the conclusion that freedom is just an illusion and that at bottom all that we do and say and think is determined in advance by natural and social forces over which we exercise no choice. The basic error of this view is well exposed by Marcel: 'To make a representation of ourselves which takes things as its model, we make it impossible for ourselves, by definition, to attach the least meaning to the word "freedom"; we have accordingly to take refuge in some determinist conception which implies an active misunderstanding of what we are . . . My freedom is not and cannot be something that I observe as an outward fact; rather, it must be something that I decide.'[6]

Basically similar considerations underlie Kant's treatment of the third antinomy of pure reason, in which he sets side by side a proof that 'there is no freedom; everything in the world takes place solely in accordance with laws of nature', and a contradictory proof that 'it is necessary to assume that there is also another causality, that of freedom'.[7] The antinomy arises through the misuse of the categories of understanding, which have their applicability only within spatio-temporal experience. They cannot in principle be applied to an originative freedom which belongs not to the phenomena of nature but to a supposed noumenal self transcending nature.

The natural sciences, by the very methods which they employ, concern themselves only with empirical phenomena and with the ways in which these are related. There is no place for freedom in the domain which the sciences explore. So it is sometimes supposed that the sciences support a universal determinism and that the belief in freedom is unscientific or even anti-scientific.

But this is quite mistaken. For the reasons already given, there is no way in which science could take cognizance of freedom, but on the other hand it is freedom that makes possible the scientific enterprise itself. The relation between science and freedom has been lucidly treated by Austin Farrer. 'The whole mass of natural fact as we have put it together,' he declares, 'is the product of an enterprise that knows itself as free.'[8] Freedom cannot indeed be discovered by science or vindicated at the end of an empirical investigation. The defence of freedom is rather that it is the presupposition of every science, investigation and argument. The denial of freedom is a self-contradiction, the *reductio ad absurdum* of the arguments that lead to the denial. For all argument and all science require the activity of judgment. We have to decide between the true and the false, the valid and the invalid, the probable and the improbable, and we have to make these decisions on rational grounds. If the determinist were right, then rational discrimination and science itself would become impossible. Our beliefs (including a belief in universal determinism) would be products of causes beyond our control, not beliefs arrived at by rational judgment. We would believe this or that proposition not because we judged it to be true on rational grounds, but because of our psychological history, because of the influence of cultural factors and social pressures, because of the chemistry of the body or the mechanism of the nervous system or whatever it might be. That such irrational factors do enter in is not in dispute, but to suppose that our beliefs are entirely determined by such factors undercuts the possibility of rational judgment and finally eliminates the distinction between truth and error. A belief which eliminates the very possibility of discriminating between true and false cannot itself claim to be true. Thus, although one cannot prove freedom because this would entail an illegitimate objectivizing of freedom, one must assume freedom as a postulate of any rational investigation.

We have been considering here the claim that freedom is a presupposition of the exercise of rational judgment, of discrimination betweeen truth and error, but perhaps it is even more obvious that freedom is a presupposition of the moral life. We acknowledge responsibility for our acts, we hold others to be responsible for theirs, and it would make no sense to do so unless we believed that those acts were really acts of a moral agent and not just happenings. We assume that they have been freely chosen with the intention of bringing about some state of affairs envisaged by the agent. I have mentioned that Kant showed that arguments which seek to establish the freedom of the will run into contradictions because they are trying to press into the service of speculative reason categories that have their application only within the sphere of the empirical. But when he came to consider practical reason, Kant redressed the balance. The freedom which cannot be demonstrated by argument is a postulate of our everyday moral acting. In other words, our assurance of the reality of freedom depends on our direct awareness of the exercise of freedom, and our constant assumption that both we and others have this freedom. To deny this would undermine morality, and Kant even seems to accept that this freedom is, as we have said, a breach in nature. He writes: 'This principle (the principle of free action) had not to be searched for or discovered; it had long been in the reason of all men, and incorporated in their nature, and is the principle of *morality*. Therefore, that unconditioned causality, with the faculty of it, namely, freedom, is no longer merely indefinitely and problematically *thought*, but is even as regards the law of its causality definitely and assertorially *known*; and with it the fact that a being (I myself) belonging to the world of sense, belongs also to the supersensible world, this is also positively *known*, and thus the reality of the supersensible world is established.'[9]

However, as is the case with many philosophical disputes, so in the one between the upholders of free will and the determinists, truth is not wholly on one side. Even if we accept that there is a genuine human freedom, this freedom occurs within a setting that is already determined. Human freedom is always limited. We never enjoy an absolute freedom (I have already criticized Sartre for exaggerating freedom) and we never confront entirely open possibilities. People do speak of 'the open future', but the tragedy is that the future is never fully open, and sometimes we can only hope that it is ajar and that there is some small area of freedom. Always to some extent the future is foreclosed by the past and the present. If there is never a fully open future or a total freedom, it may seem that in many situations we are close to an absolute determinism. Human freedom is always conjoined with finitude. To be finite means to stand at a given point in space and time, to see things from that vantage point and to be limited by all the factors that have converged on that particular spot. Some philosophers talk of the 'facticity' of human existence, and by that expression they mean everything in the existence of an individual or a group which simply has to be taken over and which is not in any way subject to free choice. One's genetic inheritance, including, within certain limits, one's temperament, aptitudes and intelligence; one's position in the social and economic order; one's place in history, the apparently accidental circumstance of whether one is born in a time of peace or a time of war, a time of affluence or a time or scarcity, a time of science or a time of superstition. Of course, some of these things can be changed, at least within limits. But the point is that no individual and no generation ever begins from scratch, so to speak, or is faced with an entirely open future. The actions of earlier generations and individuals are still working themselves out, and to some extent determining what is possible now. Our own individual choices in the past limit the kind of choices that are possible for us now; for instance, a vocational choice, especially one that requires a long period of preparation and training, usually makes its effects felt for the rest of a person's life. In many societies, of course, vocation is not even a choice. It is an index of the increase of freedom in modern times that the range of vocational choices has been widened for many people, though not for all, in the industrial countries. For millions in other parts of the world, there is no such choice. But no one even in the most advanced societies is totally liberated from the past and never will be. The stubborn element of the given remains alongside freedom, to condition, limit and even frustrate it. All of us find ourselves thrown into an existence which we did not choose and the circumstances of which we did not choose, and it is from that point on that we begin to exercise whatever freedom is open to us.

I have said in the last paragraph that a person's past choices limit what is possible for him now. Paradoxically, however, this might in some cases be an index to freedom itself. If the basic freedom is to build a human life, then one's choices over the years may bring a person to the point where we can say, 'He could not possibly do that!' This would not be a restriction on his freedom, but a testimony to the fact that he had reached a point of stability where he could no longer be blown off course by some chance desire or emotion. Freedom, we have said, is quite different from chance, and has nothing to do with unpredictability.

There is another and somewhat different way in which freedom is limited. Many theologians have maintained that whatever might be true of human beings in some ideal state of existence, they are as we know them in the real everyday world in bondage to sin, and that sin is so disabling that they are not free to choose the good. In a famous treatise, Luther declared that '"free will" without God's grace is not free at all, but is the permanent prisoner and bondslave of evil, since it cannot turn itself to good'.[10] One is reminded of Paul's anguished words: 'I do not do the good I want, but the evil I do not want is what I do. Now, if I do what I do not want, it is no longer I that do it, but sin which dwells within me.'[11] If this is determinism, it is determinism of a different kind from that of modern critics of free will, but it is none the less another way in which freedom is limited. We shall have to return to this problem in connection with the topics of alienation, conscience and commitment.

For the present, however, we take note that freedom is always hemmed in and limited. There must always be a tension between human freedom and all the sheerly given factors that belong equally to human existence but stand in the way of freedom. Human beings are called to freedom, summoned to go beyond whatever condition they find themselves in to a fuller mode of personal and social being. But the factical conditions of life are always theatening this freedom, and sometimes it appears to be cut down virtually to extinction – we are hemmed in by a *plenum* in which even the tiniest empty space that might allow the exercise of freedom has been preempted. Because of this tension, freedom in the human condition is inseparable from anxiety. There is a well-known passage in the writings of Kierkegaard in which he speaks of the anxiety attendant on freedom: 'This anxiety may be likened to dizziness. He whose eye chances to look down into the yawning abyss becomes dizzy . . . Anxiety is the dizziness of freedom, when freedom gazes down into its own possibilty, grasping at finiteness to sustain itself.'[12]

Confronted with this vivid picture, one must pause. It suggests that much of the praise of freedom that one hears is far too superficial, for those who utter it are apparently unaware of the anxiety of freedom and of the overwhelming weight of responsibility which it brings. But when one becomes aware of this, one then understands Sartre's aphorism: 'To be free is to be condemned to be free.'[13] To be free is to have laid upon one human care and human responsibility, in place of the unthinking irresponsibility of the animal. The contrast between the demands of freedom and the apparently very meagre resources which finite human beings have for meeting them is frightening.

It is this apparently impossible synthesis in the human being of freedom and finitude, spirit and flesh, the unlimited and the earthbound, that has led some thinkers, as we have briefly noted, to declare man an irrational contradiction or a senseless accident or even an absurdity that does not fit into the harmonious scheme of the universe. Albert Camus gave eloquent and sensitive expression to this point of view in his celebration of the mythical Sisyphus who spent his days rolling heavy rocks to the top of a hill only to have the frustration of seeing them crash down into the valley again. Camus calls him the 'absurd hero', and he intends us to take seriously both the absurdity and the heroism. The human condition, in which the possibilities of freedom are tied and constantly frustrated by the finite and the factical, is, he believes, incurably absurd. But Camus did not go on to conclude that therefore one should resign oneself to this unhappy fate. On the contrary, no other modern writer has been more insistent on taking up the challenge of human freedom, rebelling against the factors that frustrate it and seeking a betterment of the human lot. He can even find a certain joy in his disillusionment. 'The struggle itself toward the heights is enough to fill a man's heart. One must imagine Sisyphus happy.'[14]

This may seem illogical and merely romantic. Or it may mean that so long as there remains a vestige of freedom, of transcendence, there is also hope. Or it may even suggest that a universe in which freedom occurs demands from us a more affirmative response than Camus' 'metaphysical rebellion',[15] and that we cannot rest content with the bleak prospect which he offers.

Certainly, few people would be as strong-minded as Camus in asserting freedom in the face of the absurd. It takes much less than that to discourage the exercise of freedom. Once the anxiety of freedom has been experienced, there is a tendency to flee from it. Jacques Ellul has remarked that 'whenever man has made a beginning of liberty, he has taken fright, retreated, renounced his freedom and sighed with relief at being able to put his destiny finally in the hands of someone else'. A little further on, he continues in language reminiscent of that which we have been using ourselves: 'In his vanity and boasting, man pretends that he wants to be free. Once a little freedom is offered him, however, he starts back at the sight of the void which he must now fill, the meaning he must now provide and the responsibility he must now carry.'[16] There are many examples in history of the flight from freedom. Every dictator of whom we have heard was able to wield his dictatorial power only because his fellow citizens were on their part willing to yield their freedoms. We often talk as if all over the world people were longing for freedom, but this is not so. The anxieties and responsibilities of freedom, at all levels from personal freedom to political freedom, are no sooner understood than they are shunned. People prefer the security and mediocre contentment that come from routine patterns of existence and from following the line of least resistance. 'People love slavery and authority,' wrote Berdyaev. 'The mass of mankind has no love of freedom, and is afraid of it.'[17]

Freedom, then, whether we are thinking of its many outward manifestations or of that mysterious creativity which is at its root, is a strange contradiction. It begins as a nothing which becomes very real and precious. It is earnestly desired, and yet at the same time people shrink from it and avoid it. It is creative and life-enhancing, but it can equally well be disruptive and even destructive. It brings to those who exercise it a feeling of enlargement and exhilaration, and yet, if they pause to think for a moment and gaze into the depth of freedom, they experience anxiety. These are tensions that cannot be removed. They belong to the very essence of our human condition, as finite beings thrown into a factical existence where much has already been determined. Only God could be free from the tension, because only God would have the capacity to exercise a freedom not trammelled by external givens. But whether in the case of God it makes sense to talk of either freedom or necessity is questionable.[18] However, man is not God, and human freedom will always be a conditioned freedom.

In spite of the tensions and in spite of the threats of disruption, freedom, we believe, is worth maintaining and increasing. It is so because it is essential to the human adventure. Where freedom has disappeared, humanity too has disappeared, and the human being without freedom has been reduced a member of a herd or a machine or a plant or a stone or some other object whose nature is wholly given. Such a person ceases to be that unique being who has been told to sculpt himself from the as yet uncarved material, and to make his nature out of an as yet plastic possibility. But the invitation to embark on this adventure is fraught with danger and anxiety, and this explains why in every society so many people prefer security to

freedom and unconsciously yearn for a return to the untroubled irresponsibility of the womb.

An interesting question arises at this point. Is freedom a value? It might
seem that in saying that freedom is essential to humanity, I am indeed
asserting that it is a value, even the highest value. This appears to be
Sartre's point of view, because he thinks that the worth of an action or even
of a character depends on its being autonomous, irrespective of its content.
But this, I think, is a mistake, and is part of Sartre's exaggeration of
freedom. Freedom is not itself a value, but the necessary condition for the
pursuit and realization of values. It is also the condition for the pursuit and
realization of disvalues. Without freedom, there could not be an authentic
humanity, but equally there could not be the terrifying phenomenon of
inhumanity. Freedom is therefore neutral, a conditon of value but not itself
a value. The same remarks apply to liberation, whether in an individual or
a society. Liberation is not an end but a beginning, and there remains the
question of what will come of it.

It is hardly surprising that people are attracted by the exhilaration of
freedom but put off by its anxiety. Yet, until we are prepared to accept both
aspects and measure up to them responsibly, freedom in the full sense will
escape us, and so also will that full humanity, towards which freedom is
only the first (though essential) step. I think there can be little doubt that in
recent years there has been a great demand to enjoy the benefits of freedom,
but this has not been matched by a willingness to shoulder the burdens of
the responsible and often anxious exercise of freedom. We have heard a
great deal about 'rights' of one kind or another, but very little about the
demands that are correlative with every right, and which have to be met if
the rights are to be maintained. If there were nothing but rights, the result
would be anarchy. If there were nothing but demands, the result would be
slavery. Both anarchy and slavery are enemies of freedom. It is in the midst
of these opposites that the delicate plant of freedom has to survive.

Does this mean then that freedom needs a protector? At one level, we
could say that law is the protector of freedom. John Locke remarked, 'The
end of law is not to abolish but to enlarge freedom.'[19] Freedom needs the
protection of law because, as Luther made clear, the human will is subject
to sin, and in any sinful society there are constant attempts by some
members to take away the freedom of others. Law is meant to mitigate this
evil, yet to the extent that a society is sinful, its very laws may become
perverted so that they are themselves instruments of oppression. Must we
look beyond law to God as the ultimate protector of freedom and therefore
of humanity? We have seen that some would hold that a transcendent God
is incompatible with a true human freedom. This question cannot be
decided now. But what we can say at this stage is that if God is real, he
relativizes all human powers and institutions, even the state, and so

undermines the claim of any one of them to be an enslaving absolute. To this extent at least, he is the protector of freedom.

Perhaps even at this point we can go rather further, and return to the question raised almost casually at the end of our discussion of Camus, whether a universe in which freedom occurs must not evoke some affirmative response; whether, so to speak, freedom may not be a kind of *vestigium Deitatis* in the world. Perhaps God is so far from being the enemy of freedom that he is its author, in the sense that he has not filled the world with his creation but has left over some of the uncreated nothing, so that humanity can be his partner in the continuing work of creation. We tend to think exclusively of freedom as a right, as something to be claimed so that God may seem to stand in the way of it. But if we have learned that freedom is just as much a demand on us and a responsibility, then we can understand Berdyaev's statement that 'freedom is not something which man demands of God, but that which God requires of man'.[20]

The traditional natural theology saw the traces of God in his created works. I am suggesting that we can also see him in the work he has left unfinished, in the freedom and openness that remain. And a God who is seen in this second way is far more interesting and exciting from a human point of view. The God of natural theology and of philosophy has always been suspect among the religious, because as the First Cause or Supreme Intelligence or Great Mathematician, he seemed remote from human interest and also from the God of the Bible. His creation, however wonderful its beauty and order, could hardly be more than a glorified toy – like, say, these intricate clockwork models of the planetary system which we sometimes see in museums. The clockwork universe and even the natural universe as we conceive it today in far more complex ways can be an object to be admired and contemplated for its interest, ingenuity and beauty. But there is no personal communion with it, no response.

But if we suppose that there is a breach in this structure, so that some of the creatures are not just part of nature but are themselves centres of freedom and creativity, then God's creation could no longer be considered as, from his point of view, a toy or even a work of art. It would become a potential partner with God able to respond to him and to join with him in a continuing work of creation. Of course, since freedom is in itself neutral, the free creatures of the universe might turn against God. Man is God's risk. But even when one allows for the risk, how much richer is a universe that can freely respond through some of its members than one which can be no more than an object of contemplation, however infinite its interest!

These remarks also have some consequences for interpreting the biblical tradition that man is made in the image of God. What is this image? Some have seen it in rationality. The human being exercises reason; this distinguishes him from the other creatures and reflects, on the finite level, the

Supreme Intelligence that framed the universe. But rationality is not, as we have seen, to be taken as the *differentia* of humanity, nor is God adequately represented as Supreme Intelligence. Others have claimed that the image of God in man is dominion. This is even less satisfactory. It goes on the assumption of a monarchical God whose basic attribute is sovereignty, and sees man as his vice-gerent, charged with subduing and exploiting the earth. In place of either of these interpretations, the image of God in man should be understood as the human share in the mystery of creativity. The comparison between human freedom and divine creativity was already briefly expounded near the beginning of this chapter, and will be developed further in what follows.

III

TRANSCENDENCE

Some years ago there appeared a book by Alistair Kee with the title, *The Way of Transcendence*. The subtitle explained that the book was offering a version of Christian faith without belief in God. The conjunction of transcendence with the dismissal of theism is interesting. It reflects the difficulty which many people have nowadays in believing in God, understood as a transcendent being, yet at the same time the main title of the book reaffirms the need for transcendence, though for a transcendence understood as a quality of human life. We are soon told what this quality is. The person embarked on the way of transcendence is engaged in 'a kind of life for which he must consciously decide and for which, if he decides, he must strive with all his determination.'[1] It is a thoroughly active understanding of transcendence, and suggests the picture of climbing a mountain trail and overcoming the force of gravity that holds one back. Kee contrasts with the way of transcendence what he calls 'the way of immanence', the way of drift and conformity in which one decides nothing for oneself but lets one's life be formed by passing appetites, social pressures, the latest fashions and so on. The contrast may well remind us of the ancient Christian teaching about 'the two ways' – the way of life and the way of death (*Didache*) or the way of light and the way of darkness (*Epistle of Barnabas*). The way of transcendence and the way of immanence brings before us in modern terminology what has long been recognized as a fundamental human choice. But I mention this language about the way of transcendence chiefly because it affords a very good example of what has been called 'relocating transcendence',[2] that is to say, finding the *locus* of transcendence in the human existent rather than in God.

Considered as an attribute of humanity, transcendence is closely related to freedom, and our discussion of transcendence will be largely a further exploration of the themes introduced in the preceding chapter. If freedom is the original or primordial openness of the human being, transcendence is the continuing process of creativity and development which flows from that freedom. The word 'transcendence' means literally 'climbing across' or 'going beyond' or 'exceeding the limits'. It is essentially a very dynamic idea. To the extent that transcendence belongs to human beings, they are always on the move and always crossing the boundaries which at any given time circumscribe a human existence. Just as in the physical world, as we move through space towards the horizon, that horizon turns out not to be an impassable barrier but opens out on new horizons, beyond which we may pass in turn, so in the history of a human person or a human society one horizon after another is crossed. It might be thought that these horizons are in time rather than space, and it does seem to be the case that temporality is a necessary condition of human transcendence. But it is going too far to say, as Jürgen Moltmann does, that we should regard 'the future as a new paradigm of transcendence'.[3] It is not just the future alone or our passage through time that constitutes transcendence. There are many ways of transcending. Involvement in the world around us, relations with other people, religious or political commitment, are all modes of transcendence. We could say that transcendence is the 'becoming more', and when we speak of this 'more', clearly we do not mean a quantitative more, but a qualitative more, a deepening, enhancing and enriching of life, or, if one prefers, a fuller, truer humanizing of life. Transcendence means pushing back the horizons of humanity itself.

In our Western culture, we have probably been more concerned with pushing back the horizons of nature, through voyages of exploration first on the earth and then in space, and through the investigations of the natural sciences, than with exploring the reaches of the human spirit. Of course, the expansion of knowledge is also a mode of transcendence on the part of man. But it is only a part of a much larger enterprise, and though the West has excelled in its scientific achievements, it has lagged behind other cultures in probing the possibilities of humanity itself. These cannot be known in the same way as we know the phenomena of nature.

Does humanity come at last to a boundary that cannot be transcended? Is death such a boundary in the case of the individual? Or is there no limit to the possibilities of this being who is impelled by the quest for 'something more'? Sartre wrote that 'man is the being whose project is to be God'.[4] If this is so, then Sartre rightly drew the conclusion that it is a self-contradiction. Yet there seems to be in humanity such a strange blending of the finite and the infinite that one cannot rule out *a priori* that the transcending of every horizon opens a new horizon to be transcended in turn, and that there may be no end to this.

Many writers on the human condition have, during the nineteenth and twentieth centuries, discussed the question of human transcendence, even if they have not actually used the term 'transcendence' itself. This distinguishes modern views from those of an earlier time, when there was thought to be a fixed unchanging human nature. However, one has to qualify this statement by noting that in early Christianity, at least in the Eastern churches, there was something very close to the modern conception of human transcendence.

But it was the Enlightenment, with its ideas of historicity, relativism and progress, that ushered in modern views of man and was a powerful influence in breaking down older static ways of thinking of humanity. A new impetus was given by the rise of evolutionary theory, for if *Homo sapiens* has arisen out of subhuman origins, is it not reasonable to suppose that there lies ahead of him a goal which would greatly surpass the humanity that we now know and which might even be designated 'superhuman'? Admittedly, those philosophers who have written about transcendence have offered a great many different accounts of it. Yet these are not just rival views. As I have already said, human transcendence is such a multifaceted phenomenon that it can be seen from many angles, so that any account can hardly avoid being partial. It may be useful to pass in review some of the major descriptions and interpretations, emanating from quite a wide range of philosophical traditions.

Let me begin with Nietzsche. On the one hand, he was receptive to the naturalistic influences of evolutionary theory, while on the other he can be seen, with Kierkegaard, as one of the founding fathers of modern existentialism. For Nietzsche, humanity is a transitional form, and such love as he can have for the human race derives only from his belief that human nature as we know it is perishing and being transformed. The mixture of contempt and aspiration for humanity finds expression in sentences like the following. Zarathustra declares: 'I teach you the superman. Man is a thing to be surmounted. You have trodden the way from worm to man, and much in you is still worm. Once you were apes, and even yet man is more ape than any ape.'[5] But soon we find him saying: 'Man is a rope stretched between beast and superman – a rope over an abyss. Perilous is the crossing, perilous the way, perilous the backward look, perilous all trembling and halting by the way. Man is great, in that he is a bridge and not a goal. Man can be loved, in that he is a transition and a perishing.'[6]

Of course, in determining Nietzsche's attitude to the human, much depends on what interpretation is to be placed on the notion of the 'superman' or 'overman' (*Übermensch*). Has man been entirely surmounted and thus replaced when one comes to the superman? Or is the superman simply man brought to perfection? Where lies the decisively significant division – between man and superman, or between both of these and the beast? According to Karl Löwith, the idea of the superman (which had already appeared in German philosophy before Nietzsche) has its roots in the Christian idea of the God-man, now dechristianized in a secular philosophy.[7] Now, according to Christian theology, the God-man remains fully human – indeed, in him we see true humanity for the first time. If this holds also for Nietzsche's superman, the Nietzsche is not finally misanthropic, despite all his contempt for the ordinary run of human beings.

Nietzsche's understanding of humanity as a transitional mode of being continues to make itself felt among some later existentialists. Indeed, the very word 'existence', as they use it, has taken on a meaning very like that of transcendence, for 'existence' has taken on the very active sense of 'standing out' or even 'going out'. But these writers use the word 'transcendence' as well.

Thus Sartre sees man as fundamentally the desire *to be*. But, as the fragile being-for-itself that is without the security and solidity of being-in-itself, man lacks the being that he desires. 'Such,' writes Sartre, 'is the origin of transcendence. Human reality is its own surpassing toward what it lacks.'[8] Man is the desire for self-subsistent being, and this means, as we have already noted, that he is the desire to be God. But this notion of God, Sartre believes, is self-contradictory. 'Human reality therefore is by nature an unhappy consciousness, with no possibility of surpassing its unhappy state.'[9] Thus, although Sartre thinks of human beings as self-transcending, their transcendence must eventually be frustrated.

We may contrast with Sartre's view of the matter that of another philosopher of existentialist tendency, but this time one who is a theist and a Catholic, Marcel. Like Sartre, he sees the need for transcendence arising from a dissatisfaction with life as it is, but he explicitly differentiates his understanding of transcendence from Sartre's.[10] He contrasts transcendence with immanence, and while he accepts that from one point of view transcendence can be understood as the movement of the human spirit upward and outward, we cannot confine our view to the human reality alone. Human transcendence is a going out to another, to a transcendence beyond the human level. 'The term "transcendence",' he says, 'taken in its full metaphysical sense, seems essentially to denote an otherness, and even an absolute otherness.'[11] Here we seem to be moving from human transcendence to divine transcendence. Yet, in spite of this and in spite of his talk of an 'absolute otherness', Marcel does not deny that there can be an experience of transcendence in human life.

A further important difference between Marcel and Sartre is that whereas the latter sees the struggle for transcendence as a highly individual affair, Marcel stresses the importance of the interpersonal. Our fidelity to one another is itself a transcending of the boundaries of the individual self, and this also means that transcendence can be experienced as grace as well as struggle. 'The descent into personal relationships is at the same time an ascent into transcendence.'[12]

In spite of the very considerable differences among them, the three philosophers just considered, Nietzsche, Sartre and Marcel, are in agreement in thinking of transcendence as fundamental to being human, and also in thinking of it as related to the whole human person and embracing all its dimensions. Transcendence they see as related to the central *desire to be*, and it is because of their concentration on this that these three may be grouped together and loosely designated 'existentialists'. They provide a good sampling of the existentialist understanding of transcendence, and we do not need at this point to call any more witnesses from that tradition. But the concept of transcendence is employed by other modern philosophies very different from existentialism – indeed, it is the occurrence of this idea right across the spectrum of modern philosophical anthropologies that makes it so important. Each philosophical tradition, however, has its specific interpretation of transcendence, deriving from its own insights and interests.

Marxism is an obvious example. The idea of transcendence was clearly expressed by Marx, though without the use of the term itself, when he wrote: 'Since, for socialist man, the whole of so-called universal history is nothing but the formation of man by human labour, the shaping of nature for man's sake, man thus possesses a clear irrefutable proof that he is born of his own self, a proof of the process whereby he has come to be.'[13] This may seem to be an exaggerated view of transcendence as the self-creating activity of humanity and to be even more anthropocentric in its understanding of history than is existentialism. Surely man did not ultimately create himself or the nature which is the object of his labour? But Marx would not have allowed the validity of a question about ultimate origins, for, in his view, such a question would belong to the idle speculative philosophy which he had rejected, not to the philosophy which is tied to activity in the world.

The mention of labour in the sentence which I have quoted from Marx indicates the special aspect of transcendence that impressed him. It reflects a view of the world in which economic and material factors are the ultimate determinants of history – and even if this is again an exaggeration, it stands as a needed corrective to philosophers and theologians who, on their side, have exaggerated spiritual and intellectual factors, to the virtual neglect of the material foundations of life. Marx was to write at a later time that 'the mode of production in material life determines the social, political and intellectual processes in general'.[14] We have then to ask whether this so-called 'economic determinism' is not inimical and contradictory to any idea of human self-transcendence and of the freedom which such an idea seems already to have assumed. I do not think this question is susceptible of a simple answer. It is a difficulty not peculiar to Marxism. Christian theology, for instance, has to reconcile human responsibility and divine providence.

A fuller discussion of these matters could come only after we had gone into the problem of alienation. But for the moment, it may be pointed out that, for Marx, labour or work is not just material production. If it has become such, it has lost its true character. Labour is, at least ideally, creative and satisfying, and a source of human dignity. John Plamenatz writes: 'Work in the life of man is not only what has to be done, systematically and daily, to procure what satisfies material wants; it is also what meets, or should meet what Marx calls the need for self-affirmation.'[15]

Not only the idea but the actual term 'transcendence' is in wide use among later Marxist or neo-Marxist writers. Marcuse, for instance, draws attention to the social and political meanings of transcendence, almost totally neglected by the existentialists, including those who break out of individualism to the level of the intersubjective. Marcuse defines 'transcendence' as follows: 'tendencies in theory and practice which, in a given society, "overshoot" the established universe of discourse and action toward its historical alternatives'.[16] 'Critical reason' has an important part to play in judging the inadequacies of the existing order and creating dissatisfaction with it; this in turn liberates the transcending drive towards an alternative order. What Marcuse attacks is precisely the materialism of Western societies, absorbed as they are in technology, consumption and the 'standard of living'. He calls this mode of life 'one-dimensional thought and behaviour', and claims that it 'prevents transcendence and confines ideas and actions to the given system'.[17]

Leaving Marxism, we find that in a very different philosophy, namely, Thomism, the idea of transcendence in its dynamic sense and as applied to the human being has become very important in the past few decades. The movement known as 'transcendental Thomism' has in fact become the main intellectual force behind the most adventurous Roman Catholic thinking in the period leading up to and following on Vatican II. Bernard Lonergan may be taken as an exemplar of this philosophical development. He believes, like Aristotle, that the human being has an innate desire to know. 'There is an intellectual desire, an *eros* of the mind. Without it there would arise no questioning, no inquiry, no wonder.'[18] This sentence alone is enough to indicate the intellectual bias in Lonergan's approach to the question of transcendence, which, as we shall see in a moment, is basically to be understood as the asking of questions and the passage from one question to another.

It might seem then that for Lonergan man is the desire to know rather than the desire to be. But this would not be quite accurate, for he explicitly connects knowing and being. He can say that 'being is the objective of the pure desire to know',[19] and since this is offered as a definition of being, we could say that at this point being is made dependent upon knowing. Later on, however, he tells us that 'since cognitional activity is but itself a part of the universe, its striving to know being is but the intelligent and reasonable part of a universal striving toward being'.[20] In a key passage in which he writes about transcendence, he brings both of these points together in a remarkable description of the movement of transcendence, a passage which presents in concentrated form the major ideas of his philosophy. He declares:

> Transcendence means 'going beyond'. So inquiry, insight and formulation do not merely reproduce the content of sensible experience, but go beyond it. So reflection, grasp of the unconditioned and judgment are not content with mere objects of defining, supposing, considering, but go beyond them to the universe of facts, of being, of what is truly affirmed and really is. Moreover, one can rest content with knowing things as related to us, or one can go beyond that to join the scientists as searching for knowledge of things as related to one another. One can go beyond both present science and common sense, to grasp the dynamic structure of our rational knowing and doing, and then formulate a metaphysic and an ethic. Finally, one can ask whether human knowledge is confined to the universe of proportionate being, or goes beyond it to the realm of transcendent being; and this transcendent realm may be conceived either relatively or absolutely, either as beyond man or as the ultimate in the whole process of going beyond. Clearly, in spite of the imposing name, transcendence is the elementary matter of asking further questions. It means a development in man's knowledge relevant to a development in man's being.[21]

I have quoted this passage in full because of its importance in clarifying what Lonergan and other Thomists understand by transcendence. Although it seems clear that transcendence is not just a matter of knowing but also of being, nevertheless the passage indicates the basic role assigned to knowing in Lonergan's thought. We must notice also his mention of a transcendent realm beyond man, which places Lonergan with Marcel against Sartre and Marx and suggests that transcendence is not to be exhaustively understood in human terms, even if we begin with the human drive towards transcendence.

Perhaps one should mention a fourth type of philosophy at this point, namely, the process philosophy associated with the names of Whitehead and Hartshorne. Its whole dynamic way of thinking about the world has much in common with the views we have been considering. But process philosophy bases itself on an understanding of nature as a whole, rather than human nature, and it does not seem to me to have contributed much to the understanding of human transcendence or even of human existence generally. If it has something to tell us about transcendence, then, as we shall see, this concerns divine rather than human transcendence.

I have given examples of several very different types of modern philosophy which in the end produce very different doctrines of man, and yet all are agreed on the importance of transcendence, the teaching that the human being is in a process of transition towards new forms of existence, or, to put it in another way, that the human being is unfinished and confronts an openness in which he has still to shape himself.

Are these new forms of existence also higher or better forms? Is the contemporary stress on human transcendence a reappearance of the doctrine of progress? I do not think that either existentialism, Marxism or Thomism teaches a doctrine of automatic progress – in fact, some existentialists are also pessimists. Yet perhaps there is a standing temptation to fall into a belief in automatic progress if one begins from the notion of transcendence. The very word suggests a movement upward. But the most perceptive philosophers have been well aware that human beings can slip back as well as move forward. Still, whatever the direction of the movement may be at any given moment, existentialists, Marxists and Thomists seem to be agreed that there are as yet unfulfilled human possibilities, and that there is no way of saying just how far these possibilities extend. The acknowledgment of these possibilities can be seen as a ground for hope, though admittedly a vulnerable hope.

When we took note that the modern dynamic view of humanity in transcendence contrasts with the earlier view that there is a fixed human nature, I did mention that nevertheless it is in accord with a still older understanding of the human being – the doctrine of man that came to expression in early Christian theology, especially in the east. Heidegger remarks that 'the idea of "transcendence" – that man is something that reaches beyond himself – is rooted in Christian dogmatics.'[22] He makes this remark in a passage where he has just quoted that famous sentence from the Hebrew account of creation: 'Then God said, "Let us make man in our image, after our likeness." '[23] There were, admittedly, Christian thinkers (including Augustine and others in the West) who understood the creation of man in quite a static way. Man, they thought, had been created already mature and perfect, manifesting the divine image, and then he had fallen into sin and the image of God in him had been defaced or even totally obliterated. But many of the early Christian theologians of the East had a very different understanding of the image of God in man – a much more dynamic understanding which already anticipated modern views of humanity as a self-transcending being.

Irenaeus is a good illustration of the ancient Christian understanding of humanity embarked upon a course of ever new enhancement of being (though certainly with the possibility of slipping back or failing to achieve). While accepting the biblical teaching that man was made in the image and likeness of God, he did not think that this means that man was made perfect in the beginning. On the contrary, 'created things must be inferior to him who created them . . . they come short of the perfect. Man could not receive this perfection, being as yet an infant.' The image of God, in other words, was given as a potentiality, into the realization of which man might grow – though equally, through sin, he might slip back from it. Mistaking the parallelism of 'image' and 'likeness' in the Hebrew for two distinct concepts, Irenaeus seems to have supposed that man's original endowment was the potentiality for growing towards God (this was the 'image'), and that the goal would be the glory of closeness to God, the realization of the potentiality (this was the 'likeness'). So actual human life is the progression, though it may be interrupted, from the potency of the image to the fulfilment of the likeness. In Irenaeus' own words: 'Now, it was necessary that man should be in the first instance created; and having been created, should receive growth; and having received growth, should be strengthened; and having been strengthened, should abound; and having abounded, should recover from the disease of sin; and having recovered, should be glorified; and being glorified, should see his Lord.'[24]

About this teaching on the progressive unfolding of humanity towards deity, Geoffrey Wainwright has remarked: 'Following Irenaeus, the Greek fathers made an exegetically improbable but doctrinally valuable distinction between 'image' and 'likeness' . . . God's gracious calling of humanity to communion with himself includes the initial and fundamental capacity, the aided progress in time and the final and eternal realization.'[25] It should be added, of course, that many of these early writers did not hesitate to call the final realization the 'deification' of humanity.

This dynamic view of humanity found in early Eastern Christian theologians has its roots in the New Testament. Paul can claim that Christians 'beholding (or reflecting) the glory of the Lord, are being changed into his likeness from one degree of glory to another'.[26] Rather similarly, John declares: 'We are God's children now; it does not yet appear what we shall be, but we know that when he appears we shall be like him, for we shall see him as he is.'[27] This language does suggest something like an unending progression towards God, while the Second Epistle of Peter speaks explicitly of becoming 'partakers of the divine nature'.[28]

At this point, we shall leave for the present the topic of human transcendence in order to reflect on a different use of the term. In a theological context, there is more likely to be a mention of the transcendence of God than of the transcendence of man. It may be worth noting that this theological usage is a surprisingly modern one. Only since about the middle of the nineteenth century have theologians been accustomed to talk about the transcendence of God, though the usage is now standard. Is the idea of divine transcendence in any way related to the kind of transcendence about which we have been thinking up till now?

This is a difficult question to answer, and in fact contradictory answers are given to it. Some theologians see God as the goal of human transcendence, while many philosophers would hold that a transcendent God must be the enemy of human transcendence. Here we have a new form of the problem that already emerged in our discussion of freedom.

First of all, we have to define more closely what is meant when we speak of the 'transcendence' of God. The term is generally used to refer to the *otherness* of God – to all those ways in which his being is and must be different from the being of man and all other creatures. So when we think of God as transcendent, we think of his absolute priority and exaltation over all created beings, his power and majesty, his mystery and incomprehensibility. Unless God were transcendent over creation in these many ways, he would not be God and he would have no claim to the unreserved adoration of the creatures. Incidentally, in speaking of God as transcendent 'over' the creation, I am acknowledging that it seems impossible to get away from the metaphor of height in expressing the idea of transcendence. The transcendent God is naturally described as the Most High.

Biblical religion has laid great stress on the transcendence of God, unlike some Eastern religions which have stressed rather his immanence. But if God were wholly and utterly transcendent, and nothing else, if he were wholly other and thus utterly beyond understanding, how could we say anything about him or know anything about him or even believe anything about him, or how could he have any significance for human life? There must also be a sense in which God is accessible and near to his creation. By the divine 'immanence', we mean the closeness of God, his indwelling of the creation and his activity within it, his affinity and concern with humankind. All these characteristics too would seem to be necessary to the very idea of God. For how could we worship a God who was merely different, or merely numinous power? Would he have any claim upon us or any right to the name of God unless he were a God who cares, indeed, a God who cares so much that he draws near to his creatures and in a real sense identifies with them? God is paradoxically both the furthest and the nearest.

Of course, to say that anything is 'necessary to the very idea of God' – and I have claimed that both transcendence and immanence are necessary – is to presuppose a certain history of the idea of God. Perhaps there was a time when sheer absolute power was constitutive for the concept of deity. This may have been the case with the God of the Aztecs and with many other ancient deities. But that would represent a stage in the history of religion and a type of religion that has long been surpassed. It has been surpassed not only in the Christian experience of God but in the experience of other religions besides. Once human beings have attained a certain level of spiritual development, the very meaning of the word 'God' has come to include mercy and love as well as power. When one reflects on what possession of these attributes implies about God, one is driven to say that in him there are both transcendent and immanent aspects.

Transcendence and immanence are opposites, but they are opposites which seem to imply each other, like convexity and concavity. Sometimes transcendence may be stressed, sometimes immanence, but both belong to any viable concept of God. If God were wholly transcendent, and nothing else, or wholly immanent, and nothing else, he would have ceased to be God, in any sophisticated understanding of the word. When we study in depth the immanent, the finite, the creaturely, and, above all, the human reality within this immanent order, we find that it points beyond itself or even seeks to pass beyond itself. It contains intimations of the transcendent. On the other hand, the transcendent would be utterly unknown did it not in some measure communicate itself in the immanent order.

There is no contradiction in believing that God is both transcendent and immanent. A Christian theologian who devoted much attention to these questions, J. R. Illingworth, illustrated the relation of God to the world by the analogy of the relation of human selves to matter. We transcend matter, for we have material things at our disposal and (within limits) have mastery over them; but, as selves, we are also immanent in matter, essentially immanent in our bodies and secondarily in the environing universe. Illingworth believed that in an analogous manner God both transcends the material order and is immanent in it. He transcends it as its creator and governor. But he is also immanent in it – primarily immanent (incarnate) in Christ and secondarily immanent in the whole creation.[29] One need not agree with everything in Illingworth's theology or in the idealist philosophy which undergirds it in order to acknowledge that he makes out a good case for reconciling divine transcendence and divine immanence. A similar case is argued from a different philosophical background among process philosophers and theologians. Following Whitehead, they speak of the 'dipolarity' of God and also make use of the mind-body analogy. Incidentally, a corollary of these views of transcendence and immanence in God would seem to be that the act of creation is to be understood not only on the analogy of making (as if the creation were wholly external to God) but to some degree on the analogy of emanation (God's going out from himself into the creation).

We are now in a position to come back to the question about the relation of human transcendence to divine transcendence. Christian theologians, both ancient and modern, have answered the question by claiming that God, the transcendent reality, is the goal of human transcendence. We have seen that some of the philosophers we have considered would go along with this – the Catholics Marcel and Lonergan, and perhaps to them we could add the radical Protestant (as he calls himself), Karl Jaspers, who speaks of transcendence (*Transzendenz*) as that realm of being which lies at the limit of man's existential possibilities.[30] But over against the theologians and theologically oriented philosophers who see divine transcendence as the 'whither' of human transcendence stands the impressive protest of those atheistic philosophers who hold that divine transcendence is incompatible with human transcendence. God cannot be the fulfilment of man's transcendence, but only its suppression. The transcendence of the human, they believe, demands the abolition of the divine. 'Evil I declare it, and hostile to mankind, this doctrine of the One, the Perfect, the Unmoved, the Sufficient, the Imperishing.'[31] Admittedly, these words of Nietzsche seem to envisage a God who its utterly and wholly transcendent. But in the face of such a God (if indeed we have not to acknowledge frankly that he is a faceless God), we can understand the demand for relocating transcendence in the human being, and for challenging the illusion of a divine transcendence which could only be inhibiting and an obstacle in the way of human transcendence.

Is there any way of resolving this apparently fundamental conflict? It could only be resolved if it were found possible to develop a non-alienating or non-oppressive conception of divine transcendence, and this would mean an understanding of divine transcendence that could be seen as liberating and encouraging *vis-à-vis* human transcendence, rather than as the ultimate control that has already settled everything in advance, including the very goals of man's transcending freedom.

It can hardly be denied that many theologians have indeed represented the transcendence of God in ways that have been alienating and oppressive, and that there has been a standing tendency in Christianity to revert to the God of the Aztecs and others, the God who expresses an ideology of power. Divine transcendence has been conceived in static terms as God's absolute lordship over the creation. To some extent we have seen that this view must be modified by taking seriously God's immanence alongside his transcendence. But we must go further still. I think we found a clue when, in a mention of the act of creation, I claimed a place for emanation (with its suggestion of participation) alongside the analogy of making (with its suggestion of sovereignty).

This can be developed by taking the active transcendence that we know in our own human experience as the analogical clue to the transcendence of God. Then we would think of the divine transcendence not as the static otherness and aloneness of the One, the Perfect, the Sufficient and so on, but of God's active transcendence, in the sense of his capacity to go out from himself towards new goals. Would this not be closer, in some ways, to the living God of the Bible, the God who is realizing his purposes in history? Charles Hartshorne talks of God's 'surpassing' himself, and writes: 'The higher forms of power are not those which inhibit the freedom of others, but rather those which inspire appropriate degrees and kinds of freedom in them, the power of artists, prophets, men of genius and true statesmen. God is the unsurpassable inspiring genius of all freedom, not the all-determining coercive tyrant.'[32] Here we at least come in sight of a God 'whose service is perfect freedom', and thus in sight of an affirmative relation between human transcendence and divine transcendence.

IV

EGOITY

The word 'egoity' means the condition of being an ego or a self. This is the condition of every human being, even if he or she has never reflected upon it. Everyone says 'I' – 'I am,' 'I do,' I believe,' and so on. Who or what is this 'I'?

It will be remembered that in our discussion of freedom, I introduced the Greek term *hegemonikon* and said that it seemed to be just the right word for referring to the person who exercises human freedom.[1] I translated it as the 'leading edge' of a person, and went on to say that it is the conscious, rational, discriminating, unifying, purposeful element in the human being that leads us in one direction rather than another. It is this directedness that makes the difference between human action and mere natural happening, and that allows us to speak of freedom rather than randomness. There is directedness too in the idea of transcendence, and this seems to be recognized when we say that there can be retrogression as well as transcendence. I have used 'leading edge' as a translation of *hegemonikon* rather than the common translation 'ruling principle', not only because 'leading' or 'guiding' is a close rendition of the Greek but because I wanted to stress the notion of direction.

Very primitive animals – sponges, for instance – have no distinct head region. But quite far down in the evolutionary scale, among certain lowly worms, there emerges the phenomenon of cephalization, the distinction of a head end from a tail end, and this of course is characteristic of all higher animals. With this there has also emerged direction, and especially the distinction between forward and backward. In *Homo sapiens* the distinction between forward and backward has developed to an immeasurable extent beyond its primitive origins, and is now more than a spatial distinction. It is true, of course, that the human being faces forward and that in the head region are located the brain, the sense organs and the speech organs, and so all of the higher functions. But the leading edge is no longer exhaustively describable in biological functions, and the forward direction is no longer only spatial but has taken on many connotations relating to life and growth and values. The leading edge is now the conscious self or ego, the self which can say 'I'. Certainly, this self or ego is closely associated with the brain and other organs, and may well be inseparable from the body, but in our waking hours there are going on in this ego innumerable activities and experiences of a different order from anything that can be described in biological categories – perceptions, reasonings, speech acts, moral decisions, communications, emotional reactions and an indefinite number of other ingredients that go to make up what we call 'mental' life.

We could also call this ego the 'control centre'. It unifies (or seeks to unify) the many strands in human experience, it remembers, projects, learns, selects, and does a hundred other things besides. Admittedly, it is sometimes not in control, and sometimes, in pathological cases, there may be more than one centre. In the experience of all of us, there are conflicts within the ego. But there could be no normal human experience, no freedom, responsibility or transcendence, but for the *hegemonikon*, the leading edge which finds expression in the pronoun 'I'.

It is important that the 'I' should not be understood only or even primarily in intellectual terms. This has to be said because, since the time of Descartes, there has been a strong tendency in Western philosophy to identify the ego, or at any rate the essential core of the ego, with the subject of cognition. 'I think, therefore I am.' Here thinking is taken to be the essential human activity. At an early stage in this book,[2] however, the definition of man as the rational or thinking animal was questioned, and criticized as too narrow. Many philosophers today would agree with this criticism of Descartes. They might agree with John Macmurray when he suggests that 'we should substitute the "I do" for the "I think" as our starting point,'[3] for action, which, as intentional, is always more than mere happening or process, includes thinking and is a richer concept. Perhaps one has even to go beyond Macmurray to do justice to what constitutes an ego. But to take even Macmurray's line is to fly in the face of much of the European philosophical tradition, for it is to put practical reason before pure reason.

Descartes not only made thinking the essential characteristic of the 'I', he annexed this thinking to a special kind of substance, the *res cogitans*. There are two kinds of finite substance, *res cogitans* and *res extensa*, mental substance with the distinctive property of thinking and material substance with the distinctive property of extension. The fact that he used the same word *res* for both of them indicates that he gave them roughly equivalent ontological status, and that moreover he conceived them both on the analogy of a thing (*res*), a solid enduring object. Something of that analogy lurks behind the notion of *res cogitans*, no matter how subtle the substance of this entity is supposed to be. If some philosophers have criticized Descartes for his stress on thinking, far more have attacked him for his dualism of thinking and extended substances. He has become a whipping boy for Marxists, empiricists, existentialists and Christian theologians alike. One of the most sustained attacks has come from Gilbert Ryle, who spoke of the Cartesian view 'with deliberate abusiveness as the dogma of the ghost in the machine'.[4] He argued that the basic error of the Cartesian view is a category mistake, because it represents the facts of mental life as if they belonged to a logical type or category which is the counterpart of the physical facts (as is indeed clear from the use of *res* to signify both), whereas they belong to another type.

I agree myself in rejecting dualism, and there are of course many other strong arguments against it, as well as the one just cited from Ryle. But I think it is possible to reject dualism without falling into a reductionist understanding of the self, such as is common among empiricists. I should say at this point that I do not believe Ryle was so much of a reductionist as some of his critics believed. He says quite plainly, 'Men are not machines, or even ghost-ridden machines. They are men – a tautology which is sometimes worth remembering.'[5] Still, there is a reductionist tendency in empiricism, and I think we can perceive clearly what it is if we go back to the father of modern empiricism, David Hume. He believed that the self is a fiction, and that at any given moment there are only the contents of consciousness. To quote his argument in summary fashion: 'There are some philosophers who imagine we are every moment intimately conscious of what we call our *self*. For my part, when I enter most intimately into what I call *myself*, I always stumble on some particular perception or other, of heat or cold, light or shade, love or hatred, pain or pleasure. I never catch myself at any time without a perception, and never can observe anything but the perception.'[6] The revealing words in the sentences quoted are, 'I never catch myself at any time without a perception,' that is to say, I never catch the *subject* of the perception. But what would it mean to catch the subject? It suggests an activity like spinning round so quickly that you could perceive your own back. There is, in fact, to use Ryle's expression, a category mistake here, though of a different kind from the one found in Descartes. The mistake in this case is to try to turn a subject into an object, to try to find the subject among its own perceptions and impressions as if it were another entity of the same order. No wonder the self or ego turns out to be elusive, and when I look for *myself* among my perceptions, I find nothing but the perceptions.

Of course, this is not for a moment to deny that there are what Ryle calls 'higher order actions',[7] that is to say, actions which are directed upon other actions. For instance, I may play chess; then I can think about myself playing chess, and perhaps criticize the way I played; I can even think about myself thinking about my playing chess, and the series could be indefinitely extended. This might be taken to mean that the self can indeed be objectified and that there is no limit to such objectification. But, as Ryle recognizes, the 'I' keeps retreating before this process of objectification – 'my commentary on my performances must always be silent about one performance, namely itself'.[8] He claims that what thus eludes becoming the object of comment is not privileged, for a moment later it may be objectified. But this is surely to confuse subject and object and to treat them as of the same logical type. Is the self which is objectified genuinely comparable with the self which is subject – or, if one prefers, the self which is agent? No higher-order action reduces or abolishes the subject self, which immediately becomes the subject of that higher-order action. There is no way in which I can catch this subject of my acting, thinking and feeling, and bring it within the area of objectifiable fact. Hume was right in saying that one can never perceive the self among one's perceptions, but the reason for this is not that the self is a figment of some philosophers' imaginations, but that the actively perceiving self (subject) belongs to an entirely different category from anything that can be perceived (object), and that no act of violence can turn the former into the latter.

It is at this point that we find the Achilles' heel of empiricism. As a method for the investigation of natural phenomena, empiricism has amply proved its worth. But it fails when the attempt is made to apply it to personal life. Empiricism can be successful only when that which it is investigating can be objectified and spread out for scrutiny as an object. But there must always be a spillage, so to speak; there is always the residue, which is the investigator himself, that cannot be brought within the objectifying purview. Empiricism provides a successful way of approach to the problems of nature, but it cannot give an adequate account of that being who has transcended nature, namely, the human being. The being who says 'I' is a breach in the texture of the merely natural.

It was some such breach that Ian Ramsey was recognizing when he maintained that 'saying "I"' is 'logically odd' and cannot be brought within the logic of our ordinary assertions about the world.[9] Although he was sympathetic to empiricism, his Christian apologetic consisted in showing that there are elements of personal experience that cannot be adequately contained in the empiricist framework. If he continued to think of himself as an empiricist, it was only because he had modified his empiricism by incorporating into it many insights derived from philosophies of a more personalist kind.

Our discussion of the 'I' has been reminiscent of part of the discussion of freedom earlier in this book.[10] We found then that freedom too cannot be detected by empirical investigation. It is not another empirical phenomenon, so it tends to be dismissed as an illusion. We can no more discover it than Hume could discover *himself* among his perceptions. But we did hold, following Kant and others, that freedom is a presupposition of our responsible activities. Is this not also the case with the elusive self or 'I'? I cannot objectify this 'I' – that would be the most elementary of category mistakes, and would change the 'I' into something else. But do I know something only through objectifying it? Is there not a self-awareness that comes before objectification? I believe that there is. It is what Sartre has called the 'pre-reflective *cogito*',[11] thought other writers have named it differently. It is called 'pre-reflective' because it has not yet reflectd on the self as an object, yet is the pre-condition that there may be any such reflection. It is the subject's awareness of himself as subject – as subject of thought, initiator of action, exerciser of freedom. It cannot be empirically demonstrated, but is a necessary condition of our ever engaging in any empirical demonstration.

We began this chapter by asking about the meaning of the word 'I'. We found ourselves speedily rejecting the belief that the 'I' or self is a substance, at least, if 'substance' is understood in the Cartesian sense of *res*, that is to say, on the analogy of material thinghood. In this rejection, we found ourselves in agreement with empiricists such as Hume and Ryle, but when we came to consider their accounts of selfhood, we parted company with them also. Their accounts were too reductionist, and led to the virtual elimination of the most characteristic features of selfhood through the attempt to objectify the 'I' as a complex of observable behaviour. The empiricists were correct in turning from a Platonist or Cartesian doctrine of a substantial soul to a more Aristotelian account of the soul as dynamic form, but they went wrong in trying to eliminate the subjectivity of the self and the privileged access which each ego has to its own inner consciousness. John Macmurray has pointed out that attempts have been made to understand the self on the analogy of a material thing, then on the analogy of a biological organism, but his own view is that we can begin to understand it only if we employ fully personal categories, and that these are *sui generis* and irreducible to anything else.[12] With this I agree. Cartesian and empiricist accounts of the self must both yield to a distinctively personalist phenomenology, which will take account of all the dimensions of selfhood.

Perhaps the first thing to be said about a self is that it needs time. It is through and through temporal. We may recall Sartre's claim that the human being begins as nothing, and although he exaggerates the point, it is certainly true that a self does not appear ready made, but needs time and experience in which to make itself and to transcend into its possibilities. If it is the essential mark of a material thing to be extended in space, it is essential to a self to exist over a stretch of time.

But we must note that the relation of a self to time is a peculiar one. A material thing too exists in time – indeed, we are told that an atom requires a minimum of time as well as a minimum of space in which to exist. But the peculiarity of a human self is that it lives in awareness of time. We have noted Dobzhansky's speculation that human awareness of death is a major difference between man and the animals.[13] To know that there is an end, death, is to live in a span of time. Animals, we may suppose, live from moment to moment or, at the most, from one brief episode to another. Human beings are always living in a span of time, which may be more or less extended, from the so-called 'specious present' to an entire lifetime. Through memory, we bring with us our past; through anticipation and the projects of the will, we reach out into our future. This is the basis of that feeling of identity which belongs to a self. However much I have changed or my circumstances have changed, I recognize myself as the same self, the same strip of history that I remember from childhood and that I keep projecting into the future. This is what John Dunne calls 'bringing time to mind', and he says that it leads to 'a dilation of the present'.[14] If you like, this can be understood as another form of transcendence. The human person transcends the moment into a span of time, he transcends brief spans into longer spans, he comes to understand that there is for him a span that begins with birth and ends with death, his lifetime. And with that there is also the possibility of understanding that one is even now engaged in producing a biography. To put it in another way, one is engaged in the lifelong task of becoming a person, of sculpting the raw material of life into a truly human shape. Incidentally, although the words 'self' and 'person' are often regarded as roughly synonymous, I think the distinction can be made that whereas the self or ego is present from the beginning of life as the 'leading edge', as I have called it, the word 'person' indicates a stage in the development when some stable characteristics have emerged. This would seem to be implied in talking of the self having the task of becoming a person. It might be more accurate still to say that the goal is to become a person-in-community, for no person exists in isolation, though a self may try to do so, and in so doing diminish its own personhood. To be a person-in-community further implies that the self's transcendence of the moment does not stop even with the recognition of one's own lifespan, but goes on to an awareness of living in history.

I have briefly sketched the temporal basis of selfhood, and have indicated how it is related to such 'subjective' feelings as death awareness, living in a span, and the personal identity that says 'I' throughout a lifetime. But now I must draw attention to another peculiarity of a self, namely, that it has very indefinite edges. A solid material thing, whether it be a rock or an artefact, is bounded by a fairly definite surface. A self, on the other hand, transcends itself in all directions and is likewise penetrated from all directions. It is constantly projecting itself forward in time into its possibilities, and these as yet unrealized possibilities belong to the self as well as what it actually is, so that we can say that the self is always more than it is, or, in another sense, less than it is. It never quite coincides with itself; that is to say, it never fits entirely within a definite boundary, but keeps spilling over. That is the understanding behind the philosophical exhortation: 'Become what you are!' Similarly, the human being transcends into other persons. 'In its own intrinsic structure,' writes Marcel, 'subjectivity is already, and in its most profound sense, intersubjective.'[15] This relation to others is a two-way traffic, for their being also enters into mine, and sometimes it may even be the case that when I think I am myself, I am only reflecting others. One must also recognize the extension of the self into the regions of the unconscious. Around the luminous centre of consciousness, the *hegemonikon*, are areas that are subconscious and unconscious, and out of them come memories and desires that also claim to belong to the self.

The fact that the self has indefinite edges and never quite coincides with itself draws attention to another peculiarity – the internal relations of the self. I can be related to myself. This finds expression in everyday language: 'I am angry with myself'; 'I would not trust myself in such a situation'; 'I was not myself when I did that'; 'At the interview I tried to be myself'. No simple analysis would cover all these cases. These, and many others, would have to be considered one by one. But I do not think the empiricist account of them in terms of higher order activities which objectify earlier activities is at all adequate, or that being angry with myself or not trusting myself is at all the same as being angry with James or not trusting Philip. Rather, we have to say that within the self there is both unity and conflict. There is unity, because what 'I' may reject is still 'myself', an *alter ego*, so to speak. Yet the very use of that expression, *alter ego*, implies the conjunction of identity and otherness within the self – something I have tried to express earlier by saying that I never quite coincide with myself. Perhaps I am striving to coincide with myself, that is to say, to realize those possibilities of existence with which I have identified myself and towards which I project myself. But, as long as I live, conflict is never overcome, and the identity is continuously threatened by otherness. We see this in extreme form in those pathological cases where there may be in an individual two or more selves striving for the mastery and possibly dominating him in turn – the schizoid situation of a Dr Jekyll and Mr Hyde. Yet something analogous is known in ordinary experience. The position of the ego as the leading edge is challenged by some would-be *alter ego*. In our discussion of freedom, I quoted the extraordinary words of Paul: 'If I do what I do not want, it is no longer I that do it, but sin which dwells within me.'[16] This cannot be read as determinism in the ordinary sense, for Paul would not have felt any guilt about his sin if it had been some purely extraneous power that had taken over his life. The sin 'dwells within' him, that is to say, it is part of his self. Yet somehow it is not his 'true self', it has for the time being ousted the 'I' from its leading role.

But how can we talk of a 'true self' or a 'false self'? We do commonly use such language, and we find it also used by professional psychiatrists like R. D. Laing in their discussions of schizophrenia. It is interesting to note that while Laing uses this language primarily in respect of pathological conditions, he says that 'every man is involved personally in whether or to what extent he is being true to his "true nature" '.[17] The answer which I wish to give to the question about a 'true nature' and a 'false nature', a 'true self' and a 'false self', a 'true humanity' and a 'false humanity', is in terms of that direction or directedness which is given with human existence itself, and of which we are from the beginning dimly aware, becoming, we may hope, more explicit aware of it as we go along. We have several times already taken note of this directedness,[18] but much more remains to be done in exploring it, especially in connection with the idea of conscience, which still lies ahead of us.

There is, however, a question to which we could apply the test of directedness right away. How is egoity related to egoism? The term 'egoity' is primarily a descriptive term. It points to a basic structure in every human being, the presence in him or her of an 'I' or ego or self, a 'leading edge' which is conscious, discriminating and purposeful and which, within the range of options that are still free, is constructing a life story and forming a person of one sort or another. By 'egoism' is meant a philosophy or ideology which puts the interests of the self before all others. The term is generally used pejoratively, but it should be remembered that there have been a few philosophers, both ancient and modern, who have actively advocated egoism, and many more who, while not advocating it, have believed that egoism is the 'natural' condition of the human being and that behaviour that appears to be altruistic is in fact dictated by concealed self-interest.

It does seem to be the case that egoity, the fact that each human being is a centre, sets up a tendency towards egoism, in which each makes his own centre absolute and evaluates everything from that point of view. The tendency is so strong that William Temple equated it with original sin. It is the temptation to put oneself in place of God, the temptation of the garden of Eden: 'You shall be as gods.'[19] But the tendency is to be resisted. Temple writes: 'I am in a state from birth in which I shall bring disaster on myself and everyone affected by my conduct unless I can escape from it.'[20]

But why should he say that the tendency is disastrous and we ought to escape from it, if it arises inevitably from the universal human condition of egoity and is so strong in everyone? Here we strike again upon one of those tensions or even contradictions that belong to humanity. Egoity sets up a tendency toward egoism. But egoism is self-defeating. The egoist sets himself up as the centre. He seeks to draw everything into himself and to make everything and everybody serve himself. But even in doing so, he is diminishing his humanity. He sets out to secure his ego, but in the process he stifles it. It is the deadly sin of gluttony on the grand scale, and the egoist is finally choked and suffocated. For we have seen, in our earlier studies, that the natural direction of the human being is outwards – this is the meaning of transcendence. The egoist, on the other hand, is concerned with his own centre. He is *incurvatus in se*, curved in upon himself, which was Luther's way of expressing the nature of sin. So instead of achieving his aim of self-aggrandizement, he slips back into a subhuman existence.

But the whole situation can be read in another way. The fact that inevitably I see the world from my own unique centre can be understood in terms of my finitude. In that case, it means that I have to become part of a larger whole. My outlook is distorted so long as it is confined to the narrow vision of the 'I'. My ego is only an abstract fragment, and to fulfil myself, I have to get out of myself. Admittedly, this is dangerous, and we have taken note that human beings tend to retreat from the hazards of freedom and transcendence.[21] Yet only by taking the risk of transcendence can a full humanity emerge. In the first place, the fragmentariness of the individual must be overcome by his joining himself with others. Finally, perhaps, he must transcend towards God and find his true centre there. Over against the temptation to become God is the Christian teaching that the human goal is to participate in the life of God.

Egoism proves to be a false direction in which to seek the realization of humanity. Only through losing the narrow egocentric self can a fuller humanity be attained. The ideals of self-fulfilment and self-renunciation are not contradictory, for in a remarkable way they coincide. It is above all Christianity that has understood this human paradox. Hans-Martin Barth has well said of its founder that he was one 'whose sacrifice for his fellow men in the last resort knew no limits', but that he was also one 'who burst the bounds of what had previously been seen as human fulfilment'.[22]

V

EMBODIEDNESS

All human life, as we know it, is embodied. Every human being is a body, made up of material substances, though, as we can equally well say that every human being *has* a body, we do not simply equate him with his body. We could also say that all human life is incarnate; it takes place 'in the flesh', in the sphere of the material and the spatio-temporal. Because of the special associations of the word 'incarnation' in Christian theology, it could be misleading to use it in a general way, yet in a sense the miracle of 'the word made flesh' is to be seen in every human being, where freedom, transcendence and rationality are conjoined with and manifest themselves in and through a material organism which belongs to a quite different order of being.

In the preceding chapters, we have dwelt chiefly on the 'spiritual' aspects of humanity, especially freedom, transcendence and the conscious ego which gives direction to life. We did indeed take note of the oppositions that are present in any human being: the area of his freedom is surrounded by a vast, already determined background, his possibilities for transcendence are inseparable from possibilities for regression, his egoity is from the beginning ambiguous. In turning now to the embodiedness of human beings, we are correcting the balance, and fighting against the universal tendency to take too grand a view of man by so exaggerating his spirituality and rationality that we forget that it is all firmly embedded in a material substrate which can be both supportive and threatening. However far human beings may have proceeded along the path of transcendence, they take their bodies with them as a permanent heritage from their humble origins in the dust. They remain part of the physical universe and subject to its laws, however much they may have adapted it to their own needs.

The familiar contrast that we make between body and soul focuses many of the polarities of human existence and overlaps them. When we speak ofthe soul, we think of that luminous centre of conscious selfhood which says 'I'. Yet we saw in the last chapter that the boundaries of the self are not sharp, and that it fades into a kind of penumbra at the edges of consciousness. The body is not something alien, but belongs to this wider self, and though some of its processes are quite unconscious, others obtrude on our awareness. The body is acknowledged as 'mine', yet there is a measure of ambivalence in this. We have already noted the peculiarity of our language, which allows us to say both that I *am* a body and that I *have* a body. We would never dream of saying, 'My body is hungry.' We say, 'I am hungry,' and here we seem to identify ourselves with the body. Yet, when we talk of someone 'having' a body, we seem to have introduced the idea of difference between him and his body, and to have recognized that he is somehow more than his body. This is another example of that identity in difference and difference in identity, that self-relatedness or failure to coincide with oneself, which we have already noted in many contexts. Incidentally, although many writers on the philosophy of man have drawn attention to the oscillation in language between being and having a body, I am not aware that any have pointed out that the same ambivalence occurs in talking of the soul. It is just as natural to say of someone that he 'has' a soul as that he 'is' a soul. The human being is from the beginning both body and soul, and neither exhausts his being. They can be in conflict, and they have sometimes been regarded as irreconcilable opposites, so that one has to choose between the soul and the body. This is certainly not a view that I would share, yet one can see how it might easily arise, given the original polarity in man of body and soul. The views being developed in this book point rather in the direction of bringing body and soul into a synthesis – indeed, this is one important aspect of the task of becoming human, in the fullest sense of the word.

We find Kierkegaard writing in one place: 'Man is a synthesis of the soulish and the bodily. But a synthesis is unthinkable if the two are not united in a third factor. This third factor is the spirit.'[1] Admittedly, this brings difficulties of terminology. The word 'spirit' is not to be understood here as some metaphysical spiritual substance, as if the body were somehow to be volatilized into ether. 'Spirit' here is to be understood much in the sense that I have myself used the word 'person', as when I pointed out that such biological phenomena as sexuality and death, without in the least ceasing to be bodily, are at the human level, transformed from *merely* biological phenomena into profoundly meaningful events of personal life.[2] But whether one uses the language of 'spirit' or of 'person', to talk of a 'synthesis' of soul and body cannot mean the abolition of the body.

In the discussion of the ego or self, I have already criticized Cartesian dualism. Body and soul cannot be regarded as two parallel *res*, things or substances, and I accepted Ryle's contention that a dualism of this kind rests on a category mistake. But I went on to say that I did not find Ryle's own account of the matter to be satisfactory. Ryle (like empiricists generally) is so eager to bring everything within the area of the objectifiable and publicly observable and so within the area accessible to empirical investigation, as to overlook or falsify the elusive subject that refuses to be reduced to an object. Category mistakes are not the monopoly of those who want to talk about spiritual substances. They belong also to those who want to reduce the spiritual or personal to a material thing or the adjective of a material thing. Perhaps the crudest category mistake in the history of philosophy was that of the Enlightenment *savant* who declared that the brain secretes thought as the liver secretes bile! The old-fashioned behaviourist psychology was not much better. Ryle has sometimes been called a 'neo-behaviourist', but I doubt if this does justice to his own protestations that he is *not* reductionist in his treatment of the human being – protestations which I was careful to quote in the earlier discussion. Nevertheless, one is left with the suspicion that any empiricist account of the ego, self, soul or whatever it may be called, is bound to have a reductionist tendency, and that there lurks in it a fundamental confusion of the categories of subject and object. I would find myself in general agreement with William Barrett's criticism of Ryle. While Barrett acknowledges the cogency of Ryle's attack on 'the ghost in the machine' and his achievements in clarifying our talk about consciousness, he goes on: 'In attempting to dispel the ghost from the machine, we have banished more that we wanted to. We have become behaving organisms rather than conscious subjects. To be a conscious subject is not at all to be a Cartesian subject; but it is also much more than being a behaving organism.'[3]

To reject the view that the soul is an independently existing substantial entity that somehow 'inhabits' the body and interacts with it, does not mean that one has then to accept that the soul is merely the behaviour of the body, a dependent epiphenomenon. One can accept (to use the language of Aristotle and Aquinas) that the soul is the 'form' of the body, without supposing that this form is determined by the body. Rather, this is a dynamic form that becomes the *hegemonikon*, the leading edge or governing centre that gives direction. In the complex being that we call a human being, we can get rid neither of the materiality of the body nor of the transcendent characteristics of the soul, and we cannot absorb either into the other. They exist in synthesis, even if the synthesis is imperfect or uneasy. And if this synthesis is a person, must we not agree with John Macmurray that it is *sui generis*, not to be reduced to a substance or an organism or whatever it might be?[4] Ryle himself seems not far from this position when he writes with some irony: 'Man need not be degraded to a machine by being denied to be a ghost in a machine. He might, after all, be a sort of animal, namely, a higher mammal. There has yet to be ventured the hazardous leap to the hypothesis that perhaps he is a man.'⁵ The exploitation of the ambiguity of the word 'man' in the last sentence of this passage may remind us of the parallel ambiguity in the adjective 'human' mentioned at the very beginning of this book.

Suppose, then, we agree to say that the human being is a psychosomatic unity, of a unique kind that we call personal. It may be replied that this formula solves nothing. Perhaps not, but it offers at least an approach to the subject of the embodiedness of human existence that is not obviously biased towards idealism or materialism or reductionism. It has the advantage too of beginning not with two hypothetical entities, mind and matter, that have to be put together, but with unitary human beings as we know them, though their unity is always a matter of degree, and within it we can distinguish the polarities of body and soul, as indicated in the adjective 'psychosomatic'.

This understanding of the human being as a single reality of which the mental and the physical are two aspects or poles seems to have considerable empirical evidence in its favour. Although a mental event, a conscious thought or feeling, is of an entirely different order from a physical entity, the two seem to be intimately correlated in human life. If someone is hit a blow over the head, he may lose consciousness altogether. If he indulges to excess in alcohol or drugs, his consciousness becomes confused or distorted. If certain parts of his brain are artificially stimulated, this again will affect his consciousness. On the other hand, there seem to be states of mind that have effects on the body. Deep-seated anxieties can inhibit the use of limbs or other faculties, and their removal takes away the inhibition also, so that it appears like a miracle of healing. A settled serene disposition often goes along with good physical health. Of course, it might be difficult in some cases to say what is the cause and what is the effect. But it is enough for our purpose simply to note the close correlation, and the evidence that this is not just a dependence of soul on body but seems to be a reciprocal relation in which each pole influences and is influenced by the other.

But while modern empirical knowledge supports the view that man is a psychosomatic unity, this has been from ancient times the teaching of the Judaeo-Christian tradition. The older of the two creation stories in Genesis tells how God 'formed man from the dust of the ground, and breathed into his nostrils the breath of life'.⁶ Dust and breath are there in man together from the moment of his creation. There is no suggestion here of a pre-existing soul that 'falls' into matter and is contaminated by it. The material body is an integral part of the whole human being. The fall into sin is only subsequent, and that is a fall of the entire human being, both soul and body. As the story is told in Genesis, it suggests that the primeval sin included both pride and sensuality.

This unitary conception of the human being continues through the

Hebrew Scriptures. It has often been pointed out that in the classic period of Hebrew religion, there was no belief in immortality (for the shadowy existence of Sheol could not be counted as such). Life was believed to be bound up with the body, and while the Hebrew ideal stressed the spiritual qualities of righteousness and mercy, these were to be exercised in the context of long life and material prosperity. Even as late as the time of Jesus, the Sadducees were clinging to this traditional this-worldly ideal, and believed it to be the authentic faith of the Jewish people. Of course, already in the time before Christ other ideas were beginning to establish themselves, and we find them in the deutero-canonical literature of the period. Some Jews, under Greek influences, were accepting the belief in an immortal soul that would survive the body. Though good men seem to perish from the earth, 'the souls of the righteous are in the hand of God',[7] and they are at peace. But the doctrine of an immortal soul independent of the body does not fit well with the Hebrew tradition. When the sufferings of the Maccabean wars drove the Jews to think seriously about life beyond death, they could not conceive such a life without the body as an integral part of the human being. Thus, far more congenial to their tradition than any doctrine of an immortal soul was their own solution of the problem in terms of belief in the resurrection of the body. At first sight, this may seem a more primitive and inherently less plausible belief than belief in an immortal soul that will survive without the body. Yet it could be argued that the Hebrew belief in resurrection is more profound than the Hellenic belief in immortality. It is so because it recognizes that a body is essential to a personal existence.

Some modern philosophers have speculated what existence as a disembodied soul might be like, and their findings are not encouraging. P. F. Strawson, for instance, points out that while it is possible to conceive one's soul surviving its body, one would then be in a very extraordinary condition. There would be no perception of a body related to one's experience, one could not be perceived by other people, and there would be no way of initiating changes in the physical world. Two consequences seem to follow. Such an existence would be utterly solitary, and the individual so existing would have to think of himself as a *former* person and would have to live on the memories of his past, for there would be no new perceptions or social contacts. As these memories gradually faded, life would become more and more attenuated. Strawson reasonably concludes: 'Disembodied survival, on such terms as these, may well seem unattractive. No doubt it is for this reason that the orthodox have wisely insisted on the resurrection of the body.'[8]

Well, whether for this reason or for others, Christianity certainly did insist on the resurrection of the body, and turned this item from the Jewish heritage into one of its major articles of faith, embracing both the resurrection of Jesus Christ and the general resurrection at the end of the age. Paul did not hesitate to make resurrection the key issue on which Christianity stands or falls.[9] As christology developed in the church, there emerged another powerful motive for acknowledging the importance and worth of the body. I mean, the doctrine of incarnation. The Word had taken a body, and this conferred an unprecented dignity and importance on the material world and on the human body in particular. It is surely a striking fact that as Christianity extended itself through the Hellenistic world, it consistently resisted the pressures of docetist and gnostic sects that in one way or another denied the true embodiment of the word in Christ.

Admittedly, Christianity was less successful in resisting pressure to transform belief in resurrection into a belief in immortality of the soul. At an early stage in Christian thought, the influence of Plato made itself strongly felt, and for him it is the soul that is the true human reality. It would not be unfair to say that throughout its history Christianity has lived in an uneasy compromise between resurrection and immortality. The former has remained its official doctrine, but the latter has stubbornly maintained itself alongside it, and in fact the popular belief of Christendom has been a form of dualism, corresponding to the more sophisticated form that came to expression in the philosophy of Descartes. But in recent decades the development of biblical theology and the sometimes exaggerated opposition that has been perceived between Jewish and Greek ideas has recalled Christianity to a more unambiguous affirmation of the body and of the material world generally as essential to a fully human and personal existence as well as being implicit in its own most authentic tradition.

Incidentally, these questions about the body in human existence, whether it is integral to such an existence or whether the soul is the reality and the body only a temporary adjunct, cannot be dismissed as merely metaphysical or theological speculations. They afford another important illustration of how theories about the human being translate themselves into action and so become part of the very reality they profess to describe, shaping it one way or another. The Judaeo-Christian tradition has, as we have seen, accepted the body and the material world generally as part of God's original creation and therefore good. A care for man's material well-being is therefore built into this tradition and has expressed itself in a great many ways, from Israel's prophetic concern for social justice in the economic order to Christian medical missions in modern times. But religions which have taught that the body or matter in general is evil or illusory (for instance, both gnosticism in ancient times and certain Eastern religions of the present) have believed that salvation is possible only for the soul, and that such salvation consists in an escape from the imprisoning body into which the soul has fallen and thereby had its original purity contaminated. Such religions encourage a contempt or hostility for the body and tend to be indifferent about the material conditions of life. In each case the belief about the human reality itself moulds that reality.

Yet even to say this is to draw attention again to the ambivalence that seems to enter into every aspect of the human condition. A body-affirming and world-affirming religion can degenerate into a preoccupation with material well-being, as has in fact to a large extent already happened in Western countries. Some historians have claimed that science, technology and even capitalism have their roots in the biblical tradition, especially in the doctrine of creation and the divine command 'to subdue the earth'.[10] The point should not be exaggerated, but it does seem evident that the world-affirming character of biblical religion has stamped itself on Western civilization, and now that religion and the sense of the world as divine creation have declined, we are left with the secularized materialist consumer mentality of the technologically advanced nations. It is worth noting that while Christianity did take an affirmative attitude to the material world, it produced a corrective from within itself, namely, the asceticism of the religious life. This first appeared in Eastern Christianity, always less attached to the world than its Western counterpart, but the religious life developed in the West as well. It would no longer be considered a 'higher' form of Christianity, but is seen today as 'a sign of contradiction', that is to say, as a corrective to excessive absorption in material and bodily well-being. A reverse dialectic can be seen in some eastern religions. Whereas the main tradition in Hinduism has been mystical and other-worldly, reforming movements in modern times have sought to improve the physical conditions of life.

We have seen that both modern thought and the Judaeo-Christian tradition agree that the human being is a psychosomatic unity, and reject the various dualisms that have been so dominant at one time or another. But we are still far from grasping what is meant by 'psychosomatic unity'. We tend to lean to the view either that a human being is an animated body or that he is an embodied soul. It seems hard for us to grasp that there is an irreducible category, namely, that of 'person', which is a unity, though for certain purposes we may wish to consider this or that aspect in abstraction. I think this is what Strawson also is saying when he declares: 'The concept of a person is logically prior to that of an individual consciousness. The concept of a person is not to be analysed as that of an animated body or of an embodied anima.'[11] The unity is expressed in a somewhat different way by Sartre. He writes, 'There is nothing *behind* the body, but the body is wholly "psychic".'[12]

It is perhaps worthwhile at this point to recall the teaching of a philosopher of an older generation, Schopenhauer. Like Macmurray, Ryle, Heidegger, Sartre and other twentieth-century philosophers, Schopenhauer in his day criticized and rejected the dualistic account of body and soul as distinct substances that are somehow conjoined in human life. If he had been able to read Sartre's words quoted above, he would doubtless have agreed with them. For Schopenhauer, the whole body is the seat of will and so of man's psychic life. The interesting point is that he locates the tension or polarity between the soulish and the bodily *within* the psycho-somatic unity which is a human being. He was impressed by the fact that the brain and the genital organs are situated at opposite poles of the body. This represents the tension between knowledge, the intellectual and spiritual life on the one hand, and what he called 'will', understood as blind urge or desire, on the other hand. To quote his words: 'The genital organs are, far more than any other external member of the body, subject merely to the will, and not at all to knowledge. The genitals are properly the *focus* of will, and consequently the opposite pole of the brain, the representative of knowledge. Knowledge affords the possibility of the suppression of willing, of salvation through freedom.'[13] The point is especially interesting if we remember that in introducing the idea of a *hegemonikon* or leading edge in the last chapter, I mentioned the phenomenon of cephalization or the development of a head region in evolution. But I also indicated that the boundaries of the ego stretch away beyond the luminous centre of consciousness, so that it may be invaded by desires and impulses which, in a sense, belong to it and yet may be in conflict with its policies. It is important not to be misled by Schopenhauer's peculiar use of the word 'will'. When and if I use the word 'will' myself, I understand it in a more Kantian sense and would associate it with consciousness, the ego, the self. Indeed, the will simply *is* the self in its initiation of action.

If the body is wholly psychic, if it is an integral part of a person and, if we may so express it, an outlying area of the ego, so that when it invades the centre, we say 'I am hungry,' not, 'My body is hungry,' then there would seem to be two ways in which we learn about the body. We can learn about it from the study of other people's bodies. This is no doubt how we first learn the configuration of a human body, its elegance and powers of movement. On a more sophisticated level, we learn about it through anatomy, physiology, biochemistry and so on. But because we ourselves have bodies or are body-souls, we learn about the body also from our experience of our own bodies. The physiologist tells me what goes on in the body when I am hungry or angry, but it is only through my own experience of being hungry or angry that I can attach full meaning to these words. A doctor can explain exactly what goes on in the body during a heart attack, but only someone who has experienced a heart attack knows it as an item in his own conscious history. He knows it in a way the doctor does not, unless the doctor too has suffered one. So it would seem that even the body cannot be wholly objectified or wholly known from the outside. It is part of the whole human reality, just as essential a part as what we call the mind. So it can be fully known only in a human way. To choose a more cheerful illustration than that of a heart attack, we might ask whether any treatise on the physiology of respiration could tell us what it is like to stand on a mountain and freely breathe in the cold clean air. In such a moment, it is possible to feel at home in the body, to know it as part of oneself and to experience the unity of the whole person. We talk of the *joie de vivre*.

But it is also possible to feel not at home in the body and to experience tension and alienation between the conscious centre of the self and the body. Though I have been stressing that the human being is a psychosomatic unity, this unity is a potentiality rather than a ready-made actuality. We recall Kierkegaard's belief that the human task is to effect a synthesis of body and soul. Though one may reject metaphysical dualism, there is still the task of synthesizing the different and possibly conflicting tendencies within the human person.

Now let us consider some of the specifically bodily contributions to human life. The next few paragraphs can be contrasted with our earlier speculation on what a disembodied existence might be like.

First, the body is the source of sensations, and I have in mind particularly sensations of sight, sound, touch, taste, smell, temperature and whatever else tells us about the physical world around us. The body of each one of us is located among other material things, and can both act upon them and be acted upon by them. From the beginning of life, we are in interaction through our bodies with these material things. We can admire them, use them, possess them, destroy them or deal with them in innumerable other ways. On the other hand, they can supply our needs, or they can threaten and injure us, or they can be indifferent. To belong in a world through having or being a body is essential to the human condition. It is essential to our well being, yet at the same time it inevitably exposes us to disease, injury, subjection to subpersonal forces, eventually to death, as our own bodies participate in that constant coming into being and passing out of being which is characteristic of the changing configurations of matter and energy in the physical universe.

Second, the emotions are closely connected with the body. In anger, for instance, adrenalin pours into the bloodstream. In some other emotions, the bodily basis may not be so clear, but some such basis there would always seem to be, and our emotions would seem to be just as important a way of relating and responding to our environment as are sensations. One difference would seem to be that while our senses make us aware of particular objects in the environment, emotions relate us to situations. It is hard to say whether the emotion is produced by the situation or whether it intuits the situation. An emotion of fear, for instance, is produced by some threatening situation, but one could also say that it intuits the situation as threatening. I speak here of 'intuition' because one does not infer that the situation is threatening; one may not use words at all, but reacts 'instinctively', as we say. Emotions are in this way a mode of sensitivity. Through the emotions we 'read' the environment and make the appropriate response, or at least prepare to make it. We can therefore agree with Sartre that 'emotion is a way of apprehending the world'.[14] Elsewhere, he says, 'what an emotion signifies is the totality of the relationships of the human reality to the world'.[15]

Emotions then are not just subjective moods, and they do not come and go in a purely arbitrary way. They are related to varying situations in which we find ourselves. Also, while it is true that one cannot feel an emotion at will or, on the other hand, banish at will an emotion that has arisen, it is also true that the emotions can be trained. We can learn to be more sensitive to certain kinds of situation, and we can learn to control emotions like anger. The emotions play an important part in relating us to the environing reality, and just as our thoughts about it can be true or false, so our emotions may be appropriate or inappropriate. John Macmurray, one of the few British philosophers who has attended to this topic, asks: 'Since our feelings refer to what is outside them, to some object about which they are felt, why should they not refer rightly or wrongly to their object, just like thoughts?'[16] Our emotions, like our thoughts, are 'intentional'; that is to say, they refer beyond themselves to situations in the world.

A little reflection too shows us that the emotions are by no means disordered or capricious. They fall into well-defined families, within which one emotion fades into another closely related one, and each is appropriate to its own kind of situation. They form, as it were, an emotional commentary on the events of life, and this commentary is not negligible in the management of life. Most languages are extraordinarily subtle in the rich vocabulary they possess for distinguishing the nuances of emotion. English, for instance, has so many words for referring to the gradations and modifications of fear – terror, panic, revulsion, horror, fright, alarm, dread, awe, reverence and many others. Or consider this series expressive of the heaviness of boredom and emptiness, taken from Pascal and left untranslated in his eloquent French: *l'ennui, la noirceur, la tristesse, le chagrin, le dépit, le désespoir*.[17] There is what we might call a 'logic' of the emotions. It was of course Pascal who wrote: 'We know the truth not only by reason but by the heart; it is in the latter way that we know first principles. The heart has its reasons that reason does not know.'[18]

These may seem exaggerated claims to make for the emotions, and perhaps Pascal would not have put them so starkly had he not (like some of the other philosophers we have mentioned) been in conscious opposition to Descartes. Pascal was a noted mathematician, but he believed the attempt of his fellow-mathematician Descartes to make mathematics the paradigm of all knowledge to be utterly mistaken. What he claims for the emotions is to be understood in this context. It then shows itself to be a plea for the whole person – emotion as well as reason, body as well as soul. What is being advocated is not an emotionalism, but simply the claim that one cannot ignore the emotions and the intuitions which they provide. Sometimes these intuitions are mistaken, just as our sense-perceptions can be mistaken or our chains of reasoning. The deliverances of the emotions need to be subjected to the critical scrutiny of reason. But our understanding of the human situation will be vastly impoverished if the testimony of the emotions is neglected. The whole human being is Dionysian as well as Apollonian, and if we take away either, we are left with a half-man or half-woman.

The emotions display a dialectic similar to that which we have met in other aspects of human life. Some of them may be broadly called affirmative, because they express an affirmative attitude to the surrounding world – such as trust, contentment, joy, affection. Others are negative and opposite to these – suspicion, dissatisfaction, sorrow, resentment. Perhaps if either class of emotion wholly prevailed, human life as we know it would come to an end, for if there were either unbroken contentment or unrelieved despair, there would be no incentive to go any further. I say, 'human life as we know it', that is to say, temporal life, for some thinkers have imagined a complete fruition which would be life in eternity rather than life in time. But this is not something we can consider at this point.

However, if we look at the other possibility, the unrelieved despair that would follow from the complete domination of the negative emotions, we could see that as paralysing any further activity. We need what Tillich called the 'courage to be',[19] and perhaps we can have that only if the affirmative emotions are more fundamental than the negative ones. The tension between the two will, however, always be felt in temporal existence. We may recall how, in our discussion of freedom, we noted that the exercise of freedom is accompanied by both exhilaration and anxiety.[20] Some writers have in fact stressed anxiety as the most revealing human emotion, yet are not joy and courage to be taken as equally revealing of the human situation, perhaps even more fundamental, since they are affirmative? Are not the very presence of joy and courage in human life the mute evidence of a trust in the order and meaningfulness of being? Ricoeur goes so far as to call joy and anxiety 'ontological' emotions, because they seem to light up and intuit not just this or that situation, but the human situation in its totality. It is, however, joy, or, strictly speaking, 'joy in and through anguish' that he takes to be the fundamental emotional index.[21]

Third, the body is the seat of certain desires, which arise out of its own bodily processes. We have already seen that although physiologically the

activities associated with these desires are similar to animal activities, they
have in the human being become personalized. Human beings 'make love',
as we say, they do not merely copulate. They eat rather than feed. Eating
and drinking become social occasions for personal intercourse. These
various activities have ceased to be merely animal and have been integrated
into the lives of persons. They can indeed belong to the most intimate
aspects of personal life, and to the extent that this happens, we have an
example of the 'synthesis of body and soul' of which Kierkegaard wrote.

But here too conflict and alienation can occur. There are false forms of
asceticism which deny the body and its natural desires. They are held to be
intrinsically evil, and become a matter for shame and guilt. More commonly
the desires of the body are overindulged or perverted into unnatural
channels, as happens in alcoholism and drug abuse. Here body and soul
have sprung apart, and the leading edge of the person has become enslaved
to the desires of the body and had its place usurped by them.

Fourth, the body is the basis for our relations with other people. It is
through the body that we become aware of their bodies and communicate
with them. Speaking and hearing, gestures and facial expressions, physical
contacts, are the obvious ways in which we relate to others. Again, the
possibilities are twofold. On the one hand there are love, trust, friendship,
respect, true community; on the other, hate, envy, malice, competition,
egoism. We have briefly glanced at these possibilities in our earlier
discussion of egoity. At this point we simply note the further complications
that arise when we explicitly acknowledge the role of the body in these
relations, but the whole question of human interpersonal and social
relations is so important that it will call for specific and extended treatment
later.

We have now seen something of what it means to exist in embodied
form. There can be no question of thinking of the body as evil or a mere
appendage or habitation of the self. It is an integral and essential aspect of
the whole human being. The reason for this is that only through a body do
we relate to a world, whether of things or persons. And no one could be a
person apart from such relations.

VI

COGNITION

Western philosophy, at least since the time of Descartes, has been intensely preoccupied with epistemology. What do we know? How can we know? How can we know that we know? These questions are, of course, of the very highest importance. Yet, it will be remembered that I declined to take man's rationality as the starting point for an exploration of the human condition.[1] I did so because the cognitive or intellective activities have to be set in the broader spectrum of personal existence, and if we isolate them, we turn the human being in all his concreteness into the abstraction of a knowing subject, a mere point of consciousness not so much in the world as over against it and taking it for its object. That is something less than a human being, but philosophy's long preoccupation with epistemology has tended to encourage the belief that a human being is pre-eminently a knowing subject. On the contrary, it has to be asserted that knowing is a mode of being. No doubt it is a very important way of being, but there are other ways besides. We should remember a dictum of J. G. Hamann: 'Do not forget the noble *sum* on account of the *cogito*.'[2]

Still, we must not forget the *cogito* either. Although we began our study of the human by considering freedom, we soon found that the exercise of freedom demands a whole range of cognitive activity on the part of the free agent, otherwise it would be indistinguishable from sheer randomness. Cognition is essential to human transcendence. Even to know the world is, in a manner, to transcend it. To know oneself is likewise to transcend oneself, though we have seen in our criticism of Ryle that we know ourselves not just as objectified (though we can know ourselves that way) but, more fundamentally, in a pre-reflexive awareness.

We must do justice to the whole cognitive aspect of the human being, but in order to do this, we must break out of a very narrow conception of knowledge that has become something like a dogma in the West. I mean, of course, empiricism. Let me not be misunderstood at this point. I have already indicated, in a criticism of the Marxist rejection of empiricism, that I have no quarrel with it as such and indeed welcome empirical investigation.[3] My objection is to the attempt to bring all knowledge within the sphere of the empirical, or, perhaps I should say, to extend the claims of empirical investigation so as to deny that there can be any genuine knowledge outside its scope. In particular, I have denied that this is an adequate approach to the knowledge of the human reality itself. The empirical method, as practised in the natural sciences, has proved to be enormously successful, and it can usefully be extended to some aspects of human life. But I think we have already seen that what is most distinctively human, for instance, freedom, transcendence, egoity, are not objectifiable phenomena, or not wholly objectifiable phenomena, that can be brought into the empiricist net.

Again, one has to recognize that there are narrower and broader varieties of empiricism. The narrower variety tends to identify experience with sense-experience, and to acknowledge as meaningful only concepts which refer to sensible phenomena and propositions which are in principle capable of being verified by sense-experience. I would find myself much more in sympathy with broader types of empiricism where, let us say, interpersonal, moral, aesthetic and even religious experience are recognized alongside sense-experience, but when the spectrum of experience is made very broad, the continued use of the expression 'empiricism' has been made quite vague.

The narrower type of empiricism received perhaps its classic and certainly its most extreme formulation in Alfred Ayer's *Language, Truth and Logic*, published in 1936. For two or three decades this form of empiricism, known as 'logical positivism', had an enormous vogue. According to its teaching, our knowledge is confined to the realm of that which is observable by the senses. The only exceptions are the propositions of logic and mathematics, but these were held to give no information about the real world. From the beginning, however, critics noticed that there is a serious incoherence in this extreme form of empiricism. One of its pillars is the doctrine that the only meaningful propositions are those which are in principle amenable to some form of verification by sense-experience, but then this basic tenet itself does not fall within the class of meaningful propositions. The scepticism of Ayer, like the scepticism which we noted among those who deny the freedom of the human person,[4] turns out to be self-destructive. As Husserl once remarked, 'Every genuine scepticism, whatever its type and orientation may be, can be recognized by this fundamental absurdity, that in the argument it uses, it presupposes implicitly as the conditions for the possibility of its validity, precisely that which it denies in its own theses.'[5] Ayer and others who shared his position introduced various modifications into their empiricism, but even today, although there may be few who would call themselves logical positivists, there is still among many philosophers a hankering after empiricism in what I would regard as an injuriously restrictive and reductionist form.

I propose therefore to spend a little time in criticizing the empiricist theory of knowledge, for I believe it distorts our understanding of the human reality, which is the main theme of this study. In pursuing this criticism, I shall refer to two books in particular, Karl Popper's *Objective Knowledge* and Michael Polanyi's *Personal Knowledge*. Apart from the fact that both are by distinguished philosophers of science and both make far-reaching criticisms of the conventional empiricism, these two books might seem at first sight to have little in common – indeed, their very titles might seem to indicate a fundamental opposition. Yet when we look into the matter more deeply, we find that there is more of convergence than of opposition, and that they represent a kind of pincer movement on the citadel of empiricism.

Popper's critique begins from his dissatisfaction with induction. Incidentally, he reminds us that Hume too had questioned the validity of induction. Very briefly, the theory of induction is the view that our knowledge begins with the observation of particular instances of phenomena. As we observe more and more instances, we take note of repetitions, similarities, regular connections and so on, and we go on to formulate general laws and to construct theories. Hume had already pointed out that there is no logical justification for moving from even a large accumulation of specific instances to the formulation of a general law, but he tried to find a psychological justification in the association of ideas. Popper is far more radical: 'There is no such thing as induction by repetition.'[6] He denies that we begin with pure observations – 'the bucket theory' of the mind, he calls it, which seems to be much the same as the *tabula rasa* of which the older empiricists spoke. 'There can be no pure observational language.' Our observations are from the beginning being interpreted in terms of our expectations, theories and myths. We are not passive receptacles receiving sensations. We do not just observe – we observe this or that, something that is of interest and about which we already have questions or expectations or beliefs.

What then does Popper put in place of the conventional theory of induction which, as he believes, he has discredited? His own view assigns a much more active and even creative role to human understanding. He calls it the 'searchlight' view of the mind as opposed to the bucket view, thought, of course, the language is tendentious. Yet I think Popper is far more convincing in his account and also puts the findings of science on a more secure foundation than any theory of induction can provide. Popper believes that we are constantly forming hypotheses and theories to solve the problems that arise in experience. It does not matter where we get these theories from – they may be bold imaginative constructions, and it is because of the importance of the imagination in Popper's view of knowledge that I have stressed the *creative* role of our minds. If the old view was that we glean some theory from the observation of phenomena and then try to *verify* that theory by making subsequent observations, Popper may be said to turn this right around. We confront the phenomena with our theories, and then try to *falsify* the theories in the light of facts. To falsify a theory is not to show that it is utterly worthless or a waste of time. The very process of critical discussion leads to new ideas and points to better theories. No theory is finally true. The best we can look for is verisimilitude, and approximation to the truth. A theory which explains more and has been falsified at fewer points than another theory has to that extent more verisimilitude. For instance, Einstein's theory has more verisimilitude than Newton's. But the older theory is not just superseded. To a greater or lesser extent, it is incorporated into the new.

An important point that arises out of these considerations has been well expressed by Brian Magee: 'Popper knows that interesting truths consist of quite staggeringly unlikely propositions, not even to be conjectured without a rare boldness of imagination.'[7] In other words, the significance and informative and explanatory content of a theory is proportional to its vulnerability. The proposition about which no one is going to disagree is the proposition that has very little interest and is perhaps little more than a tautology. But, as we have noted already, even a 'high risk' theory, though it may be eventually falsified or falsified in some respects, will through its very richness have advanced understanding in the course of the critical discussion to which it has been subjected. It is obvious too that this recommended procedure of the attempted falsification of an imaginative hypothesis is far more likely to be intellectually productive than attempts to verify some initially probable theory. If we try hard enough to find verification for a view, it is only too likely that we shall persuade ourselves that we have succeeded. 'It is easy,' writes Popper, 'to obtain confirmations or verifications for nearly every theory – if we look for confirmations.'[8]

Popper was writing with the methods of the natural sciences in view, but his teachings may well have implications for other branches of human knowledge. He himself believed that the criterion of falsifiability is a useful way of marking off science from theories that might appear scientific but are in fact pseudo-science. Thus he criticized both Freudianism and Marxism as being, at least in part, pseudo-science. They profess to be scientifically based, but there is no way in which they could be falsified, for they interpret every event in accordance with their own presuppositions, and then claim it as a verification. On the other hand, Antony Flew's attempt to apply the falsification principle in the case of Christian theology rests on a misunderstanding of what Popper was about.[9] His falsification principle has the function – among others – of unmasking the pretensions of enterprises which claim to be scientific and are not really so. But since Christianity never claimed to be 'scientific' in the sense in which we use that adjective of the natural sciences, then to show that Christian theology is unfalsifiable (assuming that one could show this) would only amount to showing that theology is not what in fact it has never claimed to be, namely, a science of the same kind as geology.

In fact, the relevance of Popper's epistemology for theology lies in quite a different direction, and has been well brought out by John Rodwell.[10] First, there is an obvious parallel between the imaginative theories which Popper sees as fruitful in the sciences and the imaginative myths of religion. In both cases, there may appear to be low probability, the richer the content, yet it is such exercises in imagination that stimulate thought and evoke insight. We might expect Popper to have some sympathy with Kierkegaard, who opposed all attempts to reduce Christianity to a few general truths and saw its strength and continuing interest precisely in its paradoxical character. Second, Popper has surely discredited once for all the so-called 'genetic' fallacy, which judged the truth of a doctrine by its psychological or sociological origins. He has shown that the value of a hypothesis is not affected by the question of whether it has been formed from observation or imagination, from metaphysics or mythology. Yet there are still critics of Christian theology who have not learned this simple truth, and think they are discrediting Christian doctrine if they can find links between it and the Hellenistic mystery cults or Roman emperor worship or some other Near Eastern mythology. Third, and here it is perhaps the theologian rather than his critics who has to learn from Popper, our hypotheses, whether scientific or theological, have to be submitted to rigorous critical discussion. Only so do they yield anything in them of value. This critical discussion, in both science and theology, is, one may hope, a progressive one. It never arrives at final truth, but one may hope that it leads nearer to truth, that it advances in verisimilitude, to use Popper's expression.

But now let us return from these comparisons to the main lines of Popper's philosophy. His aim is objective knowledge. What does he mean by 'objective knowledge'? To some extent, the expression can be read as part of his polemic against empiricism. In spite of its pretensions to objectivity, empiricism from Hume and Berkeley on has marked a turn to the subject. It is the experiencing subject who becomes the source and centre of knowledge. Furthermore, if the doubt which first Hume and then Popper have cast on the validity of induction is justified, the claims of the empiricist to knowledge of the real world are seriously undermined indeed. Popper introduces the paradox of 'epistemology without a knowing subject'.[11] Knowledge, as he sees it, is like a tradition which develops a life of its own. Admittedly, knowledge begins as the result of human effort and achievement, but then it generates its own problems. There is a parallel here to what both Heidegger and Gadamer have claimed about language. The utterance of a philosopher or of a poet always contains more meaning than he is aware of in making it, and it becomes capable of yielding fresh interpretations of which its original author did not dream. Popper points to something even more important. Even the most original and creative thinkers derive far more from this tradition of knowledge than their own input into it. This feedback he relates in turn to human self-transcendence. He is, of course, talking about transcendence in knowledge, so his remark would apply chiefly to that mode of transcendence which we found in the philosophy of Lonergan and the transcendental Thomists and which has a distinctively intellectual bias. But since I do not wish to separate the intellectual from the other modes of human transcendence, I would see the kind of feedback that Popper mentions as influencing all modes of transcendence. Indeed, near the outset of this inquiry,[12] I noted how every theory of the human 'by a kind of feedback mechanism, influences the reality which it studies'. In the light of Popper's epistemology, we can now see more clearly the importance of this. We can see why it was right to resist any attempt to confine the study of the human to the empirically given, for the imaginative theory itself brings about change and, one may hope, transcendence in the human reality.

We have still not followed to the end the implications of Popper's concept of objective knowledge. It becomes objective in the sense that it is actually embodied in space and time, in the form of books, tapes, films and so on. Again there is a parallel with Gadamer, who emphasizes the importance of writing in detaching ideas from someone's understanding and giving to them an independent existence as a 'text'. Now Popper at one point visualizes two hypothetical situations. In one of them, all scientists and intellectuals are wiped out in some catastrophe, and there are no records left. Any survivors would have to begin from nothing, and make the long and painful climb through barbarism once more to culture and civilization. In the second case, libraries survive, and preserve the objective knowledge on the basis of which civilized life can be restored much more quickly.

But while one can acknowledge that there are important insights in Popper's teaching about objective knowledge, it seems to me that in the illustrations just quoted, he has stretched the thesis beyond what it is able to bear. First of all, the objective knowledge which survives in libraries is surely only a potential knowledge so long as it remains locked away in the books. If there were nothing but mice and cockroaches running around the library, then the books would eventually moulder on the shelves without anyone being any the wiser. The knowledge would only be actualized and set to work again if some human minds appropriated the contents of the books. In his justifiable anxiety to correct the lurch toward subjectivism which he believes to be inherent in empiricism, Popper goes too far in talking of 'epistemology without a knowing subject'. We are not confronted with a disjunction between 'objective' and 'subjective', for knowledge – at least, knowledge about facts in the world around us – needs both a subject and an object. It is true that Popper supposes that as well as the libraries, 'our capacity to learn from them' would have to survive the catastrophe. But this leads to a second criticism. We have to ask the question whether it would be possible to learn only from libraries. We could put this question in another way by asking whether it is possible to learn without a teacher. Is there perhaps an inescapably personal element involved in the transmission of knowledge? Is it possible to pack all knowledge, including skills and techniques, into books – or even into books supplemented by films, tapes and the like, though with these one does seem to be bringing in something of a personal element? To learn how to think, how to conjecture, how to observe, how to engage in critical discussion and so on would seem to demand not just textbooks but a community of learning, or a tradition, not just in the sense of a body of objective knowledge handed on, but a living continuing succession of teachers and learners. Perhaps if human beings joined the mice and cockroaches in the library, the knowledge in the books would still remain locked up and inaccessible unless these human beings had once themselves been trained in scholarship and research by other human beings.

These reflections bring me to the other writer on epistemology mentioned above – Polanyi. Popper and Polanyi are by no means to be considered as merely opposed to one another, though they differ at many points and it might seem as if the ideals of 'objective knowledge' and 'personal knowledge' are irreconcilable. Polanyi is quite explicit in asserting that his recognition of a personal dimension of knowledge is not to be understood as subjectivism. 'Comprehension is neither an arbitrary act nor a passive experience, but a responsible act claiming universal validity. Such knowing is indeed *objective* in the sense of establishing contact with a hidden reality.'[13] Popper too, as we have seen, stresses the activity of the knower – we do not just observe, we observe this or that, and this or that is what we have chosen to observe. But it is Polanyi who brings out in detail the personal contribution to and participation in the act of knowing. It is hard to believe that after reading him carefully, anyone could still believe in the 'detached' observer or the 'value-free' investigator. These are not, as is sometimes supposed, prerequisites of science, but are perpetuations of the Cartesian speculation that there is a pure thinking subject, a point without extension and whose function is pure observation.

In Polanyi's view, knowledge demands art and skill as well as pure thought. 'I regard knowing as an active comprehension of the things known, an action that requires skill.'[14] It requires too a relation to a tradition and to a whole background of implicit awareness – 'tacit' knowledge, as Polanyi calls it, and about this I shall have more to say in a moment. Other personal factors in knowing are the imagination of the investigator (also stressed by Popper) and his commitment to his theories (reminiscent of Popper's point about the vulnerability of fruitful hypotheses). 'Personal knowledge,' writes Polanyi, 'is an intellectual commitment, and as such inherently hazardous. Only affirmations that could be false can be said to convey objective knowledge of this kind.'[15]

Let us now return to that imaginary situation envisaged by Popper. Scientists, scholars and their equipment have been wiped out, but libraries have survived and with them objective knowledge. Polanyi's stress on the personal dimensions in knowledge make it clearer than one would gather from Popper that the knowledge contained in the libraries remains only potential until there are some people around with the capacity to appropriate it. But, even more, Polanyi lends point to my second criticism of Popper, that even if there eventually were people in the library, they might be incapable of appropriating the knowledge contained in the books unless there were teachers to bring them into the living tradition of the community of learning. I come back to the idea of 'tacit' knowledge. Our language never describes anything completely and without remainder, yet we are not just unaware of what has not been expressed. Around the focal point on which I have concentrated attention, there is a penumbra of what Polanyi calls 'subsidiary' awareness. Certainly, our language can be made more exact and our descriptions more detailed, but there will always be something more that is unspecified and indeed unspecifiable. So there is no way in which all knowledge could be made objective in a library. Even if most of the *content* of knowledge could be so specified, the art or skill of knowing would still escape. 'An art which cannot be specified in detail cannot be transmitted by prescription, since no prescription for it exists. It can be passed on only by example from master to apprentice.'[16] Elsewhere he writes: 'All arts are learned by intelligently imitating the way they are practised by other persons in whom the learner places his confidence.'[17] Polanyi gives a very good example of this, namely, that 'while the articulate concepts of science are successfully taught all over the world in hundreds of new universities, the unspecifiable art of scientific research has not yet penetrated to many of these'.[18] There are, of course, hundreds of other examples from non-academic pursuits. Japanese distillers might have a recipe for Scotch whisky made available to them, they might even have a Japanese town renamed Inverness so that they could print 'Distilled in Inverness' on their labels, yet perhaps the only way in which they could produce an authentic Scotch whisky would be for several generations of them to serve their apprenticeships in Scottish distilleries.

I wrote above that the theories of Popper and Polanyi were like a pincer movement threatening the core of conventional empiricism. We can now see the truth of this, for surely some of the central dogmas of empiricism have been put in question. Here are seven basic critical questions that are raised for the upholders of the empirical theory of knowledge:

1. Whether knowledge begins from observation.

2. Whether there is a valid logic of induction.

3. Whether the ideal of scientific detachment is feasible beyond a very narrow range.

4. Whether the thinking subject is an artificial abstraction from the concreteness of the self.

5. Whether all knowledge can be put into propositions or given clear conceptual expression.

6. Whether knowledge of facts ('knowing that . . .') is the basic form of knowledge.

7. Whether the empirical sciences present us with a kind of paradigm to which all authentic knowledge should conform or seek to conform.

To attempt to answer all these questions in any detail would require a book in itself, and in fact both Popper and Polanyi have given answers. I think, however, that we have ourselves gathered enough in our reflections on cognition to be able to give some brief answers that are very relevant to our inquiry into the nature of a human being and that liberate us from the constricting limits of a narrow empiricism. Thus, in answer to the seven questions listed above, I would make the following replies:

1. That some knowledge does *not* begin from observation.

2. That conjectures and imaginative hypotheses (even, and perhaps especially, improbable ones!) may be more fruitful than inductive generalizations.

3. That in many subjects, and not least in the study of humanity itself, the ideal of detachment is a hindrance.

4. That knowledge is a function of an active self participating in a world rather than the data collected by an abstract thinking subject.

5. That there are various kinds of tacit knowledge, ranging all the way from the skills of craftsmen to the insights of artists and even the visions of mystics, and these cannot be put into propositions expressed in clear and distinct ideas.

6. That knowledge of facts expressed in propositions is one kind of knowledge among others, and has to be considered in the context of more direct forms of knowledge by participation, including knowledge of things, knowledge of other people and knowledge of ourselves.

7. That finally the concept of knowledge is far broader and richer than the narrower type of empiricist epistemology is prepared to concede.

The seven propositions just stated constitute a kind of manifesto for a more human concept of knowledge. It should be added that 'more human' certainly does not mean 'more subjective', but rather the opposite, for the broader concept of knowledge being advocated rests on a correspondingly broader apprehension of the reality with which we are confronted. Let me give some examples, then, of this more broadly based knowledge.

To begin with, there is obviously a knowledge in art. The great painter, employing admittedly observation, but also imagination, sensibility, skills, perhaps many other unspecifiable elements, enables us to participate in his vision of reality. What he shows us can be expressed only on his canvas and could never be fully put into words. But is it possible to deny that it is a form of knowledge, or to dismiss it as 'non-cognitive'? Or what are we to say about knowing other people? Surely it is not an accident that we use the word 'knowing' for this relation. But it is a very different kind of knowing from knowing a fact. Admittedly, to know some facts about a person may well be a help to knowing him in a more direct way, but to know someone is much more than knowing facts about him. To know another person is a relation that involves participation and reciprocity, so that it can be truly said that only in knowing others does anyone ever come to know himself. It was Buber who pointed out that this kind of knowing can be extended even to things.[19] I can know a tree or a mountain (as poets do) in a way that bears some analogy to my knowing a person. The thing is there not just to be studied as a natural object or to be used for my own purposes. It is there as something I encounter within the same world to which I belong, something I can appreciate for its own beauty and dignity. This is no romanticism or subjectivism, still less a nostalgic revival of animism. It is letting something be what it is in itself, and surely this is a form of knowledge and a participation in truth.

This whole book is, in one of its aspects, a plea for a wider concept of knowing. I have insisted that to know the human reality (and what knowledge can be more important?) one has to go beyond empirical investigation to participation and imagination. One has to break out of the rigid subject-object schema. Even to know the environing world in its fullness, the knowledge of the artist is needed to supplement that of the scientist. Before the modern era, it was clearly understood that knowing requires participation. St Thomas Aquinas declared: 'A thing is known by being present in the knower; how it is present is determined by the way of being of the knower.'[20] Perhaps he should have added that it is also determined by the way of being of that which is known. Increasingly, however, it has come to be believed that genuine knowledge is knowledge of facts which stand over against us as objects. They are to be known in detachment. Of course, the quest for knowledge of facts has been enormously successful. One can only be amazed and filled with admiration at the phenomenal growth of scientific knowledge in modern times. How much more we know about the facts of the universe today than ever before! Yet we are almost choking on all the new knowledge. We talk about the 'information explosion', and it seems likely that it will continue to increase exponentially. But unfortunately there seems to be another kind of knowledge where we have made no progress at all or even have slipped back. We do not know how to handle the information, we do not know how to regulate our own words and behaviour, we do not know how to relate to one another or how to build a just, cohesive, fulfilling society. Even the cleverest and most powerful among us do not know how to handle inflation, unemployment, racialism, crime, poverty, terrorism, the threat of war. The first kind of knowledge is knowledge of facts, the second – which is also called wisdom – tries to see beneath the surface of the facts, to discern inner qualities and essential relationships, to perceive the 'really real', and to act accordingly. This kind of knowing cannot readily be formulated and perhaps much of it must remain tacit. But it cannot be denied that it is knowledge, and knowledge of the highest importance for human life.

In other times and other places, it was not knowing facts but knowing people that was taken as the paradigm of knowing. 'Now Adam knew his wife Eve, and she conceived . . .'[21] Here the intimate personal relation of man and woman in sexual union is simply expressed by the verb 'knew', the literal translation of the Hebrew *yada'*. It is an indication of the extent to which we have fallen away from that understanding of knowing by union and participation that modern translations of the Bible substitute quite different ideas, and fail entirely either to comprehend or express what was meant by 'knowing'. The Jerusalem Bible has, 'The man had intercourse with his wife Eve.' How clinical, impersonal and post-Cartesian! The New English Bible is worse still. 'The man lay with his wife Eve.' Here a personal relation has been reduced to a physical one, to a physical posture for which the Hebrew gives no warrant.

Knowing other people certainly deserves to qualify as a quite fundamental form of knowledge, and no epistemology which omits it from consideration can be other than onesided and incomplete. How much knowledge, both explicit and tacit, flows from knowing another person, is incalculable. It is through knowing another that I come to know myself, through knowing myself that I come to know others, through knowing others that I come to know a world.

A question that must be raised is whether the broadening of the concept of knowledge in the ways suggested above, together with the acknowledgment of a personal dimension in all knowing, does not undermine the ideal of a knowledge that is universally valid and free from all prejudice. But can one really suppose that for finite human beings such an aseptic impersonal knowledge is possible? We have already seen reason to question the notion of a 'detached' observer making 'value-free' judgments. We have to face the limitations that the finite human condition itself imposes on our knowledge. 'The overcoming of all prejudice, that global demand of the Enlightenment,' writes Gadamer, 'will prove to be itself a prejudice, the removal of which opens the way to an understanding of our finitude.'[22] We can see things only from our position in history, not *sub specie aeternitatis*.

The effects upon knowledge of personal and cultural factors have been differently described. Calvin supposed that though it would be wrong 'to charge the intellect with perpetual blindness', nevertheless sin and self-interest frequently lead it astray; and he made the further point, borne out by some of my own remarks above, 'that it frequently fails to discern what the knowledge is which it should study to acquire'.[23] Marx, on the other hand, drew attention to the phenomenon of ideology, the fact that our theories are influenced by class and economic interests. 'The production of notions, ideas and consciousness is from the beginning directly interwoven with the material activity and the material intercourse of human beings.'[24] A more general account of the relations of interest and knowledge has been offered by Habermas. Knowledge, as he sees it, is constantly penetrated by extraneous assumptions, and this is true even of what purports to be positivism. 'Interest' he defines very broadly as basic orientations arising from the social and material conditions of human life.[25]

But the recognition of personal, social and even ideological elements in knowledge need not plunge us into a complete relativism or scepticism. There are two remedies, though perhaps they have to be administered together. One is to become aware of our interests, presuppositions and prejudices. The other is to ensure that all interests and social groups have an opportunity of expressing themselves, so that they can correct one another. Human knowledge will never be purely impersonal, value-free or interest-free, but it is possible to eliminate one-sidedness and distortion.

One further point remains to be made before we conclude this chapter on cognition. In the broadened concept of knowledge which I have proposed, we have found room for inter-personal knowledge and the kind of knowing that belongs to art. We can also find room in it for the knowledge that belongs to religion. We have already noted the parallel between tacit knowledge and the ineffable experience of the mystic. A similar parallel has been drawn between the stress I have laid on imagination and the place in religion of myth and symbol, whereby language is stretched beyond its ordinary uses to become the vehicle of spiritual truth. Perhaps most striking of all is the fact that religious knowledge is close to what I have called wisdom – the knowledge of human affairs which I contrasted

with the knowledge of facts. Religious knowledge is never a bare speculation about God, but always has its human and practical aspect. The fuller
discussion of the place of religion in human life will be deferred until later
in the book.

VII

HAVING

We have seen that human beings are always embodied and that their lives are inextricably bound up with the physical universe. Only a false spiritualizing or an untenable metaphysical dualism would seek to minimize the role of the body and therefore the importance of the material in human existence. It is true that what is most distinctive in a human being, his freedom, is in a sense a transcending of the body, so that the human being is not exhaustively described in terms of his body; yet freedom and egoity are not found apart from embodiedness. We have therefore turned away from any ascetic or purely spiritual ideal for humanity, while at the same time acknowledging that the relation to the material world is fraught with ambiguity and is even threatening.[1] It is the relation of the human being to material things that we now have to consider in more detail.

Actually, there are many ways in which we relate to material things. We can know about them, be curious about them, admire some of them and despise others, find them agreeable or disagreeable, consume them, destroy them and so on. But perhaps the most fundamental relation between a human being and a material thing is the relation expressed by the word 'having'. If I have something, it is at my disposal and, within limits to be considered later, I can do what I like with it. If I have food, I can eat it or store it or share it with someone; if I have a book, I can read it or lend it or donate it to the library or just leave it on the shelf; if I have a house, I can live in it or rent it or entertain people in it, and so on. Since all these other activities are made possible only if one *has* something, we see how fundamental this relation is in everyday life. This is borne out by the fact that in very many languages the next commonest verb to the verb 'to be' is the verb meaning 'to have' or else some periphrastic construction expressing possession. Each language likewise has an imposing battery ofpossessive pronouns and adjectives – 'mine', 'my', 'yours', 'his', 'hers', and the like.

The evident preoccupation with having or possession might seem to be *prima facie* evidence for the truth of the Marxist belief that economic factors have the ultimate say in shaping human life. Even before Marx, the classical economists had invented the figure of 'economic man', the individual who acts rationally and systematically in the pursuit of acquisitive and egoistic ends. Such an economic man may have been considered an abstraction and a fiction, but it is a fiction that comes uncomfortably close to real life. No doubt the emphasis on the material and economic factors in life was needed as a corrective to exaggeratedly spiritual understandings of man. In spite of the biblical doctrines of creation and resurrection, the strong Platonist influence in Christianity fostered what has been called a 'psychological unhappiness with matter',[2] against which first Feuerbach and then Marx protested with their own exaggerated materialism. We may recall, however, that Marx did not believe that people work merely for economic reasons, for work is or ought to be a means to self-affirmation.[3]

That a minimal level of having is essential before one can speak of a truly human life is surely something that would be universally acknowledged. This minimum cannot consist simply in food, shelter and other utterly basic necessities, for even animals need these things to survive. For the distinctively human to emerge, more is needed. If one's whole time were occupied in the struggle for physical survival, there would be no time for play or thought or personal relations, on which the whole fabric of a distinctively human existence has to be reared. What that basic level of having is, it is probably impossible to say, for it varies at different times in history and in different parts of the world. The level of having that enabled our ancestors to emerge from savagery to a tolerably human existence thousands of years ago is obviously different from what is required for human dignity in an affluent society of the present time, and that is different again from what is required in another part of the world where the development of material resources may hardly have begun. What is regarded as a luxury at one stage may have become a virtual necessity at another, and what may once have been a privilege may eventually become a right. Television, for instance, was a luxury only a few decades ago; a little earlier than that, there was no such thing. Today, television sets are common in the poorest homes, and the most backward countries have used part of their meagre resources to set up television networks. It could be argued that anyone who is to be a fully responsible human inhabitant of this planet in the late twentieth century *needs* a television set to bring him instant information about what is going on throughout the world. Unfortunately, the ambiguities of having are also clearly shown by this illustration. Television not only brings information about what is going on in the world, but inundates us with dubious entertainment and subtle advertisements which together may be creating false values and unrealizable desires. In addition, television can be a powerful instrument of propaganda, and that is no doubt the explanation of why some countries that can barely provide food for their people will nevertheless provide a television service. If television is an example of a luxury becoming a necessity, education illustrates the point about a privilege becoming a right. In a society still struggling for the basic necessities of life, books and the leisure for study can belong only to a few, but in modern society, education is the right of all, to the extent that they can profit by it.

These remarks on the minimal level of having required for a decent human life raise the question of property. We might say that property is the institutionalized form of having. In the broadest legal sense, 'property' includes one's rights as well as one's material possessions,[4] and this perhaps excuses my coupling in the last paragraph such diverse items as ownership of (or access to) a television set and the right to basic education as belonging to the minimal level of having in a modern society. John Locke, who believed that everyone has a title to 'all the rights and privileges of the law of nature', understood 'property' in the very broad sense just described, when he wrote that everyone has a power 'to preserve his property – that is, his life, liberty and estate'.[5] In contemporary society, where the production of services has greatly increased in relation to the production of material goods, this broader sense of property has a new relevance. The level of having is to be measured not just by the possession and consumption of material goods, but also in terms of such 'invisible' goods as vacations, entertainments, health care and the like. Thus, although we shall be understanding the term 'property' chiefly in the restricted sense of material possessions, we should not forget that such possessions are usually accompanied by a fringe of important, though less tangible, benefits.

The importance of having in human life, together with the strength and waywardness of the acquisitive instinct, is seen in the extent and complexity of the laws governing property. Economist Frederic Benham writes: 'Nearly all states try to prevent their subjects from killing and injuring one another and from forcibly taking one another's possessions, and try to see that contracts are carried out . . . It is generally agreed that the institution of property is desirable. Nobody prefers "the law of the jungle".' Actually, it may not be so generally agreed as he supposes that 'the institution of property is desirable' or that it overcomes 'the law of the jungle', for in some cases it may merely legitimate gains that have been made under something very close to jungle law. Benham himself remarks that no one would want to deprive a person 'of the exclusive right to the use of a purely personal possession, such as a toothbrush', but he does acknowledge that it is a controversial question 'whether means of production, such as land and railways and factories, should be owned by the state or by private persons'.[6]

We cannot avoid becoming to some extent involved in controversial questions about property and the economic life of humanity generally. But a *caveat* must be entered before we go any further. It can be no part of a study like this to offer a detailed economic prescription. That is a matter for the economist, and it will vary from one situation to another. Yet it does not follow that we are restricted only to innocuous generalities. The study of human nature and the search for human fulfilment can provide some criteria by which to judge whether concrete economic and political programmes are likely to advance or retard such a fulfilment.

We have agreed so far that there is a minimal level of having or a minimal standard of living that is apparently essential for the fulfilling of human potentialities. Below that level, the pressures of deprivation are such that the development of distinctively human activities, social, intellectual, artistic, religious and so on, is barely possible. The conditions of life are, as we say, dehumanizing. But then the question has to be asked whether a rising standard of living brings with it a rising quality of life, that is to say, a fuller and more truly human life. It is not obvious that this is the case. No doubt, in popular expectation, the 'good life' is a life of unlimited having, but it is not at all obvious that happiness increases with affluence or that humanity is enhanced by having. Furthermore, as standards of affluence rise, there are always some people – usually large numbers of people – who get left behind, so that the level of having remains very uneven, and one can even speak of the 'haves' and the 'have-nots'. There is the obvious disparity between the industrialized nations and the undeveloped nations, and in both groups there are more or less wide disparities between individual levels of having. So one has got to ask not only whether the unlimited production of wealth is a good thing for the furtherance of a truly human nature, but also about the ownership and distribution of existing wealth.

Let us take the second of these questions first. It is, of course, a bitterly contested question. We find that there are those who champion the rights of private property and of individual economic enterprise, those who would abolish private property and centralize economic control in the state, and those who believe that a so-called 'mixed' economy is best for humanity as a whole.

Considering that we have made freedom the starting-point for our study of humanity, it might be thought that this would favour the first of the three positions stated, the one that maximizes individual initiative. But this would be to forget that I insisted that freedom must be responsible, that rights are correlated with duties and that freedom is in no sense to be equated with anarchy. Freedom is not sheer permissiveness or *laissez-faire*, whether in economics or anything else.

But let us hear a spokesman for *laissez-faire*. Andrew Carnegie, by birth a Scotsman who founded a vast industrial empire in the United States, published in 1889 an article proclaiming 'The Gospel of Wealth'.[7] He affirmed his belief in the sacredness of private property, the right of free competition and the right of free accumulation of wealth. These things need no excuse, he claimed, because they benefit the whole human race in the long run. Inevitably, those who are gifted with business acumen – and Carnegie himself was supremely gifted in this respect – will do very well out of the system. He acknowledged too that it will be necessary for these leaders to hold down wages, and that some individuals are bound to suffer in the process. But these inequalities are, so to speak, growing pains that have to be endured if mankind as a whole is to move out of universal squalor. The man who becomes immensely wealthy in the process has a duty to use his wealth for the common good in works of benefaction. Both from such benefactions and from the material development flowing from industry, society as a whole will attain a much higher standard of living than it had before.

Carnegie's essay is a good illustration of Weber's thesis which connects the rise of capitalism with the Protestant ethic. In fact, Carnegie's views were shared by many American preachers of his time. These views cannot be simply dismissed. The United States is the country where free enterprise has had most scope, and it is also the country where the bulk of the population enjoys a higher standard of living than can be found anywhere else. Moreover, virtually every major American city has its parks, museums, art galleries, colleges and other amenities that have been gifted by some local captain of industry. Carnegie himself not only benefited American cities, but founded free libraries all over his native Scotland and also set up a large fund to assist Scottish youngsters of modest means to go to university.

Yet when that has been said in favour of *laissez-faire*, some things about it are unacceptable. Carnegie understates the suffering attendant on this type of industrial expansion. More serious is the ruthlessness of the industrial pioneer himself, and the spirit of competitiveness and acquisitiveness that he disseminates through society, where others dream of emulating him. And it is clearly wrong that such enormous economic power should rest in the hands of one man or a few men, even if only that same concentration of power could confer some of the benefits that society received at the hands of Carnegie and other public-spirited capitalists. And were there not others who were not public-spirited, and whose names we do not know because they used their wealth for private ends?

While the United States remains the bastion of the free enterprise system, it is surely significant that even there the free-for-all of the nineteenth century has been greatly modified by increasing state intervention into the economic sphere. On the one hand, industry has been more and more regulated by legislation designed to make its operations fairer, safer and more responsive to the needs of all engaged in it or affected by it. On the other hand, graduated taxation and corresponding welfare benefits have done something to reduce the gap between the haves and have-nots. (However, some claim that the gap has actually widened.) In any case, there has in fact been a retreat from the extreme of *laissez-faire*.

Let us now look at the opposite case. Marxism calls for the abolition of private property and for the centralization of economic control in the organs of the state. Marx saw nineteenth-century industrial society from the opposite end from Carnegie, and his prescription was likewise opposite. The evil of private property, in Marx's view, is that it deprives the worker of the affirmation of his humanity which he ought to find in his work, for it separates him from the product of his work, which belongs to the factory-owner. 'The right of property turns into its opposite; for the capitalist, it becomes the right to appropriate values created by others, while for the worker, it means that his own product does not belong to him.'[8]

Marx obviously has a good point here, and we shall come back later to consider his views on the alienation that takes place in the worker.[9] But the problem about Marx's critique is that his complaints would seem to apply just as much to a socialist system or state capitalism as they do to the case where the means of production are privately owned. A vast industry in public ownership separates the worker from his product just as effectively as does a private corporation. Working for state-owned British Leyland would seem to be, in Marx's own terms, neither more nor less alienating than working for General Motors. John Plamenatz makes an ironical comment: 'If we look at the symptoms and causes of alienation as Marx described them, they would appear to be just as evident in the Soviet Union as in the United States. It would seem to be against the interest of any communist government in the world today to encourage a close study of Marx's early writings.'[10]

Other points made by Marx similarly apply to industrial society in general, not to any particular form of it. For instance, both Marx and Engels believed that the division of labour was alienating and dehumanizing. They may well have been right about this, but it does not appear to have anything to do with the question of public or private ownership. It has to do with the scale of industry, and in mass societies like ours, where industry has to be geared to the needs of millions of people, division of labour is inevitable. Marx's criticism is applicable to large-scale industrialization under any system, and puts in question whether the heaping up of wealth enhances our humanity or alienates us from it. That is a question which we shall face later in this chapter, but the question with which we are concerned at present is the question whether private property is a threat to a truly human existence.

I think we have to reply that the case has not been made out, and that the large publicly owned industrial establishment has no advantage over its privately owned counterpart. Perhaps it is even at a disadvantage, for that which belongs to the state is peculiarly faceless, whereas the private industrialist may have some kind of social conscience and may also feel impelled by his own interests to keep his work force happy.

It is interesting to note that just as we found that in the United States (and even more so in Western Europe) there has been a retreat from sheer *laissez-faire* in the direction of state control, so in some communist countries there has been a retreat from sheer collectivism in the direction of reinstating some private enterprise and the incentives that go with it. In the agricultural communes of China, for example, when the peasants have worked the allotted number of hours on the common fields, each is at liberty to work on a holding of his own. From this holding, he may both support his own family and sell any additional produce on the open market. It is of further interest to note that this combination of care for the common good with an outlet for private initiative was recommended in China centuries before Marx. In the fourth century BC, the philosopher Mencius was asked by a prince for advice on the organization of his territory. He recommended that each square-mile tract of land should be subdivided into nine smaller squares. The central square would be the public field, and each of the surrounding eight squares would be allocated to a family. Each family would work on the central square before attending to its private business.[11]

Does the retreat from unbridled *laissez-faire* on the one side and from rigid collectivism on the other signify a convergence on what is called the 'mixed' economy? Let us remember that this question is being asked not with a view to deciding what is the most efficient economy (a matter which expert economists must decide) but with a view to deciding what kind of economic system best allows men and women to develop as far as possible their human potential. What I have called 'unbridled *laissez-faire*' does violence to the humanity of some because of the inequalities and injustices which it permits; while what I have called 'rigid collectivism' may well satisfy the basic physical needs of all but deprives them of their freedom. The Irish statesman Garret FitzGerald has well expressed the dilemma: 'The insensitivity of some liberals to economic injustice is more than matched by the insensitivity of some socialists to individual freedom.'[12] Are we finding again that the way forward for humanity is a dialectic between extremes?

It may be useful at this point to go back behind the modern quarrel between the extremes of *laissez-faire* and doctrinaire socialism to an older European tradition. St Thomas Aquinas taught that it is man's duty 'to care for and distribute the earth's resources', though ultimately these belong to God the creator. Because man has this delegated responsibility, Aquinas says that 'it is not merely legitimate for a man to possess things as his own, it is even necessary for human life, and that for three reasons. First, because each person takes more trouble to care for something that is his sole responsibility than what is held in common or by many. Second, because human affairs are more efficiently organized if each person has his own responsibility to discharge. Third, because men live together in greater peace when everyone is content with his own. We do, in fact, notice that quarrels often break out amongst men who hold things in common without distinction.'[13] But although the right to property is defended here, the very fact that the earth belongs ultimately to God means that no property right is absolute. So a little further on we find Thomas saying: 'In the case of necessity, everything is common. Therefore a person who takes somebody else's property which necessity has made common again, so far as he is concerned does not commit theft.'[14]

But can this medieval teaching (some of it, indeed, goes back to Aristotle) have anything to say after several industrial revolutions? I think it can and must, if we are to have a more responsible attitude towards the material world. I believe that in principle it makes more sense than either *laissez-faire* or Marxism and has more regard to the needs and aspirations of humanity. But it also has the virtue of going behind that fatal dualism of subject and object which appeared in the seventeenth century with Descartes, Locke and company. The representational thinking which they introduced set things over against us as an alien realm for exploitation, domination and consumption. Any sense of participation in the world was lost. There cannot, of course, be a simple return to Thomism (even as dressed up by its modern exponents), but we must recapture the sense of belonging within one world comprising persons and things, and perhaps this means the one world of God. Incidentally, it is something like a Thomistic understanding of property that underlies the so-called 'mixed economies' of Western Europe. These seek to achieve a fair balance between individual liberties and the needs of the community as a whole, and therefore curb free enterprise in the interests of the common good, while at the same time protecting individual freedom against the totalitarian pretensions of the state.

Obviously, the detailed working out of the concept of the mixed economy and the problem of getting the right balance between the individual and the community or between freedom and planning is a matter that has to be left to experts in economics and politics. But the general character of this type of economy is one that must be preferred over both *laissez-faire* and socialism by those who are concerned that human beings should be able to live truly human lives in a supportive human community.

We have been discussing the institution of property and the question about the ownership and distribution of property, but it will be remembered that we have still a further and more radical question on our hands – the question of how far having, in any form, is an enhancement of human being, or whether it is even a diminution and a threat. The question may be posed in the form of the relation between being and having. *Being and Having* was in fact the title of a book by Gabriel Marcel, in which he analysed, contrasted and compared these two basic possibilities of the human person. The question of being and having has been taken up by other writers, such as Erich Fromm, but none of them have surpassed Marcel in perspicuity. Marcel acknowledges the necessity of having – just as we ourselves have taken note that a minimal level of having is essential to being. But on the whole he finds being and having in tension with one another. Having objectifies, whereas being participates.[15] (The connection between having and the empiricist theory of knowledge becomes apparent at this point.) Having strips a thing down and makes it disposable, whereas being respects the mystery of being in that which is other. Yet the paradox is that having does not succeed in externalizing that which is thus objectified and made disposable. 'The self becomes incorporated in the thing possessed.'[16] As a person increases his possessions, his being becomes more and more bound up with these possessions, he is beset by anxiety that he may lose them and they become a burden and a demand on him. One can have the proof of this today in any great city, where the affluent have to go to great lengths to protect their possessions from crime. The extreme irony of the situation occurs when beautiful *objets d'art* have to be locked away in safes and bank vaults and can no longer be enjoyed and admired except in a few rare moments when they are fleetingly and anxiously exposed to view.

As Marcel also says, 'our possessions swallow us up'.[17] It is as if we were being sucked back into the subhuman world of things. The human being emerged as a breach in the world of things, a centre of freedom, creativity and transcendence, but there can come a point when he is reabsorbed into that world and his life is enslaved to it. It would seem that just as there is a minimal level of having, beneath which a truly human life seems scarcely possible, so there is a maximal level, above which we are stifled with the abundance of possessions and a dehumanizing again takes place. We find ourselves again having to seek a way between the extremes. We have to remember too that just as we have seen that the floor of material well-being (or the minimal level of having) is relative to different historical and cultural situations, so the ceiling is relative.

The threat that arises from having lies in the fact that the satisfaction of every desire seems to kindle new desires and new expectations and we get caught up in what moral theologians have called 'concupiscence' – an excessive desire which can deprive us of our autonomy and drags us along in spite of ourselves.

We have noted in passing that objectification is common to the desire for possession and the empiricist theory of knowledge. There can be little doubt that modern science and technology have both been motivated by the acquisitive instinct and then in turn have stimulated it. Technology gives birth to new and artificial desires and becomes increasingly something that is self-propagating and withdrawn from human control. It is impossible today to be against technology, for without it life would become impossible for millions of human beings on this planet. But precisely because it has become indispensable, it is important for us to be critical of it. Neither science nor technology is neutral or value free. They are already guided by interests, more or less conscious, and they are having a profound effect on the nature of the human being – sometimes good, sometimes bad, more often ambiguous. We may recall Marcuse's warning that the technological society tends to produce the one-dimensional man, the man whose horizons are limited to having and the consumption of goods, and who has become incapable of transcendence.[18]

The problem is compounded by the realization that, on a relatively small planet like earth, limited resources cannot sustain unlimited production of goods. No doubt some of the predictions of coming disaster have been exaggerated and no doubt in the past human ingenuity has shown itself capable of surmounting crises, so that one may hope for comparable miracles in the future, yet even so it would be foolish not to heed the warnings. The drive towards having, possession, use and enjoyment, has to be tempered by a new respect for things as having a being of their own, and a new realization that man's ownership is not absolute but more like that of a steward. Both of these points were implicit in the Christian doctrine of creation, and the erosion of that doctrine has not led to human emancipation vis-à-vis the material world but rather to a state of alienation. It is alienation from the world, in which we no longer participate but merely use; alienation from one another, as we quarrel over the possession of things; and a deep inward alienation, to the extent that we have surrendered the freedom of being to the compulsions of having.[19]

But is there anything that can be done about it? Are we not all caught in the spiral of concupiscence? Is there any possibility of maintaining oneself between that floor of having, below which humanity is threatened by dehumanizing deprivation, and that ceiling of having, above which the threat is a dehumanizing excess of consumption – especially if these levels keep changing?

Perhaps what can be done is to protest against the acquisitive instinct and the consumer mentality by a moderate form of asceticism. It would not be motivated by any Manichean fear or devaluation of the material world as such, but would be, like Christian asceticism, a 'sign of contradiction', that is to say, a protest against the prevailing tendencies and the evils that they have brought in their train, in the hope of eventually setting up a more balanced and dialectical attitude to wealth and possessions. In the earliest Christian community, goods were held in common so that the needs of the poorer members might be met; but this was a voluntary 'communism' that had nothing to do with the communism of the modern totalitarian state.[20] At a later time, not all members of the church but those who entered the religious orders and took a vow of chastity continued the witness of non-attachment to possessions. What I have called here 'non-attachment' is well expressed by A. M. Ramsey as 'using and yet not clinging or exploiting, enjoying and yet being apart.'[21] He tells us: 'Asceticism can be true or false. The distinction is between asceticism which knows that the created world is good, but disciplines the use of creatures so as to avoid being dominated by them, and asceticism which flees from the world or flesh or sex on the view that they are evil.'[22]

When I recommend a 'moderate' form of asceticism, I have in mind only a simplified life style and an avoidance of 'conspicuous consumption'. Though I have made a comparison with Christian asceticism, the appeal is just as much to the non-Christian as to the Christian, for it is based simply on considerations of humanity and envisages a multidimensional rather than a one-dimensional human being. There is already a widespread acknowledgment of the rightness of the appeal, in face of the inequitable levels of having now prevailing in the world, the future problems that will arise from pressure on scarce resources, and perhaps above all the damage being done to human nature by the ever increasing preoccupation with having.

The asceticism of which I have been writing would be exercised by individuals and relatively small groups. This might seem to be a mere trifling with the problem, unless their witness, as a sign of contradiction, could induce a collective asceticism. But is it realistic to believe that nations, corporations and labour unions would restrain themselves? Perhaps they would, especially if they could be shown that it is in their own interest to do so. But this will be further discussed when we come to such topics as sociality and love.[23]

VIII

SOCIALITY

Although in our studies of the human being we have up till now been thinking usually of the individual person, we have at several points been confronted with his inescapably social nature. Thus, in discussing freedom, we could not ignore the fact that it has to be exercised in social and political situations which sometimes protect and encourage it, sometimes suppress it. We have also seen that one important aspect of human transcendence is transcendence towards the other person. We have had to distinguish between egoity, as part of the condition of every human being, and its hardening into a harmful egoism. Likewise, we have seen how having brings us into relation with each other and is frequently a source of conflict. In all of these cases, we have been catching sight of one of the most radical tensions in the human being, the tension between the individual and the social poles of that being.

In the course of human history, it would seem that these two poles have been more often opposed to each other than brought into harmony. There have been times of collectivism and times of individualism. In a collectivist society, the individual is virtually deprived of freedom and self-direction. He becomes a mere unit to whom is assigned a function that will serve the social whole. The individualist, on the other hand, asserts the right to be himself, but he tends to carry this to the length of disregard for others. The contemporary world presents extreme examples of both collectivism and individualism. There are countries so regimented and controlled that individual freedom is minimal, and there are others where individualist preferences have been carried to the point at which there may even be a threat to the stability of society. But it is more complicated than that. The same extremes can be found within the same country, perhaps even among the same people in different aspects of their lives.

Both views have had their philosophical advocates. Hegel believed thatthe state is more truly a person than any individual citizen. His English disciple, Bosanquet, went so far as to claim that it is only by a misuse of language that we call the solitary human being an 'individual'. For him, the individual is 'something complete and self-contained',[1] so that the term is more applicable to some great whole, such as the state, than it is to a fragment, such as an isolated human being. On the opposite side, we find Kierkegaard attacking the Hegelian conception and upholding the dignity and even ultimacy of the individual human being. He declares bluntly that ' "fellowship" is a lower category than "the single individual", which everyone can be and should be'.[2] We may be reluctant to follow either Hegel or Kierkegaard, and we may believe that the former's 'state' and the latter's 'individual' are alike abstractions, but this will not solve the problem of reconciling these two poles of our being. Both sociality and individuality belong ineluctably to humanity; each has its just claim, and neither can be absorbed into the other without damage to the human being.

Let us consider first the pole of individuality. We have seen already[3] that every human being is characterized by egoity, by which I meant that there is a leading edge or luminous centre which gives direction to each person's life. We have seen too that the ego or self cannot be completely objectified. It always preserves something of subjectivity, inwardness and privacy. No one can look directly into another person's mind or see things through another person's eyes, and no one can fully disburden and reveal himself to another. No doubt there is a tragic potential in this separateness of human beings, yet it is also the necessary condition for the joy and richness of personal relations, which could not arise if there were no subjectivity. Up to a point, each one's subjectivity can be opened to another in intimacy, yet there will always be that which is inaccessible and inexpressible and which on this very account adds to the depth of the relation. There is an inwardness in every human being constituting the core of his or her individuality.

Individuality is constituted not only by the inner subjectivity of each human person, but also by his or her uniqueness. For all the billions of human beings that exist or have existed on the earth, each one is a unique being, not only numerically but qualitatively. Even their bodies bear a stamp of uniqueness – the human face, which seems to come in an infinite variety of forms and by which each human being can be recognized and named. In his discussion of angels, Thomas Aquinas claimed that every angel is a distinct species.[4] Although his reasons for saying this would not apply to human beings, one is tempted to say the same about them. To be sure, they all belong to the same biological species, but can persons be classified as if they were organisms? Is not each one unique? This is again part both of the grandeur and of the tragedy of the human condition, for it means that each person is irreplaceable. This confers on each one the dignity and value of that which is unique and irreplaceable; but it also means that each one, when removed by death, never comes again. Of course, a human being can be replaced if we think of him only in functional terms, as a soldier or worker or whatever. But as a unique person, he comes only once.

Each human being then has a self-identity that differentiates him from every other. He says 'I', he calls 'mine' a particular strip of history, which extends through memory into the past and through anticipation into the future, and to which he is giving shape and direction by what he is doing in this present moment. So each human being is a unique irreplaceable centre of freedom and creativity, engaged in his or her task of fashioning a unique human life-story. At the same time, each one has his unique givens and his unique situation, and these constitute, as it were, the raw material of the life-story and also the limits to what is possible for that human being. Just to contemplate the seemingly infinite range of human beings and the immense potentialities of each one is (or should be) in itself enough to generate that profound respect for the individual, his worth and dignity, that have to be defended against every attempt to transform him into a mere unit in some impersonal system, be it economic, political or even metaphysical.

But however impressive is the individuality of each human being, equally striking is the essential sociality of each one. In the famous words of John Donne, 'No man is an island.' Individualist philosophers of the Enlightenment taught that society had been formed by individual human beings coming together and giving up some of their 'natural rights' in a social contract. But it seems more likely that individuals emerged from a social matrix. We become aware of the face of the other long before we see (and then only indirectly) our own faces. But perhaps it would be no more correct to say that society is prior to the individual in an ontological as distinct from a chronological sense, than to say that the individual is prior to society. Both the social and the individual poles seem equally original in the being of man, and their tension is there from the beginning as one of the factors contributing to the dynamics of human life.

An insight into these relationships is already evident in the creation story in Genesis. 'God said, "Let us make man in our image . . ." So God created man in his own image, in the image of God created he him; male and female created he them.'[5] The implications are that the image of God (the image, that is to say, of archetypal personal existence) requires for its manifestation not just an individual human being, but the simplest social unit, the couple, male and female. It is significant too that the Hebrew word for God, elohim, is a plural form, reflected in the words, 'Let us make . . .' This implies that in the one God there is something analogous to a social existence, an insight later developed in the Christian doctrine of the Triune God: God is One and God is Three, he is the consummation of both individual and social existence, or, better expressed, he perfectly unites these two poles of personal existence.

Let us now briefly review some of the basic characters of all human life that point to its inescapably social character.

I begin with sexuality. Human beings come in two basic varieties, male and female. Anatomically, physiologically and psychologically, each human being is from the beginning oriented towards a relation with another. No human being can reproduce the species by himself or herself. Reproduction needs the couple, and that is to say that the very survival of the human race is dependent on a social (in this case, sexual) relation. But the talk about reproduction must not mislead us into supposing that we are concerned here only with a biological relation. All higher animals, after all, are sexually differentiated and sexually reproduce themselves. But it was pointed out at an early stage in this book[6] that among human beings, the sexual relation is never merely biological. It is a personal relation, and even when its personal dimension is minimized or almost obliterated, it does not revert to a biological relation but deteriorates to a subpersonal relation. To go back to Genesis for a moment (though this time to the alternative creation story), the creation of Eve does not take place so that Adam may have a mate for the continuance of the race, but so that he may have a 'helper'. 'The Lord God said, "It is not good that the man should be alone; I will make him a helper fit for him." '[7] The animals are brought to him, but none of them can supply the lack. Only a fellow human being can supply Adam's lack of being, and though the relation is sexual, it is more than that, for it is human, personal and social.

A second characteristic of every human being that points to his social nature is that he belongs in a family. I put sexuality first because it seems to be the basis for all social life, yet what comes first in the life-story of every individual is that he or she is born into a family. From the very beginning, he is surrounded by others and in relation to others, especially to the mother. The first reality that he knows is a personal reality other than himself. He knows this reality before he knows himself as distinct from it, before he says 'I'. He knows it too before he knows the impersonal reality of the material world – a point which reinforces some of my earlier remarks about the nature of cognition.[8] Compared with animals, the human being has a very long period of dependence, and the more advanced a country is, the longer is the period of dependence and nurture. During that time, others are entering into the very fabric of an individual's life – first, the parents, then teachers, friends and all the influences of a given society and culture. We call this 'education'. Certainly, a good education is one that draws out the child's own potentialities and helps him become what he has in him to become. Yet, when that has been conceded, the input of society into the individual will always preponderate over what may be elicited from him. Of course, if there is nothing but input, then education has been abandoned and reduced to manipulation and propaganda. But even where these distortions are studiously avoided and the freedom of the child is allowed maximal expression, he will still receive far more from society than he brings from his own resources, and this is necessary for survival. Knowledge, skills, patterns of behaviour and so on have to be learned from those who have themselves already had experience of living as human beings on this earth. We may be reminded at this point of Popper's claim that even the most creative genius owes more to the collective human wisdom than he will ever put into it,[9] and of Polanyi's recognition of the importance of the personal teacher-student relation in the transmission of skills.[10] This problem of the tension and possible conflict between the social and individual contributions to personal formation will encounter us again in an acute form when we come to consider conscience.[11]

A third indicator of our basic sociality is language. It is often said that it is the capacity for language that constitutes the main difference between man and the animals. At least one can say that man is in a unique way a linguistic being and that language enters into virtually everything that he thinks or does. Even so-called 'tacit' knowledge presupposes a knowledge that can be formulated in words. One of the functions of language – though it is certainly not the only one – is communication. It follows that there can be no private language, for language can communicate only if there is a shared vocabulary and syntax. No individual could have a language of his own, and even languages spoken by small tribal or ethnic groups are tending to become extinct in the modern world, where the need for worldwide communication is pushing us in the direction of a universal language, either an artificial language or, as seems more likely, a natural language such as English, already the lingua franca of large areas of the globe.

A fourth pointer to the inescapably social character of the human being is provided by the fact of economic interdependence. Our earlier discussion of having and of man's relation to things[12] has shown us that in the economic sphere the interests of individuals inevitably intertwine, though more often than not they are in conflict. But the economic phenomenon which most clearly demonstrates human sociality and interdependence is the division of labour. Perhaps there was a time in the dawn of human history when each individual did everything for himself – secured his own food, made his own clothes, built his own shelter and so on. But it soon was discovered that it is much better for each to acquire skill in some particular occupation, and then to exchange his products with others. The result is a higher economic standard of living, though the price (if it is a price) is the surrender of individual self-sufficiency and its replacement by interdependence. Of course, this account of the matter may be as much a myth as is the story of a social contract. But whether there ever was a time of individual self-sufficiency does not matter. The point is that in every historical situation, economic interdependence is a fact, and that interdependence has reached a higher level today than at any previous time. Marx and Engels were both critical of the division of labour, especially the division between mental work and physical work, and regarded division of labour as one of the causes of alienation. Apart from the fact that the billions of people on the earth today can survive only through the intricate division of labour, this division ought not to be alienating them but teaching them their inescapable solidarity and interdependence, even if they are slow to learn that lesson. But the complaint of Marx and Engels raises another point – whether the division of labour, by riveting each individual to a particular task, sometimes a monotonous task, has not tipped the balance too far in the direction of collective interest over individual interest. Marx and Engels did in this connection speak of a society in which it would be 'possible for me to do one thing today and another tomorrow'.[13] At this point we are again confronted by the dilemma of the modern technological world. We can only survive and enjoy a reasonable level of having through an intricate network of production, and this also stresses our solidarity and interdependence; but inevitably this limits the freedom of the individual and requires of some individuals that they become little more than parts of the machinery.

I have advanced four considerations to show that each human individual, in spite of all his uniqueness, is inevitably involved with others in social relations. Perhaps the four factors I have mentioned are so many manifestations of that fundamental transcendence that belongs to every human being, the need to go beyond every state in which he finds himself. One aspect of that transcendence is transcendence towards the other person or persons. Paradoxically, only through transcendence towards the other does the individual ever fulfil himself.

'Where there is no "Thou", there is no "I".' The quotation is actually from Feuerbach,[14] though in recent times we are more likely to have heard this truth expressed in very similar words by Buber. In view of what has just been said about the sexual, family, linguistic and economic life of man, it might seem so obvious that there is no 'I' without a 'Thou' that the point is hardly worth making. But the stubborn egoism which is a perversion of our inescapable egoity, and the individualism which has been so strong in the West since the Enlightenment, make it necessary to stress even the obvious, that no man is an island, that there is no 'I' without a 'Thou', that there is no truly human existence without community and that community is not an extra that gets added on but is of the very essence. When indeed people do rebel against individualism, they are more likely to turn to an equally subhuman collectivism than to the genuine reciprocity of persons-in-community.

Buber's philosophy provides an impressive vocabulary for describing the interaction of the individual and social poles of the human being and for depicting what a true 'I-thou' relation might be. 'Distance' and 'relation' are twin concepts used to elucidate a genuine community of human beings; if each individual, to be a human person, must be in relation to another, this relation can never be an absorption but must leave room for a distancing that respects the other's freedom and inwardness.[15] 'Dialogue' is a favourite term with Buber, and implies a genuine give and take, a willingness to recognize that the other has truth as well as oneself and a willingness to listen to it, a desire to confirm the other as well as to be confirmed by him.[16] There is also the idea of the 'between', almost, one might say, a 'field theory' of human relationships in which the individual centres of selfhood are firmly located in the network of interpersonal relations. 'The fundamental fact of human existence is neither the individual as such nor the aggregate as such. Each, considered by itself, is a mighty abstraction . . . The fundamental fact of human existence is man with man. I call this the sphere of the "between". Though being realized in very different degrees, it is a primal category of human reality. This is where the genuine third alternative [to individualism and collectivism] must begin.'[17]

We have seen in an earlier chapter that Buber was prepared to acknowledge that a person may relate even to a tree in a manner analogous to the intimate way in which he relates to another person as a 'Thou'. He is right in holding that a thing of nature or of art need not be merely an object for exploitation or curiosity, and that some kind of communion with it is possible. However, he is not advocating romanticism, and he recognizes that one's experience of a thing is normally very different from one's encounter with a person. Things are usually experienced in the dimension of the 'I-it', not the 'I-thou'. They are objects to be handled, possessed, manipulated and finally disposed of. The danger in human life is not that there will be a burst of romanticism whereby things will be treated as quasi-persons, but that there is a constant tendency to reduce persons to things, to degrade them from an 'I-thou' to an 'I-it' relation. I suppose the ultimate degeneracy of the 'I-thou' to the 'I-it' would be slavery. In that case, a person has been turned into a thing. He has become the possession of another and the instrument of another. He has been deprived of his human freedom and dignity (even if he may still preserve some inward freedom). But the humanity of the owner cannot remain unaffected by the denial of the humanity of the slave. The ambiguities of the master-slave relation were, of course, exposed by Hegel in a famous analysis,[18] but I think that Buber's explorations of the interpersonal adds a new depth to the discussion. If it is indeed the case that there is no 'I' without a 'Thou', if everyone needs the confirmation of dialogue with the other, the distance and the relation of community, the vivifying atmosphere of the 'between', then to deny and seek to diminish the humanity of the other is to deny and diminish one's own humanity.

As an acceptable social institution, slavery has been virtually abolished throughout the earth. But it does not follow that forms of dependence and servitude scarcely distinguishable from slavery do not still exist, or that the desire to possess and exploit the other has grown any less. It does not follow either that new forms of dehumanization have not come in and that they are doing damage to us all. What is one to say, for instance, of the functional conception of man, the view that sees him as the sum of the various roles that he plays, but leaves out of account the person himself, the leading edge, the unique centre of freedom and creativity? When this is left out and the human being is dissolved into a collection of roles, then the respect for the inward individual core has gone. Men and women are evaluated for what they do, not for what they are. Even the lover becomes the sexual partner, whose worth is to be judged by performance. This functional view of man is the opposite of the Christian view that human beings are not saved by works but are acceptable in themselves, because each one is a bearer of the divine image with all its potentialities. Elizabeth Moberly has rightly observed that 'the idea that one is justified by grace through faith rather than by works is an assertion of the priority of being over doing'.[19] But it is an assertion rarely heard in the modern world.

Although we have seen it to be the case that relations to others are an inescapable aspect of the human person and necessary to his very existence as a person, it cannot be denied that these relations easily degenerate, and they may militate against a true humanity just as often as they promote it. Against Buber's affirmative account of the 'I-thou' relation, we may set the equally subtle but depressingly negative view that we find in Sartre.[20] The other makes me his object, then I seek to recover myself by absorbing the other. This sets up an endlessly frustrating love-hate relationship in which each vainly tries to possess or be possessed by the other. Perhaps this frustration of human relations is a more realistic description of what actually is the case in many human situations than is Buber's description of the 'I-thou'. Yet, from what we know of our own possibilities, we could have no hesitation in saying that it is Buber who describes the *truly* human. What Sartre with his talk of possessing and being possessed omits is the 'distancing', as Buber understands it, that is to say, the respect for the inwardness of the other, which is not to be invaded or subjugated. This inwardness is not the frustration of interpersonal relations but their enrichment.

There is, of course, a further major difference between Buber and Sartre, and that concerns the ontological status which each assigns to the personal and the interpersonal. Buber is a believer in God, so that, in his often quoted words, 'Every particular "Thou" is a glimpse through to the eternal "Thou".'[21] Even God does not absorb the finite person but rather confirms its being. For Sartre, on the other hand, persons exist in a godless, indifferent, even nauseating universe. For him, a God (apart from being self-contradictory) would be oppressive. But certainly God, as Buber conceives him, is not oppressive. He is rather the enabler of genuine interhuman relationships, the author and sustainer of the 'between', the guarantor that the personal and interpersonal have ultimate worth and significance. Perhaps it is only in some such ontological setting that human relationships can come to their full flowering.

Buber is sometimes criticized on the ground that his account of the 'I-thou' relation deals only with the most intimate human contacts and has nothing to say about one's relations to society at large. The criticism overlooks the fact that Buber was intensely concerned with larger questions, such as the question of peace, but it does draw our attention to the importance of *scale* in human relations. Obviously, one can enjoy an 'I-thou' relation with only a relatively few people. What does sociality imply beyond that inner circle?

In the first instance, there is the wider circle of people with whom we come into contact in the pursuit of our daily tasks and pleasures – the bank clerk, the taxi driver, the shopkeeper and so on. Especially in the rush and bustle of modern urban life, the tendency is to treat them as mere functionaries or even machines, for what is the difference between cashing your cheque across the counter or drawing your money from an automatic dispenser outside the bank? Can we be surprised that some people's daily work alienates them from their humanity? Harvey Cox once suggested that in casual relations of this kind, an 'I-you' relation is possible, one less intimate than an 'I-thou' relation, but one which still respects the humanity of the other.[22] I would agree with this, and would add that perhaps the relevant virtue here is *courtesy*. This may not be a very highly regarded virtue, but what is fundamental to it is recognition of the other's dignity as a person. Courtesy does not even need words, so those who tell us that their time is too valuable for such niceties need not be alarmed. Courtesy consists primarily in a certain demeanour towards the other, a demeanour which conveys recognition and respect. It should not be despised or treated as merely cosmetic. Julian of Norwich speaks frequently in her writings of the courtesy of God himself towards his creatures.[23]

But beyond even these casual meetings, there are millions of others with whom our lives are entwined. Even if we wished, we could not avoid standing in some kind of relation to them. At this point the social pole of the human being is at its most distant from the individual pole, yet we have seen that both must have their rights in an adequate understanding of humanity.

What kind of relation is possible, when we think of society on the large scale? Obviously, it cannot be the direct type of relation we know at the level of individuals and small groups. We are talking now about the relation to people, most of whom we shall never actually meet, so the relation must be indirect. It is in fact mediated through structures, institutions, associations. Social and political structures form part of the environment with which we have to come to terms, just as much as do nature, things and other individual persons. Structures, institutions and large associations often strike us as impersonal, sometimes even as inhuman. However disordered relations between individuals may be, they seem rarely so ruthless as relations between nations or between powerful groupings within nations. The human being is essentially social, yet the pressures and demands of society seem to threaten the very humanity that it ought to enhance. In Reinhold Niebuhr's words: 'The community is the frustration as well as the realization of individual life. Its collective egoism is an offence to the individual's conscience; its institutional injustices negate the ideal of justice; and such brotherhood as it achieves is limited by ethnic and geographic boundaries.'[24]

Here again we seem to have struck on still another contradiction in the human condition, and one that seems well nigh irresoluble. By his very nature, man must create social and political structures and institutions, yet as soon as these have been created, they acquire a life of their own; they no longer serve human life but tyrannize it and dehumanize it. How many millions of people have lived or are even now living under régimes that stifle them and make for many a decent human life almost impossible? For a secure and worthwhile life, man needs the state or *polis*, he needs law and government and all the apparatus of a structured society, yet throughout history these have shown a tendency to become oppressive, and at any given time, including the present, they are for probably the majority of people on this planet more a framework of bondage than a means to freedom and the enhancement of life. Man is an inescapably political animal, but he has not so far found the way to integrate his political life with his needs and aspirations as an individual.

Is there any hope of solving the problem? Perhaps we should remember that it constitutes a problem only for those who recognize the individual as well as the social pole in the human being – it is not a problem for political extremists of either the right or the left, for whom the individual is expendable as the price of some collectivist system. There are various possible approaches to a solution. I shall consider two. One of them may be called realistic, the other is more idealistic or even mildly utopian.

The realistic approach takes the view that national states and powerful associations within such states (such as trade unions, employers' associations, political parties and the like) are motivated only by self-interest, and that politics is therefore a power struggle. No group will obtain justice except by struggle. So those who are concerned that individuals and minority groups should have reasonable freedom and opportunity, and who believe that structures and institutions should exist for the sake of man, not man for the sake of institutions, see the problem as one of curbing the inevitable abuse of power. The excesses of political and social oppression are to be prevented by ensuring that power is not concentrated into a very few hands. On the international scene, the balance of power (or, as some would say, now the balance of terror) has long been recognized as a way of ensuring that no single state or bloc of states could exercise dominion over other countries. Within national states, especially democratic and pluralist countries such as the United States, power is as widely distributed as possible. There are checks and counter-checks, and this does ensure a rough justice and a broad humanizing of structures, while there are ways of redress for individuals or groups who may suffer from some features of the system. It may well be that this balancing of powers and interests is the most realistic handling of the situation and the best that can be achieved in resolving the tensions between individuals and society and between different groups within a society.

I have called this the realistic approach, and acknowledged that it may be the best solution practicable, but I have mentioned that there is a more idealistic or utopian approach to the problem, and it cannot just be dismissed. I quoted above some remarks of Reinhold Niebuhr, who was very much a realist in ethics and stood opposed to every form of utopianism, romanticism and sentimentalism. No one was more committed than he to the cause of a free and just society, but he firmly believed that large social groupings are guided only by interest and can be checked only by power. But was that too pessimistic a view? I would like to think so. Gene Outka writes: 'Groups are not as incorrigible as Niebuhr supposed. He selected with tiresome regularity the elements of conflict in group relations, and neglected both actual and possible areas of cooperation. It may be more difficult for groups to suspend their own interests to the extent desirable than it is for individuals, but Niebuhr appears to deny even the possibility of such suspension.'[25]

If our concern is not just to describe human beings as they are but to criticize the existing state of affairs and to consider imaginatively the still unrealized possibilities of humanity, then we do not need to rest satisfied with the realist view of man and society. We have to ask whether, just as individuals learn or can learn that egoism is self-destroying and that there is no 'I' without a 'Thou', social and political groups can also learn their interdependence. It is at this point that religion again becomes relevant. In

Christianity we hear of the kingdom of God and even of a new creation, and although these are eschatological concepts and therefore, as Niebuhr claimed, not realizable in history, they may nonetheless exert a pressure on historical forms of society and help to transform them.

But should the church be involved in politics? Should there not be separation of church and state – a fundamental tenet of modern liberalism? But just as a matter of historical fact, the church has for most of its history been involved in politics. That happened almost immediately after it gained licit status under Constantine. The historian Eusebius of Caesarea was perhaps the first to develop the theme of the solidarity of church and state. 'In his writings,' claims Aloys Grillmeier, 'a political theology seems more and more to have gained the upper hand.'[26] In much of European history, the church was closely associated with the ruling class, but in recent times it has in various parts of the world allied itself with leftish movements. The involvement with politics is inevitable, for the business of religion is to bring salvation to men, and since no man or woman is an island, no man can be saved on his own. He can be made whole only along with others, and this includes not only other individuals but the structures and institutions that enter into the lives of all of them. As I have written elsewhere, 'the idea of "individual salvation" is really a contradiction in terms',[27] though, regrettably, one has to say that sometimes the church has conceived its mission to be the rescuing of individuals from the *massa damnata* of mankind, rather than the salvation of humanity. Religion, with its deep insights into human nature, knows the magnitude of the problem, and keeps alive the hope of transformed individuals living in a transformed society. This is more than any political vision, but it has a political dimension.

On the other hand, those who are suspicious of religion becoming involved in politics do have some reason for their attitude. Too often religion has become the dupe of a political force and has conferred a certain sacrality upon it. It is much easier for the church to be used for political ends than for it to exert a humanizing influence in politics. Therefore the church ought never to ally itself with any particular party, though individual Christians may do so. The church must maintain a critical freedom in politics if it would help to bring us beyond the mere balancing of power and interests to a genuine reconciliation and cooperation. Of course, the best service that the church can render towards building a new and better society is just to manifest such a society in its own life. For the church has its own structures, institutions and organization, formally comparable to structures in the secular world. Can it show that these can be humanized, that authority can be wisely exercised, that even a very large association of people can pursue ends other than those dictated by self-interest? Admittedly, the church has often failed in these matters, and shown itself to be prone to all the perversions that we see in secular society. Ecclesiastical politics have been as appalling as any. But in the early centuries of its history, before the Constantinian settlement, the Christian church existed as a kind of 'counter culture' on the margin of Roman imperial society, and showed how thitherto warring groups could discover a new solidarity.[28] Perhaps there is still such a possibility, that could take us beyond the provisional and precarious balancing of interests to a genuine reconciliation.

IX

LANGUAGE

When I raised the question about what is distinctive in the human being, we could not fail to take note of the Greek view of man as *zōon logon echon*.[1] This expression is usually translated 'rational animal', and I rejected this as too narrow a definition of the distinctively human, since rationality does not exhaust personality. But another translation of the Greek is possible. The human being is the 'living thing that has speech'. A strong case could be made for holding that it is language that is the distinctive mark of humanity. 'Man's relation to the world is absolutely and fundamentally linguistic in nature,' declares Hans-Georg Gadamer.[2] Rationality needs language, but language is broader than rationality and corresponds to the whole range of personal being. Language may be poetry as well as argument or description, it can express emotion and resolution as well as give information. Of course, it might be said that animals too have language. Such diverse creatures as bees and dolphins are well known for having developed forms of language, and many other creatures exhibit rudimentary forms. Yet these animal analogues to language are so restricted as compared with the seemingly endless possibilities of human language that here we have a difference of degree so vast that it has become a difference in kind. Human language transcends animal language just as human personality transcends the psychology of even those animals that stand nearest to man. There is a qualitative difference between the two.

What is language? A moment's reflection shows us that this is a most extraordinary question. Admittedly, every question must presuppose at least some idea of what is being asked about, for otherwise we would not even get the length of asking the question. But in the case of the question, 'What is language?' much more than a vague idea is implied. In order to ask the question about language, we have to use the very language that we ask about. 'What is language?' is already a highly complex example of language – phonetically, lexically, semantically, syntactically and in other ways besides. It needs a considerable measure of linguistic competence just to be able to ask this question. Perhaps the only answer that can be given is to bring to speech the tacit or implicit understanding of language which the questioner must already possess in order to ask the question.

One of the most astonishing phenomena of human life is the fact that at a fairly early age every normal human being learns a natural language – English, French, Chinese or whatever it may be. Not only does he learn to make and recognize intelligible sounds – words, syllables, phonemes – and to amass a vocabulary, he does something even more astonishing in mastering a grammar, the system of intricate relationships whereby these sounds are built into meaningful sentences and the sentences in turn into stories, arguments, poems and so on. Yet all this is unconsciously absorbed, in the sense that there is no *explicit* knowledge of grammatical relationships and the very words 'grammar' and 'syntax' are still unknown. This linguistic competence is a striking example of tacit knowledge.[3] One may contrast the way in which a child learns his native language with the way in which at a later time he will learn a foreign language, for instance, Latin. Now he will have to come to grips explicitly with grammar and learn a metalanguage about parts of speech, cases, moods and so on. But for centuries people who could neither read nor write and knew nothing of formal grammar were able to speak and understand highly complex languages, and some who were without formal education were even able to compose superb poetry on the basis of their tacit knowledge of the language. One is further astonished by these facts when we note that in the period in which languages have been written down, the past four thousand years or so, the general tendency has been for grammar to become simpler, even though vocabularies have vastly expanded. Modern Scottish Gaelic is syntactically simpler than Old Irish, modern Greek than ancient Greek, Hindi than Sanskrit. Admittedly, the spoken language is usually simpler than the written language, but nevertheless ancient peoples had implicit mastery of highly complex systems of language.

How does one account for this impressive linguistic competence which, universally in children and frequently in adults, lies below the level of conscious explicit awareness? Does it tell us anything about the nature of a human being?

There is no doubt that language is learned, yet there would seem to be equally no doubt that there is an innate disposition to language. The child, as we say, 'picks up' language. He does not just repeat what he hears, like a parrot or a myna, but is soon making up his own sentences, having mastered the rules for constructing meaningful combinations of words. Piaget has claimed that there is a definite period in the life of the child, approximately the same in cultures all over the world, in which the development of linguistic competence takes place. Chomsky has used the expression 'generative grammar' for those rules of syntax which enable the construction of meaningful sentences rather than just strings of words. More generally, writers who have taken a structuralist approach to linguistics have talked about a 'depth grammar' and contrasted it with 'surface grammar'. This depth grammar is held to be a deep structure of the human mind comprising the 'theoretical or abstract system of relationships which determines the narrative on the level of manifestation',[4] that is to say, it underlies the surface grammar of the actual natural language (English, Latin or whatever it may be) in which the sentence or story finds expression. This deep generative grammar is also in some sense a universal grammar, for in spite of all the differences of surface grammar among the natural languages, there is fundamental agreement about what makes sense and what does not, and the affinity is evidenced by the fact that we can translate out of one language into another, even into another that belongs to an unrelated family of languages.

Is this a reversion to a doctrine of innate ideas, in the manner of Descartes? Sometimes we get the impression that it is, and certainly it challenges empiricist notions of language. Yet the most plausible interpretation of the structuralist theory of language is as little tied to the Cartesian belief in innate ideas as it is to the rejected empiricist belief in a *tabula rasa*. It is much more compatible with the Kantian theory of a twofold source of human knowledge – the logical structure of the mind (the categories) on the one hand, and the intuitions of sense on the other. 'Our nature is so constituted,' he writes, 'that our *intuition* can never be other than sensible . . . The faculty, on the other hand, which enables us to *think* the object of sensible intuition is the understanding. To neither of these powers may a preference be given over the other. Without sensibility, no object would be given to us, without understanding, no object would be thought. Thoughts without content are empty, intuitions without concepts are blind.'[5] These remarks of Kant may, with appropriate modification, be applied analogously to the problems of language which we have been considering. Language could never come into being were there not some *a priori* structure, whether we call it 'depth grammar' or by some other expression. Yet it is an empty potentiality until the human being to whom it belongs finds himself growing up in a human situation where a natural human language is spoken. It is some such situation that Edgar McKnight has in mind when he talks of 'a combination of innate and historical factors maintained in equilibrium'.[6]

The twofold root of language is recognized also in the philosophy of Heidegger. In his early period, he considered talk or discourse (*Rede*) to be a fundamental way of being of the human existent (*Dasein*).[7] But later we find him suggesting that man could not have invented language, and making the grammatical point that 'the infinitive carries a privileged position in language as a whole'[8] – the infinitive being that part of the verb which has been, so to speak, decontextualized, stripped of tense, person and number, and so of a relation to a concrete human situation. Language comes to be described as 'the house of Being' and we are told that 'before he speaks, man must first let himself be addressed again by Being, taking the risk that in response to this address he will seldom have anything much to say'.[9]

But is not this an unnecessary mystification, perhaps a modern counterpart to ancient myths telling of how man learned language from the gods? On the other hand, it might be the case that these early myths represented a dim realization of the mystery of language and of the human being himself as *zōon logon echon*. In any case, it could all be given a naturalistic explanation. The intricate structures of the human brain, including the structures that make language possible, are themselves developed out of universal structures of matter and energy, so that they must reflect the basic structures of the world. We could even speak of a 'language' or 'grammar' of nature, which would consist of the basic laws of physics and chemistry, and, at a more complex level, the genetic code which carries the information for the building up of living organisms and their parts, including the human brain. Surely, this is a language of nature. So it is far from fanciful to see the roots of language as penetrating far back beyond human experience, both individual and social, into the very structure of reality itself.

Incidentally, the development of writing during the past few thousand years has brought out the latent autonomy of language. When something is written down, it becomes a text and has attained a relative independence. It is no longer possible to consider it merely as the product of a speaker's subjectivity, for it has been detached from him and from the human situation in which he produced it. It has been decontextualized, and in process of time the original intention of the person who uttered the words may be forgotten or obscured, while the language itself may yield new meanings that were not originally envisaged. 'Not occasionally only, but always,' writes Gadamer, 'the meaning of a text goes beyond its author; that is why understanding is not merely a reproductive but a productive act as well.'[10] Although the autonomy of written texts (and presumably also of fixed oral traditions) is a phenomenon appearing in the history of natural languages, it does lend some support to the view shared by Heidegger and the structuralists that there is an autonomous root of language that cannot be conceived as a human invention.

But that brings us back to the question of how this root of language is to be understood – in naturalistic terms as a reflection of the 'grammar' of the physical universe, or in a more 'spiritual' way as, perhaps, the language of

God? Since we have set our face from the beginning against any dualism, and have held that the human being is a psychosomatic reality, in one sense a product of nature but in another a being who has transcended nature, we cannot be satisfied with either a naturalistic or a spiritualistic answer to our question. Even if language is ultimately the gift of God (so that to some extent the old myths would be vindicated), it is a gift that has been transmitted through the physical universe, evolution and history. Some people might feel that the naturalistic explanation is adequate, others may feel that one has to go further.

This talk of the 'language of God' may remind us of a celebrated passage in one of Bishop Berkeley's dialogues. One of the speakers, Alciphron, says: 'I have found that nothing so much convinces me of the existence of another person as *his speaking to me.*' He goes on to explain: 'What I mean is not the sound of speech merely as such, but the arbitrary use of sensible signs which have no similitude or necessary connection with the things signified; so as by the apposite management of them to suggest and exhibit to my mind an endless variety of things, differing in nature, time and place; thereby informing me, entertaining me, and directing me how to act, not only with regard to things near and present, but also with regard to things distant and future.'[11] These words of Berkely seem to me to describe very well the meaning of 'grammar' in the foregoing discussion. Berkeley himself goes on to develop an argument from design which would not perhaps find much favour nowadays. But my own argument is that the very fact of language with the strong indications that its 'grammar' has its roots in transhuman reality is evidence of an ordered universe, and this is part of what we mean when we speak of God. Whatever Nietzsche may have had exactly in mind, I think he was speaking truly when he said, 'I fear we are not getting rid of God, because we still believe in grammar.'[12]

Of course, belief in a universal order is only *part*, as I said, of belief in God. It is a not inconsiderable part, as it would seem to imply a fundamental trust in reality. But to justify God-language, there must also be the possibility of communion on a level not lower than personal. The language of physics and chemistry, even the language of the genetic code which some would subsume under physics and chemistry, cannot rank as a language of God. We could speak of a language of God only if there were the possibility of saying 'Thou', that is to say, of perceiving and responding to a depth of meaning beyond the physical. We recall Heidegger's assertion that 'before he speaks, man must let himself be addressed by Being'.[13] The German verb *ansprechen*, which I have translated here as 'address', could also be translated as 'claim'. In either case, it refers to a reality with which human beings have some affinity and with which there is the possibility of some intercourse, a reality that can address us and even claim us. This would be no faceless mechanism that has left its traces in the depth grammar of the human brain or mind, but a creative reality not less than rational and personal, whose image is reflected by human beings.

Is this a baseless claim, or are there evidences that the innate capacity for language among human beings signifies a deep affinity between them and the environing reality that has brought them forth and the possibility of communion with that reality? I see at least three evidences that this is so.

One is religious experience, the fact that many men and women have claimed and still do claim to be addressed or encountered by an Other whom they call God and whose 'word' they believe themselves to have heard in and through the events of this world. Some may say this is only a widespread illusion, but it is evidence that has to be considered, and the place of religion in human life will be examined by us in due course.[14]

Next, there is the evidence of modern science, which has moved far from the mechanistic views that were current in the nineteenth century and has been revealing in the universe a complexity of structure not hitherto imagined. Atoms are not solid particles whose accidental collocations and collisions might produce the anomaly of thinking beings. It looks far less likely than it once did that human beings are some kind of surd in the universe, and far more likely that they, with their minds and values and languages, are bringing to expression realities that have their roots in the structures of the universe itself so that, as Peacocke has observed, we are pointed to man's total involvement with the world around him.[15]

Finally, if there is a fundamental grammar underlying our natural languages and reflecting the structure of reality, is it not significant that all languages have their God-talk – stories of God or the gods or the holy, and rules for using this talk? It is remarkable too how much there is in common among the various forms of God-language. Language is not just for talking about things or biological needs. It is creative and expanding, and from an early time, even at the level of the mythological, it has embraced a realm that transcends everyday material phenomena. Perhaps this constitutes the basis for the ontological argument for God's existence, though it has to be noted that we have not just a concept of God but, at least potentially, an entire grammar. God is already there in language.

I turn now from these somewhat speculative but surely important questions about language to its functions. It would be hard to say how many functions belong to language, but I propose to examine five that seem to be of special importance and, in their several ways, shed light on what it means to be a human person.[16]

The first function of language that calls for mention is *expression*. Through language, human beings express themselves. We recall that every human being is a unique centre of existence, yet he or she is at the same time embodied in a world of things and is a participant in human society. Language is our opening to the world and to others. There are, of course, openings besides language, such as perception and action of every kind, yet perceptions and actions are themselves given shape and expression through language, and sometimes language is itself action – it is performative, in J. L. Austin's sense of the word.[17] Grammatically, some utterances look like statements, but in fact we use them to bring about new states of affairs in the world, that is to say, they are actions.

It is possible for us, no doubt, to come pretty near to being purely cognitive subjects and to express only what we observe. Many philosophers have in fact treated the human being as if he were wholly, or at least primarily, a subject of cognition, with the world constituting the object of his cognition and remaining unaffected by it. But that is a mere abstraction from the concrete reality. Language normally expresses the whole range of our interaction with the world, emotive and practical as well as cognitive, personal as well as impersonal. Even when we come nearest to being mere observers, it is impossible to screen out altogether the personal dimension. As we have learned in an earlier discussion,[18] there is no way of knowing the world that can completely dispense with the contribution of the knower. To put it in another way, any knowable universe is bound to include knowers as part of its intrinsic constitution – a point known sometimes as the 'anthropic principle'.[19] Even if there is, as we have seen likely, a universal grammar, this is encountered only as embodied in some natural language which cannot help expressing something of the human point of view and the multiple interests of mankind. Admittedly, in modern times attempts have been made to reduce language to a calculus and to construct artificial languages that would as far as possible abstract from the human element. But apart from the fact that such languages always have to be explained in some natural language, they are too formal to express the multifacetted reality that we know in human experience.

The point is well illustrated by William Barrett, who points out that the greatest language philosopher of modern times, Ludwig Wittgenstein, began his philosophizing by employing the precisely constructed language of the *Principia Mathematica*, but finally abandoned it for the less precise but far more richly expressive language of ordinary speech. 'The attempt to understand language itself through the model of a single paradigmatic language – and that a formal language that is artificially constructed – is fruitless. It does not show us the multiple uses that language serves in the actual flow of life. It is like looking at a landscape through a grid and then carving out its parts in geometrical form without following the natural contours of the terrain. In the next and mature period of his thought, Wittgenstein sought out these living contours within language as we use it.'[20]

Next, we consider the function of *referring*. Our language is normally directed at some reality about which we are wanting to say something. It is aimed at things in the world, or at people, at political situations or other complex realities, at the universe itself or even at God. It is the case that very occasionally language seems to be almost devoid of reference. A highly abstract poem might have its point in the texture of the sound, but it is significant that such a poem is virtually untranslatable. In the vast majority of cases, language refers within the public domain, so to speak. Out of the undifferentiated background of entities of which we are aware, directly or indirectly, at any given time, language isolates and brings to notice that about which the speaker wishes to say something. This way of understanding the referring function of language corresponds to what we have earlier called (following Popper) the 'searchlight' theory of know-ledge.[21] Our language lights up what we are talking about and brings it into the focus of attention. The chief rival to this understanding of language is what may be called the 'picture' view, according to which language is like a picture and is true if the elements in the picture and the way they are related show correspondence with the fact about which one is speaking. This picture theory of language, though once widely held – it was favoured by both Russell and the early Wittgenstein – is nowadays seen to be inadequate. It may have a rough applicability to relatively simple facts in the physical world, but there are wide areas of human language which cannot be subsumed under the 'picture' model. These would include, at one end, talk about sub-atomic particles, and, at the other, theological discourse about God. Such language cannot 'picture' its referend, yet it is certainly uttered in the conviction that it refers to a reality beyond the subjectivity of the speaker, and we also find that it 'lights up' that reality for us. Admittedly, we cannot, as it were, beam our language directly in such cases, and we do in fact make use of symbols, metaphors, analogies and the like. But to the extent that such language does bring what we talk about out of its hiddenness into light, then it has a claim to truth, which the Greeks called *aletheia*, precisely 'unhiddenness'. The function of referring in human language is another evidence of the basic human tendency toward transcendence – that man reaches out to relate to realities beyond himself, and there is no obvious limit to his outreach.

Communication is a third basic function of language. When we were discussing human sociality, we noted that language is an evidence that human life is essentially social.[22] There could hardly be a private language, for the very notion of language implies a linguistic community. It is important that we now correlate our understanding of communication with what we have previously learned about human community. We have seen that both relating and distancing, both outreach towards the other and respect for his or her inner integrity, are characteristic of a rightly ordered community of persons. It follows that communication can never be simply the transmission of an idea from one mind to another, especially if there were any hint of domination or manipulation in such transmission. Communication is rather an act of sharing. It proceeds on the assumption that there is already a sharing – the sharing of personal and rational being, the sharing of a common world, the sharing of interests and so on – and the specific aim of the communication is to extend that area of sharing. If the referring function of language is to light up some aspect of reality, then the communicating function is to let the other share the illumination. The aim is to let him see something for himself, even if one is hoping to persuade him to adopt a certain attitude or policy of action.

These remarks show us again how inextricably intertwined are the moral and intellectual strands of the human being. Even in a scientific community, where the purely cognitive interest may be paramount, that interest can never be separated from the other human and personal interests of the members of the community. Any intellectual enterprise demands as a condition of its success integrity and fidelity among those taking part in it. It needs much more than the collection and exchange of information.

A fourth function of language is *articulation*. The units of language cohere with one another to form ever larger wholes. Words form sentences, sentences are joined together in stories, arguments, theories, poems, dramas, belief systems and so on. These linguistic wholes are closely correlated with areas of individual or social experience, and it seems doubtful that these areas could be unified without the articulation made possible by language. We noted, for instance, that every individual human being is characterized by egoity, and it was no accident that we introduced this topic by the linguistic observation that everyone says 'I'.[23] The 'I' is constituted by a luminous centre surrounded by a penumbra which is also acknowledged as belonging to the 'I' and which extends both in space and time. But would any sense of egoity, beyond perhaps a fleeting momentary awareness, be possible apart from the articulation provided by language? Could one have a memory of the past, or could one form projects for the future, apart from the use of language that relates all these together as belonging to the same ego? Beyond the life of the individual, the life of society seems also to require linguistic articulation. The state, for instance, is held together by its constitution and its laws, and these have to be expressed in language. Is not the idea of the world itself, as some kind of unity, dependent on language and on the fact that human beings have named and described and related the multitudinous phenomena that confront them through the use of language? I do not mean that language creates all these unities. Perhaps language can articulate and bring into intelligible relations the swirling chaos of experiences only because there is some order there to be discovered, and we have indeed seen reason to believe that the roots of language may go back to some structure that is there in the very nature of things. But if language does not actually create these articulated systems, it certainly makes them accessible to human beings. Without language, we could be aware neither of the unities of human life, actual or potential, nor of the breaches in unity.

Language has, finally, the function of *creativity*, opening up new areas of knowledge and experience. Language is not static but keeps growing and deepening. It does not just describe things as they are, but through imagination and symbolism opens up new levels of awareness.

It is not easy to make a clear distinction between thought and language. The two are not identical, for clearly one thought can be expressed in an indefinite number of languages, as when I say 'I am cold', 'J'ai froid', 'Mir ist kalt', 'Tha mi fuair' and so on. Yet it would seem that the thought must be expressed in *some* language. On the other hand, we have made some use in the foregoing pages of Polanyi's idea of tacit knowledge, and have seen good reason for believing that there is such knowledge. Could we suppose that thought or thinking, in the sense of insight, leaps ahead of language, as it were, yet language is always close behind and our new thoughts find expression in new language? Perhaps the most primitive human languages were very severely restricted in what they could express – maybe information about hunting and gathering, just as the language of the bees indicates where nectar is to be found. But from these beginnings, human language has developed almost infinite possibilities. Poets, prophets, scientists, students of human nature and many others have contributed to that development and it goes on still today. Anyone who has regard to the enormously increased range which language has developed over the centuries and millennia will find any positivist attempt to set limits to language a most implausible venture. Language in its creativity and flexibility is one of the most powerful factors in the whole adventure of human transcendence.

The objection may be made that the account of language given in this chapter has been far too much idealized. All the virtues and benefits of language have been extolled, and it has even been represented as a kind of divine self-communication that is given with the very structure of the human being. I could not altogether deny this charge of one-sidedness, for I have been trying to show the essential contribution that language makes to the fulfilling of the human potential, and I have spent too little time over the failures and abuses of language. But the ambiguities which show themselves in every aspect of human nature are there in language also. Just as I said that the chapter on 'freedom' might equally well have been a chapter entitled 'bondage', and the chapter on 'transcendence' one on 'retrogression', and the chapter on 'egoity' one on 'egoism', so the chapter on 'language' might have had a less prestigious title – say, for instance, 'gossip' or 'lies' or 'misrepresentation' or 'slander' or any of the numerous other perversions of our talking together. If language can express and bring into the open the thoughts and feelings of the human person, it can also dissemble them and frequently does so; if language can light up the realities of life, it can also obscure them by becoming a mere exercise in pretentiousness, degenerating into what Heidegger has called 'idle talk';[24] if language can be the vehicle for genuine human communication, it can also be the instrument of lies and propaganda, and does in fact stir vicious passions and inflict terrible wounds; if language can articulate human life, it can equally well fragment and disrupt it; if language can be creative, it can also be sterile and destructive, perpetuating outworn values in the form of popular 'sayings' which masquerade as traditional wisdom.

The complaint is frequently heard that we are today living in a time when language has decayed. I mentioned Heidegger's indictment of 'idle talk', and we find him expressing the fear that in an age dominated by technology, it becomes customary to talk of everything as a possible object of control and manipulation. 'This process of unrestrained technological objectification,' he writes, 'naturally also affects language itself, and its determination. Language is deformed into an instrument of reportage and calculable information. It is treated like a manipulable object, to which our manner of thinking must conform.'[25] It could hardly be denied that the popular press, the advertising agencies, the mass media (especially television) have committed terrible sins against language, and therefore against the human race, 'the living beings that have speech,' and these sins have often been excused by appeals to 'freedom of expression'. Yet here one must concede that the risks of the misuse of language cannot be avoided if there is to be an extension of communication and information beyond an educated élite to the people at large. Actually, we find Heidegger going on to the more hopeful reflection that 'the saying of language is not necessarily an expressing of propositions *about* objects. Language, in what is most proper to it, is a saying *of* that which reveals itself to human beings in manifold ways.'[26]

Language may in fact be alienated from its true place in human existence, and that would be part of the more general alienation of the human being from his humanity. But is alienation the last word? Or does language, with its inbuilt norms of truth and fidelity, point us beyond alienation?

X

ALIENATION

The word 'alienation' has been very widely used in the nineteenth and twentieth centuries. But as Frank Johnson, editor of an important symposium on the topic has said, ' "Alienation" is an atrocious word.' He explains why: 'Most terms which possess scientific bite are characterized by a reasonable specificity of denotation, a clarity of meaning within particular disciplines, and an absence of serious internal paradox or ambiguity. None of these belong to the word "alienation".'[1] The term has been used by philosophers, psychologists, sociologists, writers on politics, theologians and educators, and has passed into popular usage. Among those different types of people using the word, it has borne different senses, though there has been a measure of underlying similarity. A further source of confusion arises from the differing valuations when one speaks of alienation. Generally, alienation is taken to be a bad thing – for instance, by Marxist politicians and by Christian theologians. Indeed, some of the latter come near to equating it with sin. But sometimes alienation is a neutral phenomenon, neither good nor bad. Occasionally, it is represented as something that may be aimed at as desirable, as when William Barrett expresses the view that 'in the nineteen-sixties, the young aspired to alienation, cultivated it as a way of life and proclaimed it as their defiance'.[2] Incidentally, the very fact that we recognize that human beings can be alienated from their humanness is a confirmation of the point made at the beginning of this book, namely, that the adjective 'human' is itself not so much a descriptive as an evaluating word which implies some norm or ideal of humanity. We must begin then with some clarifications, and perhaps a brief history of the concept will be helpful.

The word 'alienation', in its most basic sense, means either the process of becoming other, or the state of having become other. If something has simply become other than it has been, then the term is neutral, as when we speak of the alienation of property. This simply means that there has been a change of ownership. But often the word means that something has become other than it ought to be, and then the word carries a negative valuation, as when we say that a child's affections have been alienated from its parents. In this case, we might use a more definitely valuating term, and talk of 'estrangement'.

If we take our survey back as far as Hegel, we find that in him the idea of alienation is fundamentally a metaphysical idea. It is necessary to the world process, for the Absolute Spirit must externalize and finitize itself in that which is other than itself in order to know itself in and through this other. 'Spirit is alone reality. It is the inner being of the world, that which essentially is and is *per se*; it assumes objective, determinate form, and enters into relations with itself – it is externality (otherness) and exists for self; yet, in this determination, and in its otherness, it is still one with itself – it is self-contained and self-complete, in itself and for itself at once.'[3] Again, he writes: 'Spirit is knowledge of self in a state of alienation of self; spirit is the being which is in the process of retaining identity with itself in its otherness.'[4] Obviously, there is a certain tragic aspect to this. In itself, the divine life of Absolute Spirit could be conceived as an undisturbed unity, but in actuality it is going out into the finite, so that from the beginning there has been sacrifice in spirit. Yet if this is necessary to the world process, then in some sense it is a blessed sacrifice – and with this one may compare the Christian paradox which has described as *felix culpa* both the fall of man and the cross of Christ.

This tragic element is reflected in human experience in that particular phase of the unfolding of the finite spirit which Hegel calls the 'unhappy consciousness'. This unhappy consciousness is 'the alienated soul which is the consciousness of self as a divided nature'.[5] This awareness of an alienation that is within the human spirit and which knows that the Absolute Spirit is not undisturbed unity but is already sacrificing itself in going out into the otherness of the finite because of the necessity of its own nature is 'the bitter pain which finds expression in the cruel words, "God is dead!"'[6] That phrase, 'God is dead!', was later to be made notorious by Nietzsche. But Hegel is simply quoting a Good Friday hymn by Luther, in which by a startling but theologically orthodox exercise of the *communicatio idiomatum*, the death of Jesus on the cross is spoken of as the 'death of God'. We should not forget this occurrence of the phrase in Hegel, for we shall see that one of the main contentions of the philosophical analysts of alienation in the nineteenth century was that God is an alienating influence in human life. We have ourselves already noted the difficulty of reconciling human transcendence with divine transcendence, and I said at that point that reconciliation seems possible only if one can form a non-oppressive concept of God.[7] This may well mean a more thoroughly christianized concept of God, in which the suffering and death of Jesus are taken seriously as moments intrinsic to the divine life itself.

But the immediate development from Hegel was in a different direction. Feuerbach, while accepting Hegel's view that the subject must externalize itself and know itself in and through the other, located this process not in Absolute Spirit but in the human being. He neatly turns Hegel upside down. It is the human being who 'projects his being into objectivity, and then again makes himself an object to this projected image of himself thus converted into a subject, but as an object of an object, of another being than himself'.[8] What we call 'God' has no reality in itself. It is simply a projection of an idealized human nature. The true end of humanity is not God but humanity itself. But this is concealed from the religious believer, even in Christianity where the doctrine of the incarnation has made God into man. The result has been the alienation of the human race from its own true nature. All that is best in the nature of man has been ascribed to God, while human beings have thought it right to denigrate themselves, as in doctrines of original sin. Particularly objectionable is the Lutheran teaching on *sola gratia* – that human beings have no merit of their own and owe everything to the grace of God. 'Luther,' declares Feuerbach, 'declares himself to be for God and against man. God is everything to him, man nothing.'[9]

It could hardly be denied that some of Feuerbach's criticisms do strike home. His remedy is to get rid of God, so that humanity may take back into itself the virtues which it had externalized and alienated in the imaginary being of God. Perhaps it was historically necessary to do that, since we know ourselves only through our dealings with the other. But the alienation has now become harmful and diverts human effort from human goals. We have to learn that 'theology is anthropology, the object of religion expresses nothing other than the deified essence of man'.[10] Feuerbach sums up his purpose thus: 'to transform theologians into anthropologists, lovers of God into lovers of man, candidates for the next world into students of this world, religious and political flunkeys of heavenly and earthly monarchs and lords into free, self-reliant citizens of the earth.'[11]

Though there are social and political allusions in the last quotation, it was left to Marx to develop the political and economic dimensions of the concept of alienation. In part, he agreed with Feuerbach that concern with the illusory goals of religion had alienated human beings from their true goals. Thus, 'the abolition of religion as the illusory happiness of the people is required for their true happiness'.[12] But in the main, his view of alienation was very different from Feuerbach's. The latter had seen religion as a major factor in the shaping of society and politics, but for Marx religion was a symptom and belonged to the superstructure. The realities of life are economic, and – as we have noted already – the human being affirms himself through his work. Religion cannot be abolished so long as the conditions which give rise to it remain, but if alienation could be overcome at the level of economic life, then religion would simply wither away. What then is this basic alienation? It is the alienation of the human being from his work and the product of his work. His labour, in which he ought to be affirming himself and finding satisfaction, has, under capitalism, become a commodity that is bought and sold and put to use without regard to the worker himself. He has become degraded to part of the industrial machine.

We have taken note at an earlier point[13] that although Marx inveighed against the capitalist system as he knew it in the nineteenth century, his criticisms have some force in any modern industrial society, capitalist or socialist, though of course some of the worse abuses of the nineteenth century have been removed, at least in Western nations. But division of labour, resulting in some cases in very monotonous work with no clear relation to the product; mechanization, which again separates the worker from his product and turns him into a machine minder; market forces, which compel people to produce goods in which they have no interest; above all, perhaps, the vast scale of modern industrial enterprises which makes the ordinary worker feel like an insignificant unit in a great impersonal organization – these are some of the economic factors that produce alienation and prevent that self-affirmation in work which Marx believed to be necessary for a truly human life. The problems, however, are endemic in any modern technological society, and neither capitalism nor socialism can provide a doctrinaire solution.

One has, perhaps, to add still another alienating factor that may prove to be increasingly difficult to handle – unemployment. Advances in automation and computerization have already eliminated many of the more monotonous tasks, but they have also meant that industry can get along with a smaller labour force. It is quite possible that this trend may continue, and that the number employed in regular work in advanced societies may continue to decrease. Some utopians have promised a coming age of leisure, but they have not considered the strain and divisiveness that must arise in any society where some work and some do not, or whether Marx's point about the connection between work and self-affirmation points to a permanent characteristic of human nature or whether it can be transcended. Throughout this book I have gone on the assumption that human nature is a changing nature, but we should be clear that it would need a very profound change and probably a slow and painful one to wean men and women away from their need to affirm themselves in some regular productive work. At this point we have to recall some of the problems that confronted us when we considered the place of having in human life,[14] and to ask whether ever-rising economic production should have the priority that we accord to it, or whether this must not be weighed against the threats of alienation and estrangement from a truly human life.

I cannot accept either that the expression 'truly human' here begs the question, for however much Marxists, Buddhists, Christians and so on disagree about some aspects of a 'true humanity' or a fulfilling society, they are all agreed about some of the obvious and widespread ways in which many human lives are brutalized or deprived of meaning at the present time.

But we now return to our summarized history of the concept of alienation, and we move our sights from Marx to his near contemporary, Kierkegaard. 'Alienation' is not part of the Kierkegaardian terminology, yet the phenomenon or some aspects of it was one of which he had an acute awareness. His whole philosophy can be seen as an attempt to break out of such alienated forms of existence as pretence and superficiality to a genuinely human mode of being. I give three instances from his writings. In his *Concluding Unscientific Postscript*, he contrasts the objective truth of propositions that can be learned out of books with the inward truths of life that can be learned only in an act of passionate appropriation. In *Fear and Trembling*, the contrast is between the conventional morality based on rules and customs with the agonizing decisions of conscience, typified by Abraham's response to the command to sacrifice Isaac. In his *Attack on Christendom*, the profoundly Christian Kierkegaard bitterly assails the ecclesiastical Christianity of Denmark, for it has, he believes, reduced Christianity to doctrines and history, whereas it is properly a matter of the will. Since truth, morality and religion are close to the centre of human life, Kierkegaard's contention that we meet them for the most part in alienated forms in the modern world must be considered just as revolutionary as Marx's assault on the political and economic fabric of society.

The revolt was carried to its furthest length by Nietzsche. For the sake of human freedom and transcendence, all the old alienations must be abolished – God must be declared dead, the old tables of the law must be broken and conventional norms of right and wrong replaced, there must be a transvaluation of all values. If Feuerbach had been right, then the path that led to Nietzsche should have been the path to liberation and the overcoming of alienation. But in fact, it leads to a new and very profound alienation. 'What did we do when we loosened this earth from its sun? Whither does it now move? Whither do we move? Away from all suns? Do we not dash on unceasingly? Backwards, sideways, forwards, in all directions? Is there still an above and a below? Do we not stray, as through infinite nothingness? Does not empty space breathe upon us? Has it not become colder? Does not night come on continually, darker and darker?'[15] This picture of an utterly contingent world, where we have moved away from all suns and there is neither up nor down and the centre is everywhere, is sometimes called nihilism.

Hans Küng has suggested that with the nihilism of Nietzsche the attempt to liberate humanity from the alienating power of an oppressive God reached its end and perhaps even came to a turning point.[16] Patrick Masterson, who has carried the story down to Sartre, in whose philosophy the human being is finally alienated not only from the cosmos but even from his fellow human beings, makes a similar point when he writes: 'We have seen how the rejection of God in defence of the transcendence, creativity and liberty of man has been accompanied by a frank admission of the obscure, unvindicated and ultimately uncertain outcome of this creative autonomy of man.'[17] Our brief survey has brought before us many forms of alienation or alleged alienation, and it is not at all clear how they are related. But none of the philosophers mentioned or all of them together have offered a solution to the problem of alienation. It seems rather to grow worse, and certainly the solution is not nearly so simple as the abolition of God.

Keeping in mind the historical background that has been adumbrated above, let us now attempt a more systematic analysis of alienation. I shall discuss four aspects that are of special interest from the point of view of this book.

Let me begin with the neutral sense of the term 'alienation', that is to say, with the mere possibility of otherness, short of actual estrangement. Whether one should even speak of 'alienation' at this level is doubtful. We are concerned rather with the ground of alienation or with what makes alienation possible, but obviously that is an important topic.

It will be remembered that in the earlier discussions on egoity and embodiedness, we found ourselves in agreement with the majority of contemporary philosophers in firmly rejecting any metaphysical dualism in the human being.[18] In particular, we turned away from Descartes' dualism of mind and body, res cogitans and res extensa, and insisted that the human being is a psychosomatic unity. But to affirm the unity of the human being is not to deny that there are internal distinctions within that unity (as is indeed implied in the term 'psychosomatic') or that the unity may be subjected to strains and disruptions and may in fact never be fully actualized.

It will be interesting to recall the biblical account of the creation of man, for there we find the acknowledgement of a duality along with the denial of a dualism. The duality is represented as essential to humanity itself, and that which makes the difference between men and women on the one hand and animals on the other. The duality is introduced in symbolic or mythological guise: 'Then the Lord God formed man of the dust from the ground, and breathed into his nostrils the breath of life.'[19] Other ancient myths tell similar stories, and see in the human being the conjunction of earth and breath, or, in more sophisticated language, matter and spirit. But although such stories point to a fundamental duality in humanity, they are not necessarily dualistic in their underlying philosophy. The occurrence of such myths from the earliest times shows that men and women have always understood themselves as complex beings, standing in a tension between two component elements. But only some of the stories developed this primordial consciousness into a full-blown metaphysical dualism, and certainly the biblical story did not.

It is important to note that in the biblical story the fundamental duality is present in man in his original condition, before there is any mention of a fall into sin. The two component elements, the dust and the breath, are embraced within a unity, and both belong equally to the primordial humanity. In a genuinely dualistic mythology or philosophy – the various forms of Gnosticism, to which I shall be referring later, are examples – body and soul are utterly foreign to each other. They have come together through an unhappy accident or through demonic contrivance, and they remain in irreconcilable conflict in every human person. Only the soul is recognized as the truly human element, and salvation is understood as the escape of the soul or spirit from the imprisoning body. But in the biblical narrative there is no hint of such dualism. Body and soul are with equal primordiality constituent of the whole human being, and then salvation is understood as the resurrection of the body, a renewal and transformation of the human existent in all its dimensions.

However, the use of the expressions 'body' and 'soul' is not suitable in talking about the Genesis story, for they import too much of a metaphysical flavour into it. Originally the story simply expresses the felt complexities of human life. The 'dust' symbolizes the given in human existence, all the enduring links that tie us to the natural order. But as well as the given, we are conscious also of possibility, freedom and creativity, symbolized by the 'breath of life'. The most obvious given item in a human existence is the body, but the given does not simply coincide with the body. On the other hand, the presence in man of possibility and freedom constitutes an openness in his being. He is not simply a given, but has the possibility of becoming other than he is at any particular moment. Thus the awareness of otherness and the possibility of otherness are present in the human being from the beginning. If there is a neutral sense of 'alienation' as simply 'becoming other', then we are now beginning to see what this is, and how it constitutes the condition for the emergence of alienation in its more definite and usually harmful forms of estrangement.

A classic analysis of the fundamental duality of human existence is provided by Kierkegaard. He relates it to the phenomenon of anxiety, and sets it in the context of an exegesis of the biblical story of the creation and fall of man. What emerges in Kierkegaard's analysis is not yet alienation in the full sense, but rather, what makes alienation possible. Kierkegaard's own question is: 'What makes sin possible?' (Later we shall consider the relation between sin and alienation). He regards the Genesis story of the fall as describing an event or development in the life of every human being – the passage from innocence to sin, or from the unbroken wholeness of a merely given existence to the felt tension between a given state and an unrealized possibility. Since this is also the transition from animality or near animality to humanity, then we can again see why original sin might be designated *felix culpa*. But strictly speaking, we are not yet at original sin, but at that still more original breach or duality in human nature that makes sin possible, at what I have called alienation in the neutral sense of the term.

Innocence, according to Kierkegaard, is ignorance. It is really a pre-human condition, in which the human being has not yet emerged as spirit with freedom and responsibility, but is still determined in a natural condition. In innocence, there is peace and repose – but not quite. There is a stirring, a malaise, a sense of instability. This is what Kierkegaard calls *Angst* or anxiety. 'This is the profound secret of innocence, that at the same time it is anxiety.'[20] He says explicitly that anxiety is not guilt, but perhaps it is the premonition of the possibility of guilt. We can recognize in Kierkegaard's descriptions what I have called the sense of otherness or alienation in its neutral sense, the anxiety attendant on being launched out of the given into the insecurity of freedom.[21]

The illustration which Kierkegaard gives of this transition from the innocence of dreaming to human moral consciousness is the awakening of sexuality in the individual. In this, of course, he is still following the Genesis story. There is a malaise not properly understood, a premonition which finally issues in the sensual act and so in the loss of innocency and a changed quality of existence. But this introduction of sexuality into the analysis may be unfortunate, since it could easily mislead us into supposing that Kierkegaard is moving in the direction of a dualism of body and soul, and is advocating a form of asceticism. That this is not the case can be seen from what he says a little further on, where he declares that the human task is to accomplish the synthesis of soul and body. Such a synthesis is the very opposite of any dualism.

A more recent thinker who has written in an illuminating way on the neutral basis of alienation is Paul Ricoeur. He talks of 'fallible man', that is to say, man as 'fragile and liable to err'.[22] We are not yet talking about 'fallen man', but about the conditions which would make a 'fall' of man possible. According to Ricoeur, fallible man is characterized by a fault in the very heart of his being. (The words 'fallible' and 'fault' are, of course, cognate.) But this fault is not a moral fault, though it is the ground for the possibility of moral fault. The original fault in humanity is more like a geological fault, that is to say, a discontinuity, a break in the wholeness, the presence of otherness in identity.

It now becomes clear to us that the source of alienation in the human being is the same as the source of transcendence. In the discussion of transcendence, we did indeed note that the possibility of advance seems to be inseparable from the possibility of retrogression.[23] When we talk of alienation, we are considering the negative possibilities that can flow from the same source as human transcendence. If the latter outweighs the former, then we might be justified in calling alienation a 'happy fault'. But we are still only at the beginning of exploring it.

We turn now from that neutral, primordial discontinuity in the human being, which is the condition of the possibility of the various forms of alienation, to an actual and negatively evaluated form. Again we take our lead from the Bible, and its concept of sin. We may begin by reminding ourselves that sin is not the same as guilt or moral fault. There may be sins – such as the failure to perform religious duties – which are not moral faults, and even when a sin includes some moral delinquency (and this will be true in the majority of cases in a modern society) the sin is more than the moral fault, for it includes a religious dimension. Strictly speaking, one can only sin against God. The Psalmist therefore was correct when he said, 'Against thee, thee only, have I sinned,'[24] though his sin, and presumably most sins, are at the same time offences against fellow human beings.

Sin has been understood under many images. It has been seen as a stain, which must then be washed out; or as a missing of the mark, the sense of the Greek word *hamartia*; as a breaking of the law; or as a transgression of the divinely ordered scheme of things. No doubt these images all draw attention to some aspects of sin, though some of them have become somewhat archaic, as has indeed the concept of sin itself. In recent theology, an attempt has been made to refurbish the concept of sin by bringing it into relation with the concept of alienation. Paul Tillich, for instance, has interpreted sin in terms of alienation, though he prefers to use the word 'estrangement'. This way of looking at sin directs attention away from sinful acts or sins to sin as sinful condition. It is the condition of being estranged in one's actual state from what one might be. It is a fall, not in the sense of a deterioration from a superior state, but in the sense of a falling short of the possibilities of a human existence. Awareness of sin therefore brings with it the question of overcoming the alienation. In Tillich's words, 'it is the question of a reality in which our self-estrangement is overcome, a reality of reconciliation and reunion, of creativity, meaning and hope'.[25]

It is important to note that although we usually think of sin as it relates to the individual, there is also corporate sin. Indeed, the Hebrew prophets spent more time denouncing the sins of the nation than those of individuals. We have seen that social and political structures have their impact on the quality of human life, and that this impact may be alienating. The worker may be alienated because of the economic system, or again, the functional view of men and women is also alienating to the extent that it leads to a devaluing of the personal. The problem about corporate sin is that of assigning responsibility or – which is equally important – that of *feeling* responsibility. Corporate sin is, in Schleiermacher's words, 'not something that pertains severally to each individual and exists in relation to him by himself, but in each the work of all, and in all the work of each'.[26] The sources of corporate sin are no doubt the same that produce the sin of the individual – egoism (which can be that of a group as well as of an individual), greed, pride, desire for power and domination, and so on. In the case of individuals, however, it is much easier to assign responsibility and culpability, and for this reason corporate sin tends to be overlooked and unacknowledged.

I have said earlier that sin is essentially a religious or ontological phenomenon, rather than a moral one, even if it usually includes moral fault and offence against the fellow human being. I gave assent to the acknowledgement of the Psalmist that sin is against God and alienates us from him. But in the subsequent discussion, more stress seems to have been laid on the human alienations associated with sin than on the supposedly basic alienation from God. But while in the concept of sin it is *aversio a deo* or turning from God that theologians have regarded as primary, other alienations go along with it. The sinner is estranged from himself, in the sense that he misses and falls short of his own potential, while there is also estrangement among individuals and groups, in the form of a failure to achieve a true human community. God was supposed to be the judge who punished human sins, and this is a mythological way of saying that sin, which is primarily a breach with God becomes its own punishment as its consequences are worked out in human life. These consequences are disruption and estrangement on both individual and social levels in the life of the being whose task is the synthesis of body and soul, that is to say, of the manifold constituents that enter into his being.

But is this threefold correlation of alienation from God, alienation from others, and alienation from oneself, really a fact of human life? Certainly, many theologians have talked as if it were. But have they made this assumption too easily? We recall the opposite view of the nineteenth-century atheistic philosophers discussed earlier in the chapter. They held that it is precisely the relation to God that alienates men and women from themselves and from their neighbours, and they believed that if God could be eliminated, that would take us far towards the elimination of alienations on the human level.

Is there any way of settling this head-on clash? I have conceded that a concept of God which has been influential in the West and which may be called the 'monarchical' view of God can be oppressive and is difficult to reconcile with belief in human freedom and transcendence. I also think that such an understanding of God is sub-Christian, and that when the concept of God is more fully christianized, it is so far from being oppressive that it becomes an encouragement to human transcendence. Our brief survey of the history of the concept of alienation has in fact suggested that atheism is no cure, but rather brings in its train even more severe forms of estrangement. We have seen clear evidence for this in the philosophies of Nietzsche and Sartre. Even clearer evidence has been provided by those political regimes of the twentieth century in which dogmatic atheism has been part of the official philosophy. As Hans Küng has remarked, 'After the experience of National Socialism and Communism, modern atheism has lost much of its credibility.'[27] Incidentally, although I have spoken of 'dogmatic atheism', it is a well known fact that atheistic ideologies such as National Socialism and Communism tend to develop quasi-religious trappings and even substitutes for God. This is perhaps not surprising if we were right in surmising that God is already there in the grammar of human speech and thought, or, as Jung expressed it, he is present in the human mind as an archetypal idea.

To pursue these questions further, we turn now to another form of alienation – the sense of being alienated from the whole scheme of things. Perhaps this is a form of alienation from God, though it may be experienced rather as alienation from the cosmos. It is the sense that human life is an isolated phenomenon, unable to find any kinship in the surrounding world. Whether we call this alienation cosmic, ontological, theological or religious, it is perhaps the most profound alienation of all.

It is a strange but undoubted fact that at various periods of history people have been seized with an overwhelming mood of ontological estrangement. They have felt alienated from the universe which, in extreme cases, has impressed them not just as indifferent but even as hostile and demonic.

A very interesting example of this is provided by the movement (if it may be called a movement) loosely called Gnosticism. Partly religious, partly mythological, partly philosophical, Gnosticism flourished over wide areas of the Near East about the time of the rise of Christianity. In some of its forms, it coalesced with Christian elements.

To the Gnostic, the world was utterly alien and demonic. Awareness of duality had become in this case a thoroughgoing dualism. 'Light' and 'darkness' were the two great Gnostic symbols. The human soul is a fragment of light, but it is imprisoned in a material body which is itself part of a world of darkness. Men and women are lost and alone, strangers in a vast alien world.

Hans Jonas has used the expression 'cosmic nihilism' to describe the mood of the Gnostics. That mood finds expression in many fragments of Gnostic writings which he quotes. It will be enough to cite one example:

> Having once strayed into the labyrinth of evils
> The wretched soul finds no way out.
> She seeks to escape from the bitter chaos,
> And knows not how she shall get through.[28]

Other times and other cultures have their periods when a sense of lostness and abandonment seems to prevail. There was a time of unrest and pessimism in Chinese history that produced poems like the following:

> I look beseechingly to Heaven
> But find no pity there for me.
> For long, no peace has been our lot.
> Heaven grinds us on this millstone.

Another in similar vein runs:

> Unjust, unjust the might of Heaven,
> To grind us in this black assize;
> Unpitying, unpitying indeed,
> To lay on us this monstrous guilt.[29]

But to people in the West, the parallel to the 'cosmic nihilism' of Gnosticism is found in the philosophy of Nietzsche. We have already noted some main features of his philosophy, but Nietzsche was a poet as well as a philosopher, and the following verses give poignant expression to the feeling of alienation in a world in which God has died and everything is growing darker and colder. Indeed, if one did not know the provenance of these lines, they might easily be mistaken for a Gnostic fragment:

> The world's a gate
> To deserts stretching mute and chill.
> Who once has lost
> What thou hast lost stands nowhere still.[30]

Of course, long before Nietzsche brought the mood of alienation to its extreme and most sensitive expression, it had been building up. Already in the seventeenth century, the vastly expanded universe of the new astronomy was provoking the feelings expressed by Pascal: 'The eternal silence of these infinite spaces fills me with dread.'[31] In the nineteenth century, the poet Hölderlin was writing of the departure of the gods and of the consequent feeling of forlornness on the part of human beings. In English literature, there is something like a parallel in Matthew Arnold:

> The Sea of Faith
> Was once, too, at the full, and round earth's shore
> Lay like the folds of a bright girdle furled.
> But now I only hear
> Its melancholy, long, withdrawing roar.[32]

One could go on and talk of Kafka and Beckett and Sartre and dozens of other literary figures who have given expression to modern humanity's deep sense of alienation from the world in which we have to live. But perhaps that era of extreme alienation is passing. The world as interpreted by the science of the twentieth century is in many respects less intractably repelling than was its nineteenth-century counterpart. Furthermore, the metaphysical dualism which underlies all these views from Gnosticism to Sartre is not very convincing – it seems inherently improbable that there are two opposite cosmic principles. But finally, it is a question whether human beings themselves can endure to live permanently over against a universe which displays only impersonal necessity and faceless mechanism, and gives no hint or signal of having any affinity with the personal life of the human being. Let us agree that we cannot return to the naive faith of pre-scientific times. But is there any way to find again the fundamental trust which dualism, atheism and nihilism together destroyed?

Sociologist Peter Berger mentions the deep need that human beings have for believing that the world is an orderly and meaningful affair and not foreign to our human concerns. He introduces an illustration which makes very clear what I mean by ontological alienation. I quote the passage in full:

> A child wakes up in the night, perhaps from a bad dream, and finds himself alone, surrounded by darkness, beset by nameless threats. At such a moment, the contours of trusted reality are blurred or invisible, and in the terror of incipient chaos the child cries out for his mother. It is hardly an exaggeration to say that, at this moment, the mother is being invoked as a high priestess of protective order. It is she (and, in many cases, she alone) who has the power to banish the chaos and to restore the benign shape of the world. And, of course, any good mother will do just that. She will take the child and cradle him in the timeless gesture of the Magna Mater who became our Madonna. She will turn on a lamp, perhaps, which will encircle the scene with a warm glow of reassuring light. She will speak or sing to the child and the content of this communication will inevitably be the same: 'Don't be afraid, everything is in order, everything is all right.'[33]

Berger goes on to point out that although the scene he has described is an everyday and even trivial one, it has deeper implications. 'Everything is in order' is a metaphysical statement. He says: 'The formula can, without in any way violating it, be translated into a statement of cosmic scope: "Have trust in being!" '[34] But to have trust in being is an important part of what is meant in religious language by belief in God. It implies belief in a cosmic order that is not alien or indifferent but is supportive. I have myself described religious faith as 'faith in being', an expression very close to Berger's, and have said of such faith that 'it looks to the wider being, within which our existence is set, for support; it discovers a meaning for existence that is already given with existence'.[35] Similar expressions can be found among many contemporary theologians of diverse backgrounds – 'fundamental trust' (Küng), 'ground of confidence' (Ogden) and so on.

Berger claims that 'at the very centre of the process of becoming fully human, at the core of *humanitas*, we find an experience of trust in the order of reality'.[36] But then the question arises whether this trust in the order of reality is perhaps an illusion, induced by our need to overcome alienation and ontological insecurity. And certainly we have to acknowledge that the world presents an ambiguous face. Some features do indeed point to an order that can be trusted, but others to dark, chaotic, threatening forces. One may eventually decide to make a fundamental act of trust rather than of distrust, and one might think there are better reasons for such a decision, but one could never reach conclusive proof. It remains a matter of faith or belief, albeit a reasonable faith. It seems also to be the case – though the reasons for this are obscure – that there are periods of history when the faith in cosmic order is eroded and a sense of cosmic alienation takes its place, as we have seen with Gnosticism and nihilism.

Need one, however, choose between a fundamental act of trust and, on the other hand, some bleak atheistic or nihilistic view? Is this not an over-dramatizing of the situation? Do not people live by limited acts of trust and in limited areas of meaning, and these have value regardless of what the ultimate human situation may be? To those who would speak in this way, I think Hans Küng has addressed a very pertinent question: 'How can it be meaningful to take a single step, if the whole journey is absurd?'[37] To express the matter in another way, does not the taking of a single step imply the faith, however weak or tentative, that the whole journey will make sense? We shall come back to this in later discussions of commitment, belief and hope.

One's theological or metaphysical stance is not merely an academic question but has obviously profound existential consequences and affects the whole 'feel' or 'tone' of life. If the final reality is alien to human aspirations, then there must be a deep sense of alienation pervading the being of humanity. If the final reality is trustworthy, then there is an equally deep sense of belonging. But it would be a shallow unreflective faith indeed which sought to sweep doubts and anxieties under the carpet and to promise undisturbed peace and joy. All religion knows the dark side of human existence (Hegel's 'unhappy consciousness') and its 'peace' is neither a facile acquisition nor an unthreatened possession. For instance, in Christian theology, over against alienation is set a theology of atonement and reconciliation, teaching that only through costly struggle and suffering can the division be overcome.

We recall our question about whether there is a correlation among the different forms or levels of alienation. Does cosmic or ontological alienation produce in turn social alienations and alienation of the individual from himself? Do periods when this cosmic alienation is strongly experienced also exhibit powerful alienations and polarizations within society? On the other hand, does cosmic trust or religious faith build social trust and social hope? Does belief in reconciliation to being encourage reconciliation among human beings? There are no easy answers to these questions, but we have seen some considerations that would point to affirmative answers, and we shall see more as we continue our explorations.

But now let us look at some further aspects of alienation. We have still to consider the alienation of groups within a society. For instance, until recently and even to some extent today, black people have been excluded from the mainstream of American society. They have been alienated both in the sense that they have lived in separate neighbourhoods and gone to separate schools and churches, and in the sense that feelings of mutual suspicion and resentment have developed between them and the white majority. A parallel case was that of the Jews throughout much of European history. They were compelled to live in ghettos and excluded from many aspects of public life. To the extent that these forms of alienation meant injustice and inequality, they are now universally admitted to have been wrong, and vigorous if belated attempts are made to put matters right. On the other hand, there is resistance on the part of the alienated groups to mere absorption into the mainstream. Their distinctive traditions and way of life are threatened and could easily be engulfed in the featureless mass culture of the industrial world. And so some of them believe that a measure of separateness is desirable. Thus, as I said earlier, we cannot assume that alienation is always bad. There may be groups which consciously stand out from a given society, defying the values of that society and challenging what passes for 'common knowledge' in that society. They may believe that in the long run they will not only preserve something they care about themselves, but will also render a service to the society with which they are in conflict. Such would be the position of the rebellious youths of the nineteen-sixties, or of those who have entered the religious orders as a 'sign of contradiction'.

The ambiguities of alienation at the social level can be seen if we take an actual example, and recall some of the ways in which the Christian church has related to society at large during its history.

Christianity began as a fringe group. For the first three hundred years of its existence, the church was an alienated minority. About that period, historian K. S. Latourette writes: 'From the beginning, Christians felt themselves in opposition to what they called "the world".'[38] He goes on to describe some of the ways in which Christians voluntarily kept themselves at a distance from the mainstream of social activity. They did not enlist in the army, as they were opposed to bearing arms. They did not take part in the public sports and amusements. They did not join in the celebration of holidays and festivals, because these – as indeed had most public occasions – had pagan elements included in them. They would not burn incense in honour of the emperor. On the other hand, the imperial authorities frequently persecuted the Christians, because they did not conform, and to the voluntary isolation which the Christians took upon themselves, one has to add all the discriminations that society made against them. Eusebius of Caesarea mentions Christians who were excluded from housing, public baths and markets – forms of discrimination that have been known in modern times.[39]

But while there was alienation between the church and society at large, ancient alienations were being overcome within the church. In particular, differences of racial and ethnic background, of social position and of sex, were being reduced and abolished by a new spirit of reconciliation. Perhaps if the new spirit of Christianity was to survive and develop, it had first of all to show the possibility of an alternative society, as it were, nurtured in marginal communities.

But with Constantine and the fourth century, the picture changes. The one-time alienated and persecuted minority becomes first a tolerated religion and then the religion of the state. Now there is identification with society, and some Christians even engage in persecution of the remaining pockets of paganism. Eusebius, who has claims to be considered the first political theologian, was lavish in his praise of the new order: 'All things were filled with light, and all who before were sunk in sorrow beheld each other with smiling and cheerful faces. With choirs and hymns, in cities and villages, at the same time they celebrated and extolled first of all God, the universal king, then they also celebrated the pious emperor, and with him all his divinely favoured children.'[40] The new relationship with the empire meant that some of the good influences of Christianity could now be released from the ghetto into society at large. Athanasius, for instance, talks of the reform and purification of society at this time.[41] Yet the close identification of church and state was full of danger. The coupling of the names of God and Emperor in the last sentence that I have quoted from Eusebius was fateful for the future of Christianity.

Although there were many ups and downs, for something like fifteen centuries Christianity remained the dominant spiritual force in Europe and was closely identified with the whole social and political fabric. That was the phenomenon which we now call 'Christendom', and in retrospect we can see the ambiguities of that period. So long as the church was an alienated sect, it kept alive its ideal of a new humanity, but had no power to influence the wider society; when it attained power and influence, its ideal faded, and it in large measure conformed to the values of the society with which it had identified.

The uneasy relationship between church and state has obvious connections with the conflicts which we have noted earlier in this chapter of alienation, especially the conflict between those who hold that humanity must overcome its alienations by its own efforts, principally through the growth of science and technology and release from the illusions of religion, and those who hold that this is far too superficial a recipe and that alienations on the human level can be resolved only if there is an overcoming of ontological alienation and the attaining of a fundamental trust in being, which is not far from what the religious call 'faith in God'. This is the deep cleavage in the world today. It is experienced not only in the West as between Christian and secularist viewpoints, but also in the struggles between Islam and secularism in the Middle East and between Buddhism and secularism in the Far East. It is, of course, something far more subtle than a straight fight between atheism and religious faith, and one cannot simply identify with either the one side or the other. As I have said earlier, there can be no return to the naive faith of an earlier epoch. A new faith has to incorporate the genuine insights of science and of the whole spirit of secularity.[42] But if faith were to disappear in a sheer secularism, then humanity would be gravely impoverished, and the alienation that comes with atheism is more acute than any ever induced by religion.[43]

Confining our attention to the West, while recognizing that what we see there can be paralleled throughout the world, I would like to draw attention to the perceptive analysis offered by the historian Martin E. Marty. He speaks of a schism in the West, and explains it as follows: 'In the middle of the nineteenth century, people who had acted in concert to make up Christendom finally divided into mutually opposing parties. One set devoted itself to religious and ecclesiastical concerns; the other was increasingly preoccupied with the secular.'[44] But the situation resulting from the break-up of Christendom varies in different parts of the West. On the continent of Europe, and especially in Eastern Europe, the breach has been sharpest. The church is confronted by atheistic ideologies and has been in many cases subjected to persecution and discrimination. The situation is in some ways reminiscent of its sect-like beginnings in the Roman Empire, though it is important not to romanticize this, as some writers on 'secular Christianity' have tended to do. England, by contrast – and perhaps one could add the Netherlands and the Scandinavian countries – has been the scene of what Marty calls 'mere secularity'. Religion is ignored, rather than attacked, but it is nevertheless pushed into a ghetto. It may be significant that all of the countries in this group treated religion as a department of state, and have retained their monarchies along with their nominal allegiance to the state religion. Thomas Cranmer, a major architect of the Church of England, inherited the enthusiasm of Eusebius for associating God and the king. His biographer writes: 'The phrase "God and the king" appears continually in Cranmer's letters, and it was indeed rare for him to write the name of the Almighty without bracketing it with that of Henry VIII.'[45] But most ambiguous of all is the position in the United States. There is official separation of church and state, and according to the textbooks, America with its high technology and affluence should be the most secularized society in the world. Instead, religion seems to flourish more than in any other advanced Western society. But Marty believes that the outward flourishing of religion covers over a deep alienation. American religion has itself been secularized and made to conform to the realities of the secular order. I suppose the extreme example of this would be the 'gospel of wealth', to which I have alluded earlier.[46] It may be, however, that although Marty's strictures apply to much American religion, there are also evidences of a social critique among the churches, and this could lead to a healthier situation.

One point that emerges quite clearly from this analysis is the extraordinary persistence of religion, in spite of all the pressures against it. Also, we have seen no compelling reasons for accepting the thesis that religion is an alienating influence in human life. On the contrary, we have seen that a fundamental ontological trust is a prerequisite for the overcoming of alienation. But there is still a long way to go in search of a situation where human freedom and transcendence can flourish to the full, and yet there can also be a relation to a reality that transcends humanity.

XI

CONSCIENCE

Alienation, as we have already seen,[1] implies the consciousness that human life is in one respect or another not what it ought to be, that there is a falling short or a missing the mark or an estrangement or a state of sin or however we may express it. The sense of alienation is therefore a disclosure of the human condition in some of its aspects, and the very awareness of alienation raises the question how it may be overcome, so that what has been lost (or not yet gained) may be restored (or attained for the first time). It is at this point that we must take into consideration the place of conscience in the human being, for conscience is an intimate way in which we are disclosed to ourselves, and, in its affirmative function, points us towards what we ought to be or ought to become. In saying 'what we ought to be or become' rather than 'what we ought to do', I am implying that at its deepest level conscience has to do with the formation of character and personhood, rather than with the doing of discrete acts, and I hope that the justification for this interpretation will emerge in what follows. Of course, person and act are closely connected. As Aristotle remarked, 'moral virtue comes about as a result of habit'.[2] Through habitual action, a stable character is formed, but there comes a time when, reciprocally, one's character leads into courses of action compatible with it. I want to stress the importance of character and personhood, for we have already seen reason to believe that the functional view of the human being which equates him with his acts is itself an alienating misunderstanding and misses the full depth of the personal.[3]

The English word 'conscience' is derived from the Latin *conscientia*, which in turn translates the Greek *syneidesis*. The Latin and Greek words are closely similar compounds, and the root meaning is in each case 'knowing with'. Originally, these words had no connection with moral issues. They were used very generally for 'awareness' or 'consciousness'.

It was among some of the ancient philosophers that they acquired the special sense of 'knowledge of right and wrong'. Paul introduced the term into the Christian vocabulary when, in a famous and much discussed passage, he argued that although the Gentiles did not have the law which God had revealed to Moses, they had a kind of inward law in their very being, and this inward law, at least in a general way, seemed to prescribe the same kind of moral conduct as did the law of Moses. 'When Gentiles who have not the law do by nature what the law requires, they are a law to themselves, even though they do not have the law. They show that what the law requires is written on their hearts, while their conscience also bears witness and their conflicting thoughts accuse or perhaps excuse them.'[4]

Even if no special word for 'conscience' is used, the presence in human beings of an inward sense that guides them is universally recognized. To cite an example from a very different culture, we find in classical Chinese philosophy the claim: 'Everyone has within him the principle of right, what we call Tao, the road along which we ought to walk.'[5]

But although the presence of conscience in the human being is universally acknowledged, there is much less agreement when people try to say what conscience is. There must be few aspects of human nature about which more divergent accounts have been given than conscience. Sometimes the stress has been on knowing, and conscience has been represented as primarily rational and cognitive. A classic example of this type of interpretation is provided by the English philosopher Joseph Butler. Human nature, he taught, is a bundle of instincts. Some of these, man shares with the animals, some of them are peculiar to himself; some of them have the purely selfish ends of the individual in view, but others are conducive to the common good. Conscience is the rational selective principle which permits some instinctively motivated courses of action to be realized, while others are restrained. In Butler's words, conscience is 'a principle of reflection in men by which they distinguish between, approve and disapprove their own actions'.[6] At the opposite extreme from the position represented by Butler, we find accounts of conscience which represent it as essentially irrational and as consisting in feeling. If we confine ourselves to the English philosophical tradition, this other view is well represented by John Stuart Mill. He describes conscience as 'the internal sanction of duty'. It is 'a feeling in our own mind; a pain more or less intense, attendant on the violation of duty'. In 'properly cultivated moral natures' the pain is felt so intensely that it becomes impossible to do the wrong act. We are confronted with 'a mass of feeling which has to be broken through in order to do what violates our standard of right', and it would be so painful to break through this mass of feeling that in fact we are restrained from the violation.[7]

The two views of conscience briefly set forth in the last paragraph seem hard to reconcile, yet both may claim support in the common experience of conscience. We have all had experience of rational deliberation on moral issues and of choosing the course to which conscientious reflection has directed us. Yet many of us will also have known the kind of experience that Mill describes. For instance, I myself was brought up in Scotland in a community where strict Sunday observance was the rule. Although I soon came to reject with my mind that very negative interpretation of the Sabbath rest, for a long time I continued to feel some twinges of guilt when I did anything that went against the taboos that had been taught me in childhood.

The two views may be contrasted in many ways. The Butler view – if we may call it such – has a more dynamic character; it is future-oriented, and has at least the possibility of being creative. The Mill view is relatively static; its appeal is to the past, and it is concerned with the maintenance of standards already learned. The Butler view, again, seems to encourage autonomy and the responsible exercise of one's freedom. The Mill view, however, is heteronomous. It imposes the standards of the society in which a person has grown up, though these standards may also be represented as the command of God, as in the case of Sunday observance, mentioned above. The autonomy/heteronomy contrast may be expressed in another way. On the Butler view, one is drawn towards particular courses of action by the values one discerns. On the Mill view, one is driven rather into this course or that by an authority figure – the parent, the teacher or even, allegedly, God. There is a final contrast. On the Butler view, although he speaks of actions, the reflectively chosen actions tend to build up into larger patterns, guided by some consistent goal or ideal, and so this conception of conscience leads to the formation of character. On the Mill view, conscience is more concerned with isolated acts, and this explains in part why the guilt-feeling experienced may be out of all proportion to the seriousness of the act done or contemplated.

In drawing out these contrasts, I seem to have been using more affirmatively evaluating terms in describing the Butler view than I have used for the Mill view. But I come back to the point that both views have support in experience. Hence, they should not be regarded simply as rival theories of conscience. Rather, they are partial views, each of which stresses certain features of conscience while ignoring others, so that they would need to be integrated in a more comprehensive view. Both Butler and Mill recognize this to some extent. We find Butler saying in one place that conscience can be considered 'as a sentiment of the understanding or a perception of the heart, or, which seems the truth, as including both'.[8] Mill, on his part, freely acknowledges that conscience is a 'complex phenomenon' and that the feeling of which he speaks has to be connected with 'the pure idea of duty'.[9] Still, even if Butler and Mill allow for modifications, they present very distinctive and, it must be said, one-sided accounts of conscience.

A partial help towards finding a more comprehensive view of conscience comes from Sigmund Freud, though I would stress that this help is only partial. Freud developed on the one hand his theory of the superego as a 'special criticizing and forbidding function' in the mind.[10] This superego is not indeed identical with conscience, but is said to have conscience as one of its functions. It is the deposit of rules concerning acceptable and unacceptable conduct that we have acquired in early life, and clearly it is very much like the Mill view of conscience described above, though Freud has, of course, developed his ideas in a different context from Mill's. But we find Freud mentioning another phenomenon which has an obvious relation to conscience. This is the ego-ideal. This, we are told, is a vehicle 'by which the ego measures itself, toward which it strives, and whose demands for ever-increasing perfection it is always seeking to fulfil'.[11] Here, it would seem, we are moving closer to the Butler view of conscience, and there are also resemblances to what we called 'transcendence' in an earlier discussion.[12]

Some of the contrasts which I mentioned above between the views of Butler and Mill could be applied with slight modifications to the differences between ego-ideal and superego in the thought of Freud. But only some of the contrasts would apply, not all of them. The trouble is that Freud did not go far enough in developing the notion of the ego-ideal. With his strong determinist tendencies, he had to account for everything in terms of the past. Thus, although the very notion of an ego-ideal is oriented to the future and the new (something 'toward which we strive', in Freud's own words), he deprives it of the possibility of any genuine creativity by effectually annexing it to the superego, so making the ego-ideal too a deposit of the past. 'No doubt,' he says, 'this ego-ideal is a precipitation of the old idea of the parents, an expression of the admiration which the child felt for the perfection which it at that time ascribed to them.'[13]

Certainly, the ego-ideal does not appear from nowhere, and presumably some element of hero-worship has a part in its formation. But is that the whole story? Is there not also a creative, imaginative element of novelty by which the ego transforms these influences of the past into an ideal that is truly a goal and not a deposit? It has been pointed out that the word 'creativity' is very rare in Freud's writings.[14] The nearest he comes to recognizing a true creativity is when he writes on art. For instance, in his well known essay on 'The Moses of Michelangelo', he acknowledges that the sculptor has done more than reproduce the Moses of tradition; 'he has added something new and more than human to the figure of Moses'.[15]

Thus, although Freud, when he introduced the notion of the ego-ideal, was moving towards a richer, more integrated conception of conscience, he never actually reached it.[16] The dynamism of conscience springs from the felt conflict or, at least, tension between those aspects of conscience which, in Freudian terminology, are designated the ego-ideal and the superego, the creative, imaginative projecting of a moral goal and the static inheritance from the past. The first is concerned with creating value, the second with staying within guidelines. But Freud's account of the matter makes the tension or conflict impossible, because both the ego-ideal and the superego are referred back to the parents, and both are treated as deposits of the past. The basic error of this view is that it makes any advance in morality unintelligible. It would seem that advances in morality are most likely to occur when someone's personal ideals come into conflict with the generally accepted *mores* of society. But such a conflict is only possible if the personal ideal is in some respects independent of the *mores* and so morally transcendent. This implies that there must be the possibility of a creative projecting of ideals that have not been wholly inherited. Only so can something new be brought into the situation. But Freud's quasi-mechanistic view of the human mind appears to exclude this. Human attitudes are explained in terms of the past that has shaped them – the past of the individual and even the distant past of the race. It is hard to see how, on such a theory, men and women could ever break out of the traditional scheme of customs and laws and out of the traditional value-system underlying that scheme.

But the indisputable fact is that they do break out, and any adequate theory of conscience must help us to understand how innovation and creativity are possible. It is to existentialism rather than psychoanalysis that we must turn for such a theory. In particular, the philosophy of Martin Heidegger offers an understanding of conscience which goes far towards gathering up in one comprehensive view the fragmented aspects of the phenomenon of conscience, as we have seen them in the theories so far considered. The Heideggerian view of conscience has respect both to that emotive, irrational pressure which tends to keep us within the established ways of the society to which we belong, and also to that creative capacity whereby a human being can, as it were, leap ahead of himself into a new self-understanding. This way of thinking about conscience also coheres rather well with the dynamic view of human nature that has been built up in the earlier chapters of this book, in terms of becoming, freedom, transcendence, egoity and so on. But at some points we shall come into conflict with Heidegger, since his anthropology differs in some important respects from the one developed in this book.

But let me first expound in a more detailed way some of the things that Heidegger has to say about conscience. His typical way of describing conscience is to say that it is a 'call' or 'summons'. Admittedly, this may seem at first sight to be very similar to our common talk about the 'voice' of conscience. But whereas the 'voice' is generally understood as giving information or pronouncing judgment, the 'call' is a summons and is altogether more dynamic. Indeed, according to Heidegger, the call of conscience is one that a person rarely hears, for it is usually drowned out by the voice, and that voice Heidegger calls the 'hubbub', that is to say, it is the voice of conventional morality, the standards, rules and values of society at large. It expresses the conduct that 'they' approve and expect, and the word 'they' is used here by Heidegger as we often use it in daily speech for the confused, impersonal, anonymous mass existence of modern society. 'They will expect me to do this.' What 'they' judge, value, demand and expect is the voice of conventional morality and constitutes what is commonly understood as conscience, but it is not, in Heidegger's belief, the true or authentic conscience. The true call 'must do its calling without any hubbub and unambiguously'. This authentic call is one that penetrates through the hubbub and calls the individual out of the crowd and out of the ways of the crowd. It does not enforce conventional morality. Its function is rather to bring the person called into a new self-understanding. 'The call is from afar to afar. It reaches him who wants to be brought back.'[17]

Who is it that is called? Clearly, it is the individual human being, lost and overwhelmed in the crowd, conforming his life to patterns that 'they' have adopted and imposed on all, suffering guilt feelings if he departs from the accepted standards, even if his reason has rejected them. Who does the calling? Not, in this case, society. Nor is it God, conceived as an external supernatural power. The call originates within the self. It is only because we are so deafened by what 'they' are saying that when we do sometimes hear the genuine call of conscience, it seems to us so strange that we think it must have originated 'out there'. But the call is, Heidegger believes, the call of the authentic self to the actual self. This, of course, implies a complex understanding of the self, according to which it is always more than its empirical actuality at any given moment, for its possibilities belong to it as well. Conscience is the summoning into the most authentic possibilities of the self. What then is the content of the call? Although Heidegger, as we have seen, claims that the call is unambiguous, he nevertheless also denies that there is any definite content to it. The public conscience, the voice of society, does have a definite content – the commonly accepted rules of conduct, standards of value, measurements of prestige and so forth. But one must turn away from these, for the way to true humanity or authentic selfhood does not lie through conforming. Indeed, that would mean precisely *losing* oneself in what 'they' have already decided, becoming another stereotype in a society which has fixed each one's station and duties. There is no content to the true call of conscience, for it is not already laid down what one is to become. To be made to a pattern is not to exist as a human being endowed with freedom, transcendence, cognition and all the rest, but to become like a manufactured object. Human beings have still to create their humanity and to learn the full range of their possibilities. Therefore the summons of conscience cannot have its content fully defined in advance.

This teaching about conscience is a heady wine, and it needs a cool brain if one is to swallow the draught without becoming intoxicated. For the teaching seems to abolish at a stroke the whole structure of conventional morality and to put in its place nothing at all. It seems to have carried relativism and individualism to their uttermost limits. Is morality just a matter of subjective preference?

I would not wish to deny that the doctrine is a dangerous one, and that it has been and probably will be abused. There are obvious echoes of Nietzsche in Heidegger. For Nietzsche too was contemptuous of conventional morality: 'The voice of the herd yet lingereth within thee. And when thou wouldst say, "I have no longer a common conscience with you," it shall be grief and pain unto thee.'[18] Likewise he summond men and women to a new morality, the content of which he leaves undefined: 'None yet knoweth what is good and evil – unless it is he that is a creator! But a creator is he that createth man's goal and giveth earth its meaning and its future; he it is that first maketh good and evil to be.'[19] And before Nietzsche there was Kierkegaard, justifying Abraham's readiness to set aside morality and his own natural affections in order to sacrifice his son Isaac at the command of God. That command suspended ethics – indeed, ethics was standing in the way of Abraham's fulfilling his primary duty to God; and Kierkegaard makes it clear that his duty to God was identical with his duty to himself.[20] Is there not something intolerably élitist and egocentric in all these cases? Has not the illusion of the superman, free to spurn the accepted moral standards of ordinary people, infected Kierkegaard, Nietzsche and Heidegger alike? It may not be accidental that Nietzsche's ideas were one factor contributing to the rise of National Socialism and that Heidegger was for a time an adherent of the party. For is it not necessary that such theories lead into moral nihilism?

On the other hand, if Heidegger's teaching about conscience and morality seems comparable to Nietzsche's, it could be argued that it is also comparable to Jesus Christ's. For Christ too seems to have taken rather a poor view of conventional morality as too much tailored to the tastes of a sinful society, riddled with mediocrity and hypocrisy. Significantly, he called his friends and disciples from among those who were excluded from respectable society. The most impressive sections of his teaching take the radical form: 'You have heard that it was said by men of old . . . but I say unto you.'[21] And there is elusiveness too in the new morality which Jesus taught. He did not lay down definite rules, but, to some extent at least, left his followers free to find out what love might demand of them.

The point is that ethical openness and flexibility seem to be a necessary condition of the possibility of any ethical advance. Certainly, this brings with it the risk of ethical anarchy or nihilism, but otherwise we could only keep on repeating the same stifling patterns, transmitted from generation to generation. If there is to be any creativity and progress in the moral life, then sometimes an individual conscience, understood as the call of an as yet unrealized ideal of humanity, must rebel against the collective conscience, understood as what 'they' approve (Heidegger), the herd instinct (Nietzsche), the public (Kierkegaard), the superego (Freud).

In the conflicting modern theories of conscience, we witness the unfolding of the ambiguity already present in the language first used to designate this phenomenon – the language of *syn-eidesis* and *con-scientia*. We have seen that these terms convey the meaning of a 'knowing with'. In the first instance, this is a knowing with others; it is one's participation in that understanding of right and wrong that prevails in a specific society and by which one must abide in order to be acceptable in that society. But as individual persons begin to have a measure of independence and are no longer simply items in a collective body, then conscience can also become a knowing with oneself, a fundamental self-disclosure in which one becomes aware of the tension within oneself between the actual empirical self and the authentic or ideal self on which one's aspirations are projected. It is this new level of conscience that makes possible the criticism and then perhaps the transformation of the social *mores* expressed on the first level of conscience. A dynamic and creative element has been introduced, based on the capacity of the individual for rational and moral reflection. Unless we recognize this aspect of conscience, then, as I have indicated above, it is very hard to see how we could account for moral progress.

I have cited Heidegger's theory of conscience as the one which, I believe, is most adequate in taking account of the two modes of knowing-with. But I also said that we would have to part company with him on several issues. I think that there are three major criticisms that have to be made, and the theory has to be amended accordingly.

The first and most obvious point is that Heidegger (and likewise Kierkegaard and Nietzsche) is far too individualist. These men scarcely conceal their contempt for the voice of the herd or for those utterances of conscience which represent conventional morality. To some extent, that attitude is understandable and even, up to a point, justifiable. No doubt, most people are all too ready to accept unreflectively the moral standards of their group and to be less than responsible moral agents. We have noted earlier that although human beings are inescapably social, individuals usually have a greater moral sensitivity than do groups.[22] So we need individuals with 'nonconformist' consciences if we are not to lapse into moral stagnation. But Heidegger's account gives too much weight to the individual over against society. He sees all the weaknesses of public morality, but does not allow for the redeeming features of collective experience and even some flashes of collective wisdom. If it is true that there must be moral criticism and creativity on the part of individual persons, that someone must say, like Luther, 'Here I stand!', surely it is also true that such an individual must allow his own moral reflection to be subjected to the criticism of the society and of other individuals within the society. It is out of this kind of interaction that new moral insights can be gained, and without it, the individual may be guilty of monstrous egoism.

This leads to a second criticism, that Heidegger does not sufficiently recognize the fallibility of conscience. The public conscience is dismissed as what 'they' say, and the call that comes through its hubbub from afar is counted the true conscience. But self-deception in matters of conscience is only too easy – as Bishop Butler was well aware, in spite of the high view he held of conscience. Perhaps people rarely or never choose evil in the full awareness that it is evil for themselves, thus deliberately going against the inner call, but they are experts at dressing up the evil as good. The call that summons me to break with conventional morality may be a veiled egoism even though I sincerely believe that I am being summoned to my authentic selfhood.

Was it really the call of Being that led Heidegger in 1933 to identify the destiny of the German people with National Socialism, and was there no hidden ambition behind this – perhaps to become the great national philosopher in Germany's hour of need? Or what are we to say of Kierkegaard's decision to break his engagment to Regina Olsen? He sincerely believed that this 'suspension' of the ethical was justified by a higher moral imperative, as he thought it had been in the case of Abraham. But may there not have been in the background a secret desire to escape the responsibilities of marriage? Yet how can one rule out the possibility of some self-deception or latent selfishness? Someone might very well persuade himself that what is most convenient or most advantageous to himself is the 'call of Being' or the 'voice of God', though it conflicts with what ordinary morality demands. At any rate, our best safeguard against self-deception would be once again to let our individual consciences be criticized by the public conscience which, despite its limitations, cannot be merely dismissed. The person who wants to break with conventional moral norms is driven to self-criticism as well as to social criticism. F. H. Bradley once declared that a direct outrage on common morality is rarely justifiable, for 'common social morality is the basis of human life . . . upon its foundations are erected the ideals of a higher social perfection, but common morality remains both the cradle and the nurse of its aspiring offspring'.[23]

Yet sometimes it will be the case that after both social criticism and self-criticism, the moral pioneer will decide that the time has come for him to break with conventional morality on one point or another, for the growing edge of moral sensitivity is more often to be found in the consciences of individuals than in the social group. As Reinhold Niebuhr was never tired of saying, the group is 'more arrogant, hypocritical, self-centred, and more ruthless in the pursuit of its ends, than the individual'.[24]

A third criticism of Heidegger is that he does not sufficiently allow for moral weakness in the face of the demands of conscience. He certainly does acknowledge that for most of the time the individual person is lost in the crowd and that 'they' do the choosing for him, and that this state of affairs can be reversed only if the individual brings himself back to himself from his lostness in the crowd. But if he has already surrendered his freedom, how is he to do this? Heidegger's reply is paradoxical: one must choose this choice, one must want to have a conscience.[25] But how is this possible? How can one break out of the enslavement to what 'they' have already decided? Heidegger does not adequately consider the bondage of which Luther speaks, and which we noted in our discussion of freedom,[26] nor does he consider Paul's experience of impotence in face of the *alter ego* of sin, of which we have also taken note.[27] The question has to be faced at this point whether, as many moral philosophers have argued, morality needs to find its completion in religion, in the sense that we can only truly hear and respond to conscience through grace. But we shall defer this question until we come to the discussion of commitment.[28]

At present, I come back to the question whether there are any norms for the kind of conscience we have been considering. If the norms of society are rejected or assigned a secondary rank, are there any guidelines left? We remember that Heidegger denied that the authentic conscience has any content, and up to a point we found ourselves agreeing. One has still to discover the content of a true humanity and the shape of a more human community than we know at present. If there is to be growth into these as yet unexplored regions, then there cannot be available rules, norms, duties, laws, values, comparable in their definiteness to those of the inherited morality. The very notion of creativity in morals implies that there must be openness and the absence of a rigid legalistic framework. Rather than knowing a set of neatly prescribed duties, one needs the fundamental experience of the moral obligation to become a truly human person. The duties will emerge in the light of this. 'The chief thing,' wrote Kierkegaard, 'is not whether one can count on one's fingers how many duties one has, but that a man has once felt the intensity of duty in such a way that the consciousness of it is for him the assurance of the eternal validity of his being.'[29]

But it does not follow that therefore we are plunged into a complete relativism, or that the distinctions of right and wrong, good and bad, have disappeared or become quite arbitrary matters. It is the case that some existentialist philosophers, from whom I would certainly wish to distance myself, have written in ways that suggest thoroughgoing relativism and arbitrariness. When they insist that their ethic has no content, they seem to imply that the call to authentic selfhood could summon one to be, let us say, a Nazi or a Marxist or a Christian or a criminal or a Buddhist, and that these are equally valid options; for what is important is not the content but the form of one's existence, and in particular that it is freely chosen by oneself. If a person realizes his own possibilities, he has become a truly human person, and since each individual is unique, there can be no one pattern. Just as these philosophers object to God as the alleged enemy of human transcendence, so they object to anything like universal moral ideals. Sartre, in one phase of his career, came pretty close to such views, but we have already criticized his exaggerated idea of what constitutes freedom and his belief that freedom is the highest value.

From the beginning, I have set alongside human freedom certain 'givens' that are equally constitutive for our human nature, and which our exercise of freedom has to take into account. These givens rule out some ways and direct us along other ways. The human being is creative of himself, but at no point is his freedom to create absolute. Some ways lead to his fulfilment and to higher or fuller levels of humanity and personhood; other ways diminish his being. These remarks, incidentally, apply just as much to society as they do to individuals. This means that the givens are not sociologically explicable, even if particular expressions of them are. As soon as these givens receive some definite shape as laws or customs or concrete ideals, they are made relative to a historical and cultural situation. But what is not derived from that situation is the fundamental directedness of human life, the given fact that there are ways forward and ways backward, a direction towards a fuller humanity and a direction toward a diminished humanity. It is this directedness that is known at the deepest level of conscience. We may call it the ontological or metaphysical basis of conscience. The human being, we have seen, is not constituted with a fixed nature, to be regulated by unchanging laws. There is an openness and fluidity in his being, so that he can go out into novelty and find new and more fulfilling modes of existence. But he becomes aware that the direction in which he moves is not a matter of indifference, that his freedom is not sheer randomness but is exercised in rationality and responsibility. Some directions enhance his being, others threaten to destroy it.

We have met several of the givens of human nature in earlier chapters, and at this point we may remind ourselves of them. They constitute, as it were, the parameters of human freedom, and any call of conscience must have regard to them, for only so can such a call be a summons to a more truly human existence. If these givens are ignored, then the summons is a sham and its end is not fulfilment but destruction – as in the case of the

Nazis, for instance. There are at least half a dozen such givens. They correspond roughly to the various forms of alienation noted in the last chapter, and in each case an affirmative relationship is needed for the overcoming of alienation.

1. We have more than once seen that no individual can become a truly personal existent without affirmative relations to other persons. There is no I without a Thou, and egoism is the perversion of egoity.[30]

2. Human life is bound up with its material environment and a true humanity requires a right relation to that environment. We have seen that this implies at least a minimum of having, yet there must also be a respect for the material world, since sheer exploitation and concupiscence enslave the person who goes that way and diminish him.[31]

3. The body constitutes a special case within the material world. All human existence is embodied and we have seen that Kierkegaard thinks of human fulfilment as the synthesis of body and soul. The body is a given, and either despising the body or indulging the body takes us away from a full humanity.[32]

4. The inescapably social nature of humanity involves us not only with other individuals but with institutions. These too are givens with which we have to come to terms. Tyrannous institutions on the one hand and anarchy on the other adversely affect the quality of human life. The search for humanity has to adjust individual freedom to appropriate forms of institutions.[33]

5. Many people, myself included, would say that a relation to God is also a constituent factor in a truly human existence. Admittedly, this point has not been established with the same cogency as the four already mentioned, and we have agreed that only a non-oppressive God can encourage the transcendence and growth of humanity. But we have also seen how the absence of a relation to God, what we have called 'cosmic alienation', can slip into a paralysing nihilism that utterly devalues humanity.[34]

6. The five givens I have mentioned point humanity in affirmative ways and afford a minimal content for conscience. These cannot be absent in any ideal of human existence. But I want to add another given which has a negative character and is also significant for conscience. I mean, our capacity for recognizing something as just plainly and utterly evil and destructive of everything we understand by 'human'. I am tempted to say it is the capacity for recognizing absolute evil. The example that comes to mind is Auschwitz – a production line (or, better, destruction line) planned and built for the elimination of human beings, though it destroyed in a deeper way the humanity of those who conceived and operated it. There are some things that no appeal to some inner summons could even begin to justify. To quote Peter Baelz: 'Some moral principles, such as the sanctity of human life, are so fundamental that, if a person openly flouts them, he

cannot have begun to reflect morally, even though he pretends to have acted according to his conscience. He is an evil man, not a moral nonconformist.'[35] This negative given, then, excludes some things from insertion into the content of any call claiming to be a call of conscience.

The basic givens which impart a sense of directedness to the human quest for an authentic humanity correspond to the Judaeo-Christian idea of an 'image of God' in men and women, an idea which we have already mentioned in the discussion of transcendence.[36] But this is not an image for copycat imitation. It is rather, shall we say, man's obscure awareness in the depth of his being of the direction of the human pilgrimage towards a fuller mode of existence. Within the parameters of the givens, there is an infinite variety of concrete ideals, as wide as the infinite variety of human beings. We do not have to choose between the anarchy of those who claim that everything is permitted and the legalism of those who want to impose inflexible laws and patterns. As Maurice Wiles has well expressed it, there are two emphases: 'In the first place, there is the recognition that there are certain basic characteristics written into the context of human life which mean that we cannot simply make of it whatever we choose. However little we may be able to spell them out, it is important that we should acknowledge that they exist . . . But the second emphasis is an equally serious recognition of historicity, change and becoming as fundamental features of human experience. Even if man's being provides the basis for the norms of his becoming, it should not be understood to prescribe the precise form that the becoming should take.'[37]

Similar considerations arise in relation to the traditional doctrine of a 'natural law'. It originated among the Greeks and was later incorporated into Christian moral theology. The natural law has no clearly definable content, for as soon as it is given such a content, it becomes a positive law which is historically and socially conditioned. The natural law is rather the criterion that is ontologically prior to every positive law, so that sometimes one has to say paradoxically that the laws of a society are unjust.

The actual moral life is lived in the tension of the two levels of conscience – the call to authentic humanity and the pressures of the public value system, the natural law and the positive law, the image of God in man and the concrete cultural situation. Sometimes it may be necessary to give more weight to the one side, sometimes to the other. In our own time, the tension between the two modes of conscience has become acute, and society is polarized between those whose consciences are dominated by the traditional *mores* and those whose experience of conscience takes the form of a summons out of the accepted ways. In a time of rapid change and unprecedented choices, it seems desirable to give more weight to the adventurous, forward-looking and creative form of conscience, and certainly it ought not to be suppressed. But in the end we need both forms in their interaction, for every individual moral insight needs to be criticized against the accumulated moral wisdom of society.

I have been talking in fairly general terms about moral advance and the emergence of new ideals of humanity, but in the course of history this has been a fairly concrete matter. There have been a few 'representative persons', as we might call them, who have taught and usually also exemplified a way of life which has then attracted others who have seen in it a manifestation or even a revelation of authentic humanity. I mean especially the founders of the great religions, Jesus Christ, the Buddha, Confucius and others. Their insights were further developed by disciples, and these few human beings have had an incalculable influence in forming the consciences of millions of others. These have been the moral pioneers of the race, and their creativity remains unexhausted. But the tension that we noted in society between the summons to the new and the influence of the established ways is paralleled in the religions, where the innovating thrust of the founder is eventually stabilized and even petrified in systems of law or moral theology. Then there has to be a return to the sources, and new disciples have to recapture or even discover for the first time insights of the founders. At present in the Christian church, the tension between those who recognize that the changing nature of humanity and of the world calls for new moral thinking and those who stand firmly by the tradition is just as acute as is the tension between progressives and traditionalists in society at large.

But if these representative persons, as I have called them, have formed the consciences of millions of others, does this not mean that they have imposed a heteronomous ideal which is just as opposed to moral autonomy and authenticity as is the herd morality represented by the collective conscience? I do not think so. These representative persons are far from being stereotypes. They have an openness and freedom about them, so that to follow them does not mean to engage in slavish imitation, but to follow in a direction they have opened up, where our own consciences, illumined by theirs, have to find in our own time the solutions to our moral problems. To say that these men have formed the consciences of others does not mean that they have imposed anything upon them (even if their 'churches' have). It is a reciprocal matter. They awaken the consciences of their disciples, but they can do so only because these consciences were already summoning to a true humanity, which the disciple now recognizes in the representative man. I come back to the point that there are ways forward and there are ways backward, and that our consciences are illumined by these representative persons because they have already recognized them as representative. If, for instance, Paul speaks of Christ as 'the image of the invisible God',[38] this is possible because he already has some understanding of that image in his own being.

I have talked of 'representative persons' in the plural. Does this mean that there are several ideals of true humanity? Presumably it does. We have seen that within a particular tradition, such as Christianity, there is a freedom and openness that allows for many different forms of discipleship. Likewise, within humanity as a whole, there may be several distinct types which cannot be combined in a single ideal of humanity but which complement and enrich one another within the total society. I mentioned above, Christ, Buddha and Confucius. One cannot follow these three paths simultaneously and has to set out on one of them or on some other quite different path. But one can respect each of these ways, and recognize that in each of them humanity is enhanced. But let me insist again that not just any way can lead to human fulfilment, even if it is pursued with the utmost intensity and resolution. Only moral insanity would choose the way of a Hitler or a Stalin or a Casanova, for these ways lead to the diminution and extinction of humanity. Our consciences may be weak and fallible, but they provide a basic orientation in the quest for humanity and can be illuminated and strengthened.

XII

COMMITMENT

In recent decades, the notion of commitment has been prominent among students of human nature. Commitment has been known by a variety of names and understood in a variety of ways, but there is a wide measure of agreement that some basic commitments are needed for the formation of a mature human person. Though we shall have to consider the meaning of 'commitment' in detail, at this point it can be said provisionally that a commitment is the acceptance of a continuing obligation to pursue some goal or policy of action. As we have seen already,[1] the freedom which begins as empty space or absence of constraint is not abolished but given shape and direction by the development of stable attitudes and policies of action.

Psychologists and psychiatrists have in various ways stressed the importance of commitment. Jung and his followers talk of 'individuation', said to be like a narrow path which must be chosen and pursued between the false alternatives of absorption into the collective and rejection of it.[2] R. D. Laing has mentioned the need of his patients to establish a firm sense of identity in face of the threat of 'engulfment'.[3] Rollo May has shown the need for will and commitment if love, especially sexual love, is to be fully human and mature.[4]

Many philosophers too have been stressing the role of commitment. We can divide them into two groups. Some, like the psychologists, have prized commitment because it unifies the self and rescues it from the various forms of alienation. Thus Heidegger believes that the summons of conscience leads into 'resoluteness' in the face of finitude and death.[5] Marcel talks of 'fidelity', especially toward other people.[6] Sartre sees the human being 'engaged' in his freely chosen projects.[7] But there is another group of philosophers who point to the role of commitment as an indispensable element within the philosophic quest itself. They reject (as we have seen reason to do) the notion of 'value free' inquiry, as if philosophy or science could be somehow clinically isolated from the rest of human life. Maurice Blondel wrote about the work of the philosopher: 'One must be involved, at the risk of losing everything; one must be compromised.'[8] The words appear in the introduction to his first major book, which was also his doctoral thesis presented to the University of Paris. A commentator mentions that he was grilled for four hours before a packed audience by his examiners, who did not like what he was writing![9] Just about the same time, William James was writing about the 'will to believe' and the need to take intellecual risks.[10] Another American, Josiah Royce, was developing a different aspect of commitment in his 'philosophy of loyalty', and maintaining that 'all scientific research depends on loyalty to the cause of the scientific community of interpretation'.[11] More recently, Michael Polanyi has elaborated the importance of commitment in scientific research.[12]

To the testimony of psychologists and philosophers must be added that of theologians. There is an obvious relation between commitment and faith. For a long time this was obscured because of the tendency to identify faith with belief in propositions. But from Kierkegaard onwards, first among Protestants and then among Catholics, it has become increasingly recognized that faith is an attitude of the whole person and includes an act of trust or commitment, which can perhaps be only imperfectly expressed verbally as a belief. Of course, theologians always made the distinction between *fides qua creditur* and *fides quae creditur*, between the act of faith and its content. But the earlier insistence on orthodoxy as right belief overshadowed the more existential understanding of faith as commitment. The latter, however has now asserted itself. Bultmann, who stresses the place of decision in the complex phenomenon of faith,[13] may be taken as typical of many other contemporary and recent theologians.

Will, resoluteness, engagement, loyalty, faith and so on – these are all different, and each one of them may appear in different forms. But they all resemble one another, and it may be that the term 'commitment' is the word which most effectively draws our attention to the ground of their resemblance. What then do we mean by 'commitment'?

I have already suggested as a provisional definition, 'the acceptance of a continuing obligation to pursue some goal or policy of action'. An obligation is a bond, something by which I am bound. It is therefore in one sense a limit on my freedom, but if it is a bond that I have freely accepted, then it has become part of a mature freedom in which energies are directed into chosen channels and not capriciously dissipated. In accepting a commitment, therefore, one binds oneself to another person or a group of persons, or to an ideal or a cause or even an ideology, and one seeks to let one's own actions and energies serve the object of the commitment. It is clear that such a commitment involes the whole person, his thinking as well as his acting, his feeling as well as his judgment. Sometimes whole groups of persons may be committed to some common goal, but it will be easier to study the structure of commitment in the individual, while remembering that the acceptance of commitments is the most obvious way in which the individual transcends his mere individuality. The sharing of a commitment is one of the strongest forces in the formation of community. This kind of commitment has been well described by Royce: 'Loyalty is the willing and thoroughgoing devotion of a self to a cause, when the cause is something that unites many selves in one, and which is therefore the interest of a community. For a loyal human being, the interest of the community to which he belongs is superior to every merely individual interest of his own.'[14]

Let us now try to spell out more fully the nature of this bond or attachment to which in a commitment we submit ourselves and devote our energies. We can discern in it three aspects. It is self-forming, self-transcending and self-limiting.

First, then, a commitment is important for self-formation. We have seen that every human being has the task of forming a self or becoming a person. We have acknowledged that no one begins from a purely open situation and that there are many givens. Some of these givens, like the need for a relation to others, are common to all human beings; others, like the conditions prevailing in a certain society at a certain time, are common to a whole generation; still others, like one's specific genetic inheritance, belong to the individual alone. To a large extent, it is the case with all of us that our selves are already determined by hereditary, cultural and environmental factors about which we have no choice. But there are areas that are unfinished and undetermined, and within the limits of what is open to us, each one has to shape the raw material of his life and achieve what he can of personhood and character. Each one has to establish his identity and not just suffer the fate of engulfment. He or she becomes aware of the summons of the authentic self or ego ideal or whatever it may be called, and seeks to move nearer toward it and to identify with it. 'Though much of what we are is due to our particular psychological make-up and cultural context,' writes Stanley Hauerwas, 'our character should be formed by our own effort rather than as a passive response to our particular environment.'[15] Choice of a vocation or career, the formation of friendships, the acceptance of a religious faith or a value system of some sort – these are important decisions that contribute to the building up of a character and personhood, and that help to make someone one kind of person rather than another kind, and that eventually make him or her the unique person that he or she is.

It should be noted that when we speak of commitments, we are thinking not of isolated or once-for-all decisions, but of persistence along the line opened up by the initial decision. That is why the word 'continuing' was included in the provisional definition of 'commitment'. Even when someone undergoes a decisive conversion, one often finds that it is followed by subsequent new moments of conversion, transforming the dramatic moment into a stable and enduring frame of mind. A commitment implies a measure of consistency, and we only properly speak of a commitment where there is such consistency over a period of time. More and more, the committed person's thoughts and energies flow along some channels rather than others. This lets us see the importance of commitments for self-formation. Commitments give shape to the raw material out of which character and personhood are to be built, and they give direction to our constructive energies.

Although there is hovering in the background of these commitments some ideal of the self which has captivated us and with which we are seeking to identify, the commitments are in fact to objects other than one's own self. Persons of depth and character do not come into being through deliberately aiming at an ideal self in some egoistic or narcissistic way. 'The true aim of the soul,' wrote William Temple, 'is not its own salvation; to make that the chief aim is to ensure its perdition.'[16] Likewise Hegel criticized the pietistic ideal of the 'beautiful soul'. Such a soul, he claimed, 'lives in dread of staining the radiance of its inner being by action and existence, and to preserve the purity of its heart, it flees from contact with actuality'.[17] So although I have said that commitment is a factor in the formation of selfhood, any inwardly directed pursuit of an ideal self is the very opposite of a life of commitment. Character and personhood are formed not by a direct attempt to cultivate them (this would be a form of egoism and would be retrogressive) but through commitment to ends that lie beyond the self. These ends will certainly be consonant with some particular understanding of what a human being is and ought to be, perhaps with one of the 'representative types' mentioned in our discussion of conscience.[18] But the formative power of such commitments lies in stretching the self beyond any narrow egoism.

These remarks are already bringing us to the second aspect of commitment proposed for discussion: self-transcendence. We have seen in earlier chapters, especially those on egoity and sociality, that no human being finds satisfaction and happiness purely within himself or herself. That is not only a fact of experience, it is more. It is an *a priori* condition arising from the very way in which human beings are constituted. Paradoxically, self-formation and self-transcendence go together. In Reinhold Niebuhr's words, 'Consistent self-seeking is bound to be self-defeating; on the other hand, self-giving is bound to contribute ultimately to self-realization.'[19] Each one of us comes into being in a world of things and persons, and we have to come to terms with these, even if it is only in a minimal way. When

I speak of 'commitment', however, I certainly have in mind something more than a minimal way of relating to the world and society – we might even say a maximal way, a way of frank and conscious engagement.

I call it a 'maximal' way, for commitment is no casual or transitory relation to the environing reality, but a serious and purposeful relation to it. One might think, for instance, of the commitment of the scientist who devotes himself to the investigation of some area of physical reality, or of commitment to a career, or to a political cause, or to a friend or marriage partner. These all imply self-transcendence. The human being is impelled to look beyond himself and to form stable relations with entities beyond himself. He has to go out from himself and know himself as belonging to a reality greater and deeper than himself. There may be no limit to the length he has to go. The human being, though finite, seems to have, as Schleiermacher put it, 'a sense and taste for the infinite'.[20] That may mean that in the long run he has to find a relation to God as the ultimate and all-embracing reality, but even leaving that aside, we see that every limited commitment is already taking the individual out of his mere individuality. Because it goes so much against our first unreflecting instincts, we cannot dwell too much on the paradox that 'whoever would save his life will lose it; and whoever loses his life . . . will save it'.[21] The more a human being pledges himself and engages himself beyond himself, the more firmly he is established as a truly personal being; whereas the more he seeks to defend and consolidate the inner centre of his being, the less personal he becomes and the more he resembles a subhuman form of life.

A further important point that has to be made in considering the self-transcending aspect of commitment is that this self-transcendence seems to manifest itself most clearly and completely when the object of the commitment is another person, so that the commitment itself is a person-to-person relation. It is true that a cause, an ideology, a career all draw a person out of himself and relate him to a larger reality, but where the object of the commitment is impersonal, the commitment may turn to fanaticism (as is often the case in politics) or to ambition (as may happen with a career). Of course, it cannot be denied that the cult of a hero may also become fanatical. But would not a commitment to someone who himself or herself manifested a true and deep humanity, a commitment of love and self-giving, be the highest self-transcendence of all?

If this is so, then one might be tempted to claim that the Christian commitment has an advantage over most of its rivals, whether other religions or secular ideologies, because it focuses upon a person, Jesus Christ, rather than on a world-view or a socio-political doctrine. The point has in fact been made by some apologists, notably Hans Küng.[22] But it would have to be seriously qualified, because the person of Christ has itself become so intertwined with causes, institutions, heterodoxies and orthodoxies, that the Christian commitment too, whatever it may be ideally, has often been understood in primarily impersonal terms and then turned into a fanaticism.

We come now to the third aspect of commitment: self-limitation. At first sight, this might seem to contradict what I have just been saying about commitment as self-transcendence. Can a commitment be both self-trans-cending and self-limiting? I think it can, and both of these aspects need to be taken into account. In discussing self-transcendence, we noted that the human being seems to have a taste for the infinite, but he always remains himself finite. He cannot himself become infinite, certainly he cannot become God, even if in some sense he might eventually participate in the divine life.[23] The human being has limited time, limited experience, limited wisdom, limited resources, limited capacities. He must therefore limit his commitments also. No one can spread himself out in all directions. Every commitment, if it is a commitment in any depth, must also be a renuncia-tion, for if one's time, energies and capacities are limited, one can only commit them in a certain direction by diverting them away from another direction. 'The more steadfast I am in my resolve,' writes Michael Zim-merman, 'the more I understand my finitude.'[24]

If, for instance, one commits oneself to a particular career or vocation and is determined to make a success of it, then one has to concentrate on that, even if one has other aptitudes and has felt the attraction of other possible careers. Or if one has committed oneself to a particular religious faith, this too demands a single-mindedness, even if one feels deeply and freely acknowledges the truth and wisdom to be found in other faiths. Admittedly, there have been a few great geniuses like Leonardo da Vinci who were in their time 'universal men' and seemed to excel in everything. But they are very rare indeed, and in the contemporary world probably no longer extant. The man or woman who dabbles in a great many pursuits without really mastering any one of them, the dilettante, as we call such a person; or the syncretist who mixes half a dozen great religious traditions and takes none of them with ultimate seriousness – such persons display a shallowness that is far from genuine commitment.

John Eckhart wisely observed: 'A man must ever do one thing; he cannot do everything. For if he tried to do everything, now this, now that, forsaking his own way to take another which, for the moment, pleased him better, he would soon become quite unstable.'[25] We are reminded of the New Testament stories of the man who sold all that he had to buy a field with a hidden treasure, and of the merchant who acted similarly in order to purchase one pearl of great value.[26] Indeed, the New Testament has some very harsh teaching on the theme of how a deep commitment will bring with it a correspondingly deep and painful renunciation. 'To another, Jesus said, "Follow me!" But he said, "Lord, let me first go and bury my father." But he said to him, "Leave the dead to bury their dead; but as for you, go and proclaim the kingdom of God." '[27] In the same gospel, Jesus says, 'If anyone comes to me and does not hate his own father and mother and wife and children and brothers and sisters, yes, and even his own life, he cannot be my disciple.'[28]

Commitment is bound to be painful, for its reverse side, so to speak, is renunciation. Each one has to establish a hierarchy of commitments, and concentrate his energies on those that stand at the top of the scale. There may even be one, an 'ultimate concern', in Tillich's phrase, which governs all the others. It is where commitment is limited that we see most strikingly its contribution to the establishment of a definite character and identity. Hauerwas remarks that 'the clearest example of character is one in which a life is dominated by one all-consuming purpose or direction'.[29] I think myself however that where one commitment, however admirable, is exalted to this almost terrifying level, the danger of fanaticism is great, and that a more balanced humanity requires a few basic commitments (I shall try later to say what these might be). Even a commitment to God cannot (and should not) abolish my commitment to my family or to society, as we saw in our discussion of Kierkegaard's treatment of the Abraham story.[30] I think too that, important though commitment and conscience are in the quest for humanity, there is a danger of becoming too moralistic and puritanical if one exaggerates the agonies of resolve and renunciation and forgets that a fully human existence also has its times of relaxation, play and humour. We do not have to insist on a reason for everything, and later we shall ask about the role of play, humour and art in life.[31]

One final point may be noted before we leave the topic of commitment as self-limitation. It is that the renunciations demanded by commitment should not be viewed in too individualistic a manner. As finite persons, we must all renounce some possibilities that may have attracted us, yet as persons who transcend mere individuality, we share a common life with others and can have through them a vicarious enjoyment of possibilities not fulfilled by us in our own lives. A man or woman may find as much joy in the achievement of a son or daughter or friend or even an unknown person, as in having done the same thing personally.

So far I have been setting forth a kind of phenomenology of the basic structures of commitment in fairly general terms. I believe that the aspects described can be verified in many concrete individual histories of statesmen, scientists, scholars, doctors, religious leaders, to say nothing of innumerable ordinary people whose life stories were known only to a few. Let me illustrate the point with just one illustration, but a very well known one – the apostle Paul. As far as the aspect of self-formation is concerned, it hardly needs arguing. It was his commitment to Christianity that made him the unique person he was. That commitment began with a dramatic conversion experience, then grew into a settled attitude which is reflected in everything that he says and does. Whether Paul attracts us or repels us (and he does sometimes come close to the danger of fanaticism) he is beyond question a man of character, with a strong identity given in terms of his fundamental commitment. The aspect of self-transcendence is also clearly present. Paul, the individual with a rather narrow training and outlook, becomes the principal founder of a new universal community transcending the barriers of race, culture, sex, language and social status. The very words that have become associated with him, words like 'apostle' and 'mission,' speak of that sending out which is of the very essence of transcendence. The aspect of self-limitation is clearly visible too. Because of his basic commitment, he makes many renunciations. Here one must count not only the sacrifice of a settled home and family ties, but also the painful extrication of his life from the Judaism to which he had been so passionately attached and which still mattered very much to him, as is evidenced in his theological attempts to find a place for the ancient Jewish people in the scheme of salvation.[32]

Now we return to our general consideration of commitment. In the analysis given so far, we have been thinking of commitment as already present in developed form in someone's life, but this may have conveyed too static a picture. A commitment is something living and extending itself through time, coming into existence, growing and perhaps changing in the way it is understood, maturing and sometimes fading away and dying. Let us try then to develop the concept of commitment further, so as to allow for these dynamic elements.

How does a commitment begin? People very often find it hard to say. Why did you choose your particular vocation rather than another (assuming you are one of that fortunate minority on our planet for whom there is freedom to choose in this vital matter)? Why did you become a Christian, or, let us say, a Marxist (again assuming that you have grown up in a pluralist society where such a choice was possible)? I repeat, people often find it hard to answer such questions. It is not that they have forgotten, but rather that the mental processes involved may never have been too clear to themselves.

It seems to be something like falling in love. It is not the result of some cool deliberate calculation, but something that happens to a person. One experiences a pull, a claim, an attraction. Yet it is not quite right to say that it just happens to a person, like an event that breaks in from outside and is quite outside one's control, such as being struck by a slate falling from a roof. There is an initial interest, and there is a free conscious response to the person or the cause or the career to which one finds oneself drawn. Again, although I said that the origin of a commitment is like falling in love in the sense that it is not usually the result of some cool calculation, it is not just a matter of the emotions. As something that involves the whole person, it demands thought and reflection if it is to be a responsible commitment. Impossible or utopian commitments are only a waste of time and energy, and we have to bring critical realistic judgment to bear on possible commitments. It is true that we first of all experience the pull of attraction, but we then have to ask about the resources we can bring to our response, about the possibility of bringing the commitment to realization, even about the genuine worth of the object. The realistic touch is not absent from the New Testament. 'Which of you, desiring to build a tower, does not first sit down and count the cost, whether he has enough to complete it? Otherwise, when he has laid a foundation and is not able to finish, all who see him begin to mock him, saying, "This man began to build, and was not able to finish." '[33] We are rational responsible beings, and therefore an element of reflection and evaluation comes into any worthwhile commitment that we make.

Yet this would still fall short of calculation. Commitment inevitably involves some element of risk, sometimes even of recklessness. We ought to be as reflective and responsible as we can when we take upon ourselves a commitment, but our finitude and fallibility mean that there can be no guarantees. There will always be some doubts and questions about the viability of the way that leads from the initiation of a commitment towards its realization, even some doubt about what exactly its realization would mean.

We are already moving from the question of how a commitment begins to the question of how it continues, grows and matures. And already we see that there is a difficulty here, almost a contradiction in the very meaning of commitment. We only speak of a commitment where the person concerned has taken a definite step and has quite decisively set his sights on some goal or bound himself in some relation. He has pledged himself or engaged himself, and these expressions carry the connotation of doing something definite and unambiguous. There is a vast difference between a commitment and an experiment. In an experiment we are, as we say, non-committal. We are trying something to see how it will work out. A commitment is not just an experiment. In a commitment, the committed person has projected himself or herself in the strong sense of that word, that is to say, has thrown himself or herself forward towards the future. It is more like a wager than an experiment, for though in the case of both the commitment and the experiment, one cannot be sure in advance how it will turn out; in the commitment, one has put oneself at stake, so to speak. So in a commitment there are side by side the definiteness or single-mindedness with which it has been assumed, and the provisional or tentative character of one's understanding of it. Both sides seem to be unavoidable, yet the tentativeness seems to contradict the finality and good faith. The unavoidability arises from the fact that in making a commitment, we have to leap ahead of what can be known and guaranteed, yet we feel it is right to make that leap. We cannot know the full content of the commitment or all that it is going to demand until we have embarked on it and are living it out. Of course, if we have been properly reflective and responsible in making the commitment initially, we shall not have entered it in sheer ignorance or taken on ourselves something impossible. We shall not begin to build an ambitious tower without some thought about resources. We shall not rush into a marriage without having got to know the partner in some depth. But, even so, there is much remaining that can only be worked out and understood as one goes along.

This is the testing of a commitment, but also its maturing and validation. We find that it is more difficult than we had supposed. We find that the demands are heavier than we had expected. We find that other interests are competing for our time and energy. We find that it is very painful to renounce these other interests or even to reduce them. Worst of all, we may be troubled with doubts about the value of the commitment itself and the wisdom of ever having got ourselves into it. Most of us will have known these problems, though in different contexts. They can arise in one's vocational or professional commitment, in the marriage relation, in a political loyalty, in religious faith and in many other contexts. One has certainly to be open to the possibility that a commitment will break down and that one may have to say, 'I was mistaken about this,' or, 'I have taken on more than I can manage.' But it is very important not to come to that point too quickly. Admittedly, there can be a blind stubborn persistence that is no longer fit to be called commitment and has become just fanaticism or the refusal to admit a mistake. But one must not be put off too readily. If a commitment, as we have seen reason to believe, begins in some scarcely definable way through an appeal and attraction that has seized us, may there not have been there some genuine vision that we must not too easily let go? Furthermore, is it not only through testing and even severe testing that a commitment can be fully understood and its possibilities made explicit? We may reach a stage when our understanding of it is considerably different from the one with which we set out, but this is not the abandonment of the commitment but a continuous process of growth and maturing. Something like this is bound to happen if commitments are not static but share in the dynamism of human life.

Supposing then that a person's commitments do survive the testing, that they become stronger and deeper and more mature, what is the result? The result, surely, is the emergence of character and personhood, built up around those commitments that have given the person his or her identity. As I indicated above, concentration on a single all-consuming commitment certainly produces a well-defined character, but may be in danger of becoming an obsession. There are more likely to be perhaps half a dozen basic commitments that among them give structure and stability to the person concerned. For example, there might be a marriage relationship, one or two deep friendships, attachment to one's work, a religious faith, perhaps some special interest in, let us say, a political party or one of the arts or some beneficent agency. But although a basis of serious commitments is needed for the development and maturity both of individuals and of a responsible society, the actual picture will never be quite as tidy as it appears in theory, for the commitments are always under the strain of conflicts, alienations and even chance happenings that throw human beings off course.

But has not this sketch of the nature of commitment and the formation of persons of character made it all appear impossibly difficult? Must we not again ask whether the human project is, at least for the vast majority of people, an impossibility and even an absurdity? It may be replied that everything worthwhile is difficult, and that there is nothing more worthwhile and more difficult than the fundamental human task of simply becoming human. We can cast our minds to an early stage in our explorations where we took note of Alistair Kee's distinction between the way of transcendence and the way of immanence.[34] He made it clear that the way of transcendence is a hard way in which one must be consciously and constantly striving to overcome obstacles. There is, of course, the easy option, the way of immanence. The opposite of a life of commitment is a life of drift, going with the currents and never swimming against the stream. But no one pretends that persons of depth, vision, creativity and compassion are formed in that way. They come into being only when men and women seriously engage with their environment and with one another in committing themselves to goals and relationships that can be brought into being only through difficulty, striving and even suffering.

But although the life of commitment is of necessity a difficult one, it is not impossible nor is the human project absurd. Let us remember that a commitment seems to begin not as my purely autonomous or unsupported decision, but as something that is evoked from me by attraction and appeal. Commitment begins therefore not as an effort but as a gift. Something is received before anything is given out. Every commitment is a response to someone or something that has elicited it, and in that very eliciting has given it support. We are not just committing ourselves to others, they are committing themselves to us. That is why commitment, though difficult, is not impossibly difficult.

We have to turn things around at this point and see commitment from the other end. Commitment is not an entirely asymmetrical relation. Even when one commits oneself to something impersonal, for instance, to the preservation of the natural environment, there is something in the object of our commitment which has invited or evoked it from us. It is seen as having its own dignity and beauty, and not merely as an object to be used for our convenience. When we think of a commitment to another person, say in marriage or friendship, the element of reciprocity is much more obvious. If one is also prepared to acknowledge the possibility of a commitment to God, presumably this would stand highest of all in the hierarchy of commitments, and in this case the weight has moved to the other side in a quite decisive way. The testimony of the religions is that our commitment to God rests upon his prior commitment to us. 'We love, because he first loved us.'[35] A commitment to God would assuredly be impossible if he had not first committed himself to his creatures and called them into a relation to himself, so that any commitment they make to him is enabled and sustained by his commitment to them. Perhaps indeed it is the primordial commitment of God to his creation that makes any human commitment possible.

The archetypal commitment of God not only to Israel but to the whole creation is called in the Hebrew scriptures *berith*, usually translated 'covenant'. The word originally meant a 'bond', hence an 'obligation', and is similar in meaning to what we have been calling 'commitment'. God's covenant with Israel in the Old Testament and his relation to the church in the New are both set out under the analogy of a husband to his bride, and marriage could be considered the archetypal commitment on the human level.[36] However, the covenant which God makes with his people is a unique kind of commitment, because the initiative, the enabling and the support lie so decisively on the side of God. Within the perspective of biblical religion, it is the basic fact that God commits himself to his people that makes it possible for them to enter not only into commitment to God but into commitments on the human level in the hope that these can be brought to a meaningful and fruitful issue.

One might even argue that the very fact that human beings do make commitments is itself some evidence for the reality of God. Every commitment is an act of trust. If I commit myself to protecting Mother Earth, it can only be because I believe that this planet has the values of beauty, interest and worthwhileness. If I commit myself to other persons, it can only be because I have some faith in and respect for human nature, and that faith and respect outweigh the disappointments I have had with human nature, whether in myself or in other people. In other words, the simple fact of commitment evidences a basic trust in life itself – a basic trust that we have met in other contexts also. Implicitly, such trust rejects the belief that reality is cold, impersonal, mechanical, alien, and still more the belief that it is meaningless, absurd or frustrating. But to entertain this basic trust is surely to give at least a minimal assent to part of what is meant by belief in God.

The full Christian belief in God develops this minimal assent into the theology of a God who commits himself. How do we think of this self-commitment of God, of the God of the covenant or the many covenants?

The idea is present first of all in the doctrine of creation. The creation of the world is to be understood not so much as an act of power on the part of God as rather his sharing the gift of existence. We may remember that belief in a transcendent God has been seen by many philosophers as an obstacle in the way of human transcendence.[37] But this is a misunderstanding. If creation is a sharing of the gift of existence by the Source of being, then God's transcendence is understood not as his exaltation above creation but rather by analogy with what we mean by 'transcendence' in the human being, that is to say, the capacity to go beyond the bounds of one's being to relate to another. The analogy is, of course, imperfect, for God creates the other to whom he relates. His creation has brought forth others who can respond to him – human beings, made, as the Bible expresses it, in his image and likeness. We can interpret this as meaning that these finite beings too have a share of transcendence. They have that 'sense and taste for the infinite' that lets them reach out and transcend toward God. But then they are met by his transcendence, which was prior to and originative of their own. Is not this commitment in its primordial form? This is no oppressive God, and his creating was no arbitrary act, but a caring act seeking a response, so that for him the creation had value, and from the beginning he was committed to bringing it to its flowering and fruition.

In the next place. God's commitment is implicit in the doctrine of incarnation. Whether we think in terms of a salvation history or a salvation myth or a mixture of the two, the story is the same. Mankind did not keep its side of the covenant, human beings did not respond with a commitment of love and obedience to the prior commitment of God. The covenant was falling apart. We can see the parallel with the cases we mentioned above, where human beings find their commitments are not turning out as they had hoped. I said then, however, that one must not give up too easily. So in the story, God does not withdraw from his commitment. On the contrary, he plunges in more deeply, so to speak, and identifies himself in a new way with his creation. 'The Word became flesh.'[38] We say this was a new way, yet it was simply a continuation of the way that began in creation. Perhaps we should say that it was a new unfolding and manifestation in history of the original commitment of God.

When we consider these matters, a new light is shed on human commitments. I do not mean that these are made light or easy – they will always remain demanding and difficult. But when human commitments are seen in the light of God's commitment to his creation, that does effect a transformation. There is here a support and undergirding that brings a new hopefulness into the situation, in spite of all the fallibility of our human nature, and the long history of commitments betrayed and convenants broken. It is not in vain for finite and sinful human beings to take commitments upon themselves.

The theological term which expresses what I have been talking about in the last few sentences is 'grace'. In face of the demands of conscience and the obligations of commitment, human beings are often weak and unable to do what they recognize to be their duty. What we call 'grace' is the experience of receiving a gift that gives the strength to fulfil the demand. We experience something like grace in our ordinary human relationships – there is no mystery about it, beyond the mystery that is present in all personal life. When a friend forgives, when a spouse encourages, when a child trusts – these are occasions of grace for the person so forgiven, encouraged or trusted. He or she receives something precious, and this in turn is something strengthening which enables the person concerned to give out something in return. That is why grace is so closely connected with commitment. What we receive in relations of commitment is certainly not less than what we give, and it is what we receive that makes it possible for us to give what is demanded of us. Grace is first and foremost a gift, and in its most typical form, it is the self-giving of a person. God's grace is simply his self-giving, self-bestowing, self-commitment, in his acts of creation and redemption. Since all this takes place on the personal level, there is no compulsion in it. Grace may be prevenient, but it is never irresistible. That would be contrary to its fundamentally gift-like character. Indeed, if we think of incarnation (and we ought to remember that this is not an exclusively Christian idea, but one that has parallels in Hinduism, Buddhism and other faiths) as God's supreme self-commitment and act of grace, he comes not in majesty and power but in vulnerability, and places himself at humanity's disposal. Only in some such way could God elicit the corresponding commitment on the human side and sustain that commitment through the assaults and testings to which it is bound to be submitted. It was Paul whom I took as an exemplar of the meaning of commitment, and it is also he who confesses, 'Through the grace of God, I am what I am.'[39]

The connection between commitment and grace can be seen more clearly if we look at the structure of some of the Christian sacraments. The word 'sacrament' is applied to a number of diverse rites performed in the church, but whatever the differences may be among them, they are all regarded as 'means of grace'. In several of the sacraments, solemn vows are taken, so that the element of commitment is very strongly in evidence. The particular commitments are singularly difficult ones, and therefore the vows are placed in a context of grace – ultimately, the grace of God, but proximately the supportive grace of the sacramental community. In these sacramental rites, some of the most basic features of all human commitments are brought clearly into view in both the words and ceremonial, and this is not just an institutionalizing of the commitment but a symbolic way of bringing out its significance and setting it firmly in a context of grace. It makes it clear that commitment is not the heroic resoluteness of the autonomous individual but his response to a whole complex web of relations that evoke and then sustain his commitment. The various features which we have seen to be characteristic of commitments generally can be clearly traced in the three sacraments of baptism, marriage and ordination.

We take first baptism, or better baptism-confirmation, that is to say, the entire rite of Christian initiation, whether it is ministered all at once or in two stages. It is not difficult to see in this sacrament all those structures which we saw to be typical of any commitment. There is self-formation, for the sacrament is commitment to a way of life, commitment, if you like, to one expression of the 'way of transcendence'. The public acknowledgment of faith, expressed both in the vows and in the recitation of the baptismal *credo*, confers an identity, for the candidate has pledged himself to a particular way of life and has joined himself to a particular community. Significantly, it is at baptism that he receives his Christian name. Then there is the aspect of self-transcendence. The life of the baptized person is being related to larger realities, the life of the community and even the life of God. The laying on of hands in the initiatory rite is also important in this regard, for it symbolizes an empowering and a sending, a conferring of a part in the ministry and mission of the whole church. There is likewise the aspect of self-limitation. The baptized person renounces, in the traditional language, 'the world, the flesh and the devil', for to choose one way of life is to renounce other ways that are incompatible with it. What we have seen so far are the structures characteristic of any commitment. But the sacramental form indicates that this is no bare commitment that someone is taking in his own strength – it would be little short of terrifying, if it were. It is a commitment in the context of a greater commitment, that is to say, in the context of grace, and it is for this reason that we can speak here of a sacrament. In the first place, there is the grace and support of the Christian community, in whose midst baptism normally takes place. But there is more to it than that. From Paul onwards, Christians have believed that baptism sets a man or woman on a new life, to be lived in the power of the Spirit of God, and that must finally be the ground that makes the Christian commitment possible.

Marriage differs from other Christian sacraments because it is not a specifically Christian relation but a natural one found in all human societies. But it is understandable that it has been brought into the sacramental system, for at the heart of marriage is a demanding commitment which needs the support of grace. The basic structures of the commitment are again easily recognizable. There is self-formation, for the two persons coming together and pledging themselves in an intimate relationship are taking the step which, probably more than any other that they will take, is going to form them and contribute to their development as persons. There is also self-transcendence here, for the partners are giving up their separateness to become 'one flesh' and found a new community – a community which begins with the couple and then opens into the wider community of the family. There is also the negative aspect of renunciation, for the new relationship demands the 'forsaking all others', in the traditional phrase. Marriage is a monogamous relationship, and this is no legalist taboo, but the recognition of something that we have seen as belonging to any deep commitment, namely, that we can only form such a commitment if we do not disperse ourselves in all directions but channel our resources. Promiscuity is incompatible with a truly personal sexual relation. The whole commitment is a demanding one, and to see marriage as a sacrament seems to do no more than recognize the need for grace. There is the grace which the partners give to each other, the grace that they receive from friends and from the community to which they belong, and the grace of God's constant commitment to his creation, a commitment which, we may remember, has been likened in the Bible to the marriage relation itself.

My third example is ordination. Some in the church are called to special ministries, particularly the priesthood. Even when we say that someone is 'called', we are acknowledging an initiative that precedes anything that the candidate for priesthood does for himself. He does not choose this vocation; rather, he finds himself chosen, and may even be reluctant. Of course, we have seen that in every commitment, there is something that draws and attracts the person who takes the commitment up. The by now familiar pattern of commitment repeats itself in the case of the priest. He requires formation, and this is not something that descends magically in the moment of ordination, but a process that has already begun and will continue. The aspect of self-transcendence is associated with the function of the priest as a 'representative person'. He represents God to the people and the people to God, and this is possible only because he has to stand in a close relation to both, his own individuality being subordinated to his priestly office. These extraordinary demands can be met only if there is renunciation of competing interests. The traditional Anglican ordinal spoke of 'laying aside the study of the world and the flesh'. These words do not mean turning one's back on the world in which we all live, but they do mean renouncing anything that conflicts with the priestly calling and priestly character. In the Roman Catholic Church, of course, priesthood is interpreted as requiring celibacy, a freedom from any ties that might stand in the way of the claims of the priestly life. It might seem that the demands are such as to make priesthood an impossible vocation, yet we all know that there have been and are many faithful priests serving God and their fellow human beings, and one can only account for this by recognizing that here too there is a grace that makes the commitment of priesthood thinkable and possible.

Although the discussion of these three sacramentally structured commitments has brought us into a more definitely Christian and theological context of ideas than I employed in the earlier parts of the chapter, I believe that what we learn from the sacraments is significant for all commitment, even when it takes an apparently quite secular form. Even there, something like a common grace is needed, though many people may regard it as purely human.

One last important, though nowadays controversial, question may be raised. How permanent are commitments? Are there any lifelong commitments? I did acknowledge that sometimes a commitment may break down, though I also expressed the view that one should never come to this point lightly. In the three sacraments we considered, the notion of permanence receives definite expression. Baptism includes a promise to walk in God's ways all the days of one's life, marriage is until death separates the partners, priesthood is claimed to be indelible. Are there some commitments which need a lifetime for their working out? Or do they perhaps affect us so deeply and even ontologically that we cannot give them up? Or have all such ideas become obsolete in this age of rapid change, mobility and rootlessness?

In the middle of last century, Kierkegaard was writing about permanent commitments. His list was slightly different from ours. He mentioned friendship, marriage and vocation as examples of lifelong commitments.[40] But the question has to be asked whether what was possible in the Denmark of Kierkegaard's time is possible today. Friendship might seem to be most at risk of the three relations he mentions. When most people lived out their lives in a single town or village, lifelong friendships were natural. But our society today is a highly mobile one. Many of us leave our native place and then spend various lengths of time in different cities or even different countries. We have different friends in childhood, youth, middle age and retirement. Yet against this, it has to be said that even today there are some friendships that persist, and the very mobility that separates people also allows them to keep in touch in a way that was not possible in earlier times. Vocation is another problem. In a rapidly changing society, professions and occupations may become obsolete, and in virtually all of them retraining and updating are necessary. Likewise the ideal of lifelong monogamous marriage has been put in question. Divorce and remarriage have become widespread in contemporary society, and there are some who argue that, if the children can be protected, it is a good thing to change marriage partners at certain points in life.

Obviously, there are many complicated issues in all this, and one cannot dogmatize. But I think our study of commitment shows that the really deep commitments that are capable of enriching humanity deserve to be persisted in for better or worse, and that however rash it may seem to pledge oneself for a lifetime, this is not an ideal that we should lightly surrender. There are some commitments that need a lifetime to be fulfilled. The commitment of baptism, which is simply the special Christian expression of the general commitment to become a truly human person along the way of transcendence; to be a loyal and reliable friend, in season and out of season; to be a good husband or wife, father or mother, to make a success of marriage and family; to be devoted to a vocation, whether it be that of priest or scientist or nurse or farmer; these all need a lifetime, and even at the end of a lifetime there is more to be done.

XIII

BELIEF

In discussing commitment, we have taken note that a commitment is an attitude of the whole person, involving will and emotion as well as intellect.[1] Mention was made specifically of the case of religious faith, which contemporary theologians are more likely to interpret in terms of practical trust and obedience than in terms of giving assent to a creed. We hear more of 'orthopraxis' (right conduct) than of 'orthodoxy' (right belief). Yet the belief element in any commitment, religious or secular, is of sufficient importance to merit further discussion. It belongs to our rational or intellective nature, and when it is undervalued, the way is open for commitment to turn into fanaticism or superstition. Certainly, right conduct is no less important than right belief, but the two are so subtly and intimately connected together that it is probable that in the long run we cannot have the one without the other. It is common today to stress 'belief in . . .' and to contrast it with 'belief that . . .', but there obviously cannot be 'belief in' without at least a minimum of 'belief that'. If someone believes in a political cause, he must believe that the theories behind it are true, even if he does not understand them too clearly. If someone believes in God, then he believes at least that God exists and has the sort of character that makes it appropriate to call him 'God'. So we read in the New Testament that 'whoever would draw near to God must believe that he exists and that he rewards those who seek him'.[2] But just as 'believing in' implies 'believing that', so 'believing that' may predispose us to act in certain ways. When I believe a proposition, a theory, a story, a body of doctrine or whatever it may be, I accept it as true, I have confidence in it, I am even prepared to act on it, although I lack conclusive evidence that it is in fact true. We all live much of the time by our beliefs, and there would appear to be relatively few matters on which we could claim to have knowledge in the strictest sense. For just as we have to distinguish belief from commitment, we have also to distinguish it from knowledge. When we speak of knowledge, we imply that there are sure grounds or evidences for what we know, but these are not present in the case of belief. Yet for a large part of our lives, we move in the realm of belief, and would have to agree with Bishop Butler that 'probability is the guide of life'.[3]

The lack of certainty may not worry us very much in day-to-day matters. Many of our beliefs relate only to some passing state of affairs, and may be quite trivial. I believe that the car that has just overtaken me on the highway must have been travelling at eighty miles an hour. I believe that it will be fine today, so I shall set out to climb a mountain. Other beliefs are much more serious and lasting, and may be acquired, elaborated and deepened over a long period of years. Such are a person's political opinions or his beliefs about topics that have interested him and about which he has come to care.

But people also have a core of what I may call 'transcendent beliefs'. I am using the word 'transcendent' here in a different sense from either of the two meanings assigned to it in an earlier chapter.[4] In talking of 'transcendent beliefs', I do not mean that they constitute belief in a transcendent reality, though in many cases they may do so. I mean beliefs that transcend the level at which empirical evidences could, at least in principle, be decisive for establishing the truth or falsity of the beliefs, or even for establishing a very high degree of probability or improbability. Such would be beliefs about the nature and destiny of the human being, his place and significance in the universe, about good and evil and the conduct of life, about God or the absence of God. I suppose these might also be called 'ultimate' beliefs, but that might be too pretentious an expression. So I shall be content to call them 'transcendent' beliefs, because they go beyond the level of our ordinary beliefs, and we shall also find that this terminology draws attention to links with the kinds of transcendence we have discussed earlier in the book.

It is when we come to matters of this kind that we are made very much aware of the limitations of human knowledge and of the problematic nature of belief. At the mention of transcendent beliefs, people of strongly empirical temperament may find themselves very uncomfortable and may even tell us that we ought not to admit any beliefs that transcend the limits of what can be empirically decided. But in practice such a ban cannot be put into effect. The ultimate questions do not go away, and the problems are not solved by the vanishing of the problems. The most searching critic of the old-style metaphysics began his major work with the sentence: 'Human reason has this peculiar fate, that in one species of its knowledge it is burdened by questions which, as prescribed by the very nature of reason itself, it is not able to ignore, but which, as transcending all its powers, it is also not able to answer.'[5] Kant went on to explain that he 'found it necessary to deny *knowledge* in order to make room for *faith*'[6] and the German word here translated as 'faith' is *Glaube*, which can equally well be translated as 'belief'. Kant's separation of knowledge and faith had momentous consequences, not all of them happy. Yet his main point is valid, that knowledge and faith are two different operations.

Kant, as we have noted, was also wise enough to see that the questions which, as he put it, transcend our powers, cannot be ignored. They seem to be built into our humanity, and even if only implicitly we cannot help giving answers. Even to say that one will refuse to answer is to give an answer of sorts. 'Scepticism,' as William James wrote, 'is not avoidance of option; it is option of a certain particular kind of risk. Better risk loss of truth than chance of error – that is your faith-vetoer's exact position. He is actively playing his stake as much as the believer is.'[7] It cannot be denied, however, that many people have wanted to remain on what they take to be the firm ground of knowledge and have been reluctant to take the risks of belief. To them it has seemed a scandal that the most important questions of life (or what have usually been taken as the most important) belong to the realm of belief rather than to that of assured knowledge.

Some have reacted to this situation by taking the view that since they cannot *know* the answers to such questions, they will at least try to suspend any judgment on them and remain agnostic. For instance, Bertrand Russell mentions in his autobiography that from the time when he was a young man, he was resolved not to accept any theological proposition unless it could be substantiated in the same way as a piece of scientific knowledge.[8] This is actually an impossible demand, since theology is not a natural science and does not employ the methods of natural science. It means in practice that no proposition of a theological kind could ever win acceptance and that such an agnosticism is virtually an atheism.

On the other hand, there have also been religious thinkers who have been dissatisfied with the fact that their fundamental doctrines were matters of belief, and who have felt just as strongly as Russell that we ought to *know* the answers to questions before giving assent. So they have tried hard to convert belief into knowledge, and the most obvious illustration of this is the long series of attempts to prove beyond doubt the existence of God. Even although these proofs have been more and more refined in the face of objections, and even although they retain some evidential force, it is now generally agreed that the arguments fall short of being proofs and have failed to provide demonstration. In this question of the existence of God, therefore, we have still to do with a matter of belief, not of knowledge.

But what is interesting here is that those who have attempted to construct such proofs had the same estimate of belief as did the agnostics who suspended judgment. Both groups have regarded belief as somehow inferior, unworthy and unsatisfactory, at best a makeshift that can only be made respectable if we can convert it into knowledge. There seems to be a deep craving for certainty in the human mind, and a restlessness if one has to stop short of knowledge, in the sense of that for which we have assured and sufficient evidence. As far as our everyday beliefs and our scientific beliefs are concerned, then, of course, it is both legitimate and desirable to convert them into knowledge. A scientific hypothesis, for instance, is subjected to every kind of testing, all relevant evidence is brought to bear upon it, questions are raised about its verifiability and its falsifiability, and if it stands up to all the tests applied to it, then it becomes part of current scientific knowledge, though we recognize that the word 'knowledge' is used here in something less than its strictest sense. But transcendent beliefs are not scientific hypotheses, and are therefore not amenable to the same kind of testing and cannot be verified or falsified by the same kinds of evidence. Among other differences, scientific hypotheses always refer to some limited state of affairs and therefore have a context which can supply evidence relevant to their truth or falsity, whereas a transcendent belief is more like a vision of the whole, and the whole has no context. Scientific hypotheses refer to phenomena within the world which supplies their context, but if one ventures to say anything about the 'world' itself, then there is no context.

Concerning the many attempts to prove the existence of God, Kierkegaard ironically wrote: 'With what industrious zeal, with what expenditure of time, of diligence, of writing material, the speculative philosophers have laboured to get a strong and complete proof of the existence of God! But in the same degree that the excellence of the proof increases, certitude seems to decrease.'[9] This may seem a strange thing to say, but I think that reflection will show us that it is pretty near the mark.

In the first place, Kierkegaard was acutely aware that our human experience and knowledge are finite. As much as any agnostic, he denied that we can ever attain to a demonstrable knowledge of the answers to transcendent or ultimate questions. These questions, as we have noted, ask about the world as a whole, but the human being is inserted into the world as one item in it, and he can never step out of it, so to speak, so that he can view reality as a whole. He may – and in fact he does – entertain beliefs about the whole or have some vision of the whole, but it is absurd either to demand or to offer the kind of demonstrative evidence concerning the whole that we might reasonably expect to have about some limited facts or sets of facts within the whole – the facts or sets of facts with which the sciences are concerned and about which empirical evidences may be decisive.

But, in the second place, Kierkegaard went further in his claim that, the more excellent the proof, the less sure we seem to be! Can this be the case?

I suppose one could say that if the very attempt to prove God's existence is fundamentally in error because it rests on a failure to distinguish transcendent beliefs from everyday and scientific beliefs, then it can in the long run produce only confusion and bewilderment, so that it shakes rather than establishes belief in God's reality. Again, chains of reasoning are always fallible, so that, as Pascal pointed out nearly two hundred years before Kierkegaard was writing, proofs of the existence of God may impress some people in the moment when they think they grasp the force of the demonstration, 'but an hour later, they are afraid that they have made a mistake'.[10] The result is again doubt rather than certitude.

But there is still more to Kierkegaard's remarks, and I think that he was seeing very deeply into human experience when he taught that belief is not just an approximation to knowledge (and we must remember that he was thinking specifically of what I have been calling 'transcendent' beliefs, not everyday or scientific beliefs). Transcendent belief is not an inferior or provisional form of knowledge, and it could not be such. Therefore we are wasting our time and misunderstanding the situation when we seek to convert this kind of belief into knowledge. Belief has an essential role to play in human existence, and it plays that role in its own right, so to speak, and not as a substitute for something else. Belief stretches the human being beyond himself, it sets before him visions or speculations that do not let him settle down in the comfortable assurance of the familiar and the well known. To recall William James' remark for a moment, belief assumes the risk of losing truth to be a more serious danger than the risk of falling into error.

We now begin to see the connection between transcendent beliefs and transcendence as a basic human characteristic. Kierkegaard was ahead of his times in conceiving human existence as something dynamic and human nature as something that is coming to be and is as yet unfinished. The human being is always on the move, reaching out for a completion that lies ahead. In this respect, Kierkegaard anticipated that view of the human reality which we found to be a constant feature across the spectrum of modern philosophical anthropologies, from existentialism and neo-Marxism to transcendental Thomism.[11] Thinkers from all of these groups use the word 'transcendence' for this dynamic quality of human life, and though in speaking of 'transcendent' beliefs, we were thinking of something like a logical transcendence, this has its part to play in a form of existence which can as a whole be called 'transcendence'. Such an existence was to be lived in risk, as it is constantly projecting itself into the region of the new and the untested. Risk, creativity and novelty go together. In such an existence, belief rather than knowledge must be our guide. To use another Kierkegaardian expression, there has to be a 'leap' beyond the secure region of proofs and evidences. Perhaps it is even like leaping into

Kierkegaard's 'seventy thousand fathoms of water' – a risky procedure, yet presumably a very worthwhile risk for the person who stays afloat. No actual ocean is anything like so deep, and presumably Kierkegaard exaggerated his figure to stress the qualitative difference between our everyday mental operations and the kind of belief he was trying to express. Understood in this way, transcendent beliefs are not static ancient metaphysical prejudices inherited from the past and inhibiting further thought. The opposite is the case. These transcendent beliefs are themselves aids to transcendence. We could call them 'thought experiments' or, to borrow a term from space exploration, 'probes' out beyond the familiar and the well known. They are part of the human search for a vision that will make sense of human life and give it the dignity that we feel belongs to it.

But does not this talk of dignity and feeling expose the real nature of these beliefs? Are we not confessing that they are without any cognitive basis or significance, and that they have no link with reality? Are they not just expressions of subjective longings and aspirations?

I have made several mentions of Kierkegaard, and many people believe that he did make belief a purely arbitrary matter, a leap of faith having no regard to any possible evidential material. This is an exaggerated interpretation of his views, but one can find passages in his writings where belief is closely linked to passion and truth to subjectivity, and one could argue that he completely separates belief from knowledge so that the two lie side by side in the human mind, unrelated to each other and introducing a new kind of dualism. William James too associates belief with the will and the passions, and visualizes the possibility that these may sometimes have to be our guide when evidence is lacking or is evenly balanced on either side.

Admittedly, Kierkegaard in his conflict with the rationalist philosophers of his time and James in his critique of the neo-Hegelians of his time had to be polemical in their utterances, and so they do give the impression of advocating an irrational type of faith. But it is not so simple as that. William James' pragmatic test of truth, for instance, when fully developed, is seen to be not so very far from the coherence theory of truth held by his philosophical opponents. The case is perhaps not so clear with Kierkegaard, and his position has often been caricatured, but he does explicitly say that the believer must use his understanding and that he cannot believe nonsense.[12] A fair judgment of Kierkegaard is made by Louis P. Pojman, who says of him: 'A highly rational person, he saw that reason had severe limits, and that for many of our deepest beliefs there were no full justifications.'[13] His concern was not to downgrade reason, but to combat the narrow rationalism that separates reason from the personal existence within which it functions, and so to reintegrate reason with the whole person. So Kierkegaard claims that 'in existence thought is by no means higher than imagination and feeling, but coordinate'.[14] If one eventually comes to believe in a paradox, it is not because it is absurd, but because the drive of reason itself has brought the thinker to a limit or a point of collision where he is impelled to go beyond the reach of reason. 'The supreme paradox of all thought is the attempt to discover something that thought cannot think.'[15] This implies that thought and reason themselves include a faith that carries them beyond themselves, and without such a faith they lose their drive and become lifeless. 'The thinker without a paradox is like a lover without feeling: a paltry mediocrity.'[16] The parallel between this remark and some aspects of Popper's theory of knowledge will not escape the reader.[17]

Still, for my own part I would wish to go much further than Kierkegaard in recognizing the role of critical understanding in belief – and, of course, this is also where Popper differs from Kierkegaard. In particular, I find Kierkegaard's scorning of probability unacceptable. He is right in claiming that no weight of empirical evidence, however much it is piled up, will ever establish a transcendent belief, because eventually one is going to come to the critical leap *eis allo genos*, as he is fond of saying – the leap into an ocean seventy thousand fathoms deep, and therefore qualitatively different from any ocean on earth. To give a very simple analogy (it has been used in the past by both J. H. Newman and I. T. Ramsey), suppose one keeps adding sides to a polygon, one could go on for ever and still not arrive at a circle. Yet at some point, one would make the imaginative leap, and see that the circle is the limit toward which the process is tending, though it will never get there. This suggests a relation between the evidences and the transcendent belief. The evidences will never establish the belief, but they are not irrelevant. They point in a direction; they have, so to speak, a trajectory. To that extent, they encourage the leap, and while the leap goes beyond reason, it does not altogether lack continuity with rational exploration.

Kierkegaard does even less justice to the negative significance of probability. For instance, while we may agree that there is no accumulation of probability derived from observation that would establish belief in God's beneficence, because this is not an empirical generalization but a transcendent belief, we would have to acknowledge that there might be such an accumulation of evidence that the universe is full of suffering, waste and evils of many kinds that one would be deterred from making the leap to belief in the divine goodness. One can and (I would say) should allow that there are important questions where one must go beyond the evidence and commit oneself to a belief – and, as we have seen, even the refusal to do this is to take up an option. But we can only adopt a belief responsibly if we have reflected as deeply as possible upon it, and taken account of whatever evidence may be relevant; and if our beliefs have any bearing on our lives, then some evidence must be relevant.

To assert this is quite compatible with holding, as Kierkegaard did, that the multiplication of evidence will never demonstrate a transcendent belief, but it is also to recognize much more fully than he did that evidence has to be seriously considered. To take an illustration related to Kierkegaard's interests, we may agree with him that if we possessed the most minute details concerning the life of Jesus Christ, this historical evidence would bring us no closer to establishing faith's assertion that he is the Word of God incarnate, for that is not an assertion of the same order. We might, however, believe that historical evidence about Jesus would point us in the direction of a certain estimate of his character and significance and that this might induce some people to make the leap to the assertion that 'God was in Christ' or to an equivalent assertion in an appropriate idiom. What is perhaps more obvious is that if the evidence made it seem highly probable (and Kierkegaard rightly held that historical evidence never attains to certainty) that Jesus was a hypocrite or that he was a mythical invention, then this would surely deter us from embracing the church's transcendent beliefs about him. It is probability rather than improbability that must be our guide, and even the paradox which is initially improbable must be shown to be not a sheer contradiction. There are beliefs that cannot be converted through demonstration into knowledge, but whatever beliefs we hold – and the more ultimate the beliefs, the more strongly this applies – we must hold them responsibly, and this means reasonably. We have to take account of what is compatible with the belief, and even indirectly supportive in the sense that it may point in that direction; but equally of what counts against it, and we have to weigh these evidences against one another. Some of our transcendent beliefs will stand up to this kind of testing. They will remain beliefs and they will include a leap beyond the evidence, but we shall be able to hold them without any *sacrificium intellectus*. On the other hand, it may come about that a belief has so much arrayed against it that finally we are driven to abandon it.

At this point, however, we should notice that a belief, as we have seen also in our discussion of commitment, should not be abandoned as soon as it strikes against difficulties. Belief is the intellectual aspect of commitment, or, one might say, intellectual commitment. I have said that transcendent beliefs are not the same as scientific hypotheses, but there are some analogies. Basil Mitchell has drawn attention to what he calls a 'principle of tenacity' in scientific research, and its significance for political, moral and religious systems.[18] Such a principle of tenacity 'is needed to ensure that the scientist is not prematurely diverted from a promising course of inquiry'. When he comes on data that do not fit his theoretical system, he modifies the system or introduces supplementary hypotheses. 'It is only when such devices have repeatedly failed and there is available an alternative system which gives promise of more satisfactory results, that the scientist is prepared to abandon his original position.' Similarly, in the case of a transcendent belief, one may need to stay with it through times when it appears to be highly implausible if its full content is to be understood and tested. Of course, a principle of tenacity could turn into an unreasonable stubbornness. There may come a time when a belief system has been so modified to accommodate awkward data that it has in fact undergone what Antony Flew called 'the death of a thousand qualifications',[19] and ought to be abandoned.

Two other points may be noted here. The word 'system' has appeared in the discussion. This need not mean a very tight system, but the kind of beliefs we are discussing (whether scientific, political or religious) are not solitary or isolated propositions, but bodies of interlocking propositions which have to be assessed as wholes, though clearly it is very difficult to make such an assessment. The other point arises from my remark that staying with a belief enables one to understand it better. Does this imply that it is possible to believe something without understanding it? No doubt if one is to believe something intelligently and responsibly, then what is believed must be understood. But it may be imperfectly understood, or, again, if we are talking about an entire belief system, parts of it may be better understood than others or there may be parts of it which remain opaque and which we believe on the authority of others because we think that they have understood them and seen that they belong within the system. So it does make sense to say that one may sometimes accept a belief and only subsequently understand it. Just as we have seen that a personal commitment only unfolds its content as we go along with it, so it will sometimes be the case that we must first assent to a belief and act upon it before we properly understand it. We may recall Anselm's famous words: 'I do not seek to understand in order to believe, but I believe in order to understand.'[20]

But does not this talk of a principle of tenacity that justifies us in persisting in a belief or of an interlocking system that is hard to assess for its truth or of believing in order to understand – does not this talk amount to a veiled confession that there are no reliable cognitive foundations for transcendent beliefs? For are these expressions we have used not evasive ways of saying that we are going to stick to these beliefs whatever the evidences, and that we are going to change the meaning and shift the ground of evidence when we find it convenient to do so? And does not this mean that we are going to believe what we want to believe and that these so-called 'transcendent' beliefs are no more than the expression of our deepest wishes and are devoid of cognitive content?

It has never been denied in this book that our emotions, interests and wishes profoundly influence our intellectual operations. One would have to acknowledge also that transcendent beliefs involve us emotionally in a far more intense way than most beliefs about empirical matters of fact usually do. For most people, the question whether God is in his heaven is more exciting and closer to their personal interests than the question whether there is water vapour in the atmosphere of Mars. We are ready, almost anxious, to believe some things; reluctant to believe others; indifferent about a great many others. We have already touched on the question of scepticism, especially the kind that arises from psychology and sociology and seeks to explain human beliefs as expressions of deep-seated needs, as by-products of personal histories or social pressures, and so on.[21] There is no need to deny the power and importance of such influences, but we have seen that this type of scepticism cannot be carried beyond a certain point, or else it becomes self-destructive. If all our beliefs were determined by our secret wishes, our psychological histories, our responsiveness to social pressures, then there would be no point at all in debating the claims of rival beliefs, for each person would believe only what those factors operating on him had determined him to believe. If that were the case, the question of truth and falsehood could not arise. But the question does arise, for the psychological or sociological sceptic believes that his own analysis of the situation is true. So this kind of scepticism is possible only if some beliefs are products of psychological and sociological factors, while others are judged to be true on rational grounds. The sceptic then would have to explain why his position is a privileged one, free from such distorting influences as characterize the beliefs which he criticizes. Marx, for instance, while believing that the various social classes are victims of false consciousness or ideology, made an exception in favour of the proletariat who alone understand the social reality (and this in spite of the fact that they are the most alienated class!). As one of his critics points out, this innocence of the proletariat is something Marx never justifies but simply sets up as a dogma.[22] It is neither more nor less an act of faith than that of the Christian fundamentalist who attributes an objective and absolute truth to the pronouncements of the Bible. The truth is that neither the sociologist nor the theologian is free from ideology. Yet we may also hope that neither the theologian nor the sociologist writes *only* what his interests secretly dictate. As the sociologist Peter Berger has said, 'Once we know that all human affirmations are subject to scientifically graspable socio-historical procedures, *which affirmations are true and which false?*'[23]

Transcendent beliefs do not necessarily reflect the wishes of those who hold them. It has often been suggested that belief in God is a candidate for the category of wishful thinking, but this would depend on what kind of God is envisaged. Let us agree that the indulgent God of much popular belief might well be considered a product of human imagination and deserves the kind of criticism to which Freud subjected it. But the God of biblical faith is very different. With his demand for obedience, righteousness, justice, mercy, love and self-sacrifice, he is a thoroughly inconvenient God from the point of view of those who want to live by the pleasure principle. It is hard to believe that such a God could ever have been invented to satisfy human desires (even unconscious ones) and the Bible itself tells us of many people who sought to evade this God and shut him out of their lives. On the other hand, many people might wish that such an uncomfortable and demanding God did *not* exist, so unbelief too may be influenced by one's wishes. Certainly, atheism would often seem to be the result, at least in part, of the history of the person concerned, his relation to his parents and so on. Even belief in a continuing personal existence beyond death cannot be seen simply as satisfying an egocentric desire for survival, though sometimes it may be that. The philosopher H. H. Price, who was interested in psychical research, remarks that there are wishful thinkers on both sides. He points out that while there are doubtless many people who want to survive death, others do not, for the religions have never taught that happiness is the only possible destiny that would await human beings in a life beyond. Belief in a life to come has usually been associated with judgment. Indeed, the traditional Christian view was that the majority of people would end up in hell, and, as Price says, this provided 'a very strong motive for *not* wanting to survive death'.[24]

But *ad hominem* arguments on whatever side really get us nowhere. Every belief has a psychological history and a sociological context, and these may be very interesting, but they do not settle the question of whether the belief is true or false. Most beliefs have both cognitive and emotional components. To recognize the non-rational factors and to analyse them is useful, but it never delivers us from responsible consideration of whether particular beliefs are likely to be true or false.

Now a further question arises. We have been talking about transcendent or ultimate beliefs as though they were matters of high importance, but are they really so? Are there not many people in the world who apparently get along very well, leading happy, balanced, interesting and useful lives, without ever raising questions about man's place in the universe, his ultimate destiny, and whether or not God exists? Some of them might even say that they are too busy with the duties, challenges, adventures and enjoyments of life to spend time in an apparently fruitless speculation on ultimate questions.

It is surely true that many people do not give a thought to such questions, at least, for most of the time. Yet is can be argued that even if they never make their beliefs explicit to themselves, there are some such beliefs at the back of their minds, and these are expressed in the values they pursue and the priorities they set up. Perhaps it is also the case that, as Heidegger claims, 'each of us is grazed at least once, perhaps more than once, by the hidden power of the question of being, even if he is not aware of what is happening to him'.[25] He also points out that the question may arise not only in moments of despair when things are falling apart, but equally in moments of rejoicing when things are transfigured, and even in moments of boredom when everything has lost significance. Surely we even have a duty to raise these ultimate questions, lest in our preoccupation with the immediate tasks we forget to ask where we are going or at what ends we should be aiming.

Even the agnostic or the positivist who tries to suspend belief about matters where a scientific approach to the question is impossible can hardly avoid having some creed, some ultimate or transcendent beliefs by which he orients his life. At an earlier stage, I quoted Bertrand Russell's determination to abide by the assured ways of scientific inquiry as opposed to what he took to be the unfounded assertions of religious faith. But later in his autobiography we find him saying: 'I have a very simple creed – that life and joy and beauty are better than dusty death.'[26] I doubt very much whether this creed is as simple as Russell would have his readers suppose, for it is a highly affirmative creed and there is a great deal that can be unpacked from it. I doubt very much too whether any scientific considerations are relevant to the question of its truth or falsity, or could be used to commend it. But it is, as I have said, a highly affirmative creed, and I suppose that a religious believer would gladly go along with it. However, he might feel that this was only a beginning, and that in his own creed he would want to go considerably further than Russell's very general affirmation. A Christian believer would say, 'I believe in one God' and then proceed to fill out this affirmation with the basic doctrines of his faith, as in the Nicene creed. Russell's creed may be, in the eyes of the religious believer, a very much reduced and attenuated kind of belief, but, so far as it goes, it still stands in some recognizable connection with the traditional creed of the Christian world and promotes some of the same basic values. It was not accidental that Russell's advocacy of peace meant that he often shared a platform with Christian speakers. His creed was, as I have claimed, an affirmative creed, unlike some of the anti-creeds which today seem to have broken almost entirely with the tradition and promote a kind of nihilism. There is no neat division of humanity into believers and unbelievers. Rather, there is a whole spectrum of beliefs, ranging from the 'I believe in one God' as one limiting case to something like nihilism at the other. Christians, Buddhists, humanists, agnostics, nihilists and others have their places on this spectrum, and there are many intermediate places.

Not only is there a spectrum of different contents of belief, there is also a wide range of degrees of intensity with which beliefs are held. Kierkegaard is a striking example of a man for whom belief was a matter of passionate intensity – indeed, he sometimes seems to suggest that the truth of a belief depends more on the intensity with which it is held than on its content. We have noted, however, that there are many people at the opposite extreme. They seem careless about belief and never trouble to work out their ultimate beliefs. The questions with which these beliefs deal do not bother them. Between the extremes of intensity and indifference, there is what might be called 'half-belief'. The half-believer, according to Peter Baelz, 'finds himself more often than not inhabiting a strange, bewildering and uncomfortable no-man's land between belief and unbelief'.[27] Perhaps many people today are in this state of half-belief, possibly many readers of this book. H. H. Price reminds us of the so-called agnostic's prayer: 'O God (if there be a God), save my soul (if I have a soul).' This is usually taken in a humorous sense, perhaps as an illustration of extreme intellectual scrupulosity. However, it does represent the frame of mind of someone who is between belief and unbelief. It has its serious counterpart in the New Testament story of the man who said to Jesus: 'I believe; help thou mine unbelief.'[28] Price himself says about the agnostic's prayer: 'It is a perfectly sensible prayer for an agnostic to offer, and unless he begins by praying in some such way, one cannot see how he is ever to begin praying at all, nor how he is ever to be converted from agnosticism to theism. One must start somewhere, and how else is an intellectually honest man to start? . . . After all, he is making what might be called a devotional experiment, and how else is he to do it?'[29] The expression 'devotional experiment' here obviously represents a view close to the one I expounded a little earlier – that belief is like a probe or experiment in our search for human identity.

To come back to our question, whether transcendent beliefs are really important, I think we have seen enough for me now to give the answer, 'Yes, it is important for people to have some deep affirmative beliefs about life, even if they are unable to go so far as the traditional affirmation, "I believe in one God". It is also important that, as far as they are able, people should clarify their beliefs and hold them in responsible awareness.'

Let me sum up the reasoning that leads us to this conclusion. If it is the case that man is a being who is incomplete and on the move, reaching out for a realization that lies ahead, a being with a measure of plasticity to his nature so that he may become either one thing or another, then to some extent he becomes what he believes he is, his society becomes what he believes a human society is, and even the environing world is shaped by his beliefs. If beliefs are as influential as this, then it is important to make them explicit and it is in the interests of responsible living to expose the beliefs that underlie human actions and policies. If a person has affirmative beliefs about himself and about humanity in general, then these tend to shape his life in an affirmative way; and if he has negative beliefs about himself and others, then these too tend to be translated into reality.

Belief at any level carries an element of risk, and in the case of belief at the transcendent level, the stakes are high indeed. But I do not think any of us can avoid accepting one belief or another at that level, even if we do so only implicitly or in a half-hearted way. We dare not be uncritical in our beliefs, for history is full of examples of people and even whole nations who were destroyed by false and sometimes cruel beliefs. Yet we dare not despise belief, for if people had never allowed their minds to be captivated by visions beyond what they could prove or guarantee to themselves at the time, they would have made little progress. And we cannot say that we shall sit around until belief has been converted into knowledge, for transcendent beliefs never will. They belong inevitably to our finite human condition, and every important action we do implies just such a belief.

Perhaps it is harder for some to believe than for others. There are sceptical natures, and we need them, for without their criticisms and questions, human beings of a more credulous type might be swamped by false beliefs. Perhaps it is possible for some people to get along on a more reduced basis of belief than others. Perhaps there will always be only a minority who believe with passion and intensity, though these may turn out to be the shapers of human destiny. But life itself seems to call out for some affirmative act of belief, for at least some degree of participation in the belief that found classic expression in the words: *Credo in unum Deum*, 'I believe in one God'. As even the cautious Kant acknowledged, 'human reason has a natural tendency to transgress its limits' in search of 'an ideal without a flaw, a concept which completes and crowns the whole of human knowledge'.[30]

XIV

LOVE

In the course of our discussions, we have several times seen good reason to believe that no individual can achieve human fulfilment so long as his interests are turned in on himself. He must, as it were, shift the centre of gravity by relating to other people, to causes, to institutions, to nature, to God or whatever it may be. In the two preceding chapters, we have considered specific ways in which this takes place. In talking about commitment, the question was asked whether a commitment to another person in love and self-giving might not be the highest self-transcendence of all.[1] So we now turn to inquire more deeply into the nature of love. Many people think that love is the highest of all human virtues. No doubt they remember the famous words of Paul: 'So faith, hope, love abide, these three; but the greatest of these is love.'[2]

The mention of Paul is hardly accidental, for in the Western world our understanding of love has been strongly influenced by the New Testament. If there is one subject on which Christian thinkers may still hope to get a respectful hearing, not only from other Christians but from non-Christians as well, that subject is love. Admittedly, love is not a monopoly of the Christian religion, but I would venture the claim that within Christianity love has been explored and interpreted in a depth that goes beyond anything we find in other religions or in secular philosophies. When at one point I suggested that there is a similarity between the Christian ethic and the ethics of Nietzsche, Heidegger and other secular thinkers,[3] because they all break out of legalism and encourage radical questioning of conventional morality, I might have made the point that the Christian ethic also profoundly *differs* from the others mentioned because of the key position that it assigns to love. It is not only that Jesus, Paul, John and others give profound teaching about love in the New Testament, it is above all that the life and especially the passion of Jesus Christ has been held up by the church as the supreme expression of love in human history. To some extent, that love has continued to manifest itself in the Christian community, and has been a topic for reflection by many Christian theologians.

Still, one would have to say that in the Christian church love has been more of a vision than a reality, and sometimes scarcely even a vision. In so-called Christian countries today, there would seem to be little of love. The very word 'love' has been debased, so that it is rarely understood in anything like the depth which the New Testament gave to it and has come to stand for sentimental affection or weak indulgence or simply for sexual passion, with even that understood in its shallowest forms. So even if we agree that the Christian tradition offers the most profound understanding of love, we must not assume that we already know what that understanding is.

Love needs to be correlated with understanding and knowledge if it is not to be in constant danger of degenerating into mere sentimentalism – as, indeed, it has done in the mouths of some Christian moralists who have commended an ethic of love without adequate attention to the question of what love is. Love needs two kinds of understanding. It needs understanding of itself. The Christian moralist who commends love has to go back to the sources and to seek to grasp the original vision of love before it is weakened or tarnished. He has to do even more. The New Testament teaching about love is given mainly in the form of parables, poetry and biography, but there must also be conceptual analysis. Admittedly, it may be the case that the deepest nature of love can be communicated only in story or poetry or – best of all – in the loving deed, but the quest for a conceptual understanding of love is not to be despised, for only so can we compare and evaluate the different accounts that moral theologians have given of Christian love, and only so can we compare the Christian teaching about love with other teachings. But love needs not only understanding of itself, it needs understanding of facts – facts concerning the kind of people who are the objects of love, facts about the world in which they live, and so on. It is a mistake to contrast love and knowledge or even love and technique. It is true that neither knowledge alone nor technique alone can supply the place of a genuinely human personal love, but that love will be all the more valuable if it is accompanied by knowledge of, let us say, psychology or of any other subject that helps us to understand better the human condition and ways of bettering it. As Daniel Day Williams has remarked, 'It is not loving concern alone which tells us what needs to be done.'[4] So love needs understanding, both of itself and of the world in which it is exercised.

The need for an understanding of love as well as a loving concern is reinforced when we remember that Christian love has not been without its critics. Marxists, for instance, have claimed that Christian love is too private and personal and is helpless in the face of major social problems. Other philosophers have claimed that the place given to God in Christian love is a distraction which turns away the energy of love from one's fellow human beings. If we are to find our way through these rival views about the nature of love and its place in human life, we must get down to basics in asking what love is.

In the present study of love, I propose to begin with love of that which is nearest, and then to expand through concentric circles, as it were, to the more distant objects of love. In effect, this means that we begin from self-love. It may be objected that self-love is not the starting point for any individual's experience of love, and I believe this is true. It is only through relation to another that one becomes even aware of one's own selfhood. Nevertheless, although self-love is not chronologically first, there are logical reasons for putting it at the beginning of our discussion.

A more serious objection might be that self-love is a contradiction in terms. I have been stressing the need for an affirmative relation to other people, and claiming that egoism is in the end self-destroying. How then can I talk of self-love? And is the objection not made even sharper by the fact that I have introduced the subject of Christian love and suggested that it may offer a paradigm of what love really is? Surely self-love is the very opposite of Christian love. Did not Jesus say, 'If any man would come after me, let him deny himself and take up his cross and follow me. For whoever would save his life will lose it.'[5] In another gospel, we find a still stronger expression of these ideas: 'He who loves his life loses it, and he who hates his life in this world will keep it for eternal life.'[6] Does not this mean then that self-denial, self-sacrifice, even self-hatred, rather than self-love, are the requirements and correlates of a truly Christian love?

But is it so certain that self-love and self-giving, self-fulfilment and self-denial, are so implacably opposed to one another? Even the teaching about *hating* one's life, quoted above, is tied to the idea of preserving it for eternity; and likewise the injunction to lose one's life for Christ's sake and the gospel's is part of the paradox that thereby one's life will be saved? Does not Jesus also teach, quoting the Old Testament, that 'You shall love your neighbour as yourself,'[7] where self-love seems to be made the model for neighbour-love? Furthermore, does he not teach a form of the so-called Golden Rule, 'Whatever you wish that men would do to you, do so to them,'[8] and does this not introduce a measure of self-interest?

Of course, it is possible to offer other interpretations of these sayings of Jesus and even to challenge the authenticity of some of them, and to say that he demanded only self-denial and self-sacrifice. Rudolf Bultmann, for instance, does not believe that the Golden Rule (so often quoted as a kind of summary of Christian morality!) is a genuine part of Jesus' teaching, and roundly declares about it that it 'gives moral expression to a naive egoism'.[9]

Certainly, one would have to agree that there can be no place for egoism or self-centredness in Christian love, nor was Jesus encouraging such egoism in any of the sayings attributed to him. What Bultmann calls 'naive egoism' is indeed the opposite of Christian love, as is also sophisticated egoism. But is self-love only to be understood as egoism and self-centredness? Or are we falling into the mistake of misunderstanding the word 'love' in one or other of its debased forms, so that we think that 'self-love' must mean self-indulgence or material self-interest or a prudential seeking for reward in a future life, or something else of the sort? But if love is to be understood in a deeper way, then there may be a form of self-love that is compatible with Christian love and is even demanded by it. This possibility has not been sufficiently considered by those theologians who insist that Christian love must be purely other-regarding.

There have been other theologians who have believed that self-love is not excluded by Christian love. A notable example was Augustine. He declares self-love to be an indubitable fact of human life: 'That a man does love himself and does desire to do good to himself, nobody but a fool would doubt.'[10] He adds that if someone voluntarily suffers pain and mutilation, it is not because he hates his own body but because he values something above the safety and soundness of the body. Most modern psychologists would agree with Augustine, and if a person is found who really hates himself, that is regarded as a pathological state of mind. The fact that the gospels command love to God and love to neighbour but do not command love to one's own self is explained, according to Augustine, by the superfluousness of commanding what is already the case, and the command to love one's neighbour as oneself is a recognition that self-love is already implicit in these wider loves.

One of the most forceful statements of the place and importance of self-love in human life is found in the writings of Bishop Butler. In a well-known passage, he puts the point in words that may shock many a hearer: 'When we sit down in a cool hour, we cannot justify to ourselves any pursuit, till we are convinced that it will be for our happiness, or at least not contrary to it.'[11] At first hearing, this may sound like a recipe for pure egoism, and a far remove from the Christian teaching that one might expect from a bishop. Let us agree that, as a child of the Enlightenment, Butler displays a cautious rationality which leans more towards the sober consideration of possibilities than the taking of risks – and it will be remembered that both belong to the structure of commitment,[12] and therefore to the structure of love, as itself a kind of commitment. Butler may have erred on the side of caution, though we should recognize that it may be even worse to err on the side of sentiment or impulse. But to accuse him of egoism or of representing altruism as merely a disguised form of egoism is a mistake. Butler had a very sophisticated and even exalted understanding of what self-love is. It is not self-indulgence, nor is the happiness which each is said to desire to be equated with mere pleasure. The person who lives for these things, says Butler, is rushing upon his own destruction. Nor can self-love mean the pursuit of one's own interests regardless of others, for this too would lead to the diminution and impoverishment of the self.

Butler believed that a true self-love goes hand in hand with the love of others – benevolence, as he called it. Self-love and benevolence go naturally together. Each human person is a social being, and his best interests or happiness is bound up with the interests of others.

Does this still seem to be a somewhat prudential outlook on life? I do not think so. The point is that if anyone is going to love and help other people, he has to be someone himself. Before he can give himself or sacrifice himself, there has to be something to give. He has to be at least on the way to becoming that self to which his inmost conscience summons him, and his true happiness lies in obeying that summons. Let us take the extreme case of someone who sacrifices his life for others. Let us suppose further that this is a person who does not believe in any life beyond death, so that his sacrifice has not been made for the sake of a reward hereafter or for an eternal bliss. Such an act – and there have been many such acts in warfare – would seem to contradict Butler's claim that we do not act coolly and deliberately against our own happiness. But to that it might be replied that in the act of self-sacrifice the person concerned was supremely happy. In that moment he realized his truest self, so that the moment (and now we are using the word almost in Kierkegaard's sense) had more existential weight than perhaps all the rest of that person's life.

We can also think of the matter in a negative way, which is at least suggested by Butler when he writes that 'it will be for our happiness, or at least not contrary to it'. Let us suppose that someone feels summoned to sacrifice his life for the sake of a friend. If he does not do it, then, although he will have saved his own life, he may have rendered himself permanently unhappy, for he will have lost and tarnished his truest self. We find again that self-giving and self-fulfilling, self-sacrifice and self-realization, are inextricably tangled together. A self-sacrifice for the sake of another might bring no more than a momentary flush of happiness almost at once extinguished by death, but to have left the other to his fate would destroy all possibility of happiness, for it would be experienced as a betrayal and loss of one's own self, worse than the loss that comes through death.

Let us come back now to the Christian understanding of love, and to the example of Jesus himself. He has sometimes been called 'the man for others', but this should not obscure the fact that he was someone in himself. Ritschl drew attention to this fact when he wrote: 'Christ had the honour of existing for himself; without this, how is it possible to render any real service to others?'[13] He meant that Jesus Christ had his own values, his own integrity, his own vocation, his own goals, and though he lived for others and made himself available in responding to the demands those others made upon him, his response was governed by his own central commitments. Thus, when he was told in the course of a busy day's ministry that his mother and his brothers were standing outside waiting to see him, he gave a pretty curt reply and went on with what he was doing.[14] When he sought a little peace and quiet in a Gentile region, and a woman came beseeching him to heal her daughter, he brushed her off – initially, at least.[15] Some readers of the New Testament have been scandalized by the harsh language that he used towards the scribes and Pharisees.[16] Incidents like these make it clear that Jesus' love was never sentimental, weak or servile. Certainly it was never that mawkishness which sometimes passes for Christian love, and which Nietzsche so savagely attacked. To be loving is not to be a doormat. Availability to others does not mean pandering to all their wishes. Love is not a blank cheque nor an invitation to exploitation – that would be counterfeit love, not really in the interest of the other. Just as we have seen that love needs intellect, so it must also be wedded to integrity, and this implies that love for the other demands respect for one's own self.

It is now possible for us to understand more clearly what is that self-love of which Bishop Butler wrote. 'We are,' he says, 'in a peculiar manner entrusted with ourselves.'[17] He is saying that the life of every human being is a trust, to be regarded with proper care and responsibility. The time that each one has at his disposal; the ordinary human powers and capacities that he or she possesses; the individual gifts or talents which one may develop or neglect, as in the gospel parable[18] – all these are a trust. Christians would think of them as a trust from God, but even leaving God out of the picture, everyone can agree that there is a responsibility involved in the human condition itself, with its freedom and possibilities for transcendence. Each must respect and value the trust that is given in his or her own life. No individual is going to put the world right, but each has a special responsibility for that little strip of history which is his or her own responsibility and with which, in Butler's phrase, he or she has been in a peculiar way entrusted. Each must respect and make the most of what has been thus entrusted. This is the true self-love, which has nothing to do with selfishness but is equally far removed from self-hatred. It is a necessary condition of one's being able truly to help and serve others. Perhaps it would avoid misunderstanding if we called it self-respect. It simply means that love for others is inseparable from personal integrity, and that each must treat with respect and reverence the gift of one's own existence.

Our plan is to consider the subject of love in concentric circles, so to speak, beginning with self-love or self-respect and then moving out into successively wider areas. I freely admitted that while this may be a useful logical order of treatment, it does not represent the way in which love actually arises and develops in a human life. It is the gift of love from another that first awakens the capacity for love in any human being, and first makes anyone aware of himself as a person who can be the object of love and respect. We may recall the famous phrase of Feuerbach, quoted in an earlier chapter: 'Where there is no "Thou", there is no "I".'[19] From the moment of birth and even earlier, every human being is bound by ties to other human beings. These ties constitute the core of what we may call 'natural love', the closest of the concentric circles. It provides each human being with the first experience of otherness, and so with the first experience of selfhood over against the other.

What, then, is included under the designation 'natural love'? First and most obvious, there is love within the family. To become a human person, the child needs the love and security given first by the mother, then also by the father and by the family as a whole. In course of time, the child will himself or herself take a marriage partner, and the love that binds them in this relation is the most intense and intimate of all forms of natural love. In addition, friendships will be formed with persons beyond the boundaries of the family and these may often be very deep and supportive. Natural love would include also one's love for places, for communities such as schools, colleges, churches, also love of one's own country and, stretching even beyond that, love of Mother Earth itself, with all its interest, beauty and variety.

Some Christian theologians have attempted to draw a very sharp dividing line between the various forms of natural love and specifically Christian love, and in the course of this they tend to be somewhat disparaging of natural love. They say, for instance, that whereas natural love implies a reciprocity, the lover looking for a return of love from the beloved, a truly Christian love looks for no return whatever. Or again, they say that whereas we bestow our natural love on those whom we find attractive and agreeable, a truly Christian love is quite undiscriminating and should be freely bestowed on the unattractive and disagreeable. Perhaps Anders Nygren is the theologian who has carried the distinction between natural and Christian love to its furthest length. He linked the difference between them to two different Greek words meaning 'love'. In classical Greek, the usual word for 'love' was *eros*. That word meant not only sexual love but was extended to include the love of beauty and even the mystic's quest for God. But no matter how high and spiritual *eros* might become, according to Nygren it remains egocentric. It seeks a satisfaction for the self and is a veiled form of self-love. In the Greek version of the Old Testament and likewise in the New Testament, a different word is used for 'love': *agape*. This is the truly selfless Christian love, and we are told that it is not a natural possibility for human beings but is rightly known only through the

Christian revelation. It is said to be quite discontinuous with *eros*. 'There is no way which leads over from *eros* to *agape*.'[20]

Incidentally, although Nygren's case does not rest primarily on a distinction in meaning between the two words *eros* and *agape*, we should note that it is extremely dangerous to assume that a difference in vocabulary always indicates a difference in concepts, or that a single word may not stand for several concepts. In one verse of the Old Testament, we find the Hebrew verb *ahebh* used three times for three kinds of love, the love of a man for a woman, the love of God for his people, and the love of the people for sweet cakes! 'And the Lord said to me, "Go again, *love* a woman . . . even as the Lord *loves* the people of Israel, though they turn to other gods and *love* cakes of raisins.'[21] The Septuagint translates *ahebh* by *agapan* on the first two of the three occasions quoted, and by *philein* on the third. One gets the impression that usage was fairly casual, and that precise lexical distinctions belong more to modern biblical scholarship than to the ancient writers. It is precisely in reference to Nygren's distinction of *eros* and *agape* that Oliver O'Donovan has written that 'it may be convenient for modern thinkers to label certain motifs by the Latin or Greek words which they think encapsulate them, but they should not then suppose that they have discovered a lexicographical statute to which ancient writers can be held'.[22] In fairness to Nygren, it should be noted that O'Donovan thinks that he was less guilty in these matters than some of his popularizers.

But leaving aside linguistic points and confining ourselves to matters of substance, I think it is clear that the sharp division Nygren and others have made between natural love and Christian love is exaggerated and even mistaken. Thomas Aquinas rightly held that 'grace does not abolish nature, but perfects it'.[23] It may well be true that in fact natural love is frequently sullied by selfishness, but it can be purified and transformed. I have written elsewhere that '*eros* contains in itself the seed of *agape*' or, avoiding this terminology, that 'the love that longs is transformed into the love that lets-be'.[24] So I do not accept Nygren's claim that there is no way from *eros* to *agape*. Natural love is the school in which human beings first learn something of what love is, and if they are ever going to be brought to higher forms of love, it can only be through learning the lessons of the loves that lie nearest to hand. I think it is significant that in the Bible itself, one of the earliest expositions of the love of God and one of the latest use the analogy of love between the sexes. The eighth-century prophet Hosea compares the love of God for Israel to love for a wayward spouse, while the Revelation of St John the Divine closes with a vision of the perfected church as the bride of Christ. These analogies, which of course have many parallels in the subsequent mystical tradition of Christian spirituality, would not be possible if our natural human loves had nothing whatever in common with the divine love or with the specific human love which this is said to elicit or to create by grace in the human soul.

The New Testament itself, however, gives no warrant for disesteeming natural love. The gospels represent Jesus himself as participating in several forms of natural love, as well as being a teacher and practitioner of a love that goes beyond the natural. He was born into a family, and though our information is scanty and possibly legendary, it suggests that there was love in that family. Luke tells the delightful story of the boy's pilgrimage to Jerusalem with his parents, of their anxiety when he is missing and of the glad reunion. We get the impression of mutual affection in a context of freedom.[25] Again, his universalizing of love apparently did not prevent him from knowing the intimacy of friendship and forming special links with those whose company he enjoyed. The obvious case is the 'beloved disciple' of the Fourth Gospel.[26] These two forms of natural love relating to family and friendship are brought together in the poignant scene when Jesus, nearing his end, sees both his mother and his special friend standing by the cross, and commends his mother to his friend's keeping.[27] No doubt his love eventually far transcended these natural forms, but we should not for a moment despise them or think that they are superseded or discredited by the new form of Christian love that bursts beyond all the bounds of natural love. Rather, if the essence of love is, as I have said, letting-be, that is to say, enabling and allowing the other person to become what he or she has the potentiality to be, then the way to the higher love lies through our natural loves.

Let it be admitted, of course, that natural human love is frequently perverted and rarely becomes what it might be. There are two common ways in which it can go wrong, and the New Testament teaching exposes these and points beyond them.

The first point is that natural love tends to be possessive of its object. The parent wants to mould the child and have him conform to some preconceived model. The newly married husband or wife wants the spouse to fit an idealized picture. There is at work a desire, perhaps unconscious, to make the other dependent. When love becomes possessive, it has become unbalanced, and may be harmful rather than beneficial to the beloved. The imbalance arises from a one-sided preoccupation with desire for union with the beloved. Such desire is indeed a part of natural love, but it has got to be set against another part which is even more important – what I have called 'letting-be', a respect for the otherness, freedom and individuality of the beloved. This is a special case of a point which we noted in our general discussion of sociality and interpersonal relations, when we contrasted Sartre's account of the matter in terms of possession and dependence with Buber's insistence on the need for 'distancing' – the need, we might almost say, of letting the other breathe and be himself as the unique person which he is.[28] It is the 'letting-be' type of natural love that is encouraged by the New Testament. I have already suggested that what little we can gather from the gospels on Jesus' relations with his family points to a balance of affection and freedom, and this is perhaps above all evident in incidents involving Jesus and his mother, to which reference has been made earlier in this chapter. In his dealings with human beings, he does not set up patterns of domination and dependence, but, according to the gospels, liberates men and women to be themselves. As Paul van Buren has well expressed it, 'in telling the story of Jesus of Nazareth, [the disciples] told it as the story of the free man who had set them free'.[29] This is the opposite of possessive love, but it is not discontinuous with natural love. We may say that it has brought natural love to the point where it is ready to be transformed into a fully Christian love, of which Paul says that it 'does not insist on its own way; it is not irritable or resentful . . . Love bears all things, believes all things, hopes all things, endures all things.'[30]

A second common defect in natural love is exclusiveness. Two people may be bosom friends and make sacrifices to help each other, yet they may have no time for any third person. A tightly knit family may know affection and loyalty in itself, but be cold and indifferent to those outside the circle. Love in such cases has degenerated into a corporate selfishness. This too is exposed in the New Testament, where Jesus declares: 'If you love those who love you, what reward have you? And if you salute only your brethren, what more are you doing than others?'[31] We do violence to the very nature of love if we try to shut it up – even what we call 'natural love' has in itself a drive to transcend and go beyond the limits put in its way.

So I cannot agree with those theologians who tend to speak disparagingly of natural love or hold that it is entirely different from Christian love. In its deepest and most mature forms, it is already, so to speak, on the borders of Christian love. But to say this is not to deny that with Christian love in its fullest sense a new dimension of love is opened up. All the natural loving relationships are transcended. 'Love your enemies and pray for those who persecute you!' Jesus bids his disciples.[32] And he put this into practice himself, for at his crucifixion he is said to have prayed for his executioners, 'Father, forgive them, for they know not what they do.'[33] This goes so far beyond natural love that it would not be inappropriate to call it 'supernatural love', though the use of this adjective cannot be taken to mean an absolute discontinuity between the two loves.

The new dimension in the specifically Christian concept of love is conveyed in the word 'neighbour'. 'You shall love your neighbour as yourself' is an ancient piece of Jewish teaching which is taken up in the New Testament.[34] There is nothing novel in the demand for neighbour love. But what is new and, indeed, revolutionary in the Christian under-standing of neighbour love is the way in which Jesus redefined the concept of 'neighbour'. Traditionally, the neighbour was the one who lived near by, a member of the same social, religious and ethnic group, quite likely a relative. It was, as George Caird puts it, 'a term of limited liability'.[35] Love of neighbour in the traditional sense fell within the bounds of natural love. But in Jesus' teaching, the neighbour is the one whom circumstances have brought near at any given time. He may and very likely will be a stranger, he may be quite an unattractive person, he may be of a different race or country or religion, he may even be an enemy. But his humanity is enough in itself to confer the status of neighbour. Life has thrown two persons together, and their very encounter contains the demand for love.

The *locus classicus* for an understanding of the Christian concept of the neighbour is, of course, the story of the Good Samaritan.[36] It was told in response to a lawyer who asked Jesus, 'Who is my neighbour?' An unfortunate traveller is lying by the side of the road from Jerusalem to Jericho, half dead after having been robbed and beaten up by bandits. Various people come along the road and they cannot help seeing the victim of the robbers' violence. Some of them might have been expected to help, for presumably the injured man belonged to their own community. They were all neighbours in the traditional sense of the word. There was a priest and after him a Levite, both men whose sense of religion might have reinforced a natural tendency to help one of their own people. But these neighbours were too busy or too fearful to stop, and they passed by on the other side. A Samaritan came along, a man of an alien community with whom Jews would normally have no dealings. He was not a neighbour in the traditional sense. But he turned out to be the true neighbour. He tended the sick man's wounds, conveyed him to the security of an inn and arranged for his care until such time as he had recovered. There was no natural tendency that would make the Samaritan act the part of the neighbour. Rather, he would have to overcome a natural aversion to having any dealings with someone of a rival community. But he did so, and thereby opened up a whole new dimension of love. The command, 'Love your neighbour!' had been given an inclusiveness, even a universality, that it had never had before.

We may feel that beautiful though this celebrated story is, it has not much relevance to our world of two thousand years later. The problems today are so much vaster and more complex. Fast communication and instant television have meant that all the peoples of the world have become neighbours, in the sense that life has thrown them closely together. We find not just one person lying by the roadside, for now there are millions of refugees, millions of destitute people, millions living under cruel and oppressive conditions, millions subject to persecution and so on. What has the story of the Good Samaritan to say to that kind of situation? We can understand the complaint of Marxists who say that Christian love is good only for 'ambulance work', that is to say, succouring some of the victims without getting to the roots of what victimizes them. But I think one can offer a reply to this criticism.

Actually, there is a modern sequel to the Good Samaritan story, told by Helmut Thielicke.[37] I shall tell it in a much abridged and modified form. The Good Samaritan was not satisfied with having helped the victim of the robbers. Prompted by the same neighbour love that had made him go to the wounded man's assistance, he now began to wonder about the robbers. Why had they turned to crime, rather than earning a living by an honest occupation? So he went to the mayor of Jericho and asked if he might have facilities for carrying out an investigation into social conditions in the surrounding area. He looked into housing, schooling, employment op-portunities, leisure facilities and so on, with a view to seeing what reforms and improvements were needed so that young people in that area would not be drawn to crime and violence.

I do not think I need to carry the story further. It is, I believe, a legitimate sequel to and updating of the Bible story, and a natural extension of the concept of neighbour love in the conditions of a modern urbanized society. We did see in an earlier chapter that the social life of human beings includes not only interpersonal relations but the vaster network of institutions, social and political structures and so on.[38] This too needs to be humanized, and it would only be by tackling the vast social problems of mankind that men and women today could hope adequately to continue the work of the Good Samaritan in vastly changed conditions. The socio-political implica-tions of the command to neighbour love are present in the original story, though they are not made explicit.

But it is not always easy to see how a virtue known and practised on the relatively small scale of inter-personal life is to be translated on to the large scale of social, political and economic structures, and this difficulty is especially great in the case of love with its associations of closeness and intimacy. Could one perhaps say that peace is the social virtue correspond-ing to love? The biblical tradition provides a concept of peace as well as of love. This was already well developed in the Old Testament, where the word 'peace' (Hebrew, *shalom*) did not mean simply an absence of war or violence but a wholeness that included unity and reconciliation among human beings, unity with the surrounding non-human creation, unity and reconciliation with God. This notion of peace also included justice, for there could be no true wholeness where injustice persisted. Obviously, the building of a true peace demands all sorts of things that take us beyond what we usually understand by 'love'. Among these demands are social and economic planning, the application of knowledge and technology, political action and much else besides. But the will and motivation for all this must come eventually from that universal love or goodwill towards the human race which the New Testament enjoins.

We must notice, however, that although at this point I have been stressing the need to take into account the socio-political structures which form the framework of human life and impinge on it in every area, I am not saying that in the modern world the original story of the Good Samaritan has been superseded or its teaching made obsolete. It would be very naive indeed to suppose that better social structures will in themselves solve the problems of human life – and I would have thought that history has already made this clear to us. Even if a perfect social system were devised (and does anyone really believe that it ever will be?) some people will still get hurt and some people will still go wrong. The kind of situation described by Jesus in his story will keep recurring, for sin is not going to disappear. There is in fact a danger if we get too much carried away by the attraction of political and social remedies for human ills. The danger is that we begin to think mainly in impersonal terms and see the solutions to the problems as exercises in social engineering, forgetting that we are dealing with men and women of flesh and blood and feeling. These men and women certainly need the social structures that will permit and encourage them to realize their human potential, but they also need love to make them whole. Just as the inclusive social virtue of peace is more than the absence of violence, so it is more than a well adjusted and well functioning social order. It is a true union of hearts and minds in mutual respect and goodwill. 'The peace of the celestial city,' wrote Augustine, 'is the perfectly ordered and harmonious enjoyment of God, and of one another in God.'[39]

A point that should not be missed in the story of the Samaritan is the statement that when he saw the wounded man, 'he had compassion'. It is sometimes said that Christian love is not an emotion, for Christian love is something commanded, and it is not possible to command someone to experience an emotion. This is true up to a point. Love is certainly more than an emotion, and we have seen that it includes intellect and will. Let us agree too that there are some emotions, such as personal liking, which cannot be experienced at will. But it would be mistaken to conclude from this that neighbour love is no more than a clinical beneficence. The element of compassion is present in a fully developed neighbour love. While it is true that an emotion cannot be immediately produced by an act of will, it is also true that human emotions can be trained and controlled, so that we habitually experience some and turn away from others. We can learn to be compassionate or we can learn to be cruel.

One further point calls for discussion before we can leave the theme of love and the special contribution that Christianity has made to our understanding of love. Where does the love of God come into the picture? Or should the love of God come into it at all?

The expression 'love of God' is ambiguous. It can mean God's love towards us or our love towards God. The testimony of the religious consciousness is that God's love comes first, and human love for God is a response to his love. 'We love, because he first loved us.'[40] It is the same New Testament writer who declares, 'God is love.'[41] Here the very nature of God is defined in terms of love. If love is, as we have claimed, letting-be, then one might say that the belief that God is love follows from the belief that he is the creator whose word, 'Let there be . . .' stands at the beginning of the Bible. But the New Testament belief in God's love towards his creatures is based specifically on the conviction that his nature is revealed in the life and teaching of Jesus Christ, and so the love which is ascribed to God as his nature is the love which came to expression in Christ.

We must remember that the idea of a loving God is by no means universal in the history of religion. On the contrary, it was something of a revolution in the understanding of God. Most of the gods that human beings have worshipped have been gods of power, heavenly rulers who were proud, distant and sometimes downright cruel. If one takes seriously the Christian claim that it is in Jesus Christ that God is revealed, then God is to be understood in terms of the cross rather than of a heavenly throne. Christianity, though indeed it has often fallen away from its vision, introduced a non-oppressive concept of God, whose transcendence does not conflict with human transcendence but rather elicits it.[42]

This point helps us to see where the love of God (in both senses of that expression) fits into the pattern, and provides an answer to a common objection that protests against bringing the love of God into consideration at all. The first and great commandment, both according to Jesus and according to the Old Testament, is: 'You shall love the Lord your God with all your heart and with all your soul and with all your mind and with all your strength.'[43] This commandment takes precedence even over the commandment to love one's neighbour. What justification can there be for this?

Some critics have claimed that there is set up a rivalry between love of God and love of mankind, and that by teaching people to love God, Christianity and Judaism have diverted them from the more urgent and needful task of loving their neighbours. It cannot be denied that sometimes this complaint has been justified. Religion is easily perverted, and it is possible to become so absorbed in and preoccupied with God that this world and its needs almost drops out of view. Religion could even be made an excuse for ignoring the neighbour. What about the priest, for instance, hurrying down to Jericho and passing by on the other side from the wounded man? Was he intent on performing some religious duty, so that he was too busy serving God to have time for the neighbour? What an irony! But if God is more truly imaged in the suffering Christ than in the celestial monarch who demands the homage of his creatures, there can be no rivalry between the two loves. This is explicitly taught in the New Testament. On the one hand, we find a blunt warning that any alleged love of God that contradicts neighbour love is a sham and a falsehood: 'If anyone says, "I love God," and hates his brother, he is a liar; for he who does not love his brother whom he has seen, cannot love God whom he has not seen.'[44] On the other hand, the service which faith demands in the name of its King is precisely service to the neighbour in need: 'Truly, I say to you, as you did it to one of the least of these my brethren, you did it to me.'[45]

But this does not mean that love for God is absorbed into love of the neighbour. Since God's love for his creatures comes first and is the foundation and inspiration for all other love, then this is the paradigm of love and the revelation of what love really is. Meditation on this purest and highest of all loves will not divert men and women from love of the neighbour, but will inspire it. Kierkegaard wrote: 'The love relationship is a triangular relationship of the lover, the beloved, love – but love is God. Therefore, to love another person means to help him love God, and to be loved means to be helped.'[46] So there will be times when human beings will look directly into the sun, as it were, and offer their love to God, believing that this is the best way in which their finite human loves can be strengthened and purified.

XV

ART

The last few chapters have been rather heavily ethical in tone. From alienation, we have traced a path through conscience to commitment, and on to specific forms of commitment, namely, belief and love. Are we representing human life as altogether too grim and earnest an affair? Well, perhaps not, for the way of transcendence is a steep upward path. Yet there would be something drastically lacking in the humanity of anyone who could not sometimes laugh and play, dance and sing. I did in fact promise at an earlier stage[1] that this other aspect of human nature would not be omitted from our view, and the time has come to make good this promise.

The Western mind seems to have a tendency towards an almost deadly seriousness. When we do anything, we feel that we have to justify whatever we are doing in terms of some goal at which we are aiming. When we observe things happening in the world around, we feel that there must be some reason for them and that they must be fulfilling some function in the economy of nature. No doubt such attitudes have contributed to the development of both morals and science in the West, but it has to be asked whether such moral and intellectual growth has been purchased at the cost of impoverishing the spontaneous affective side of life. Everything, both within and without, is reduced to order. Yet in that very process it all becomes less immediate, more abstract, less lively. As a medieval mystic once said, 'A rose needs no why.'

With this Western view may be contrasted the vivid sense of play in Indian thought. One does not have to give a reason for this or that event – it is simply *lila*, the divine sport.[2] Klaus Klostermaier tells a little story which well illustrates this concept of *lila*. He and an Indian companion came upon a man shouting abuse at a group of monkeys in the boughs of a tree overhanging the road. One of the monkeys had reached down and grabbed the turban from his head and now the troop was having great fun with the long strip of cloth. Klostermaier's Indian companion remarked: 'God has a very good sense of humour. Jestingly, he wants to rid us of all that is superfluous. Everything is his play, his *lila*. If only people could see that he is in everything, that everything proceeds from him, sickness and health, life and death, the turban and the monkey – would they still grieve or get agitated?'[3] The Westerner would very likely get grieved and agitated, and would seek refuge in some complicated and finally unconvincing theodicy. I do not say that the Eastern alternative of designating the events as divine play for which no reason need be given is satisfactory. People grieve and get agitated in the East too, and there are limits to play and humour. But this alternative view is, at the very least, a needed corrective to Western seriousness.

I am particularly sensitive to this Indian corrective because, having grown up in Scotland, I was early exposed to a very serious view of life. Even before the gloomy shadow of John Calvin fell over Scotland, the harshness of the climate and the bleakness of the terrain had prepared the ground for the Protestant work ethic and for a God who was far from playful. Industry and thrift were the great virtues. We all learned the lines

> How doth the little busy bee
> Improve each shining hour,
> And gather honey all the day
> From every opening flower.

The author was Isaac Watts, an English nonconformist minister who in 1720 published *Divine and Moral Songs for Children*.

I have never lost my respect for the busy little bee, but in course of time I have come to prefer butterflies. Compared with their hymenopteral relatives, butterflies are idle creatures, and no moral lessons can be drawn from them. The very names that we give to them must be abhorrent to the puritan, for they speak of worldly pomp and vanity – Peacock, Adonis Blue, Painted Lady, Camberwell Beauty, to mention a few. Butterflies do not produce anything of commercial value. But they are beautiful, and that is more than enough. (Also, they do not sting.) They do not need any justification beyond themselves, for 'the beautiful is that which has its teleology in itself'.[4] Of course, one can offer 'explanations' of the structure, coloration and behaviour of butterflies in terms of biological utility, and these explanations may be correct, as far as they go. But they are abstractions which miss the totality of the phenomenon that we call a butterfly. Such abstract explanations have their own validity, but when we attempt to give to them an exclusive or even privileged role, we achieve only what Whitehead called the 'bifurcation' of the universe.[5] This is itself a consequence of that questionable theory of knowledge stemming from Descartes,

Locke and company, which we have earlier criticized and which, among other things, made a sharp distinction between primary qualities which were alone supposed really to belong to an object and secondary qualities which were supposed to be 'in the mind' of the subject. But if we break out of that dualism and accept the concreteness and totality of experience, we can understand Whitehead's contention that the poet has as much to tell us about nature as the scientist.[6] The being or reality of a butterfly is to be learned as much from the poet as from the entomologist. Prosaic explanations touch only some aspects of the butterfly, and leave untouched the understanding that this creature is part of the play of the cosmos in its superabundant energy, that it adds to the grace and beauty of the whole and needs no justification or explanation beyond the fact that it exists.

Play is the superfluity of life, the overplus of energy that does not need to be directed to utilitarian ends. The human being needs leisure and relaxation as well as work, and perhaps he is as much himself in his play as in his work. It is true that play develops skills and builds friendships and social relationships, but these side effects, however valuable, do not belong to the essence of play. The essence lies in the spontaneity and joy of engaging in activity which one does not take too seriously. Perhaps it lies also in the sense of belonging again to nature, to physical reality, even if only temporarily. I am always somewhat suspicious of so-called 'educational' games or toys. All play is educational, but I have suggested that this is not of the essence, and if it is stressed too much, then the truly playful character of play is lost. Play has its point in itself, and the player does not need to give a reason for what he is doing. When we begin to look anxiously for a justification for play, then we have forgotten what it means to play.

Closely allied to play is humour. A human being can laugh and see the funny side of things. There are many tensions in human life that can be resolved by humour. Anyone who has served in the armed forces knows how again and again in some difficult situation a spontaneous witticism has made that situation tolerable for a time at least by switching attention from all its anxiety-producing features to whatever was funny and bizarre in it – and something funny and bizarre can usually be found.

I have been urging the case for play and humour and I think these are necessary ingredients in a truly human nature. I suspect that the most inhuman persons in history, the great tyrants and fanatics, have been people with no sense of humour or with a badly perverted sense of humour. But one also has to say that there are limits to the concepts of play and humour. When one is considering the case of a dignified citizen whose turban has been taken from him by some monkeys, then one may talk about the cosmic play of Krishna; but such talk would be very empty if the case were that of a mother whose child has been mauled and killed by a tiger. Again, a soldier's humour can sustain and encourage his companions in a tight corner; but when one of these companions is killed, humour is out of place and something deeper is required. Play is certainly needed alongside work, humour alongside seriousness, but these are not coordinates. The priority belongs to work and seriousness. Play is the foil for work, humour for seriousness.

We have more than once taken note of Marx's point that in work a person affirms himself (or ought to be able to affirm himself). No doubt he also affirms himself in leisure and play, but can he affirm himself to the same extent or in the same way as he does in work? I have already raised this question in connection with alienation and especially the problem of unemployment.[7] If, as some tell us (though they may be wrong), more and more people will be unemployed because of increasing automation and computerization, will they be able to affirm themselves in leisure, or is Marx's doctrine that affirmation takes place in work a permanent feature of human nature? I expressed doubt as to whether even our malleable human nature could dispense with the need for constructive work, and now I think this doubt has been reinforced by our consideration of play. If the human being is in process of transcendence, then satisfying work which looks beyond itself to its product would seem to be an important element in transcendence. Play, on the other hand, so far as it remains pure play and is not being exploited for some other purpose, has its end in itself. In play, time stands still and the drive to the future slows down. This is a very good thing, in the context of the seriousness of life. But could we endure play or leisure for all or most of the time? Would it not result in intolerable boredom and an end to human transcendence? Already there is far more leisure than there used to be, but the results are curious. Though himself an advocate of the virtues of play, Robert Neale describes the current situation in America thus: 'Both executives and labourers make far more money than they need to survive comfortably. Why do these executives work such long hours, take so few vacations, and mix much of their leisure with work? Why do the labourers seek overtime and engage in moonlighting? Why do holidays, Sundays and vacations fill people with such nervousness? Why do we turn leisure into labour by repairing our properties and taking gruelling automobile trips? Why do we cut short our free time in order to get back on the job early? Why does the psychiatric profession talk of "Sunday neurosis" and "vacationitis"? And why, as has been frequently observed, does unemployment lead to suicide and antisocial behaviour?'[8] Well, it may be just that we need to educate ourselves to the age of leisure. But it could also be that the human being needs a *task*.

At this point I would like to turn attention to a famous book of Kierkegaard who, I think, has some very illuminating things to say about the problems we are now considering. I mean the lengthy two-volume work *Either/Or*. The first volume presents the 'either', the second the 'or', and initially at least these are intended to exclude each other as two different ways of life between which one must make a choice. These two ways are the aesthetical and the ethical. This is one of Kierkegaard's pseudonymous writings, in which he speaks through two imaginary characters, a young man (unnamed) who expounds the aesthetical view in the *Either*, and the respectable Judge William who champions the ethical in the *Or*. 'What I have so often said to you, I say now once again, or rather I shout it: "Either . . . or, *aut* . . . *aut*," ' storms the judge.[9] But since Kierkegaard has some sympathy with both protagonists and since they presumably represent a conflict in himself, the disjunction between the two ways may not be so absolute as it is sometimes made to appear. Indeed, the loquacious Judge William gets around to talking about 'the equilibrium between the aesthetical and the ethical in the composition of personality', and claims that whatever is valuable in the aesthetical is assumed into the ethical. Obviously our own thoughts on play and humour in relation to work and seriousness were moving in a roughly similar direction, and that is why it has seemed worthwhile to pursue the question further in the light of Kierkegaard's reflections.

First of all, we have to be clear about what Kierkegaard understands by the 'aesthetical'. The reference is not only or even primarily to art, though possibly art is the culmination and highest form of the aesthetical mode of life. But the word 'aesthetical' is used by Kierkegaard in a much broader sense. The aesthetical way of life is that side of human existence which consists in feeling and immediacy. It includes the sensuous, the physical, the emotional, the romantic, and when it is seen as a type of existence in contrast to the ethical, it is also seen as eschewing seriousness and responsibility. In an extreme form, it could be described as play brought to a highly sophisticated level. The representative figure of the aesthetical life is, for Kierkegaard, Don Juan, especially as he is depicted in Mozart's opera. Don Juan is what nowadays would be called the 'playboy'. He sees no ultimate sense in life, so he lives episodically for the immediacy of each instant. 'Don Juan enjoys the satisfaction of a desire; as soon as he has enjoyed it, he seeks a new object, and so on endlessly . . . His life is the sum of moments which have no coherence.'[10] This life that lacks unity sounds rather like the life of drift which we have contrasted with the life of commitment and the way of transcendence. Yet it has its own attractiveness, especially if there is no ultimate meaning to life and if the alternatives are stated in a heavily moralistic way. The champion of the aesthetical writes: 'Under the heaven of the aesthetic, everything is light, beautiful, transitory; when the ethical comes along, everything becomes harsh, angular, infinitely boring.'[11] The butterfly and the bee?

It is curious that the anonymous spokesman for the aesthetical should complain that the ethical way is boring, for the main objection to the aesthetical way itself is finally that it runs out in boredom. The thrill of the immediate and the novel eventually wears off and life becomes intolerably tiresome. The point is illustrated with respect to love and marriage. Don Juan is the great practitioner of erotic romantic love, and it all seems so lively and exciting compared with the supposed dullness and monotony of married love. But it was surely a masterly exercise of Kierkegaard's gift for irony that led him to make the fifty-page chapter on 'The First Love' so utterly tedious that the reader has difficulty staying awake as he tries to get through it. Judge William sets the claim of marriage over against that of romantic love, but in such a way that he sees romantic love as brought to its full bloom in the context of marriage. He claims that marriage 'is the downright seriousness of love, and yet it is not cold, uncomely, unerotic, unpoetic . . . All the beauty inherent in the pagan erotic has validity also in Christianity, in so far as it can be combined with marriage.'[12] The reason that he gives for this judgment is surely correct – that love, including sexual love, needs time for its unfolding and maturing, and it is marriage that gives this time.

Either/Or, as I have said, is primarily a contrast between two ways of life, and the contrast is real enough, for the first way is determined by the immediate feeling of each moment or episode, the second demands choice in the light of conscience, commitment, intellect and will. Yet, as Judge William's words about marriage make clear, the aesthetical is not rejected (it could not be in a truly human existence!) but is given a fresh vitality within the context of the ethical.

Let us now return to the problem raised by the question of the place of play in human life. We agreed on the one hand that play is indispensable and that life would be much impoverished without it. But if there were only play, then, like the aesthetical, it would run out in boredom. Play cannot exist on its own, but only in relation to work, seriousness and transcendence. When play is integrated with these deeper aspects of human nature, it is transformed into art. Play and humour, we have seen, have their limits. There comes a point when they no longer respond to human situations that call for something deeper. But they do not just disappear. They merge with seriousness and intellect to acquire a new depth, and are transfigured into art which is perhaps excelled only by religion in its capacity for opening up the ultimate areas of human experience.

In its simplest forms, art is scarcely distinguishable from play. It too springs from a surplus of creative energy that goes beyond what is merely utilitarian. When the maker of some utensil spends just a little extra energy upon it in making its shape more pleasing or in decorating it, this is art. Like play, it is characterized by spontaneity and carefreeness. It is not directed to any utilitarian end but has its teleology in itself. Of course, it is a very long way from the simple beginnings to the Gothic cathedral or the Mozart opera or the Flaubert novel, and all kinds of new factors have entered in along the way, so that to try to define 'art' or to seek a comprehensive concept has become, I suspect, impossible. Yet the lines of continuity are traceable back to the beginnings.

The concept of 'art' would seem to be an excellent example of that class of concepts of which Wittgenstein said that they stand not for a common essence everywhere present but for a vaguer, more elusive set of relations which he called, rather happily, 'family resemblances'. As we go from one member of the group to another, some correspondences are found, some common features drop out, some new ones emerge. 'The result of this examination is: we see a complicated network of similarities, overlapping and crisscrossing; sometimes overall similarities, sometimes similarities of detail.'[13] In the last paragraph, I have mentioned three art forms that are very different – architecture, opera, the novel. One could go on to mention music, painting, sculpture, poetry, drama, all of which can be subdivided into many branches. Then there are calligraphy, flower arrangement, ballet, landscape gardening . . . the list could go on indefinitely, but they would all be reckoned as arts. Are there even 'family resemblances' that would allow one to bring together under the single concept of 'art' such a diversity of productions and activities?

Emil Brunner says of art that 'this daring comprehensive concept, which combines the arts of the eye with those of the ear, has the great merit of leading our attention to something common in them all, the element of creativity, which is detached from all usefulness and intent merely upon creating beautiful work for the enjoyment of its beauty.'[14] This remark has the merit of linking art with play and beauty, and we are already familiar with the idea that these things need no justification outside of themselves – they have their teleology in themselves, to recall the phrase used earlier. Yet even what Brunner claims as common to all art may be questioned. We have seen that although in its beginnings art is indistinguishable from play, it eventually goes beyond play in partaking of seriousness. Some art does relate to an end beyond itself, without ceasing to be art. The novels of Charles Dickens, for instance, are a critique of some features of Victorian society. They have a 'message', but this does not destroy their character as art – that would only happen when art is made into a vehicle of propaganda and the product has no value in itself. Again, it might seem that Brunner's words, 'creating beautiful work', apply to every artist. But is *King Lear* beautiful? Or the demonic fantasies of Hieronymus Bosch? Or Picasso's *Guernica* (which conveys a 'message' as well)? These are all indisputably great works of art, but if they have beauty, it is a very different kind of beauty from that of the butterfly. It is what Yeats called a 'terrible beauty' and belongs to tragedy.

Leaving aside the question whether we ought to use the term 'beauty' in such cases as those I have mentioned, could we say that the work of the artist is to enable us to perceive with a new depth and intensity the reality of that which he is representing in his art work? (Perhaps this would hold also in the case of non-representative art – the abstract painting, for instance, yields a new experience of the reality of colour and form.) That which has hitherto been hidden from us – and in our casual everyday dealings with things and people, their reality is for the most part hidden from us – is brought into the open by the artist so that we fully see it for the first time. In his essay, 'The Origin of the Work of Art', Heidegger sets forth some such understanding. He considers a Greek temple. First, the marble has to be brought out of the earth, where it has lain hidden for millions of years. Yet it is still hidden until the artist works on it, shapes it, polishes it, sculpts it, builds it up into the structure of the temple. In this process, which Heidegger calls 'setting forth the earth and setting up a world', we see the reality of the marble in all its hitherto hidden possibilities. 'Rock first becomes rock.' The temple sets up a world in which many other things are seen in their reality for the first time:

> Standing there, the building rests on the rocky ground. This resting of the work draws up out of the rock the obscurity of that rock's bulky yet spontaneous support. Standing there, the building holds its ground against the storm raging above it, and so first makes the storm itself manifest in its violence. The lustre and gleam of the stone, although itself apparently glowing only by the grace of the sun, yet first brings to radiance the light of the day, the breadth of the sky, the darkness of the night. The temple's firm towering makes visible the invisible space of air. The steadfastness of the work contrasts with the surge of the surf, and its own repose brings out the raging of the sea.

And the temple reveals the human reality as well. It gathers round itself 'the unity of those paths and relations in which birth and death, disaster and blessing, victory and disgrace, endurance and decline acquire the shape of destiny for human being'. And, of course, as temple, it also 'encloses the figure of the god' and declares itself a 'holy precinct'.[15]

It would not be difficult to apply what Heidegger says about the temple to some human reality. Consider the Trojan War. I suspect that if one had been around to see it or if some factually minded historian had left an account of it, it would not have been a very impressive affair, just another episode in the everlasting strife of petty kings and tribal chieftains in that distant age. But Homer (whether he was one person or many) has, to adapt Heidegger's language about the temple, 'set forth humanity and set up a world', that is to say, he has penetrated to the deepest human realities that are hidden in any situation, bringing out the heroism and the nobility, the meanness and the jealousy, so that out of a sordid and undistinguished conflict he has set forth a panorama of human nature that still holds its place as a superb artwork. Someone once said that Homer was fortunate to have the Trojan War as a subject about which to write an epic. This is surely quite mistaken. The participants in the Trojan War were fortunate and we are fortunate that a supreme artistic genius was at hand to turn their campaign into an immortal exposition of the human reality.

We now begin to understand why Whitehead emphasized, alongside the scientist's interpretation of reality, that of the poet and of the artist generally. The architect and the sculptor have as much to show us about marble as have the geologist and the chemist. The poet exposes the human essence of the Trojan War better than the exact historian. All see the same phenomena, but they see them in different ways, arising from different questions, different interests, different presuppositions. No one of these ways can usurp the claims of any other or demand an exclusively privileged viewpoint. The work of the artist is something like revelation. What is revealed has been there all the time, but it has gone unnoticed in our humdrum everyday experience. It needs the sensitivity of the artist to bring it into the light, so that we notice things for the first time. The word 'revelation' is appropriate in another sense. Often the great artist will tell us that his poem or musical composition or whatever it may be has 'come to him' in a flash of inspiration, though of course this does not in the least minimize the labour and technical skill that he needs in order to embody his inspiration in the particular medium of his art.

It may be useful now to pass quickly in review some of the major art-forms. We shall see how they cohere with the view of human nature that has been developed in this book, and how they have an indispensable part to play in the process of human transcendence.

Let us begin with those arts which use words. Among these a special place belongs to poetry as one of the oldest and most fundamental of all forms of art. Poetry may have begun as word play, as sheer delight in the sound, rhythms and texture of language. But, as art, it develops seriousness and becomes a major way of pushing back the frontiers of both language and thought, and so it becomes a factor in human transcendence. We have seen the importance of language as a distinctive property of the human being, and that thought and action alike are structured by language; but we have seen reason to believe also that there is 'tacit' knowledge, a penumbra that extends beyond language, as if thought were leaping ahead of the language available at any given time for its expression.[16] The figurative use of language in poetry, mythology and other imaginative types of discourse continually extends the area of the expressible, though every extension also makes us aware of the unexpressed beyond it. Shakespeare described this function of the poet beautifully and exactly:

The poet's eye, in a fine frenzy rolling.
Doth glance from heaven to earth, from earth to heaven;
And, as imagination bodies forth
The forms of things unknown, the poet's pen
Turns them to shapes, and gives to airy nothing
A local habitation and a name.[17]

Let us turn from language to music. Both language and music are addressed to the ear, and the simplest form of music, the song, combines the words of a poem with a melody. The music obviously adds a new dimension to the poem – not merely intensifying the emotion of the poem, but expressing something of its mood and insights. At a more sophisticated level, the many settings of the Mass add a solemnity and mystery to the words and gestures which greatly enhance the total meaning. But in its purest forms music leaves words behind. Sometimes such music can be purely sensuous, and many of Debussy's works are an outstanding example of this kind of music. Here a purely sensuous experience, for instance, breathing the perfumes of the night (in the *Iberia* suite), is set forth with a delicacy and sensitivity that even the poet could hardly match in words. But there is another type of music which lies on the further side of discursive thought and has sometimes been called 'metaphysical'. The adjective has been applied to the late string quartets of Beethoven, meditations which employ not words but music. Someone remarked that music is thinking without concepts. This may be a difficult notion to grasp, but it suggests a tacit knowledge in which one has come to the boundaries of language and knowledge, but the music suggests what lies beyond. An example would be Richard Strauss's *Thus Spake Zarathustra*. Admittedly, there is here a reference to a programme, the philosophical text of Nietzsche, but when Strauss ends his composition in two keys simultaneously (a stretching or even violation of the musical idiom comparable to the poet's stretching of language), he expresses in a musical way the final ambiguity or enigmatic character of the universe, and perhaps no philosophical prose (not even the prose-poetry of Nietzsche) could express the meaning of this idea so well. Strauss gives it the force of a revelation.

Finally we turn to the visual arts. As in the case of music, the visual arts may remain on the level of the sensuous, delighting in the beauties of colour and form, light and shade, spaces and textures; or they may be on the level of what we can only call the 'metaphysical', setting forth spiritual truths that escape linguistic expression. A single artist provides us with examples of both. Velazquez in his painting *Venus at her Mirror* offers a straightforward celebration of female beauty. His *Immaculate Conception* is very different. Here he manages to convey something of the mysteries of election and incarnation, of deity, humanity and femininity. Velazquez conveys far more of the essential meaning of Immaculate Conception in his painting than does the clumsy terminology of the dogma of 1854, and anyone in search of the meaning of Immaculate Conception would do much better to begin with the painting rather than with the dogmatic formulation.

Examples could be multiplied. To step outside the European and Christian tradition, the present writer would testify how impressive he found the great Buddha of Kamakura. Just to look for a long time on this statue conveys as much of the essence of Buddhism – peace, serenity, compassion, non-attachment – as one would learn from a score of books. The philosopher Karl Jaspers has written eloquently about another great Buddhist art-work, the Boro Budur, and directly relates it to the experience of transcendence, though the term here has the special nuances which belong to it in Jaspers.[18] The Boro Budur is a very complex kind of art-work, depending for its effect on architecture, sculpture, symbolism and, not least, the actual movement of the pilgrim through the spaces which it comprises. In Jaspers' words: 'Ascending higher, up archways and stairs, the pilgrim passes statues of Buddha in meaningful poses. At the top, all images cease. Cupolas and geometrical forms remain until the last cupola points at the empty sky, with which the wayfarer is left alone.' He interprets the progression as follows: 'Buddha himself must vanish as a cipher. On the lower walls, he was in plain sight, in niches; in the latticed cupolas, he began to withdraw; in the massive central cupola, he is invisible.'[19] The various symbols, indeed, the whole complex art-work, are, in Jaspers' terminology, 'ciphers', which point the pilgrim onward to the goal of his journey, the ineffable transcendence. He explicitly compares this Buddhist pilgrimage to the mysticism of John Eckhart, who moves from the concretely conceived *Deus* to ineffable *Deitas*.

Several of the examples of art-works mentioned above draw attention to the close relation of art to religion. Historically, the two have always been intimately connected, and we can see that one reason for this relation is that both art and religion are modes of transcendence. Both aim at opening the way to the deepest reality. For the artist, this is the sublime. According to Kant, ' "Sublime" is the name given to that which is absolutely great, what is beyond all comparison great. It is a greatness comparable to itself alone . . . That is sublime, in comparison with which all else is small.'[20] This definition of the sublime can hardly fail to remind us of Anselm's definition of God: 'Something than which no greater can be thought.'[21] Nowadays in a secularized world art has become for some people a substitute for religion, and one can understand this so far as art offers a revelation of the sublime and the emotional satisfaction that goes with it. But art cannot finally be a substitute for religion. Art and religion are

complementary aspects of human transcendence, and this will become
clearer through a study of religion.

XVI

RELIGION

We come now to religion and its place in human life. For millennia, that place was of supreme importance, and religion dominated and coloured all other interests. Even today, religion remains important, but in modern times the phenomenon of the religionless man has appeared and undeniably religion and religious observance have declined in many parts of the world. Is the decline of religion a process that will continue with the spread of education and science and the secularization that they seem to bring inevitably in their train? If that occurs, then it will appear that religion does not belong to the essence of the human, but has only been a phase characterizing what will come to be seen as the childhood of the race. Yet there are many considerations that point in a different direction. It has often been the case in history that just when a religion seemed to have exhausted itself and to be on the verge of expiring, it revived and launched out on a new and more vigorous chapter in its history. Even among those who explicitly renounce religion, there seems to be a need to find some substitute for it – I have already mentioned art as a substitute for religion, but unfortunately there are much more dangerous substitutes, in the forms of mass ideologies and perverted cults. It may well be the case that even if particular forms of religion grow old in course of time and are no longer able to hold their place, the religious spirit itself endures and seeks new forms, because it has deep roots in our human nature. I shall indeed try to show in this chapter that the dynamic view of man expounded in the earlier chapters of the book readily makes room for religion.

To try to expound religion and perhaps also to justify it in terms of the constitution of human nature itself is a peculiarly modern, that is to say, post-Enlightenment approach to the problem. In older times, religion had needed no other justification than the tradition, perhaps enshrined in sacred scriptures, which accounted for its origin and continuing authority by relating some story of a primordial theophany or revelation of some sort. When the traditional account was called in question, the defenders of religion enlisted the aid of reason and constructed a natural theology which was supposed to provide backing for the traditional beliefs by demonstrating the existence of God. The Enlightenment, however, called in question both revealed and natural theology. The challenge was first of all to revealed theology, for it was demanded that beliefs resting on authority and tradition, however venerable, must be justified at the bar of reason. The religious believer might then fall back on the arguments of natural theology, but the challenge was soon extended to natural theology also. The various arguments for God's existence were criticized and found to be defective. Admittedly, no one had disproved God's existence, and the various arguments have continued to be restated to meet the criticisms. But even so, as we have noted in an earlier discussion,[1] they have lost the demonstrative force that was once claimed for them. It was at this point that the philosophy of religion turned to the phenomenology of the human person in search of the foundations of religion. Perhaps this new approach could be called 'empirical' and conformed to the new emphasis on experience. But it would be 'empirical' in the broad sense of the term since there is an acknowledgment of religious experience alongside sense experience and all the other forms of experience, and we are not dealing with empiricism in that narrower sense of a specific epistemology, which we have seen reason to criticize at various points and which could not yield an adequate philosophy of religion. But, to some extent, the post-Enlightenment approach to religion is concerned not so much with the content of 'religious experience' as with the conditions of human experience and what these imply for religion. I doubt, for instance, if there is an experience of finitude, but there are many human experiences which bring home to us the understanding of our finitude. Again, there could not be an 'experience' of death, for as Wittgenstein remarks, 'Death is not an event of life, death is not lived through,'[2] where the German word translated 'lived through' is *erlebt*, which could equally well be translated 'experienced'. We do not experience death in ourselves, but we live in the awareness of it, and so in the awareness of finitude.

The modern or post-Enlightenment approach to religion from the human side had its first great advocate in Friedrich Schleiermacher, the father of liberal Protestant theology and, it would seem, of some more recent developments in Catholic theology. Schleiermacher was satisfied with neither the authoritarian orthodoxy nor the rationalist natural theology. Thus, in his famous *Speeches on Religion to its Cultured Despisers* (published in 1799) he denied that religion is either a matter of belief, as the upholders of the traditional orthodox theology claimed, or a matter of the will, as had been claimed by rationalists such as Kant, who made religion simply the handmaid of morality. Schleiermacher held on the contrary that religion is constituted by feeling. It is important to note, however, that by feeling he did not mean a merely subjective emotion, and he did not intend to deprive religion of any cognitive content. As he used the word 'feeling', it denotes a mode of self-awareness which conveys a definite understanding or intuition of the human condition before God. It is not some subjective *frisson* but – as we have seen in the case of emotions in general[3] – the awareness of a situation through participation in it.

But what is immediately clear is that for Schleiermacher the meaning of religion is to be sought not in the traditions or scriptures of the believing community or in the speculations of reason but in the deep inner consciousness of the religious person. To quote his own words: 'You must transport yourself into the interior of a pious soul and seek to understand its inspiration.'[4] What you find in such a 'pious soul' is a 'sense and taste for the infinite' and this is how Schleiermacher defines 'true religion'.[5] Such a 'sense and taste for the infinite' is obviously close to what we have been calling 'transcendence', the inner drive of the human being towards fuller being. The length to which Schleiermacher goes in interiorizing religion is shown by his assertion that religious doctrines are 'a knowledge about feeling, and in no way an immediate knowledge about the operations of the universe that give rise to the feelings'.[6] On the other hand, it must be noted that Schleiermacher never rests his appeal on the feelings of the individual, but has in view a corporate experience. Solitary religion is, in his view, a 'morbid aberration' from the fellowship of the community.[7]

These ideas from his early work are more fully developed in his systematic theology of more than twenty years later. It is in this work that we meet the famous expression, 'the feeling of absolute dependence', which is now claimed to be at the heart of religious faith.[8] (The difference between this formulation and the earlier one, 'sense and taste for the infinite', will be considered later.) As in the earlier work, doctrinal propositions are held to be transcriptions, as it were, into words of religious states of mind. But it now becomes apparent that Schleiermacher is anxious not to give the impression of making religion an entirely subjective affair, and he claims that the feeling of absolute dependence is at the same time 'a co-existence of God in the self-consciousness'.[9] As was already clear in his early work, Schleiermacher is thinking more of corporate than of individual experience. He believes in fact that the feeling of absolute dependence is universal in human experience, and this leads him to claim that once we have recognized this feeling and its universality, then 'it takes the place of the theistic proofs'.[10]

That was a large claim to make, and is indicative of the revolution that Schleiermacher had introduced into thinking about religion. There can be no doubt that his appeal to human experience infused new life into religion and theology and gave to them a relevance and vitality that had been draining away during the Enlightenment, when religion was visualized as either a dry system of doctrines based on ancient and questionable authorities, or a still drier web of speculation based on the abstract and possibly over-ambitious operations of reason. Admittedly, one had still to find out the price to be paid for the new relevance, for in spite of Schleiermacher's own intentions, it might turn out that the appeal to feeling and inner experience would mean the complete subjectivizing of religion. Invulnerability would have been purchased at the price of surrendering the claim to be making any assertions about any transhuman reality.

Schleiermacher exercised a great influence on Protestant theology through much of the nineteenth century, and his influence has revived in more recent times. As noted above, there are now many Catholic theologians who, whether or not they have been directly influenced by Schleiermacher, have come to share his way of going about religious and theological questions. It would be impossible to trace the many ramifications of Schleiermacher's influence, but there is one admirer of his work who must be singled out, because his phenomenology of religious experience carried further the line of thought initiated by Schleiermacher, and has come to be very influential in its own right.

I mean Rudolf Otto, and especially his analysis of the idea of the holy. Writing roughly one hundred years after Schleiermacher, Otto credited him with the rediscovery of the essence of religion, which cannot be reduced either to a set of beliefs or to moral conduct, but is the 'experience of this world in its profundity, the realization of its eternal content by the feeling of a contemplative and devout mind'.[11] Otto was influenced too by the rise of a science which was new since Schleiermacher's time – anthropology and especially its investigations into primitive religion. He was particularly impressed by the work of R. R. Marett, who, in his book *The Threshold of Religion*, first published in 1909, claimed that before there emerged anything so definite as a belief in spirits or the beginnings of an ethic, religion consisted in a feeling of awe which might be called forth in many different situations. Otto's own major contribution is a detailed description of the human experience of the holy, and this is taken to be the essence of religion, whatever additional characteristics it might come to have.

We have come nowadays to think of the holy largely in moral terms. Biblical religion and the higher religions in general have all given ethical content to the idea of the holy, and the type of religion fostered by the Enlightenment, as we find it for instance in Kant's *Religion within the Limits of Reason Alone*, virtually absorbed the holy into the ethical. But Otto's contention is that its deeper and more primordial meaning is non-rational and non-moral. It is this deeper level which he designates the 'numinous' and which is held to be the distinctively religious element in the experience.

The most valuable part of Otto's work is his careful phenomenological analysis of the numinous experience. On the one side are the states of mind evoked in this experience; but on the other side is the numinous reality known in the experience, and it is important to remember this, for Otto certainly does not think of the experience as some free-floating sensation in the mind, but as a way of relating to the holy reality beyond the human subject. There is obviously a close parallel here to Schleiermacher's claim that the feeling of absolute dependence is also a co-existence of God in the self-consciousness.

As is well known, Otto's analysis is summarized in the expression *mysterium tremendum et fascinans*, and we shall take a closer look at these terms.

We begin with *mysterium*, though Otto himself considers it in second place.[12] He emphasizes the otherness of the mysterious: 'That which is mysterious is the "wholly other", that which is quite beyond the sphere of the usual, the intelligible and the familiar, which falls therefore quite outside the limits of the "canny", and is contrasted with it, filling the mind with blank wonder and astonishment.' Otto seems here to be suggesting that in this kind of experience the person who has it transcends the limits of what can be ordinarily known and perceived to encounter a reality different from entities within the world and therefore itself transcendent. I think I would want to add to Otto's account of mystery a mention of its inexhaustibility. If a mystery were *wholly* other, then perhaps one could not relate to it at all. Certainly, there is a strong element of otherliness in mystery, so that it contrasts with the familiar and the manipulable. But it is not wholly unintelligible. Rather, we strike on a depth and inexhaustibility, so that however much we describe and explore, there is more beyond which always extends beyond the reach of our understanding. This point will be seen to be significant when we ask later about psychological and sociological analyses of religious experience. Religion will bring before us again that mysterious character of all human life, a mystery which we first encountered in our reflections on freedom.[13] A true mystery is an abyss which no empirical science can ever fully explore.

We pass to the next element in Otto's trio of terms, the *tremendum*. It is with this that Otto himself begins, and some of his critics have claimed that he has made too much of it, so that he is in some danger of representing the sense of the holy as little more than fear in the face of an overwhelming but unknown reality. But this criticism has certainly been much exaggerated. It is awe rather than fear that is evoked by the *tremendum*. Otto uses the expression 'creature-feeling' for the self-awareness of the finite in the presence of numinous being.[14] Clearly, this expression is related to Schleiermacher's 'feeling of absolute dependence', though Otto is in fact rather critical of the earlier theologian's formulation. Examples of what he has in mind when he talks of 'creature-feeling' are provided by Abraham's sense of himself as 'but dust and ashes' before God,[15] Isaiah's confession when he is confronted with the vision of God in the temple that he is 'a man of unclean lips',[16] and even Christ's agony in the garden of Gethsemane.[17] On this last passage, Otto comments: 'What is the cause of this sore amazement and heaviness, this soul shaken to its depths, exceeding sorrowful even unto death, and this sweat that falls to the ground like great drops of blood? Can it be ordinary fear of death in one who had had death before his eyes for weeks past and who had just celebrated with clear intent his death feast with his disciples? No, there is more here than the fear of death; there is the awe of the creature before the *mysterium tremendum*, before the shuddering secret of the numen.'[18]

We come to the *fascinans*, the third element in Otto's analysis. With this we become aware of the dialectical or even paradoxical character of religious experience, though indeed we have seen evidence that there is a paradoxical element in everything that the human being experiences. In Otto's words, 'beside that in the mystery which bewilders and confounds, he finds something which captivates and transports him'.[19] On this side of the *fascinans* belong the love, mercy, pity and comfort of the divine. But these are the ethicized expressions of the *fascinans*, which at its deeper numinous level has a Dionysian quality. Although this is an illustration not given by Otto himself, I think one might understand what he has in mind by contrasting two ways in which Christians have claimed to experience the Holy Spirit. The gifts of the Spirit are rational and ethical – love, patience, joy, peace and the like. But there are other manifestations of the Spirit that have a definitely non-rational Dionysian character – speaking with tongues and ecstatic experiences of various kinds. There is indeed a kind of borderline where the pneumatic experience is scarcely distinguishable from the demonic. Perhaps this ambiguity is reflected in Otto's choice of the language of fascination, for one can be fascinated by both good and evil.

In the later part of his book, Otto went on to claim that the human mind has a special faculty for responding to the numinous, but this is a much more speculative part of his theory. He claims that the human mind has a 'faculty of divination' and that there is an *a priori* category of the holy, the 'schematization' of which consists in its being made rational and moral. There is an explicit parallel here with Kant's theory of knowledge.[20] The speculations are interesting in making a case for the distinctiveness of religious values, but whatever one may think of them, they do not affect the value of the descriptive part of Otto's work. It remains a notable attempt to lay bare some very fundamental characteristics of man's religious encounter with the holy. Although I have used the word 'encounter' here, Otto's whole description makes it clear that this is not like a human meeting between persons who stand on the same level but more like an 'undergoing' by the human participant of the overpowering presence of the numinous, before which he is passive and receptive. The asymmetrical character of the relationship is true to what religious persons report.

Otto's analysis, however, has to such an extent acquired something like classic status that we must be careful not to overestimate it in an uncritical way or expect it to be illuminating for all the many forms of religion. It has, I think, two serious defects. The first is the great emphasis which it lays on the overwhelmingness and majesty of the numinous as the 'wholly other', with a corresponding emphasis on the human sense of finitude and unworthiness. No doubt both points do have their place in a phenomenological account of religion, but Otto presents them with a starkness which does not always belong to them. His insistence on the otherness and even the total otherness of God seems to speak of a God who is wholly transcendent, and to leave little room for the immanence of God and for those quieter, less dramatic experiences of the divine which are also reported by religious persons. A more balanced and dialectical account would make it clearer that not all religious experience is characterized by shuddering and terror. Indeed, we have seen that an exclusively transcendent God could be an alienating influence, neutralizing the human drive to transcendence.[21] If one is to do justice to the human element and be able to answer the criticism of Feuerbach and others (to which we shall turn shortly), then Otto's stress on the overwhelmingness (*tremendum*) of the divine needs to be corrected. And this brings me to the second main defect in Otto's account – a tendency towards primitivism, by which I mean that he goes behind the developed forms of religion to explore the more primitive forms out of which they have come, like the experience of the supernatural *mana* described by Marett, whose work, it will be remembered, Otto much admired. The result is that Otto lays great stress on primitive forms, and unfortunately this happens rather obviously in his treatment of the *fascinans*. It was precisely in his treatment of this topic that he had an opportunity to make a dialectical correction to his heavy stress on transcendence and the overwhelmingness of the *tremendum*. But he has scarcely mentioned love, mercy, peace and the like when he hastens on to the more Dionysian experiences of the *fascinans*, to wild and ecstatic ways of finding unity with the deity.

If these criticisms of Otto are just, then, however valuable his account of religion may be, it must be denied any normative status, and we have to set alongside it other accounts. Among these is William James' *The Varieties of Religious Experience*, with which Otto himself was familiar.

James' book, like Otto's, is probably of more value for the careful

descriptions that it offers than for its contribution towards any philosophical interpretation of religion. But the virtue of James' treatment is that he
casts his net much more widely than Otto. He makes clear the diversity of
religious experiences, though it also becomes clear from his survey that a
typology can be attempted.

He treats, for instance, of the *sense of presence*, and cites a variety of cases,
from the apparently hallucinatory instances of people who feel that there
is someone with them in the room, though in fact no one is there, to classic
instances like those of Wordsworth and Thoreau who were sensitive to a
presence in nature, so that nature seemed to them not just an impersonal
process but the sacramental expression of a spiritual reality. In the latter
case, religious experience is closely akin to aesthetic experience. What the
religious person perceives is no different from what anyone else perceives,
but he perceives it in a special way, as having in itself some kind of
wholeness and configuration, and so as bearing a meaning.[22] James also
deals at some length with *conversion experiences*. These begin with the
subject having a feeling of dissatisfaction with himself – often a feeling of
guilt or sin, or a sense of aimlessness, or a feeling of being divided within
himself. The release or healing appears to come from beyond himself,
though it may not come until he has undergone severe spiritual agony.[23]
Mysticism is another form of religion to which James devotes his attention.
In its more profound forms, mysticism would seem to be a way of the spirit
reserved to a very small minority of human beings, but it is so important
that no consideration of religion could leave it out. Even mysticism has its
varieties, but typically there seems to be the possibility of so concentrating
the mind that it is withdrawn from commerce with the objects of sense and
makes direct contact with the divine mind. Although mysticism begins
with the mind's withdrawal into itself, mystics would deny that it is
introspective or egocentric, for the human mind is itself an abyss or
mystery, the depths of which are continuous with the being of God. It was
at this point, faced with the criticisms of those who would say that religion
is purely subjective, that James, like Otto, introduced a speculative element
into his philosophy of religion, and suggested that the subconscious
reaches of the human mind constitute the area where the divine Spirit
makes contact.[24] This theory could account not only for mysticism but for
other forms of religious experience, including the two mentioned above,
sense of presence and conversion. But whatever judgment one may pass
on this particular speculation, that will not detract from the wealth of
descriptive material which he assembled and classified.

Incidentally, the proliferation of forms of experience which we find in
James' work serves as a warning against one of the dangers attending an
approach to the philosophy of religion or theology that sets out from
religious experiences as its starting point. The danger is that one particular

form may tend to be set up as a norm – mysticism, let us say, or conversion
– though in fact this may result from the idiosyncrasies of an individual.
This has been very much of a danger in the so-called 'empirical' accounts
of religion that have flourished in the United States.[25] We may contrast the
individualism of many of these American writers with the stress on
corporate experience that was characteristic of Schleiermacher. While one
must indeed take note of the astonishing varieties of religious experience
reported by individuals, it then becomes a question whether one can
discern among them some recurring patterns, and whether there is
anything like a mainstream of religious experience, 'normal religious
experience', as Martin Thornton has called it.[26]

Actually, it seems to me that there are two major streams of religious
experience. This is almost what we might expect in view of the many
polarities and oppositions that we have seen to be characteristic of human
life. The two major streams or types can be seen as complementary rather
than incompatible with one another, but one or the other is likely to be
dominant in any particular individual or even in an entire culture or
generation. In a broad way, one might characterize the two types as
negative and positive respectively. This terminology, it must be confessed,
is not quite satisfactory, for it seems to introduce an element of valuation,
though it is meant to be primarily descriptive.

The negative type is primarily determined by a sense of the fragmentariness of human existence. It takes its rise from awareness of finitude and
even of sinfulness. The human being is believed to be incapable of making
sense of his existence or of fulfilling from his own resources the demands
which his very existence brings with it – demands for moral rectitude,
authentic selfhood and genuine community. It is this profound unease or
dissatisfaction with one's condition that motivates the religious quest, in
some people at least. Human life is seen to be threatened with loss, guilt,
even absurdity, as it is caught in the conflicts of freedom and facticity,
transcendence and retrogression, responsibility and moral powerlessness,
rationality and irrationality, alienation and belonging, commitment and
drift, the taste for the infinite and the undeniable evidences of finitude. It
is in the midst of this threat of negativity that some religious persons claim
that they have experienced grace and revelation, so that the fragmentariness and contradictions of their lives have been overcome by a power not
their own, a power they call 'God'.

Just how widespread this type of experience is can be seen from the
following examples. Schleiermacher's account of religion, in its mature
form, begins from the feeling of absolute dependence. Kierkegaard's
starting point is the mood of anxiety, the deep-seated malaise which reveals
the fundamental instability of the human existent as it faces the existential
task of synthesizing body and soul. 'The idea of anxiety,' writes his

biographer, Peter Rohde, 'fills the whole of Kierkegaard's thought and writings, and the book which is perhaps his most important bears the title, *The Concept of Anxiety*.'[27] Jaspers claims that the encounter with transcendence takes place at what he calls the 'limit-situations' of life, situations such as guilt and death where the human being has come to the end of his resources and must look beyond the bounds of the natural realm. Tillich is another example of a religious thinker who takes his departure from such experiences as the feeling of estrangement or alienation from one's true existence, the ontological shock of the possibility of ceasing to be, the felt need to overcome the ambiguities of life – experiences which give rise to the existential questions to which, in turn, the revelatory experience of religion gives an answer.

One may mention also William James' distinction between the once-born and the twice-born, which roughly corresponds to my distinction between positive and negative types. The category of the twice-born includes those religious figures like Paul, Augustine, Luther, Bunyan and many others, who have to undergo conflict and dramatic conversion as they move from situations of doubt, insecurity, guilt and even despair, to the assurance of salvation. One must remember too that this type of experience is not peculiarly Christian. The Buddha's spiritual quest was stimulated by his confrontation with sickness, old age and death.

The very mention of such names as Paul and Luther indicates that what I have called the negative type of religious experience has been characteristic of some of the greatest religious geniuses, and William James thought that this is the most profound kind of religious experience. Nevertheless, I think one has to say that it is typical of some individuals rather than of others, and that it would scarcely be desirable to have too many Luthers or Kierkegaards around. This kind of religion is characteristic of individuals of a predominantly introspective type, and it flourishes especially in times of social upheaval and uncertainty, when it may captivate a generation.

The other main type of religious experience I have called positive or affirmative. I have so described it because it seems to arise from the natural drive of the human self to go beyond any given state of itself towards goals that seem to recede indefinitely. We recognize in this the inward drive that is called the 'transcendence' of the human being, and from the religious point of view, this is finally the drive towards God as the *summum bonum* and ultimate goal of transcendence. In this second type, the fragmentariness of human existence is experienced not so much as a threat of absurdity or non-being as rather the unfinished state of humanity, for the stage which any individual or the race as a whole has attained at any time is provisional. New possibilities open up ahead, and the pilgrimage has to be pursued towards a goal which is still hidden. This second type of religion has as long a history as the other. The apostle John in the New Testament is sometimes contrasted with Peter and Paul, and taken as an example of the disciple who fulfils a natural drive towards God without, apparently, any violent conversion or uprooting from his former way of life. Simone Weil has remarked about him: 'Christ granted to his well beloved disciple, and probably to all that disciple's spiritual lineage, to come to him not through degradation, defilement and distress, but in uninterrupted joy, purity and sweetness.'[28] Whether as a matter of historical fact this description fitted John is of little moment. All that is being asserted is that the type is recognized in the New Testament, though it may very well have been represented by the 'beloved disciple' who stands behind the Johannine tradition. This understanding of human religiosity has obvious affinities with that view, noted earlier,[29] that was common to many of the Greek fathers of the church, that man has been created with a potentiality for advance which would finally lead to what they called 'deification'.

As I have hinted, the two types of religious experience seem to alternate, one or the other predominating at different times. In the earlier part of the twentieth century, when much of the world was in the grip of war and political turmoil, there was much stress on the finitude and sinfulness of human life and on the phenomenon of anxiety. Barth, Niebuhr, Tillich and others among the theologians, Heidegger, Sartre, Jaspers among the philosophers, expressed such views. In the later part of the century, conditions have been more stable, though threats and corresponding anxieties lie not far below the surface. Nevertheless, the change has been enough to bring about quite an alteration of mood. Already at the end of World War II Bonhoeffer (whose influence has been much greater than his actual writings would seem to justify) was criticizing Tillich and other theologians for trying to grasp man at the limits of his life rather than at the centre, in his weakness rather than in his strength.[30] More significant by far is the work of many of the post-Vatican II Roman Catholic theologians and philosophers. They have made the idea of human transcendence central to their teaching. Karl Rahner, for instance, holds that the human spirit is 'desire for absolute being' so that 'every operation of the spirit can therefore be understood only as a moment in the movement towards absolute being as towards the one end and goal of the desire of the spirit.'[31] On this view, our human nature is seen as characterized by a dynamic openness towards God as the 'whither' of transcendence. In Protestant theology, the so-called 'theology of hope' developed by Moltmann and others has emphasized the future-oriented character of human existence, and has incorporated elements from the Hegelian and Marxist philosophies of history.[32]

But let me say again that the two types of religious experience are complementary, and stand in a dialectical relation to each other. Schleiermacher was correct in claiming *both* the sense and taste for the infinite *and* the feeling of absolute dependence as belonging to the essence of religion, though he did not adequately relate the two. Bonhoeffer was wrong in his onesided criticism of Tillich and company, as the passage of time has shown. Alienation and belonging, anxiety and joy, fear and hope, all have their place in the human condition, even if one or other of each pair may be dominant at some given time. Though in the last paragraph I have drawn a contrast between the anxiety-laden mood of the earlier part of the twentieth century and the more hopeful, humanistic mood that has succeeded it, they are in reality inseparable, they are the upper and under sides of the entire human experience. They are like the components of a binary star, revolving around each other, with now one, now the other in the foreground.

I have been writing as if religion were a normal part of human experience, and that is what Schleiermacher certainly believed, and it was from a consideration of his ideas on religion that our discussion began. But can we assume in a secular age that religion does have this kind of universality? Even since the time that Schleiermacher was writing at the turn of the eighteenth and nineteenth centuries, the rising tide of secularization has reached much higher up the beach. Are there many people today who experience the feeling of absolute dependence or the sense and taste for the infinite or creature feeling in the face of the numinous or conversion or sense of presence or mysticism? There seem to be two answers that can be given to this question.

The first is that religious experiences of the traditional kind are probably even today much commoner than might be supposed. We hear, of course, about the interest in Eastern religions, the emergence of new cults, the practice of meditation in various forms, and so on, and these seem to be symptoms of the quest for a religion or a substitute religion. But there is more reliable evidence from those who have researched into the present state of religious belief and practice. Sir Alister Hardy, with the help of several colleagues, has collected and classified over three thousand cases of reported religious experiences, including visions, locutions, sense of presence, conversions and so on. He concludes that even in a secular technological time like our own, a large number of people have a deep awareness of some spiritual reality beyond themselves. 'At certain times in their lives, many people have had specific, deeply felt, transcendental experiences which have made them all aware of this spiritual power. The experience, when it comes, has always been quite different from any other kind of experience they have ever had. They do not necessarily call it a religious feeling, nor does it occur only to those who belong to an institutional religion or who indulge in corporate acts of worship. It often occurs to children, to atheists and agnostics, and it usually induces in the person concerned a conviction that the everyday world is not the whole of reality; that there is another dimension to life.'[33] These assertions, which are backed by careful research, indicate that religious experiences are common and that many of them are similar to religious experiences known in less secular times past. It is conceded, however, that today they may not be explicitly recognized as religious or interpreted in traditional ways, though it is also claimed that these religious experiences cannot be subsumed under any other kind of experience – 'the religious experience has always been quite different from any other kind of experience'.

The second answer is somewhat different. It lays less stress on the persistence of specifically religious experiences but argues that there are many secular or everyday experiences which have a religious dimension. This answer may also in some cases be motivated by the desire to show that religion is not a separate department of life but an attitude and a way of perceiving that can pervade all experience. According to Martin Thornton, 'religious experience is ordinary experience, controlled by religious selectivity and interpretation'. The sociologist Peter Berger is among those who have sought to show that ordinary experience has a depth that may properly be called religious. He talks about 'signals of transcendence within the empirically given',[34] and mentions among other things experiences of order, play and hope. Langdon Gilkey, a theologian who has paid special attention to these peripheral or background manifestations of the holy, makes the comment: 'Ultimacy has not vanished – and could not vanish – from modern experience; on the contrary, it is present, as it always has been in human life, as a base, ground and limit of what we are, as a presupposition for ourselves, our thinking, our deciding and our acting.'[35] J. G. Davies gives many illustrations from life and literature of everyday situations of a secular kind in which, he claims, we become aware of the holy. These situations include inter-personal relations, where the irreducible personal otherness of a human being may afford, as Buber claimed, a glimpse through to the eternal Thou; political commitment, where the individual self merges itself in something greater and finds a focus there; also experiences of death, and aesthetic experiences.[36] It will be seen that these instances, cited by Davies, are paralleled in earlier chapters of this book where we have noted what might be called a 'transcendent' reference in various aspects of human experience.

There is one point, however, at which I would disagree with Davies, and I think the other writers whom I have been citing would disagree with him also. In his eagerness to direct our attention to the presence of the holy in ordinary experiences, he feels it necessary to deny that there is any specifically religious experience as such, and he is especially critical of Otto's account. I think this view is exaggerated. Surely there are distinctively religious moments in human experience, even in a secular age, when there is concentrated at the centre that awareness of the holy which ordinarily is there only on the periphery of experience. Davies and the others have done a great service in directing attention to the presence of the holy across the broad spectrum of human experience; the holy belongs not just to specifically religious experiences, but to the entire experience of being a human person, that is to say, to the transcendental conditions of all experience. Yet I think we would be able to recognize the holy in this broad sense and to place a religious interpretation upon certain aspects of ordinary experience only if we had also known the holy in concentrated form in some distinctively religious experience. Even if we were grazed and haunted by some elusive sense of a mysterious holiness present in some ordinary experiences, we would then seek a clearer, more direct awareness of something so significant and fascinating.

In the last paragraph I have introduced the word 'interpretation' into the discussion. Up to this point I have in the main been describing religion. I have tried to delimit those areas of experience that we call religious, I have considered some of the classic accounts that have been given of them, and I have attempted to trace recurrent patterns and so take a first step towards a typology. But virtually nothing has been said about the validity of religion, that is to say, about its claim to relate us to a reality other than ourselves, a reality which is usually called 'God'. It is this question of validity which is raised by our mention of interpretation, and it is this question that we must now take up.

Let us return to Schleiermacher and his attempted rehabilitation of religion. The vulnerability of his appeal to feeling or experience became apparent very quickly. Barely a generation later, Feuerbach drew what he believed to be the conclusions of Schleiermacher's theology of consciousness. He taught that the God of experience is in fact merely the experience of God, and this is an experience which refers to nothing outside of the subjectivity of the one who has the experience. 'Religion, at least, the Christian religion,' he wrote, 'is the relation of man to himself, or, more correctly, to his own nature, that is, his subjective nature; but a relation to it viewed as a nature apart from his own. The divine being is nothing else than the human being, or rather the human nature purified, freed from the limits of the individual man, made objective, that is, contemplated and revered as another, a distinct being.'[37] By appealing to feeling, Schleiermacher had removed Christian faith both from the embarrassment of resting on authoritative dogmas and from the uncertainties of relying on dubious metaphysical arguments, but had he done this only at the price of surrendering its truth claims and turning it into a purely subjective state of mind? This was the question Feuerbach raised.

Of course, Schleiermacher had no intention of subjectivizing religion in the way that Feuerbach proceeded to do. What Schleiermacher called 'feeling', he believed to be, as we have noted, an insight into, or an intuition of, the divine reality. The feeling of absolute dependence was supposed to be correlated with a consciousness of God which amounted to a co-existence of God in the soul. Schleiermacher was so confident of all this that, as we have seen, he believed that the religious experience he described rendered superfluous the traditional proofs of the divine existence, and itself gave a superior and adequate guarantee of the reality of God.

But if the religious awareness of God were able to take the place of the proofs of God's existence, it would seem that at least three conditions would have to be fulfilled: 1. the experience would have to be universal or nearly universal among human beings; 2. the experience would need to be self-authenticating; 3. (and this point is close to the second one) there would need to be fairly general agreement about its interpretation.

On the first of these points, Schleiermacher did believe that the feeling of absolute dependence is a universal one and that, as it gets clarified in the mind, it issues in God-consciousness. Perhaps religious experience was at one time virtually universal, though even by Schleiermacher's time the Enlightenment had begun to erode it. But for us in the twentieth century, it would be very difficult or perhaps impossible to claim that religious experience is universal. The period from Schleiermacher to the present has been one in which, at least in Western countries, religion has ceased to be clearly a majority attitude. The religionless human being has appeared, the convinced religious have become a minority, though it may well be the case, as Hardy's researches show, that a very large number still retain a measure of religiosity. At any rate, there has obviously been a massive drift away from religion in its explicit forms. Admittedly, to defend Schleiermacher, it would not be necessary to claim that everyone without exception knew the feeling of absolute dependence (or, alternatively, the sense and taste for the infinite). After all, there are some people who seem to be without conscience and are amoral, but that does not invalidate the claims of morality, and we would regard such people as abnormal. Similarly, there are people with no ear for music or no eye for painting, but that does not place the arts in question or make the criteria of good music and good painting something altogether subjective. Perhaps one could say something similar in the case of religion, and this might find some support in the fact, already noted, that the non-religious seem to need some substitute for religion. Even so, in many secularized areas of the West, religion has largely faded away. If in Schleiermacher's own time there was still a sufficient majority of persons practising religion for this to be counted the majority attitude, this could not be said in the West today. No doubt it would still be possible to take the line of Davies, Gilkey and the others who say that even those who disclaim any specific awareness of the holy do have religious dimensions in everyday secular experience. This may be true, and probably is true. But I must confess that I myself am always uneasy over attempts to show that the religionless person is somehow secretly a believer, because this seems to infringe the integrity of his own self-understanding and does a certain violence to him. Moreover, it assumes not only the universality of the religious experience, but also an agreed interpretation of the meaning of that experience, and this is a question to which we have still to come. For the present, I think we have to concede that religious experience is not universal among human beings. This would not mean that the capacity for religion is not universal or nearly so, but it does seem to be enough to upset the first of the three conditions we have laid down as vital to Schleiermacher's position.

We turn now to the second condition that would have to be fulfilled if Schleiermacher's claim were to be accepted. Can it be held that the religious experience is self-authenticating? Even if the experience were not universal, self-authentication would establish its claim. Some theologians have held that the encounter with God is self-authenticating. We can no more doubt its reality than we can doubt the evidence of our senses. John Baillie, for instance, drew a parallel between our experience of the material world, our experience of other persons, and our experience of God. Even though our senses occasionally deceive us, no person in his right mind doubts the reality of material things or of other persons, and we should not doubt the reality of God either.[38] But even allowing for the fact that Baillie states his case with much more sophistication than my bare summary suggests, the argument is not sound. The sense-experience which we have in the case of observing objects or encountering friends is absent when we undergo the meeting with God. The last named case, as Schleiermacher would agree, is an interior experience. But it is precisely sense-experience which seems to be checkable in a way in which inner experiences are not checkable, and which gives to sense-experience its privileged epistemological place among the forms of experience. So we fall again at the second hurdle.

We come to the third point, which has to do with agreed ways of interpretation. There is no such thing as 'raw' experience, for experience always comes to us as already interpreted in one way or another. The religious person interprets certain experiences in what can only be called a 'religious' way, that is to say, in the way that has been typical of religions from the beginnings of human history. The religious interpretation refers the experience to some reality beyond the subject of the experience, even beyond the empirical environment, to God or whatever name is used. Such experiences are taken to be the presence of God or a word from God or the grace of God or a sign of God's displeasure, or whatever it might be. For most people who prize such experiences, their value and importance lies in the fact that they are believed to proceed from God.

However, in modern times alternative interpretations have been offered. There has come into being a whole battery of human sciences which, by the very method which they employ, are prepared to interpret religious experiences in purely naturalistic terms. It is bound to give us some pause when we reflect that at earlier stages in history people were very ready to interpret even natural happenings in the world around them in a religious way. If it thundered, that was a voice from heaven; if there was a good harvest, that was a sign of divine favour; if there was a plague, that was a punishment from God; and so on. But such interpretations have been superseded by natural explanations of these events. The thunder is explained in terms of meteorology; the good crop is due to soil fertility, favourable weather and an absence of destructive organisms; the plague is caused by a pestilential bacillus, and so forth. These may be said to be relatively crude instances, but is it possible that our more sophisticated religious interpretations may also be overtaken? That sociology, whether in the manner of Durkheim or in some more up-to-date way, will account for religion in terms of social forces, influences and pressures? That psychology, probably not in the way of Freud but in an equally naturalistic and atheistic way, will account for religious beliefs and emotions in terms of the deep unconscious drives of the mind and the need for security? That anthropology will trace back (and to a large extent, it has already done so) the most exalted religious ideas to the superstitions of primitive man?

I do not want to exaggerate these points, and I believe that they often have been exaggerated by hostile critics of religion. The sciences concerned are sometimes in danger of falling into the genetic fallacy, and in any case their investigations are never so exhaustive that they could claim to be telling us the whole truth about religion. Nor is it legitimate to invoke the application of Ockham's razor, for that would simply amount to introducing a covert form of positivism which would short-circuit the inquiry and fail to do justice to the depth and complexity of the phenomena. But with these *caveats*, I would say that the work of the empirical human sciences has to be taken seriously. The psychologist, the sociologist and others have put question marks against many religious interpretations of experience that were once taken for granted, and perhaps they have even exploded some of these interpretations. If this is so, then in the long run it must be a service to religion, which cannot thrive on error. It will make it easier to distinguish genuine religious experience from bogus forms – and in talking of 'genuine' religious experience, I am obviously leaving open the possibility that in some cases the interpretation of an experience of God may be precisely that there is a God who communicates himself in the experience. But this does not excuse us from rigorously examining all proffered religious interpretations of life, and considering alternatives. Religion, after all, though extolled by its adherents as ennobling to humanity, has been assailed by critics as a source of immaturity, intellectual indolence, fanaticism, conflict and many other evils. I do not try to reckon up a balance sheet, but if religion is to stand, it can only be by facing and answering the attacks and criticisms of those who approach it with a 'hermeneutic of suspicion'. So, in answer to the third point in our evaluation of Schleiermacher's claims, we have to say that the religious interpretation of religious experiences cannot be uncritically accepted and has no monopoly.

The first round of our discussion then has been quite negative in its results. We saw that if Schleiermacher's claim that religion can be securely founded on our experience alone and that this takes the place of the proofs of God's existence, is to stand, three conditions would need to be fulfilled. But we have now found that none of these conditions is fulfilled. The religious experience is not universal. The religious experience is not self-authenticating. The religious interpretation of such experiences is not the only possible interpretation.

I think, however, that we can refine the argument somewhat and try a second round, in the hope of doing rather better. The focus will still be on religious experience as the clearest evidence and support for religion, but we shall consider ways in which the experience in question can be more fully and clearly described and so a more discerning evaluation be opened up for us. We shall not find ourselves making so sweeping a claim as that the very experience of religion can supply the place of the theistic proofs, but we shall find that it deserves serious consideration as *prima facie* evidence about our human nature and its place in the universe.

What do I have in mind when I say that the argument can be refined beyond the way in which it is stated by Schleiermacher, and that we can attempt fuller and more detailed descriptions of religious experience than he was able to offer? This is not for a moment to make light of Schleiermacher's insights or to underrate his pioneering work in approaching the problems of religion and theology through an examination of the state of mind of the religious subject, that is to say, of a human being. But undoubtedly the technique of description has been greatly advanced since his time. I refer especially to the development of phenomenology, and in particular of the phenomenology of religion. I am using the expression 'phenomenology' here in a very broad way. Although the term is chiefly associated with Husserl and the difficult philosophical method which he constructed, there were thinkers both before Husserl and contemporary with him, and especially philosophers of religion, whose methods were to all intents and purposes phenomenological, even if they did not call them such and were not acquainted with Husserl directly or conversant with the niceties of his method. One might mention, for instance, that work of Kierkegaard, cited earlier in this chapter, *The Concept of Anxiety*; and although, like all Kierkegaard's writings, it bears the stamp of his individuality and personal experience, it also tells us much about what he called the 'universal human', so that we can recognize something of our own experience in what he describes, and perhaps recognize in it through his clarification connections of which we had been unaware before. If one may use an expression which has become something of a *cliché*, he permits us to see the experience 'in depth', and one might even say that this is what phenomenology is about, at least, in its simplest form. Otto is another philosopher of religion whose method is truly phenomenological, but I do not believe that he uses the term, though he and Husserl were for a time colleagues at Göttingen, and the latter regarded Otto's work on the holy as a masterly exercise in phenomenology. Perhaps I have said enough about his work in an earlier part of this chapter to make it unnecessary to add anything here. Otto's Scottish contemporary, John Oman, though severely critical of Otto for allegedly making too much of the overpoweringness of the numinous, used a rather similar descriptive method, developed apparently independently. One of his major points in describing the religious consciousness was to stress the element of valuation in it. Other writers of broadly phenomenological tendency who have made notable contributions to the exploration of religion as found in human experience are van der Leeuw, Eliade, Scheler and Ricoeur.

Paul Tillich offers a useful summary of the phenomenological method in the following sentence: 'The test of a phenomenological description is that the picture given by it is convincing, that it can be seen by anyone who is willing to look in the same direction, that the description illuminates other related ideas, and that it makes the reality these ideas are meant to reflect understandable.'[39] This sentence is so condensed that I think it will be worth our while to tease it out somewhat.

The phenomenological description, Tillich says, has to be convincing. This means that it must present the facts of the case as they show themselves, not as some tacitly accepted theory (whether spiritualistic or naturalistic) has persuaded us that they ought to appear. Of course, I have said earlier that we can never be pure observers and that our judgments can never be entirely value-free. But that was never meant to be a warrant for one-sidedness or an uncritical *parti pris*, and indeed I suggested ways of overcoming one-sided distortions.[40] The phenomenological method is a deliberate and controlled attempt to 'bracket' or place in suspense personal prejudices and accepted interpretations, so that as far as possible we may be confronted with the facts of the case. It is this kind of careful description which pays attention to what shows itself (the phenomenon), that can help to give to non-sensory experience something of the reliability, objectivity, public accessibility and therefore evidential weight that belongs in other areas to sense-experience. Careful description, the collection of many instances, the noting of recurrent patterns and structures, attempts at classification and typology – these are ways in which there can be built up a reliable and convincing picture of religious experience generally.

I have mentioned public accessibility, and this leads us to Tillich's second point – that what is described can be seen by anyone who is willing to look in the same direction. Here again there is a parallel with sense-experience, for each of us can check the possibly erroneous information supplied by one or other of the senses by asking someone else to look or listen or employ some other sense, and tell us if he perceives what we think we perceive. But although there is a parallel, there is also an essential difference in the case of religious experience. In this case, we are not dealing with something perceptible to anyone who cares to look, but with an experience which is interior to the person who has it. It is significant that Tillich introduces the word 'willing', reminding us again that the various activities of the mind are closely connected with each other and cannot be isolated. 'Willing' means here 'paying attention', and even in sense-experience we sometimes only perceive something when we pay attention on the advice of someone else who has already perceived it. What is being asked for is sympathetic participation on the part of the person to whom the description is being offered. When he looks into his own experience, does he find that the description fits? Perhaps the description may even be illuminating for his own experience, directing his attention to something that he had never noticed before in the way that, as was suggested above, some of Kierkegaard's analyses may do for his readers. I doubt if anyone could get very far in the understanding and evaluation of religion unless he had to at least some minimal extent undergone an experience of religion and known the meaning of the holy, just as no one could tell us much about art if he himself had no aesthetic sensibility, and no one could write history without himself participating in human affairs and, as a result of that participation, being able to enter imaginatively into the experiences of characters of the past. Some of the accounts one reads of religion seem completely unreal, because, presumably, they have been written by someone who was never willing or able to attempt to understand religion from the inside.

Next, Tillich claims that a phenomenological description must show inter-relationships. This is what we have already designated by the popular expression, 'seeing in depth'. We see a situation in depth when we become aware of its configuration and how all the items in it are related to one another. Religious phenomena, repentance, conversion, sin, peace of mind, joy, anxiety, sense of presence (or absence) and so on, are not to be understood in isolation. They belong together in a complex totality of experience, in which each item relates to every other item. This is what might be called the 'logic of the heart' – an idea recognized by Pascal, and to which reference was made in our discussion of feeling and emotion.[41] The contents of the religious consciousness are not chaotic but have their own order, whether or not one would want to speak about a 'logic'. At any rate, there is an order comparable to or analogous to logic, and this becomes apparent when one tries to transcribe the felt religious reality into the verbal formulations of a dogmatic or theological system. For it soon becomes obvious that no doctrine stands by itself. In Christianity, for instance, doctrines about the person of Christ, the triune God, atonement, the nature of the human person and so forth are all intimately related. They all belong together in a belief system, and if any one of them is modified or eliminated, the shock waves run through the whole system and every other doctrine is affected to a greater or less extent. The system expresses a total vision of life and has to be taken as a whole. This was clearly seen by Nietzsche, who believed therefore that if one could destroy a single important doctrine – belief in God – the whole structure would fall to the ground. 'Christianity,' he declared, 'is a system, a consistently thought out and complete view of things. If one breaks out of it a fundamental idea, the belief in God, one thereby breaks the whole thing to pieces.'[42] Actually, Nietzsche overstates the case, for the system is not so tightly knit or strictly logical as he supposed. There have, after all, been a few theologians who have discarded belief in God and yet tried to maintain an atheistic Christianity, though admittedly they have not been very successful. The interlocking nature of religious beliefs, reflecting relations of coinherence and mutual implication in the experiences that lie behind them, also explains why the complex belief systems of religion are so hard either to verify or falsify. Particular doctrines may be vulnerable in isolation – some of them may look like nonsense – but they have their meaning and truth-claim only as part of the whole. Likewise the pre-reflective experiences that lie behind the doctrines cannot be evaluated in isolation, but have to be seen in the context of a whole way of life. Part of the purpose of a good phenomenological analysis is to show how the various moments interpenetrate and support one another in a coherent whole of experience.

The last point made by Tillich was that a good phenomenological description should also lead to a better understanding of the reality to which the experience refers. The assumption here is that the experience does refer to a reality beyond itself, and we have seen of course that some critics of religion would say that it is purely subjective and that there is no independent reality corresponding to what the religious person calls 'God'. I do not think that this question can be settled just by examining and describing the experience itself. Nevertheless, a careful investigation of religious experience does discover in it at least two characteristics which refer it to a reality outside the consciousness of the religious person. The two characteristics are intentionality and valuation. The religious experience is strongly intentional in referring its content to a reality which the religious person takes to be not only other than himself but prior to himself. By 'intentionality' is meant this tendency of the mind to refer the contents of consciousness to an objective reality. Just as much as in sense-experience or in meeting other persons, intentionality is present in religious experience. This cannot be explained away by some 'projection' theory like that of Feuerbach. It rests on something deeper, a kind of epistemological instinct which saves us from the madness of solipsism by expelling the contents of consciousness into an environment which is other than ourselves. Of course, this is not to deny that the mind contributes to the way in which we perceive extramental realities. Anyone's idea of God, for instance, will always be subjectively and culturally coloured. But there is no reason to suppose that this is all there is to God. On the contrary, the very idea of a projection implies a screen, a reality itself unseen which makes possible the projection. I mentioned also the character of valuation in religion. This draws attention to the fact that the experience of God is as far as possible removed from a mere observing or a supposedly disinterested knowledge of something. Religion relates the finite person to the holy, the sacred, the ultimate, God, the *summum bonum*, and all of these are expressions which speak of the highest degree of existential interest, of a matter of life and death. But that kind of valuation is inseparable from belief in the real otherness and indeed real priority of that which is encountered. So when one takes note of the intentional and valuational character of religious experience itself, while indeed this does not finally settle the issue, it does establish a *prima facie* case that religion, like so many other forms of human experience, is the human response to a reality other than the human mind itself.

This second round, based on Tillich's remarks on phenomenology, has, I think, yielded more affirmative results than the first round, based on Schleiermacher. The very act of clarifying religious experience, showing its structures and recurrent patterns, its coherence and its reference, is perhaps the most convincing way of commending its claims. This is not so much an argument as an attempt to describe areas of experience which each person who is prepared to examine the descriptions with a degree of openness can then recognize as actual or possible experiences for himself.

The case for the validity of religious experience can be strengthened by a consideration of the phenomenology of other areas of experience which, like religion, have a claim to validity and yet which seem by their very nature to have a depth or inexhaustibility stretching beyond what empirical psychology or sociology can explain. We may recall at this point our own earlier discussions of such topics as freedom, conscience and esthetic experience. In all of these, we came to a point where the naturalistic type of explanation no longer works. To put it in another way, the phenomenology of religion can be seen as part of the wider pattern of a phenomenology of human experience in general, and this wider pattern itself calls for the recognition that the human being has spiritual as well as natural properties. Because transcendence belongs to him, the human person must be understood in theological as well as in psychological terms. This is the truth contained in Bultmann's dictum that the problem of God and the problem of myself are identical.[43] It would be a misunderstanding to take these words in any egocentric or narcissistic sense. But they do imply that the human being, though from one point of view a physico-chemical system and from another a biological organism and from another a highly complex pattern of behaviour, is also the being with a sense and taste for the infinite, who sums up in himself many levels of being and looks like the best clue we have to the whole problem of being.

Of course, as I have said more than once in this chapter, the description and interpretation of religion cannot in itself be conclusive, not even when it is seen in the context of other and apparently supportive areas of human experience. I could not agree with those fideists who claim that the very existence of religious faith is a sufficient justification for it. They have not sufficiently considered the ambiguities of religion, the oppressive forms which it has sometimes assumed, the abuses to which it has been made instrumental. Yet, even so, the long persistence of religion in human history and its continuing influence today have undoubtedly played a major part in stretching human beings to new stature and drawing them on in the path of transcendence. Religion has a *prima facie* claim to be considered an essential element in any fully developed humanity. In Ninian Smart's words, 'we can be sure that no total picture of the nature of man can be complete unless it contains a theory of religion'.[44]

In this treatment of religion and its place in human nature, I have dwelt for the most part on religious experience, yet I have acknowledged that this can never be conclusive in establishing the validity or permanent worth of religion. I did not accept therefore Schleiermacher's contention that religious experience renders the classic proofs of God's existence superfluous. He may have been correct if he meant that probably very few people have been led to a living religious faith through being intellectually convinced by any one or all of these proofs. The proofs deal with the God of the philosophers (First Cause, Necessary Being, Supreme Intelligence and the like), rather than the God of Abraham, Isaac and Jacob or any other God whom people have actually worshipped and served. But the God of the philosophers and the God of religion are not unrelated. The God of religion must be everything that the God of the philosophers is said to be, though he is also something more. Religion is so important that anyone who embraces it must do so as conscientiously as possible. This means that he must ask critical questions and engage in critical scrutiny, and this is where the traditional theistic proofs come into play. When a religious faith has come to birth through experience, then the intellectual questions arise and the traditional proofs with their later refinements become relevant.

XVII

SUFFERING

From the beginning of this study, we have been aware of the ambiguities of human life. Every affirmative aspect of our being seems to have its polar opposite. Freedom is exercised against a background of facticity; transcendence carries no guarantee of any true progress; egoity supplies the focus for transcendence, but also the occasion for collapsing back into a hard core of inhuman selfishness; the body permits insertion into the material and social worlds, but can become a hindrance and even a tyrant; having is essential to a genuinely human life, yet at a certain point it becomes stifling; and so on. The threat of meaninglessness or absurdity has all the time been hanging over the picture of humanity that we have been building up. In the chapter on alienation, we did look more directly at some of the negative aspects of humanity, but on the whole we may have paid less attention to the 'night-side' of human existence than we ought to have done. But now that we have been considering religion with its experience of the holiness of being, perhaps even its experience of a loving God, it is right to face again the dark and negative aspects which seem to pose a challenge to all that has been said about commitment, belief, love and religion.

Suffering is everywhere. It seems to belong to the very texture of human life. Does not the universal fact of suffering raise again all the questions about the worth of life?

I should say that I am not intending to address myself to the 'problem' of suffering, still less to the wider problem of evil, of which it is usually considered a part. I have no new wisdom to offer on these topics, and do not believe that human wisdom can find a solution. I have a more modest aim, namely, to reflect on the nature of suffering and its place in human life, and to show that in most of its forms it does not nullify the worth of life. But I say deliberately 'in most of its forms', for some forms appear to be so destructive and pointless that the proper course seems to be to fall silent in the face of them.

In one of his books, Bishop John Austin Baker begins a chapter entitled 'The World's Sorrow' as follows:

> All discussions of the world's sorrow are to some extent distortions. Sorrow is at most only one half of reality. In a thousand, often surprising, ways, our humanness is matched to its environment, and enabled to find it good; indeed, the ways in which mankind finds or makes its pleasures are far more varied than its pains. There is the relish of food and drink; the satisfaction of hard, tiring work alternating with rest, leisure, sleep; the precious sense of physical health. There are the joys of love, of friendship, and of family life, the pride and excitement stirred by the achievements of one's children, fellow workers and neighbours, one's nation or race . . . There are more than enough entries for a large encyclopedia. And that in itself tells us something of enormous import-ance about our experience in the world. Are we to count only the hate, never the love; only the ugliness, never the loveliness; only the misery, never the joy?[1]

The first time I read these words, I confess that I was mildly shocked by them. There are surely many people who lack some of the good things of which Baker writes, and some who lack all of them. Yet Baker is correct in putting the world's sorrow in perspective, as against those who paint a picture of unrelieved misery. And the proof that he is correct is obvious: the human race survives and *wants to survive* in spite of all the sufferings which afflict it. Humanity wants the experiment of life to continue, however distressing some aspects of it may be. If suffering were utterly massive and intolerable, then mass suicide or at least the loss of the will to live would be the appropriate response for the human race to make. (I believe a German poet once recommended universal suicide, but his advice was not fol-lowed.) On the contrary, there is everywhere the will to live and even the zest for life. Even those individuals who end their own lives usually do so because of some particular intractable problems, not because they have turned against life as such.

Bishop Baker, I should hasten to say, was in no way seeking to minimize the truly horrific extent and depth of human suffering. It is there, not primarily as a 'problem' for philosophers and theologians, but as a chilling fact, and although it does not take away all the joy of life or turn us against life, it tempers our joy. One is never for long without some awareness of suffering, if not his own, then the suffering of someone else, and that may be quite as painful.

What then is suffering? It is the opposite of action. In action I exercise my freedom and initiate a chain of events that are designed to bring about some state of affairs which I desire. In suffering, on the other hand, something happens to me. A chain of events has been initiated outside of my control, these events impinge upon me and involve me, and they move towards a state of affairs which I do not desire. In my freedom, I act to attain an end on which I have set my mind; in my suffering, I am driven about by external forces not subject to my choice or control. When the opposition between action and suffering is put in this stark fashion, we can see how suffering puts a question mark against any attempt to make sense of human life. For life seems to be split into two parts, the part which one chooses and fashions according to one's goals, and the part which obtrudes itself like an invasion from without and may be hostile and destructive to our goals. We seem to be driven back again to the Sisyphus-like conception of the human being, propounded by Camus.[2] Are human life and human destiny pervaded by an incurable dualism which we see at its most acute in the opposition of action and passion?

Camus advocated 'metaphysical rebellion' in the face of this situation. By this he did not mean simply atheism, but a profound protest against the way things are. 'The rebel defies more than he denies.'[3] So he commits himself to the desperate effort to build up human values and a tolerable human existence in the midst of a world which threatens him constantly with suffering and death. At the opposite extreme from rebellion is resignation. We had a glimpse of that point of view when we touched on the play of Krishna. Everything that happens, joy and suffering, life and death, is part of the cosmic play. It is senseless to get agitated or to rebel or to argue about it. Once we see that there is no point to it all, that it is in fact play, we can resign ourselves and accept it all with an untroubled mind.

But if rebellion is hopeless and, in the end, no less absurd than the absurdity against which it protests, is resignation or passive acceptance any better? The first has a kind of romantic heroism about it, the second an appearance of wisdom that has set itself above life, but surely there must be a better way than either of these. I think there is. There is the possibility of realistically accepting that suffering is inevitable in the human condition, but at the same time of seeking to transform it and integrate it into human life in such a way that we come to see that life would be poorer without it. It may not be possible to integrate it without remainder. Perhaps there remains a surd, an irremovable question mark. But at least we must see how far along this road we can go.

The approach to suffering which avoids the extremes of rebellion and resignation has found its most profound and appealing expression in Christianity. It is no accident that the cross became the pre-eminent Christian symbol, at once an instrument of torture and acute suffering, and the promise of wholeness and salvation. The cross, of course, can be understood only in relation to the career and character of the crucified one,

Jesus Christ. He, in turn, has been interpreted in terms of the various theologies of atonement, which have tried to show how his sufferings and death have saving significance for mankind. Admittedly, these theologies of atonement, combining as they do elements of history, metaphor, legend and mythology, have been subject of much debate in the church and perhaps no one of them gives an entirely coherent statement of how the suffering of Jesus is transformed into a salvific event. But they do try to put into words an experience of renewal of wholeness known in the Christian community. The suffering of Jesus was considered to be *felix culpa*, a happy fault, and the same expression was sometimes used of the fall of Adam and Eve into sin. Although it is not worked out in detail, even in the various theologies of atonement, the language gives expression to the conviction, founded in the Christian experience, that suffering, sin, forgiveness and renewal bring about a quality of human life more profound, more mature and more satisfying than would have been possible in a garden-of-Eden type of existence, a life of blissful innocence untouched by suffering and sin. We also note how the evangelists in their passion narratives integrate the sufferings of Jesus into his life and mission, so that the dividing line between action and passion becomes invisible. He is said to set his face towards Jerusalem; at his trial it is his judges rather than himself who are being weighed; at the crucifixion it is his persecutors who need our pity, for they are acting out of ignorance; finally, his life is not taken from him but he lays it down. There is in all this a reversal of roles and expectations, a transformation of values in which suffering comes to belong in an affirmative way to the one who suffers. This is as far as possible from any kind of masochistic glorification of suffering, such as Nietzsche attributed to Christianity. Suffering has no value in and by itself – it rather has disvalue – but it can become integrated into human life in such a way as to increase the value of that life. Ritschl rather than Nietzsche understood the significance of Jesus' sufferings when he wrote: 'Only suffering which becomes a kind of doing has ethical value.'[4]

Let us now consider these points in more detail with reference to different forms of suffering. We may well find, however, that just as I have said that there are no final solutions to the problem of evil and no entirely coherent theologies of atonement, so there will be some loose ends in what follows.

The commonest form of suffering is, I suppose, pain, and I am thinking chiefly of physical pain. Everyone has at one time or another experienced slight or moderate pain, and a good many people have also experienced intense pain. Would anyone say, however, that pain is always bad or an unmitigated evil? Pain is often a useful warning to us that something is going wrong with the body or something is amiss in our living habits, and that we had better take appropriate action. It is hard to see that anything but pain could do this for us, and if the pain is moderate and temporary, then I should not find it too difficult to accept it as an integral part of human experience and even to be grateful for it as nature's device for alerting me to possible dangers. Again, we observe pain in other human beings, and often it is pain much more severe than anything we have known ourselves. But the fact that we have known *some* pain makes it possible for us to feel compassion for those who are suffering much more than we have done. Once more, it is hard to see that anything but the experience of pain could arouse in us a lively and understanding compassion. In this way, pain contributes to human solidarity. It delivers us from narrow self-concern and makes us feel our oneness with other human beings. Indeed, the range is extended even beyond human life. We share this planet with the animals, and we feel a certain kinship with them. We cannot know what an animal feels or what kind of consciousness it has, but the pain of an animal is so obviously analogous to human pain that at this point we feel a contact and our acquaintance with pain can awaken and deepen a sense of solidarity with living things generally – at least, with those possessing a certain degree of sentience. If we go even further, and consider cases of people who suffer severe, constant and disabling pain, we come across many who have learned through their pain to become patient, gentle, understanding and courageous to quite an extraordinary extent. Again, they would not have developed these admirable qualities apart from pain. But here perhaps we find ourselves asking whether the price has not been a very high one; and we also know that there are others who have not been able to transform pain in such ways but have been broken and destroyed by it. When suffering, then, takes the form of physical pain, we can believe that up to a point it can be integrated into character and bring into being qualities of humanity that could not otherwise be developed. But we can only say 'up to a point', for sometimes pain is so constant and intense that it numbs and dehumanizes those who suffer from it.

A second kind of suffering which everyone experiences is the suffering associated with frustration, deprivation, failure, loss, including the loss of loved ones through bereavement. Hopes are cheated, labour is expended in vain for no reward, the pattern of life that has been built up is disrupted and everything thrown into confusion. This suffering might be called mental and spiritual pain, and it is analogous in many ways to physical pain. We can see that in this area too there are benefits to be gained from suffering. If we never met with any checks and reverses, we should all too easily form an exaggerated and illusory estimation of our own powers. Sartre, as we have noted,[5] believed that the human being is the desire to be God, and since this is an impossible desire, he must suffer the frustration of an unhappy consciousness. But surely the human being who has taken even a few steps towards wisdom and self-knowledge has overcome the infantile delusion of his own grandeur and has learned the meaning of finitude. To know and accept finitude is perhaps the most important step towards personhood, but our delusions of grandeur are so strong and persistent that only the sufferings of failure, frustration and the like can bring us to a proper self-understanding. The painful experience of bereavement helps to bring before us another aspect of human finitude, namely, mortality and transitoriness. None of us are permanent features of the world, which will go on much as usual when we have departed from the scene. We learn this for the first time through experiencing the death of another, especially another who up to that point had seemed indispensable. Such experiences also teach us how much human beings depend on one another and how little any of us is completely sovereign over his own life.

Of course, as in the case of physical pain, the considerations we have just had before us apply much more easily to moderate instances of frustration and deprivation than to extreme ones. Perhaps some of us have known people who have been active, gifted and useful members of society and who through advancing age or for some other reason have found themselves more and more cut down in what they can do and more and more dependent on others, and have become so depressed about it all that they have ended their own lives. I certainly would be very hesitant to pass any moral judgment in such a case. Yet I wonder whether such persons would not have achieved a greater dignity and won a higher respect by accepting even in extreme form the finitude and dependence that are part of the human condition. Pride and arrogance, even the desire to be God, are fundamental temptations, and perhaps it is only some fairly extreme mental suffering that can quench them. Even so, as in the case of physical suffering, one has finally to say that there will be some cases of frustration and deprivation so overwhelmingly destructive that one cannot attempt to justify them and must fall silent.

A third form of suffering is guilt. This too is a form of mental or spiritual pain, but it seems sufficiently distinctive to deserve special mention. We have seen how Mill, in his account of conscience, understood it chiefly as a kind of inward pain or discomfort, either consequent on having done something wrong, or warning us against a contemplated wrong action.[6] Some people, as is well known, have been tormented for years by a sense of guilt. Sometimes it has been quite paralysing, and often the sense of guilt seems to be out of all proportion to the wrongdoing which brought it about in the first place. As a consequence, it has become a popular belief that guilty feelings are bad and that it would be a good and healthy thing if the sense of guilt could be eliminated. Let us agree that much guilt feeling has been both misplaced and excessive, and that few would wish to lay the amount of stress on sin and guilt that people did in some former times. Nevertheless, the feeling of guilt can be seen as closely analogous to that of physical pain. Just as the latter is a warning that something is wrong with the body, guilt is a warning that something is going wrong at the level of human personal being. We have several times seen that there are ways forward and ways backward, that is to say, there are directions which enhance our humanity, and there are directions which diminish and endanger it. The sense of guilt is a deterrent from following the ways towards diminution and destruction. The value and usefulness of the sense of guilt will be apparent to us if we recall the so-called 'negative' type of religious experience discussed in the last chapter. There we saw that it has been precisely through a painful experience of guilt that some people have been brought to that critical reorientation of their lives which we call 'conversion', and that some of the most outstanding religious pioneers have attained renewal by this route. I have acknowledged that sometimes guilt is disproportionate and may be paralysing. In the long run, however, guilt is more likely to be overcome by an experience of forgiveness than by an attempt to show that it was unreasonable to feel guilt in the first place. But it is usually easier to forgive than to accept forgiveness, for the latter case has to overcome the pride and self-sufficiency which we saw to be obstacles also in the transformation of the suffering of frustration and loss.

A fourth type of suffering is rather different from the others. We suffer vicariously, and this may be the most acute suffering of all. A parent, who may be able to endure a great deal of suffering affecting himself or herself, may find it much harder to endure the suffering of a son or daughter. Someone who has courageously opposed some tyranny and stood up to all the sufferings it has imposed on him and remained unbroken, may be much more vulnerable when the agents of that tyranny threaten his wife and children. The many links that bind us all in the solidarity of human society require that even those who are relatively untouched by personal suffering cannot remain unscathed by the suffering of others. If anyone did remain completely unaffected by the suffering of others, we should think that person a most inhuman monster. At this point again we see how suffering promotes compassion and concern. Nowadays our television screens bring before us almost immediately scenes of distress from all over the world, as flood or drought or war strikes some segment of the human race. There may be a danger that such scenes become so familiar that we come to accept them with indifference, but most people are touched by them. Even more are they touched by suffering that is closer to them, and many parents have been drawn more closely to each other through the suffering of a child. Of course, I am not saying that the suffering of a child is justified by what it may do for others. As I have said already, I do not want to get into the question of theodicy, since that is not necessary for my present purpose. I might feel very much like Dostoyevsky's Ivan in *The Brothers Karamazov* that there are some forms of innocent suffering that nothing can justify. But what is claimed here is something less, yet something which can hardly be denied, that the sufferings of others can awaken in us feelings of compassion and solidarity, and perhaps these feelings would not have been awakened otherwise.

I have mentioned the more obvious forms of human suffering, and have claimed that in each case the suffering is not an unmitigated evil, for it can be integrated into the character of the sufferer and so makes its own affirmative contribution to the formation of a mature humanity. At least, this is true where the suffering is not extreme. So we have seen that the discipline of suffering may promote courage and patience; that it certainly does, in many cases, increase compassion and concern for others; that where the suffering is a result of one's own wrongdoing, it may bring about a change of policy or even a religious conversion; that, in general, it delivers us from delusions of grandeur and brings us to a realistic understanding of our finitude, dependence and mortality. As Basil Mitchell has said, 'patient acceptance of suffering, infirmity and dependence is an important part of what makes men human'.[7] Does the human being need struggle, resistance and suffering for his maturing? If transcendence is like a rising path and even if there are experiences of gift and grace, there must be effort and overcoming. Sartre coined the term 'adversity coefficient'.[8] Suffering is like a coefficient, that is to say, an additional agency which, along with grace and effort, contributes to the drive toward transcendence.

What I have just been saying about suffering may seem very unrealistic. Ours is a time when the popular philosophy of life is an unashamed hedonism. Suffering is regarded as an unqualified evil, and every effort is made to eliminate it. We have become inordinately scrupulous about what we eat and drink; we are highly concerned about health; when we take exercise and play games we array ourselves in protective clothing; we try, as we have seen, to banish guilt feelings; and we even do our best to cover up the fact of death. So it becomes a question of who is realistic and who is unrealistic. The person who accepts that suffering is part of the human lot and who tries to come to terms with it and to draw from it whatever lessons it brings, or the person who vainly seeks to banish it and to live as if man could indeed fulfil the crazy desire to be God?

Of course, it is not quite so simple as that. For thousands of years, the human race has survived in a rather precarious way, suffering from disease, early mortality and poverty, most people eking out a bare existence, and this is still true of many millions today. Is it not natural and right that they should sweep away this mass of misery now that they have the powers conferred by science and technology? Is there not something morbid and masochistic in the claim that suffering is not altogether a bad thing? Yet we have to pause and ask what would happen if we succeeded in eliminating suffering, or, at least, a vast amount of suffering, for it is hard to see how it would ever be possible to eliminate death and the sense of bereavement which it brings to those who survive. Let us suppose that human lives were completely protected from beginning to end, untroubled by pain, anxiety, guilt, deprivation and so on. Would not this be like living in a cocoon, insulated from all danger, yet not really existing? Even if one were to represent it more favourably as what I have called a 'garden-of-Eden type of existence', would not this be intolerably boring after a time? Indeed, one might ask whether the craving for deliverance from every suffering and inconvenience, if pushed to its conclusion, does not reveal itself as the desire to return to the womb. There all needs were satisfied until the trauma of birth, when the child is thrust into the world and into history and begins to climb the perilous path that leads towards full humanity. Moreover, is not this excessive desire for protection paradoxically a concealed desire for death, for retreat from the threats of life in the world back into the unconscious? Freud, it will be remembered, recognized a death instinct as well as the instinct that aims at the enlargement of life. He wrote: 'If it is true that once – in an inconceivably remote past, and in an unimaginable way – life arose out of inanimate matter, then an instinct must at that time have come into being whose aim it was to abolish life once more and to re-establish the inorganic state of things.'[9] Sentience opens two possibilities which seem to be inseparable – the possibility of transcendence and the possibility of suffering. The latter cannot be abolished short of a lapse back into presentience, but it can become, at least to some extent, a coefficient in the drive toward transcendence.

Again, I have used the expression, 'to some extent'. Many will agree that 'to some extent' suffering may play an educative role in the formation of humanity. This can hardly be denied except by those who are uninterested in human freedom and dignity, and believe that all that human beings need is to be well fed, well amused and well adjusted. But what do we say when suffering is not just 'to some extent' but is total in its destructiveness and pointlessness? What do we say in the face of Auschwitz, which has become the classic case of senseless unjustifiable suffering in the modern world, and is surely without precedent in history, unless that precedent is Calvary? But could one possibly make that comparison? At Calvary, the suffering, by some mysterious transmutation, becomes redemptive and salvific. At Auschwitz too, suffering evoked in some courage, concern, self-giving and self-transcendence. Yet for many it was just senseless suffering. And what are we to say of the children at Auschwitz? Ulrich Simon remarks: 'We have no record of what the victims may have said, but it is probable that the vast majority here experienced an event completely beyond their own understanding. They could not but manifest the tragic bewilderment which is expressed by the little girl who stood next to her mother, clutching a doll to the last.'[10] 'To some extent' one can point to the need for suffering in human life, but when it reaches the pitch that it did in

Auschwitz, one can only fall silent. One cannot even blaspheme in this case, for Auschwitz was a human contrivance, coldly and ingeniously planned by modern alienated human beings who desired to be God. These human beings were, of course, destroying their own humanity even more than they were destroying their victims, for they became cold, heartless and numb, incapable even of suffering.

One falls silent in face of the excesses of suffering because there would be a kind of insensitivity in even seeming to 'explain' them. But the silence is not the silence of despair. It may be a silence that recognizes a 'more' which is inexpressible. John Hick, after recognizing the part which suffering plays in the work of soul-making, admits that there is 'a baffling problem of excessive and undeserved suffering' which has no such function. His appeal at this point is 'to the positive value of mystery'. He says, 'it may be that the very mysteriousness of this life is an important aspect of its character as a sphere of soul-making.'[11] The implication is that faith and trust need to be challenged to the utmost by that which the mind cannot grasp and rationalize.

There would seem to be a correlation between the capacity for suffering and the place of the suffering organism on the evolutionary scale. A dog suffers more intensely than an insect (if indeed the insect can be said to suffer at all), while a human being suffers more intensely than a dog. Among human beings, those who love are *ipso facto* especially vulnerable to suffering through the sufferings of others, while those who have lapsed into moral indifference (like the executioners of Auschwitz) seem to lose even the sensitivity to suffering. There is something like a law here: the higher the level of personal being, the greater the vulnerability to suffering.

Does not this imply then that if there is a God, he must suffer more than anyone else – he must, in a sense, experience the entire suffering of the world? Here we find ourselves once more in conflict with that understanding of God that so lifts him above the world and the creatures that some philosophers have claimed that he is an oppressive and alienating God. That God cannot suffer has been part of the traditional teaching about the God conceived in transcendent terms. But what sympathy could there be between such a God and human beings? If God is love, then must he not be vulnerable to suffering? Must he not be, in Whitehead's well known words, 'the great companion, the fellow sufferer who understands'?[12] Of course, this is not all that has to be said about God. He must also be the one who is never overwhelmed by suffering, but transforms it in a way of which we have some analogy in our own human experience. And all this seems to be clearly implied in the Christian belief that God is made known in and through the crucified Christ, yet crucifixion is not the end of the story but leads on to resurrection.

In this discussion of suffering, I have deliberately excluded any mention of a life beyond death or the suggestion that the sufferings of our present life might be made good and thus be given a *rationale* in some other life. This is not because I deny the possibility of such a life – the question will be considered when we discuss death and hope – but because I think it would be a fallacious type of argument. We have first of all to consider – as we have done in this chapter – the place of suffering in human life as we know it in this world, and if we find in it some affirmative characteristics, then we may be encouraged to believe that life is stronger than death, and only then may we go on to more speculative ideas.

XVIII

DEATH

In all the aspects of humanity that we have studied, we have tried never to lose sight of the fact that, however 'spiritual' he may become, however far he may transcend or however much dominance he acquires over nature, the human being remains embodied and the physical basis of his life is part of the dynamic interflow of natural forces. This means that he never escapes from certain constraints of nature. The size of a human being, for instance, is limited by the physical structure of the body. Giants exist only in legend, for there is a mechanical limit to the size of organism which the human skeletal structure could support. In a similar fashion, there is a limit to the duration of a human being. The body is such that under favourable conditions it might function for about eighty years, more or less, but there comes a time when it wears out. Better medical care keeps most people going longer nowadays than would once have been the case, but the extent to which human life could be extended is very limited. So we come to the fact of death, the fact that every human being reaches an end when consciousness is extinguished, the life processes cease and the organism disintegrates. No account of humanity can be complete if it does not ask about the significance of death. Dobzhansky, as we have noted, even suggested that it is death awareness that makes the fundamental biological difference between man and animal.[1] We have seen too that death in the human being, even if biologically it is very much like the death of any higher animal, is qualitatively different because it has been brought into the realm of the personal.[2] Death and dying enter into human experience, whether the death of others or the anticipation of one's own death, and, more than anything else, give us a sense of the finitude and even the precariousness of human existence.

There have been times when at least some people have thought it right to think frequently upon death and have surrounded themselves with reminders of its inevitable approach. No doubt these were times when the threats to life from disease and other causes were more numerous than they are now, and perhaps also when the expectation of a judgment after death weighed more heavily than in our time. Today, we seem to have gone to the opposite extreme so that death is a subject hardly to be mentioned and certainly not to be meditated upon. The older preoccupation with death is often considered to have been morbid. No doubt this may reflect the greatly increased security of life and the decline of the belief that there is anything beyond death. Yet if the older attitude may sometimes have verged on the morbid, it can hardly be right to have gone to the opposite extreme so that we avoid as far as possible thinking about what is a universal fate for human beings. It may be the case, of course, that concern about death lies below the surface. It may also be the case that although some of the older threats to life have diminished, new ones have come along. Since the advent of nuclear weapons, there has been lurking on the edges of the consciousness of many people, including young people, the awareness that death threatens in an unprecedentedly universal manner.

On the whole, however, young people do not think much about death. Everyone knows that death will eventually come, but this is a general truth with as yet little personal significance, for in youth death seems something far off. But as life goes on, death begins to obtrude itself, and it does so more and more. One's parents die, and when that happens there is withdrawn from the world a familiar presence that had always been there and on which one had counted. The withdrawal of this reliable presence may well be the event which makes us aware for the first time in more than an abstract way of the radical finitude and transience of human life. One's older friends die, and a time comes when one's contemporaries begin to die too. There comes an age when life no longer stretches seemingly endlessly in front, as it does in youth, and we realize that the future is limited. I should think that for many people in Western countries, fifty is a significant age, as far as attitudes to death are concerned. Up to some such age – and, although I have mentioned fifty, it obviously varies from one person to another – one is still, so to speak, on the way up and the interests of life have been expanding. But at some such age one realizes that one's main achievements are already over and that soon a contraction of activities will begin to take place. Death then begins to assume a reality that it did not have before. More of one's friends are dying, and we increasingly take to heart the truth of John Donne's famous words:

Here the bells can scarce solemnize the funeral of any person, but that I knew him, or knew that he was my neighbour. We dwelt in houses near to one another before, but now he is gone into that house into which I must follow him . . . No man is an island, entire of itself; every man is a piece of the continent, a part of the mainland. If a clod be washed away by the sea, Europe is the less, as well as if a promontory were, as well as if a manor of thy friends or of thine own were. Any man's death diminishes me, because I am involved in mankind. And therefore never send to know for whom the bell tolls. It tolls for thee.[3]

Wittgenstein once declared: 'Death is not an event of life. Death is not lived through.'[4] In a sense, this is obviously true. The word translated here 'lived through' is in the German *erlebt*, and could equally well be translated 'experienced'. Our experiences are 'lived through' and, by definition, death is not lived through, for it is the end of life. Yet this may be altogether too atomistic a view of the human being, as if he were an isolated impermeable individual, strictly confined to his own private experience. Donne had a more adequate understanding of a human being when he understood himself as 'involved in mankind' and sharing a wider experience so that whatever diminishes the whole was experienced by him as a diminution too. In that sense, death is experienced vicariously in the death of the other. Furthermore, even one's own death may already have entered into one's experience by anticipation, for death is not just that moment (so difficult to define in any case) when the life actually ends, but is also the process of dying, and one could say that this process has already begun in any human being. Clinical death may well be declared to be not an event of life but its end, yet as a human phenomenon death is not reducible to the medically certifiable moment of decease. In awareness and expectation as well as in our shared experience with others, death and dying cannot be excluded from our experience of life and may very profoundly affect our understanding of it.

Death presents some strange contradictions. On the one hand, it is the most certain event that will occur in anyone's biography. No one escapes death. It is the one event that can be predicted with absolute certainty about anyone. It is an ineluctable part of the human condition – so ineluctable and so tied up with the physical constitution of the human body that I think it can be confidently asserted that no advances in medicine or health care will ever eliminate death. But over against this certainty of death stands its uncertainty. It will happen, that is sure, but when it will happen or where it will happen or how it will happen – these matters are entirely uncertain. Here is the caprice of death. In some lives, it may come as a completion or perhaps as a release, and in such cases it has a kind of appropriateness. But as often as not, it comes out of season. It may come early, breaking in and disrupting a life in full course or even one which is just beginning, destroying whatever promise was there. It may come late, after years of suffering and longing for the end, or after a person's powers are spent, his mind and strength gone, so that only a subpersonal decaying organism is left – though one might say, in such a case, that this person *as a person* has died already. Again, there are so many different ways in which one may die. One may die violently through war or crime, pointlessly through an accident, unconsciously in hospital surrounded by the para- phernalia of modern medicine, quietly in one's own bed at home sur- rounded by one's family. Then there are all the varied and contrasting ways in which people meet death. Some welcome it; some meet it with calmness, equanimity, or even indifference; while for others the approach of death brings fear and anxiety. Death has innumerable forms, and it seems to be a matter of chance which one of these will eventually confront any one of us. No doubt it is largely a matter of chance, yet psychologists tell us that people to some extent contrive their own deaths. What seems like an accident may have been subconsciously invited. Or people may stage- manage their deaths – some have even written on 'the art of dying'. Some have wanted to meet death with full consciousness of this unique moment, and most people hope that they will be able to die with dignity.

We can all recall from experience instances of many different ways in which death has come to people that we have known, and it is perhaps significant that most people think of some ways of death as preferable to others, or, at least, as less undesirable. Just as we saw in the case of suffering, our judgments are relative. Death is not just a monochrome evil. We make distinctions, though it is not easy to know what the criteria for these distinctions are. Let me mention three instances that fell within my own experience in the past ten years or so.

The first case was that of a colleague, an academic in his late sixties. He had recently retired but still enjoyed full intellectual vigour and continued to teach a course in the institution he had served for forty years. One day he gave his lecture, went home and simply died, without any pain or anxious premonition. Most of his friends said it was a good way to die. There was no suffering, no long-drawn-out worries, no diminution of powers – just a quick and painless end to a life that had already fulfilled its potentialities. Of course, on the other side, one has to set the severe shock to his wife, and one has also to ask whether one would wish death to come with quite such suddenness, with no time to be aware of what was happening at such a crucial and unique moment of one's existence. Even someone who did not share the religious motivation of the Book of Common Prayer might nevertheless feel an appropriateness in the petition of the litany: 'From sudden death, Good Lord deliver us!' So it is not quite clear that a swift and painless death after one's main work is completed is preferable to any other, though it is often thought to be so.

Let me now give a contrary instance. A woman in middle life, active in many important causes, felt unwell, and the tests revealed that she was suffering from a cancer of the lung. At first she responded well to treatment and it seemed that she might recover and continue her valuable work for many years to come. But as so often happens in such cases, the symptoms before long returned, there was a protracted illness in which the disease tightened its grip and finally brought death. What are we to say about this case? Compared with the other, it was long drawn out and was attended by pain and discomfort, false hopes, disappointments, anxieties and the feeling of helplessness. But, as against these factors, the dying person was able to reflect on what was happening, and in this particular case was able to accept it in an impressive way. Her husband and children were able to adjust themselves to the impending death, and the ties of love and sympathy among the members of that family were deepened in a way that might not otherwise have been possible. So when we bring in different criteria, it is not obvious which of the two cases of death I have quoted shows a way of dying that is preferable to the other.

But does it make sense finally to talk of one way of death as 'preferable' to another? Let me mention a third case, where death was at its most irrational and inexplicable. This was a case of a couple in their early forties, with one child, a daughter of eleven. Almost simultaneously, both parents were stricken with fatal illness. The father was taken to one hospital with an incurable cancer of the stomach, the mother to another hospital with an equally incurable tumour of the brain. What can one say in a case like this? I think it is like those cases of suffering I mentioned earlier, where one has simply to fall silent, for anything that is said is just too glib and superficial. If any words are to be uttered, they cannot be the words of an individual but only the words of the liturgy that may still bring faith and courage to those are open to hear them.

When we consider the capriciousness of death, striking as it does in a seemingly quite random and wanton manner, talk about its 'appropriateness' and even relative judgments about some forms of death being 'preferable' to others, seems suddenly empty and unconvincing. We can understand why some philosophers have believed that the fact of death alone is enough to show us that human life is finally vain and pointless, an unhappy sport accidentally thrown up in the course of an endless and meaningless cosmic process. Jean-Paul Sartre declares: 'Death removes all meaning from life.'[5] This is not a comforting statement, but many people might think that it is a very honest one. All human effort, endeavour and sacrifice come finally to death, and often, as we have noted, death presents itself in bizarre and frustrating ways. Sartre, as is well known, has a tendency to exaggeration, so perhaps he was going too far in saying that death removes *all* meaning from life. Surely there are some limited areas of meaning left, even if there is no ultimate or overall meaning. But can one claim even this much? If a whole journey is meaningless or pointless, does this not infect every step on that journey? When we talk about 'meaning' in such a context as the 'meaning of life', we are talking about an embracing whole within which the several parts serve some purpose, so that they derive their meaning from the whole. So if there is no such whole, what meaning can belong to the parts? It will hardly do either to say that we must extend our view beyond the individual life and its termination by death to human society as a whole, and that in this wider context the sacrifices and achievements of the individual find their meaning. Human society lasts longer than individuals and generations, but society too will not escape death, whether the death of nuclear war or the death brought on by an exhausted and poisoned environment or the distant but apparently certain death that will come with the aging of the sun and the consequent changes in its planetary system. We have to take pretty seriously the claim that death finally voids the human adventure of meaning. Death, especially when we look beyond the death of the individual to the possible extinction of the race, does pose very grave questions about whether human life has any ultimate significance in the universe or if it is a mere by-product of forces which, from the human point of view, are godless and hopeless.

Sartre's view of death, however, is not the only one that we find among philosophers. A very different and affirmative role for death has been developed in the philosophy of Heidegger.[6] Whereas Sartre believed that death empties life of meaning (though in practice he did not follow so bleak a conviction), Heidegger taught that it is precisely death that allows human life to have meaning. If human beings were immortal and life went on for ever and ever, there could be no unifying pattern to it. It would literally be just one thing after another, an endless concatenation of contingencies, and that surely is meaninglessness. It would be like a sentence that wandered on for ever and never came to a full stop so that we never learn the sense of it; or like a piece of music that meandered on without the definite form of, say, a sonata movement or a theme with variations; or like a novel or play in which event followed event and scene followed scene without any unifying plot that eventually came to a dénouement. The point is that human life in time can have a meaning and unity only if there is an end to it, a boundary that gives a perspective within which priorities can be set and the various events and possibilities of life seen in their interrelationships as parts of a sense-giving whole. Death is a basic constitutive factor in finite human existence, and this existence is even called by Heidegger a 'being towards death' (Sein-zum-Tode). So, like some spiritual writers of earlier times, Heidegger bids us live in the realistic anticipation of death, for this allows us to see life as a limited whole and so to live with a measure of purpose and energy in the face of the end. It is an eschatological understanding of life, though I am using the word here in a strictly secular sense, since Heidegger remains agnostic about any human destiny beyond death, though he does explicitly dissociate himself from the atheism of Sartre.[7] But to use the word 'eschatological' to describe his understanding of life in the face of the end does suggest a comparison with the first generation of Christians who lived in expectation of an imminent end of the age and who, because they lived in this expectation, were perhaps the most dynamic generation of human beings that have ever existed. On this way of looking at life, it is its intensity, not its extendedness, that is really important. One may contrast this with the modern evasion of death and concern for longevity. But a life that went on for even a hundred years and was mostly taken up with trivialities would be infinitely poorer than a life which had with zest and intensity realized some meaningful pattern, however brief its duration.

The relation of death, time, finitude and the structuring of a meaningful biography can be understood in a somewhat different way as the overcoming of mere transience and successiveness, even, one might say, as the emergence of being in the midst of becoming. Whereas an animal lives pretty much in the present instant and is distracted hither and thither by successive stimuli, the human existent transcends the mere instant, and the more human he is, the more he transcends it. He extends himself through a span of time. Through memory, he brings with him his past; through anticipation, he is already reaching into his future; thus his present is never a knife-edge instant, so to speak, but always a span of time that includes both something of the past and something of the future, spilling out, so to speak, on both sides of the present moment. When one hears a sentence, one does not hear a succession of isolated words, one hears the sentence as a whole. When one is engaged in an action, even a complicated action, that too is understood and experienced as a whole. The stronger and more mature the person is, the less is he the victim to the changing influences of each succeeding instant, the greater and more comprehensive is the span that gathers his past, present and future into a unity. Actions are parts of policies, policies are coordinated to become the expression of character. This ability to transcend the instant can already be interpreted as man's taste for the infinite, to use Schleiermacher's famous expression.[8] It is already a kind of eternity within time. And one could imagine the extension of the span to include all time, gathering up all the past in a perfect memory and anticipating all that is to come, so that, in a sense, everything would be present and experienced simultaneously. This would not be a finite human experience, but it is how people have sometimes tried to imagine the eternal consciousness of God, for whom, in the words of a psalmist, 'a thousand years are but as yesterday when it is past, or as a watch in the night'.[9] But although this is not a human experience, there are analogies on the level of human experience.

It is very important to notice that the human being's taste for the infinite or the eternal should not be confused with the desire to be God, which Sartre imputes to him. That a finite being should have a taste for the infinite might seem to be an evident absurdity, yet the experience of the transcending of the temporal instant even in everyday life shows that we can make some sense of the conjunction of transience and eternity, finitude and infinity, in the human being.

No doubt there is a taste for the infinite which is at bottom a vain and insane desire to be God, in the sense of usurping God's place and making oneself an absolute. It is perhaps the oldest of human temptations. 'You shall be as gods,' says the serpent to Eve in the garden of Eden.[10] Many Christian theologians, from Augustine to Niebuhr, have believed that pride is the ultimate sin, and they have a good case, when one considers the many tyrants that have appeared in history, men whose overweening arrogance has indeed deluded them into believing that they can exercise an absolute power over the earth and their fellow human beings. One must distinguish from this a different quest, the desire not to usurp or replace God, but the desire to participate in the life of God. This is the transcendence described in an earlier chapter,[11] and although we noted that early Christian writers had spoken of the 'deification' of man, they did not mean by this the impossible project of man's becoming God in the sense of replacing him, but that humanity, made in the image of God, finds its goal in the increasing realization of that image and in a deepening communion with God. Perhaps it is only some such belief that can rescue from absurdity the paradox of a being who is through and through finite and temporal, yet who is ever drawn out of himself by the taste for the infinite and eternal.

There is another related problem that has to be sorted out at this point. Our present chain of reflection began from the thought that death, as a limit or boundary, is needed for the construction of a unified life and therefore for whatever experience of an eternity within time the human being can attain. But the biblical account of the origin of death, as told in that very story to which we have just been appealing, sees death as the punishment for sin. Adam had been told that in the day that he disobeyed God, he would surely die.[12] At first sight, it might seem that this way of understanding death is much closer to common sense than the way which sees it as a necessary limit to the kind of existence that we call human. For human beings have consistently rebelled against death and have felt it to be somehow unnatural. Thus they have had to find some explanation for the fact that people die. They have not been able to accept death as a natural part of the human condition – something which is still true, though today we do not tell an aetiological myth but surround death with a conspiracy of silence.

It may be granted that in a sinful world, death has assumed terrors that it might not have had if human beings had been less prone to sin. It may be granted too that there is a profound sense in which death, considered not just as a physical phenomenon but as the dissolution of human person-hood, can be seen as a consequence and working out of sin. But while some of the more sombre aspects of death are bound up with sin and alienation, death as an ending that is necessary and even appropriate to a finite being cannot be wholly laid at the door of sin or seen as unnatural or a punishment or a disorder in the universe. Death belongs to human finitude rather than to human sin. The point has been well made by Karl Rahner:

> If death is the consequence of the fall of the first man, this implies that, before his sin, the first man was not under the necessity of dying. This doctrine of faith of course does not mean that the first man in paradise, had he not sinned, would have lived on endlessly in the bodily life of this world. It can confidently be said that he would surely have had an end to his life; remaining in his bodily constitution of course he would have brought this life of his from within to its perfect and full maturity. In other words, Adam would have brought his personal life to its perfect consummation even in his bodily form through a 'death' which would have been a pure, active self-affirmation.[13]

So death as the final horizon would be needed to define the boundary of even a finite life that had achieved something like an eternity in time. Ideally, death would be as appropriate to such a life as the final chord to a great symphony. Something of the meaning of this can be seen in such cases as the death of Christ and the death of Socrates – cases where, *pace* Wittgenstein, death is an event perfectly integrated into life, not something that happens to a victim but, in Rahner's phrase, 'a pure, active self-affirmation'. In both cases, however, the backdrop is a sinful world whose hostility is expressed in the death alongside the spiritual attainment of the one who dies.

Death has been called by Karl Jaspers a 'limit-situation' (*Grenzsituation*).[14] It is an ultimate in human existence, bringing us to a point where we have to face the most serious questions about the meaning and goal of human life or, indeed, whether it has any meaning or goal. In this chapter, as in the preceding chapter on suffering, I have tried to show that we are not confronted with an unmitigated evil. Death, like suffering, can make affirmative contributions to humanity. We have seen that death can sometimes come as a release. We have seen that we make relative judg-ments about death, rating some forms as preferable to others. More importantly, we have seen that the vanishing-point of death seems to be necessary if there are to be structure and perspective in a human life. We have seen that there are some cases where death comes as the culmination and final glory of a life – and there are other cases where death can redeem a thitherto unworthy or mediocre life. All this, it should be clearly observed, has been argued *without any appeal whatever to the possibility of a life beyond death*. We have simply considered death as we know it in our life in this world, and we have discovered that grim and frightening though it is in many of its aspects, it also brings its contributions – some of them perhaps indispensable – to human life.

But have we not been far too idealistic in all this talk of dying with dignity, transcending the instant, building up a unified and meaningful life, constructing an ordered biography, bringing something of the quality of eternity ('eternal life') into the fleeting moments of our transience? For how many people ever achieve a life of this kind? Is not the well-rounded existence the fate reserved for a very few favoured people, while for most life is still an untidy ragbag when death comes along and puts an end to it? Even if one makes some concessions about the possibility that death may sometimes contribute something to life or heighten the awareness and direction of life, surely it remains on the whole a negative and destructive phenomenon.

I did acknowledge that there are cases of death where one can only remain silent – just as I acknowledged also in the case of suffering. There are cases where it seems impossible to find any hidden mitigation, but this fact does not take away from the mitigations that can be found in other cases. Does this final impenetrable mystery of the apparently unmitigated death bring us then to the question whether the human being can hope beyond death? As I have said above, I have held off this question about life beyond death as long as possible. To try to draw the sting of death too early or too easily is not to take seriously its threat and its finality. That is why one must consider death as we know it in the daily lives of human beings in this world. But the fact that we have found that even on this level death is not entirely dark, negative and frustrating does suggest that we can explore the possibility of a hope beyond death without being guilty of mere escapism.

— XIX —

HOPE

Human beings live in hope – indeed, I would hazard a guess that if hope were totally extinguished and there remained only a black despair, it would be impossible to go on living. There has to be a chink of light, however dim, a possibility of good, however uncertain, if there is to be any motivation to go forward into the future. For hope obviously has to do with the future. Every human life is oriented to the future, as day by day the 'leading edge', as we have called it, cuts its way into the time that lies ahead.

It is not easy to give any brief definition or description of hope.[1] It is a diffuse, inclusive concept, denoting a mood or attitude in which beliefs, emotions, imagination and purpose are all combined. It is characterized by a measure of confidence and affirmative expectation about the future, but it should never be confused with a brash shallow optimism, which is a mere counterfeit of hope. A genuine and realistic hope is usually also fragile because of its awareness of the ambiguities of the future. The person who knows hope in the face of the future will also have known the alternative mood of fear. There are some predominantly hopeful natures, and some predominantly fearing natures, but most people will have known both moods. But one of the most striking facts of human existence is that on the whole hope seems to predominate over fear, and often we are astonished to find that people whom we might expect to have been reduced to despair are still entertaining hope. This tenacity of hope is not without its significance, as we shall see.

It might seem that a mood so elusive as hope could hardly provide a firm datum for a philosophy of human nature, and still less for a general philosophy having metaphysical or ontological pretensions. However, at least two philosophers of recent times have made the concept of hope quite central to their thought, and it will be helpful if we begin by considering what they have said on the subject.

The first of the two philosophers is Gabriel Marcel, who has spoken explicitly of a 'metaphysic of hope'.[2] Marcel's view of human nature is close at many points to the one set forth in this book. It will be remembered that his name was introduced when we were considering transcendence.[3] Like Sartre, Marcel thought of the human being as in a process of transcendence, that is to say, he is, in Marcel's own expression, *homo viator*, on his way towards a fuller and more authentic humanity. But whereas Sartre conceived the goal of pilgrimage to be a self-chosen and self-made essence, Marcel was a theist and believed that the end of the human transcendence is participation in the transcendent being of God. This is not just an arbitrary speculation but is based, at least in part, on a phenomenology of the human condition. Such a phenomenology reveals that hope is present in virtually everything that we do. Marcel is not talking about grandiose hopes, but about the simplest, even trivial, hopes that enter into everyday life. 'I hope that James will come to lunch tomorrow.' This is an example of what Marcel calls hope 'of a low order', but he argues that we must pass from this experience of hope 'in its diluted or diffused state to the same experience, touched – I do not say absolutely conceived – at its highest tension or again at its point of complete saturation'.[4] Even the most trivial hopes imply other hopes and are part of a fabric of hope which in turn lets us see the world in a hopeful way. But this predisposition towards hoping implies a ground of hope beyond the human act of hoping, and it is this, in Marcel's view, that differentiates hope from optimism and pessimism alike, for these are said both to lie strictly within the province of the human ego.

The other philosopher who has made hope central to his thinking belongs to a tradition very different from Marcel's. I mean Ernst Bloch, neo-Marxist and for a long time hard-line Stalinist. His major work is entitled *Prinzip der Hoffnung*. Bloch too sees the human being in a process of transcendence, and it is hope, described in terms of creative imagination and even utopianism, that beckons him on to new levels of being: 'The human being has still much in front of him. He is constantly being transformed in and through his work. He is constantly standing before boundaries which cease to be such as he perceives and surpasses them. What is authentic in humanity as in the world waits in its potentiality, fearing frustration and hoping for success.'[5] The coupling of humanity with the world in this quotation refers to the fact that in Bloch's philosophy hope is not just a human or sociological principle but in some sense also a metaphysical principle. Not only the human race but the universe itself has hopeful potentialities awaiting realization. This might suggest that Bloch was moving toward a kind of pantheism, but it would be going too far to say this. He remained an atheist, but perhaps one could say that it was a religious or quasi-religious atheism. This is borne out by the fact that his orthodox Marxist critics accused him of 'mysticism', while such Christian theologians as Jürgen Moltmann have shown appreciation for his work. Certainly, one must question whether hope can be given so central a place without the consequence of a transhuman ground of hope – God, in traditional language.

But let us come back to hope as we find it in everyday life. At this level, most of our hopes do not even find expression in words, but they are tacitly implied in the future-oriented actions that we do. When someone sows a field or builds a house or takes a course of study or marries a spouse or brings children into the world, he or she has acted in hope. There are many implications latent in such acts. They evince a basic trust in the future, for although hopes are sometimes frustrated, they often come to fruition, and our actions are evidence for our belief (perhaps never formulated) that it is worthwhile to trust in the future. If we think of this further, we see that to act in hope also implies the belief that the world has some openness in its texture, some space for freedom and creativeness, so that even if it is only to a small extent, each of us has some share in the shaping and transforming of the world. Beyond these ordinary everyday hopes cherished by individuals or families there are larger hopes. There is, for instance, the hope of the statesman or political activist or social reformer, a hope that might embrace an entire nation or even the whole human race. The more daring and imaginative the hope, the greater must be the trust in the future. No doubt at this level there is the danger of a utopianism that loses touch with reality and then the hope might become a mere illusion. On the other hand, it is the entertaining of large-scale hopes and visions of the future that promotes the criticism of existing institutions and opens the way for change. Hope is the spur to human transcendence on both the individual and social levels. But if hope is the spur to transcendence and if hope also implies trust in the future, then the very presence of hope in the world gives the lie to the contention of those philosophers who have maintained that the freedom and transcendence of man require the abolition of God. That would be true only if God were somewhat primitively conceived as a celestial despot. Of course, one has to concede that such a conception or misconception of God has been common enough in the history of religion, including the history of the Christian church from the time of Constantine onwards. But the transcendence that is motivated by hope (and is there any other kind?) would seem to be not only compatible with belief in a God conceived in non-oppressive terms, but positively to lean towards it. I do not wish to exaggerate the point, but hope does seem to demand a trust in the future, and such a basic trust is an important element in belief in God or however we might name him. When I briefly expounded Bloch's ontology of hope, I raised the question whether such a metaphysic does not require some religious interpretation and suggested that Bloch's atheism was of a religious or quasi-religious kind. Certainly, it is in his writings that we find the words, 'Where there is hope, there is religion.'[6]

In the same passage, Bloch uses the expression 'total hope'. What would this mean? We have seen how hope can be found on many levels, from the tacit hopes implicit in everyday life to the large-scale hopes of prophets and statesmen. A total hope would be a hope for nothing less than the whole human race, a hope for the world itself. Such a hope would have unmistakable religious overtones and would demand a fully eschatological theology. This, however, would have to be free from any hint of fatalism. It would leave room for human freedom and therefore for human sin and error, so that even a total hope would retain the fragility that belongs to all hope. Only so could it encourage human transcendence towards the realization of its vision of the whole human race living at peace with itself and its environment. If the fulfilment of the goal were guaranteed by automatic progress or divine decree, that would encourage not hope but an irresponsible optimism.

We have also to acknowledge, recalling our earlier discussions of conscience,[7] that the details of this goal of human striving cannot be known in advance. They will emerge only through a history of self-discovery, creativity and transformation. That is why the religions use a mythological or symbolic language about the goal of the human pilgrimage. Christianity, for instance, expresses its eschatological hope in such expressions as the 'kingdom of God', the 'resurrection of the dead', the 'second coming of Christ' – expressions which do not convey any precise *conceptual* content, but which are not on that account meaningless, for they do point in a certain direction towards a fulfilment of humanity in terms derived from the teaching and career of Jesus Christ.

We have seen that although the final goal of humanity is hidden, there are nevertheless some givens in the human condition which indicate directions in which the goal is to be sought and warn us against following other directions. So although one cannot specify in detail what the goal is, one can make some extrapolations that are not empty. Thus I permitted myself a few sentences back to speak of a vision of a universal peace. I did so on the grounds that love or an affirmative relation to others is necessary to human fulfilment, and that peace is the social or global virtue that corresponds to love in interpersonal relations.[8] No one has yet discovered the full meaning of peace, and still less has a true peace ever been realized. How, for instance, does one reconcile the common good with individual liberty? Yet some vision of peace and a hope of its possibility are all-important if the multifarious activities and achievements of the human race are to be drawn towards a truly fulfilling goal.[9]

But is this 'total hope', as I have called it, not just a grandiose delusion?

I borrowed the expression from Bloch who has often been criticized as a mere utopian. Kolakowski passes a sharp judgment on him: 'Throughout his life he remained a literary man, deeply versed in books, dreaming of a perfect world, yet unable to explain how it was to be created, or even what form its perfection was to take.'[10] Have not we strayed even further from reality by compounding philosophical speculation with Christian eschatology?

On the contrary, I would say that it is only by the introduction of the religious dimension that one could rescue the total hope of an ideal human society from the dreamland of utopia. I did in fact in an earlier discussion[11] criticize those who believe that social engineering can usher in the perfect society. I do not deny, of course, that the work of politicians and sociologists is necessary for the amelioration of human life, but they certainly cannot bring about that radical transformation and renewal of human nature needed if the race is to achieve its full potentiality for transcendence. The symbol 'kingdom of God' does not stand for a perfected human society but for a transformed reality that is indeed a work of God, though a work that God will do only with human consent and cooperation.

Let me now make three points concerning a universal, inclusive or total hope. 1. If there is serious hope at all, then in the long run it cannot help becoming a total hope. 2. A universal hope posits the reality of God. 3. Such a hope must also be a hope beyond death.

In the first place, then, any hope tends to develop into an inclusive hope. We have seen that hope occurs on many levels, from the simple everyday hopes of the individual person onward. But we have also seen repeatedly that no individual can find fulfilment in a purely self-regarding way. 'No man is an island,' so that what diminishes others diminishes me, and what enhances others enhances me. No hope, therefore, can be purely self-regarding. It must reach out to embrace others – first, no doubt, to those to whom I am tied by bonds of natural love, but eventually to all mankind. If my ultimate hope is for wholeness or (in more traditional language) salvation, it is clear that there can be no wholeness for the solitary individual wrenched away from the human context within which he or she belongs. I can hope for myself only as part of a wider hope which eventually expands to be a hope for the human race and for the world.

In the second place, a hope so universal and inclusive could hardly be realized by finite and sinful humanity. The very existence of such a hope (and I have suggested that it is latent in every lesser hope) seems to demand a transhuman agency for the radical transformation that would be required; or, to put it in another way, a transcendent reality (God) whose transcendent being is the goal that draws out our human transcendence. There are, I think, analogies that make this way of viewing the human pilgrimage more intelligible and more credible. If we consider the evolutionary process as it has gone forward on this planet, we recognize that there have been critical epochs or even leaps when something new has emerged. The most obvious cases are the emergence of living things out of a non-living matrix, and later the emergence of personal beings out of animal life. If one had been able to observe the development of the earth, then before these emergences took place, there could have been no inkling of the novelty that would appear – indeed, it would have seemed incredible. It seems reasonable to expect that there will be comparable emergences in the future, though we cannot from this side foresee what they will be. Does the symbol 'kingdom of God' express the hope of a new emergence which would be not just an amelioration of the human condition as we know it but a transformation so radical that it could be called 'a new heaven and a new earth',[12] perhaps a new and to us unimaginable form of personal community in which social and individual interests would be reconciled? Such an emergence or transformation would, of course, be only in part analogous to those that have taken place in evolution. The latter were brought about by the 'laws' of nature, but what I have in mind is a transformation on the personal level to be brought about by personal agency – by God, as the ultimate creator and author, but also by human beings, whose free cooperation in making ready the earth would seem to be needed even by God. A new personal community cannot be heteron-omously imposed, but only inspired and accepted.

In the third place, we seem to be led to a hope that goes beyond death. The solidarity with our fellow human beings that makes us include them in any worthy hope cannot be confined to those who happen to be alive at this time, but must extend also to the men and women of the past. Furthermore, it would be a poor hope which visualized the kingdom of God as reserved for the fortunate generations of the future and had no hope to offer for the earlier generations that had suffered and died to make ready the earth. Whatever the difficulties in the way, the hope must be extended to the dead. Alongside the symbol of the coming kingdom, one must set that other Christian symbol of the resurrection of the dead. It is not easy to see what this can mean, but the logic of hope seems to demand that it should have a place in any truly inclusive hope for the world. It might be said of course, that if God is the ultimate ground of hope, then there are no limits to what may be hoped for, except the limits that human freedom sets to God himself. This may well be true, but it is too quick and arbitrary a way of settling the matter. A hope beyond death is bound to be a speculative matter, but perhaps we can get further light on it, so that it appears to be not just an arbitrary conviction but can be seen to lie within the bounds of possibility.

In the two chapters preceding this one, we have considered the place of suffering and death in human existence. I deliberately kept away in these discussions from any speculations about life beyond death or how it would affect our understanding of suffering and death. These topics were considered strictly within the limits of our temporal life on earth. I rejected the view that suffering and death make life meaningless or not worthwhile. Neither suffering nor death, we found, is an unmitigated evil, and each of them can even be said to make some affirmative contribution to the formation of a human person. At the end of each of these chapters, however, we had to acknowledge that in some of their forms suffering and death are so apparently dark and senseless that one can only be silent before them. There are cases where all arguments break down and any 'explanation' would seem to be mere insensitiveness on the part of the person who offers it. It is at this point that the question of a hope beyond death can no longer be kept at a distance. So we come back to the topic of death and to the question whether hope can transcend even death.

A hope that reaches beyond death is, of course, extremely ancient, indeed, just about as old as the human race. While sophisticated modern philosophers may say that death removes all meaning from life, the bulk of mankind was never willing to accept so bleak a conclusion. In prehistoric times, long before any records of what people were thinking had been written down, there is unwritten evidence to show that these distant ancestors of ours had been thinking about death and were already entertaining hopes that reached beyond death. That evidence comes from the manner in which they disposed of the dead. The bodies of the dead were buried with the greatest care, and often implements or ornaments that they had used in life were buried with them, as if they might still have need of them. Sometimes the bones were daubed with red ochre, the red symbolizing blood and therefore life. All this bears mute testimony to an as yet inarticulate hope for the dead perhaps as long as half a million years ago.[13]

Passing from prehistory to history, we find the very widespread phenomenon of ancestor worship and such practices as holding periodic festivals at the tombs, festivals in which the dead were supposed to participate. These practices still go on in various parts of the world today. Beliefs about death and life beyond death found expression in myths and folk tales, sometimes of very great complexity. The great civilization of ancient Egypt seems to have been to an extraordinary degree fascinated with death and what comes after death. Some of the Egyptican practices, like the mummification of bodies and the provision of the necessities of daily life for the deceased within the tomb, simply continued and elaborated the traditions that had come down from a far more remote past. But now something like a theology of the life to come begins to emerge. The ancient Egyptians believed in a final judgment and speculated on the transformation of the mode of human existence.[14]

No doubt many of the traditional beliefs about the dead would be judged

by us today to be mere superstition. Yet there is something impressive in
the persistent belief that a human life is not annihilated by death. In all the
myths and ceremonies, some very deep conviction of men and women
about themselves is trying to find expression, perhaps just the recognition
that every human being has a unique worth and should not simply perish.

In ancient Greece, the question of life beyond death was brought into
philosophy and made the subject of rational argument. Plato, impressed
with the power of the human mind to rise above bodily desires and passions
to the contemplation of eternal ideas, taught that what is real in any human
being is an immaterial, indestructible, immortal soul. The doctrine of
recollection is taken to show that the soul has preexisted life in the body
which it now occupies, and after death it will leave the body and continue
to exist elsewhere. Socrates is represented as discoursing on immortality
with his friends in the prison before his execution, and he confidently
affirms: 'Beyond question, the soul is immortal and imperishable, and our
souls will truly exist in another world.'[15] This Platonist theory of an
independently existing soul takes us far beyond the myths and folk tales of
earlier times, and has been accepted in one form or another by large
numbers of philosophers, including some who are alive at the present
time. But it can hardly be denied that there are many difficulties attendant
on it. The activities of the soul, our mental and spiritual life, are all closely
correlated with physical occurrences in the brain and in the bodily organism
generally, and it is hard to see how the soul could exist apart from the
body. We did in fact at quite an early stage in this book reject any dualism
of body and soul and maintained that the human being is a psychosomatic
unity, and we also noted that if one could imagine a soul existing apart
from the body, it is hard to see how it could relate to a world or to other
people or have any content to its experience.[16] It is through the body that
we relate to that which is other than ourselves, and there could be no
worthwhile human existence without relatedness. So even if there were an
independently existing soul, which seems improbable, it would still be
doubtful if it could sustain in any significant way the hope of a life beyond
death.

So we turn to the specifically Judaeo-Christian tradition, which speaks
not of an immortal soul but of a resurrection of the body, though one has
to acknowledge that confused elements of Platonism soon combined with
the idea of resurrection. The confusion persists in contemporary
Christianity.

It is generally agreed that in the oldest parts of the Bible there is nothing
that could properly be called a *hope* beyond death. We do find the idea of
sheol, a dim and dusty underworld where human beings would survive for
a time at least in some pale ghostly manner. I say this could not be called a
hope, for what was visualized was a minimal level of existence, a mere

shadow of what had been known on earth, like the shadowy existence to which Homer's heroes were consigned when their souls descended into Hades. It was only at the time of the Maccabean wars that a definite *hope* in a life beyond death began to take shape as part of the Jewish faith. This happened not, as with the Greeks, through philosophical reflection, but as a result of a *moral* demand. So many young and promising lives had been cut short in these wars that it seemed that this could not be the whole story. Surely a righteous God had something more in store for them. So there arose the Jewish belief in a resurrection of the dead, and whatever else it might mean, resurrection implies a full personal mode of existence, quite different from the shadowy semi-existence of *sheol*.

Not all Jews accepted these new beliefs. The conservative Sadducees denied a resurrection of the dead and stayed with the older beliefs of Israel. But hope in a resurrection of the dead grew stronger, and of course passed into Christianity. In the Christian creeds, both the resurrection of Jesus Christ and the general resurrection of the dead are explicitly affirmed.

But is not belief in a resurrection even more improbable than belief in the immortality of an independently existing soul? I think one would have to agree, if the expression 'resurrection of the body' were taken in a strictly literal sense. Few people would believe that once the body has decayed and crumbled to dust, the particles of which it was composed could come together again to constitute the same living organism. But resurrection is a symbol rather than a precise concept and from quite an early time has been understood in figurative and sophisticated ways. In his great discourse on resurrection, Paul makes it clear that the resurrection body is not simply identical with the body of flesh and blood. There would seem to be both continuity and discontinuity. 'It is sown a physical body, it is raised a spiritual body . . . I tell you this, brethren: flesh and blood cannot inherit the kingdom of God, nor does the perishable inherit the imperishable.'[17] Can we make sense of this?

Perhaps we could think of it in some such way as follows. We experience the world in terms of the successiveness of time. Things come into existence and pass out of existence, people are born and die. But is that which is past now totally non-existent? It is indeed no longer there for me, but has it simply vanished into nothing? Now we may recall a different mode of human experience to which we have paid attention earlier.[18] We sometimes transcend the mere flux of instants and experience a span of time, carrying the past with us into the present. It gives us some inkling of a possible unity or simultaneity of experience, in which past, present and future would be gathered up together. That might be the meaning of 'eternal life'. We experience this transcending of the instant only in a fragmentary way, but if there is a divine experience, then what we know only in a fragmentary way will be for God complete. The entire past remains present to him, including, we must suppose those persons who have lived in the past.

We can express this in another way. The whole world is present to God, or, we might even say, in God. But this cannot mean simply the world as it is now at this moment. Indeed, one has to ask whether it makes any sense to talk about the world 'as it is now at this moment'. If one accepts Einstein's theory of relativity, the notion of a universal 'now' has been abolished, even for a human experience that must view things from a particular location in space-time. It would be even less applicable for a divine experience, for God is not tied to any particular point.

Does this give us a glimpse of a possible understanding of the resurrection of the dead or of a hope for life beyond death? I have consistently used the expression 'hope beyond death' and 'life beyond death' rather than 'after death'. It is not that an immortal soul will go on living after death or that we shall be provided with new bodies in the future, but that the embodied lives we have lived here are eternally present to God as he embraces within himself the entire past of his creation. To be so embraced within the divine life would be the goal of human transcendence, which early Christian writers ventured to call 'deification'.

The view sketched here need not mean a merging or absorption into God. Rather, it could be understood as the most intense communion, the final vision of God. Nor need one suppose that the past which is present to God is a frozen and petrified past. Rather, as the history of the future unfolds itself and brings nearer the kingdom of God, the final consummation of his love, the past too is being healed and prepared for participation in that kingdom. We remember again that God is not tied to a point of time. The eschatological symbol of a 'descent into hell' is relevant at this point.

The paradigm case is that of Jesus Christ. His was a transcendent humanity, in which the image of God came fully to expression, so that he was even called the God-man. His followers experienced his resurrection, believing that beyond death he lived in God and God in him. They also believed him to be the first-fruits of a general resurrection of humanity.

These attempts to spell out in some detail the nature of a hope beyond death are necessarily speculative, but I have pointed out that any adequate study of the human being must go beyond empirical description to the imaginative exploration of possibilities. Nevertheless, even the most exalted hopes expressed in the sometimes florid language of Christian eschatology are continuous with those everyday hopes that already posit a ground of hope in the universe. In the final chapter, we shall look again at some of the features of our humanity that point to the transhuman reality we call God.

XX

BEING

In the posthumously published writings of Nietzsche, there occurs a striking expression which sums up very well the understanding of humanity that has emerged in this book: 'To stamp becoming with the character of being.'[1] Of course, Nietzsche meant this in a different way. For him, it meant the highest will to power. I certainly do not wish to minimize the place of will and human effort in the struggle for transcendence, but I have also found a place for grace and believe that the priority and initiative belong to the transcendent being towards which our human becoming seeks in turn to transcend. Nietzsche believed that being is always relative to us: 'Being – we have no other idea of it than that which we derive from *living*.'[2] I would prefer to say that we are relative to being, or perhaps one should say, 'correlative'. If our idea of being must come from our own living and becoming, that is to say, from the unfolding of our humanity, that is because, to begin with, our becoming derives from being and already bears an initial impression of being. As and if that initial impression is developed and made explicit in a transcendent becoming, then in that becoming there occurs a disclosure of being.

We could say much the same thing using a different idiom from the history of philosophy, and talk about man as the microcosm. On this view, the human being is a kind of universe in miniature, reflecting in his little world the character and structure of the macrocosm within which his existence is set. This view has a long history which may go back as far as Democritus, though it is in Plotinus that we meet the first full statement of the analogy of structure obtaining between the human being and the cosmos. 'For Plotinus,' according to A. H. Armstrong, 'the frontier between microcosm and macrocosm is by no means rigid and precise. The boundaries shutting off the self from the universe are largely illusory, and disappear in the higher stages of perception.'[3] Augustine combined neo-

Platonism with Christianity, and went even beyond Plotinus, for he argued that the human mind is nothing less than an analogue of the triune being of God: 'The mind is an image of the Trinity in its own memory, understanding and will.'[4] In the Middle Ages and the Renaissance, there were many thinkers, both theological and philosophical, for whom the human being was a microcosm, exhibiting on a small scale the structure not only of the natural cosmos but even of God in relation to the world, though in such cases they moved in the direction of pantheism or, at least, of panentheism. At the beginning of the Enlightenment, the idea of man as microcosm received one of its most powerful statements from Leibniz, who declared that 'every monad is, in its own way, a mirror of the universe'.[5] In the mid-nineteenth century Lotze entitled his major philosophical work *Microcosmus*, while more recently the philosophy of Whitehead and his followers has used the body/soul analogy to explicate the relation of the world to God.

It does seem that, up to a point, a fairly good case can be made out for thinking of the human being as a miniature cosmos. For instance, in the course of the many millions of years of evolution, man has summed up in himself the various stages through which the planet has passed. From one point of view, a human being is a few kilograms of various material substances, so he contains within himself the physico-chemical level of being. From another point of view, he is a living organism to whom zoologists can assign a definite place in the animal kingdom. From still another point of view, he is a person, endowed with freedom, reason, conscience and so on. Whether his participation in these spiritual qualities allows us to think of the human being as somehow reflecting God as well as the natural universe is a matter of debate. Those who hold to a strongly transcendent view of God deny that we can learn about God from the study of humanity. Barth, for instance, in his most typical utterances, regards God as wholly other to man, deplores the *analogia entis* and maintains that there is no way by which the mind could proceed from the creaturely being of man to God.[6] But one is bound to ask whether this teaching is not modified by his later talk about a humanity in God.[7] Admittedly, this humanity of God is for Barth the true or archetypal humanity and is prior to our creaturely humanity. But though it comes first in the order of being, must not our own humanity come first in the order of knowing? Surely there is some link between the humanity of God and humanity as we know it on earth. If so, then our ordinary everyday humanity must afford on the finite level some clue, however distant, to the being of God. A similar argument holds if we talk in more traditional language about an image of God in man. This doctrine certainly does not imply that there is a 'divine spark' in the human being, understood in any pantheistic way, but it does imply that there is, so to speak, a reflection of the infinite in the finite, so that some knowledge of God is to be gleaned from the creature. If it is held, on the other hand, that there is an absolute discontinuity between God and man – as there would be if the expression 'wholly other' were to be taken with complete seriousness – then it seems to me God would remain a completely unknown quantity and anything like an incarnation or a revelation through a human person would be ruled out as impossible.

Of course, it is not only those who wish to defend the absolute transcendence and otherness of God who object to any attempt to proceed by analogy from the nature of the human being to speculations about God or even about the character of the universe. Atheists are equally critical of such a move, which they regard as simply the projecting of human imaginings on a godless world. The classic example is that of Feuerbach who, as we have seen earlier,[8] believed that man projects an idealized concept of human nature into empty metaphysical space, as it were, and thereby alienates himself from his true being. Actually, the views of the transcendentalist and those of the atheist may be closer than is usually suspected. When in the nineteen-sixties some American theologians revived Nietzsche's proclamation of the death of God and believed that they could construct a Christian theology without God, it was noted that they had all been at one time devotees of the theology of Karl Barth. The connection was made clear by the statement of one of them, William Hamilton: 'It is a very short step but a critical one, to move from the otherness of God to his absence.'[9]

But is it reasonable to suppose, as Feuerbach and others like him have done, that there is a complete discontinuity between man's spiritual being and the environing reality that has brought forth humanity? If human beings appear on this earth 'trailing clouds of glory' (Wordsworth), from where do these clouds mysteriously come? It is a pretty lame answer to say with Monod that 'our number came up in the Monte Carlo game',[10] and it is surprising that a scientist who did so much himself to bring to light the intricate complex processes that go into the formation of a human being should invoke chance. Is the universe really like a casino? Even if it were, a casino is an institution in which chance has been integrated into a highly purposeful business. At the opposite extreme from Monod, we noted the confident assertion of Berdyaev that 'man contains the whole riddle of the universe and the solution to it'.[11] But this may be over-confident and carries the idea of man as microcosm to an extreme length. There is so much of the universe lying outside our field of knowledge that it might be a rash anthropomorphism to extrapolate the human pattern upon all of it. There may well be mysteries to which humanity offers no clue. We found more plausible the modest claim of Peacocke that contemporary scientific evidence points to our being 'remarkably and intimately related' to the universe.[12] The human being is not a surd in the universe, but it is not necessary either to claim that he is the clue to everything. The most inherently plausible view is that humanity, more than any other form of existence known to us on this planet, does bring to light something of the creative forces at work in the world, and to that extent man is indeed a microcosm, a becoming that bears the stamp of being.

On the basis of this affinity between the life of humanity and the wider reality within which that life is set, it is possible to construct what might be called an anthropological argument for the existence of God. This would be a cumulative argument, and indeed the several elements constituting it have already appeared scattered through the book, as we have dealt in turn with various aspects of human nature and found that some of them at least seem to point beyond themselves to a transhuman spiritual source from which they are derived.

I do not think the kind of argument that I have in mind could lead to the idea of a wholly transcendent God – and I have already said as much – but equally it would not result in a pantheistic conception or the idea of a World-soul. It could lead to a concept of God in which there would certainly be elements of transcendence, just as we can properly speak of transcendence in the human being, but there would also be a strong emphasis on immanence, and this is inevitable if we are trying to learn something of the character of God from a study of creaturely being. The task would be impossible if God were not intimately involved in his creation. The widely held monarchical conception of God as wholly above and beyond his creation needs to be moved in the direction of a more organic view of the relation between God and the world, a view in which God is seen not only as transcendent but as deeply involved in the history of his creation. Such a view, incidentally, may be more compatible than was the traditional monarchical view with the Christian doctrines of the incarnation and the triune God.

Incidentally, the view of God I am describing (sometimes called 'panentheism') would solve a problem which arose very early in our discussions. When we considered human freedom and transcendence, we found that many atheistic philosophers – among them, Feuerbach, Nietzsche, Bloch, Sartre – believed that a transcendent God stands in the way of human freedom and transcendence, and must be abolished. There is some force in this argument, which constitutes a kind of emotional component in the atheism of the philosophers mentioned. They felt summoned to rebel against God in the name of human freedom. In conceding the force of their argument, I said that it could be met only by setting against it a 'non-oppressive' concept of God, a God working and suffering in and with his creation, leading and inspiring human transcendence rather than standing over it. The concept of God that might result from the kind of anthropological argument we have been considering would surely be of the non-oppressive kind, as well as being, I would claim, very close to the God of Christian faith.

Let me now bring together the various considerations which together constitute what I have called the anthropological argument for the existence of God, that is to say, considerations drawn from our study of different aspects of human life and cumulatively directing us to a spiritual reality which is at once the source, support and goal of humanity. I think the constituent parts of the argument can best be expressed in the form of six propositions. Some of these tend to overlap at certain points, but behind each there is a distinctive body of evidence, as we shall see when we elaborate them.

The propositions are as follows. 1. Human life has brought to light more than anything else that we know the astonishing potentialities latent in the physical universe. 2. Some aspects of our humanity suggest a transhuman spiritual source. 3. The human being in certain respects transcends nature, in such a way as to provide an analogy of divine transcendence and to suggest that the goal of humanity is participation in the life of God. 4. Human beings show a natural trust in the wider being within which their existence is set. 5. There are some negative factors in human existence which can be understood as limit-situations, impressing on us our own finitude and at the same time evoking the idea of absolute being. 6. Finally, many of these strands come together in religion, in which men and women claim to experience in various ways the reality of God, and this claim has a *prima facie* case as one deeply rooted in the human condition and one which has never been disproved and perhaps never could be. Let us now consider the propositions one by one, and recall the supporting evidence for each.

1. 'Human life has brought to light more than anything else that we know the astonishing potentialities latent in the physical universe.' I am not, in the first instance at least, thinking of human powers of cognition or of that truly miraculous enterprise of the human mind, natural science, by which the secrets of the natural have been more and more uncovered. I am thinking simply of the human existent himself as an embodied being. We have seen that embodiedness is a universal human characteristic. Each one of us is a physical organism, occupying a little volume of space, subject to heat and cold, gravity, humidity and so on. Yet each of us, even in the body, is far more than merely physical. The body knows pleasure and pain, vigour and fatigue, it is sentient, percipient and cognitive. It is a microcosm in which the macrocosm has revealed itself and shown itself to be far more than matter and force or a collocation of solid atoms or however old-fashioned materialism expressed it.

I am the eye with which the Universe beholds itself,
And knows itself divine.[13]

At least, if it does not know itself divine, which would be much too pantheistic a way of expressing it, it knows itself through the human microcosm to be much more than 'matter', as that was envisaged even as late as the nineteenth century. Yet this is known in the first instance just because there are sentient, percipient, cognitive, yet embodied human beings that the universe itself has brought forth from its resources.

When one goes on from the fact that human beings exist to the fact that they have on the basis of their cognitive powers developed science, then the point made in the last paragraph is enormously strengthened. Science has changed the meaning of the word 'matter'. Matter is no longer conceived as the hard massy particles of nineteenth-century physics, still less as the inert formless *hyle* of Greek thought. Matter is an incredibly complex pattern of energy that seems to become more complex and more mysterious with every new discovery. First human existence and then human science have utterly discredited the materialism of the past and the various reductionist theories that have succeeded it. We are driven rather towards a sacramental conception of the universe. Perhaps few would go so far as the matter-mysticism of Teilhard de Chardin: 'I bless you, matter, and you I acclaim . . . not as a mass of brute forces and debased appetites, but as you reveal yourself to me today in your totality and true nature. You I acclaim as the inexhaustible potentiality for existence and transformation.'[14] This may be exaggerated, but it seems nearer the truth than the old view of matter as dead, alien and mechanical, whether that view was put forward by the sceptical philosopher or the puritan moralist.

2. 'Some aspects of our humanity suggest a transhuman spiritual source.' We saw that the first proposition might be given by some a pantheistic interpretation, but I preferred myself to speak of a sacramental universe, implying that the potentialities of the physical world originate in a spiritual reality which may indeed be present in the physical universe, yet in some respects transcends it. If asked why it seems necessary to posit this reality beyond the world itself, I think the full range of considerations pointing in this direction will only emerge as we move through the remaining propositions, but one point which belongs to the present stage of the argument is something very like Leibniz's 'principle of sufficient reason'. He himself defines this principle as one 'in virtue of which we hold that there can be no fact real or existing . . . unless there be a sufficient reason why it should be so and not otherwise, although these reasons usually cannot be known by us'.[15] Bearing in mind that last point of Leibniz, that our understanding of such things will usually be very imperfect, I still think that there are aspects of human life and human nature which must be traced to an origin that

transcends the world. I have in mind, of course, the higher dimensions of human experience, intellectual, moral, personal and spiritual. There are many things in human experience that we share with the animals and that can be explained in terms of physics, chemistry, biology, neurology, psychology and so on, though even to say that is to acknowledge the immensely rich potentialities of the universe. Sentience, perception, some forms of cognition are perhaps all explicable as developments necessary for the survival of the species.

With language it becomes more difficult. We have seen that human language is so different from animal languages as to take us to quite a new level. We have seen too that the capacity for language seems to be innate. From where does it come? From where does grammar come and the endless possibilities of human development that it enables? The whole of man's higher life requires language as a foundation. But that higher life seems to transcend the limits of natural explanation. What about conscience and moral obligation? We saw plainly enough that this can only be partly explained in terms of society and its demands, and that the most authentic kind of conscience requires creativity. Or what of knowing persons as distinct from knowing facts, of interpersonal relations and love? Is it true, as Buber claimed, that every meeting with another 'thou' is enabled by the eternal 'Thou'? To sum up, the higher reaches of human life, what is in fact most distinctively human in us, seem to posit an origin in a level of being not less than personal and spiritual transcending both ourselves and the world.

3. 'The human being in certain respects transcends nature, in such a way as to provide an analogy of divine transcendence and to suggest that the goal of humanity is participation in the life of God.' In other words, the human being is not just a microcosm but is also the bearer of the image of God. He does not just reflect or sum up in himself the macrocosmos, but has a creative share in shaping it. He is a bridge-being, finite and creaturely, yet creative and reflecting God. Herein lies the unique interest of humanity, though also its vulnerability.

These bold claims for humanity were staked out in the early parts of the book. We noted that freedom is not a natural phenomenon but more like a breach in nature, an empty space where fresh creation is still possible. Freedom passes over into transcendence, the continuing creative drive of humanity toward an unlimited goal. This drive has direction, a *hegemonikon* or leading edge, both in the egoity of the individual and in the social reality into which he must transcend. The goal is the realization in the human race of the divine image.

Humanity, as has been said, is a bridge-being, both immanent in the world and transcendent of it. God too, as we are being led to conceive him, is both immanent in the world and transcendent of it. The best evidence for a God who is transcendent of the world is that being within the world, the human being, who also participates in transcendence. These difficult and complicated relationships are well expressed by Jaspers: 'Transcendence is being that never becomes world but that speaks, as it were, through the being that is in the world. There is transcendence only if the world does not consist merely of itself, is not built upon itself, but points beyond itself. If the world is everything, then there is no transcendence. But if there is transcendence, perhaps there is something in the world's being that points to it.'[16] On the last point, the claim is, of course, that humanity is the being that so points.

4. 'Human beings show a natural trust in the wider being within which their existence is set.' Reality presents us with an ambiguous face. There are evidences that are supportive of faith in God – and we have just been considering some of them – while there are others which suggest that reality is godless. The question cannot be settled conclusively, and we have seen that on ultimate or transcendent questions of this kind, we have to rely on belief, for certainty is not available. On the whole, human beings tend to trust reality and to have a fundamental faith in being. This is not quite the same as faith in God, but it is a fundamental element in such a faith. It is something like a natural predisposition towards faith, perhaps what the New Testament calls 'faith as a grain of mustard seed'.[17] We have seen many evidences of this tendency toward faith, for instance, in the fact that people take on themselves commitments that imply not just trust in their fellow human beings but a more basic trust in the order of things, and likewise in the hope that is everywhere in human life and maintains itself even in the face of death. Of course, in most people's lives, faith varies in its strength and intensity. There are times of firm faith in God and times when this faith has become minimal and is perhaps not even as a grain of mustard seed. What is significant is that on the whole, some measure of faith prevails over doubt. As Hans Küng has remarked, 'Man is by nature inclined to say yes.'[18] Very few people have been deliberate and complete nihilists and, as Küng shows, it is probably impossible to maintain such a position consistently. Even people who find it impossible to believe in God may nevertheless have a basic faith in certain values or in the worthwhile-ness of life. Though one does not question the sincerity of their atheism, it must be a question whether their basic faith is not closer to faith in God than they realize, and that what they cannot accept are the often naive and sometimes immoral concepts of God that are all too common among those who profess to be believers.

5. 'There are some negative factors in human existence which can be understood as limit-situations, impressing on us our own finitude and at the same time evoking the idea of absolute being.' We have seen that suffering, death and various forms of alienation, such as sin and guilt, are

not unmitigated evils, but have an affirmative function in bringing us face to face with our own being and compelling us to be realistic in accepting who we are. Recognition of finitude and guilt dispels illusions of grandeur and self-conceit. But it does more. I have used Jaspers' language of limit-situations to make the point that when one comes to the limits of the human situation, there may take place the encounter with transcendent being, though certainly this does not happen automatically, as it were.

6. 'Finally, many of these strands come together in religion, in which men and women claim to experience in various ways the reality of God, and this claim has a *prima facie* case for its validity as one deeply rooted in the human condition and one which has never been disproved and perhaps never could be.' We did in fact in a long chapter examine some of the many forms of religious experience in which human beings have believed themselves to have communion with a gracious reality which gives a new depth and significance to their lives. Even though there has been a decline of religion in modern times, there are still many people for whom it is important. Its testimony cannot be lightly dismissed, as has been recognized by the philosopher Brand Blanshard, himself a severe critic of much religion: 'I do not think it is adequately dealt with by assigning it to a prescientific era or by citing Frazer or Freud. Catholics like Gilson and Maritain, Protestants like Kierkegaard, Brunner and Barth have brought too much learning and acuteness to the defence of their creeds to deserve such treatment, and these creeds continue to commend themselves intellectually, emotionally and practically to large numbers of thoughtful minds. Views so held and so advocated should receive a respectful hearing.'[19] Given such a hearing, I hold that religion remains another evidence for the reality of God as the source, support and goal of human life. It is, I believe, significant too that those who have forsaken religion have usually found a substitute, notably art, in which, as we have seen, the sublime has something in common with the holy and is a vehicle of transcendence.

The concept of God which has emerged in this last chapter conforms, I think, to what may be the only valid procedure for forming such a concept, that is, 'by treating the universal properties of created things' – in this case, the human being, the highest known created thing – 'as inferior forms of that which, in supremely excellent form, constitutes the divine nature'.[20] Further, a God so conceived as deeply involved with his creation is no oppressive God, but one whose transcendence is a goal and encouragement to the transcendence of humanity. But at this point, the search for humanity merges into the search for deity, and would call for another book.

Notes

Chapter I Becoming

1. Alexander Pope, *An Essay on Man*, Epistle II.
2. See especially, Paul Lehmann, *Ethics in a Christian Context*, SCM Press 1963, p. 85.
3. G. Ebeling, *Dogmatik des christlichen Glaubens*, Tübingen 1979, Vol. II, p. 531.
4. See Jean-Paul Sartre, *Being and Nothingness*, ET Methuen 1957; J. H. van den Berg, *The Changing Nature of Man*, ET Dell, New York 1964.
5. W. Shakespeare, *As You Like It*, II, vii.
6. N. Berdyaev, *The Destiny of Man*, ET Geoffrey Bles 1937, p. 45.
7. Jacques Monod, *Chance and Necessity*, ET Collins 1972, pp. 137, 167.
8. A. R. Peacocke, *Creation and the World of Science*, Oxford University Press 1979, p. 68.
9. J. Z. Young, *An Introduction to the Study of Man*, Oxford University Press 1971, p. 24.
10. J. Bronowski, *The Ascent of Man*, BBC Publications 1973, p. 412.
11. Theodosius Dobzhansky, *The Biology of Ultimate Concern*, New American Library, New York 1967, p. 72.
12. M. Heidegger, *Being and Time*, ET SCM Press 1962, p. 284.
13. S. Kierkegaard, *Either/Or*, ET Princeton University Press 1971, p. 218.

Chapter II Freedom

1. Jean-Paul Sartre, 'Existentialism is a Humanism', ET in *Existentialism from Dostoyevsky to Sartre*, ed. W. Kaufmann, Harper and Row, New York 1956, p. 290.
2. Berdyaev, *The Destiny of Man*, p. 25.
3. Paul Verghese, *The Freedom of Man*, Westminster Press, Philadelphia 1972, p. 121.
4. According to the *Oxford English Dictionary*, an Anglicized form of the word, 'hegemonicon', was used by J. H. Newman in 1848.
5. G. Pico della Mirandola, *Oration on the Dignity of Man*, ET Regnery, Chicago 1956, pp. 4–5.
6. Gabriel Marcel, *The Mystery of Being*, II, ET Regnery, Chicago 1960, p. 126.
7. Immanuel Kant, *Critique of Pure Reason*, ET Macmillan 1929, p. 409.
8. Austin Farrer, *The Freedom of the Will*, A. & C. Black 1960, p. 171.
9. Immanuel Kant, *Critique of Practical Reason*, ET Longmans 1883, pp. 199–200.
10. Martin Luther, *The Bondage of the Will*, ET James Clarke 1957, p. 104.
11. Rom. 7. 19–20.
12. S. Kierkegaard, *The Concept of Anxiety*, ET Princeton University Press 1957, p. 55.
13. Sartre, *Being and Nothingness*, p. 129.
14. A. Camus, 'The Myth of Sisyphus,' in *Existentialism from Dostoyevsky to Sartre*, p. 315.

15. A. Camus, *The Rebel*, ET Hamish Hamilton 1955, p. 23.

16. Jacques Ellul, *The Ethics of Freedom*, ET Mowbrays 1976, p. 91.

17. Nicolas Berdyaev, *The Beginning and the End*, ET Geoffrey Bles 1952, p. 216.

18. See Vladimir Lossky, *The Mystical Theology of the Eastern Church*, James Clarke 1957, p. 45.

19. John Locke, *Of Civil Government*, ed. W. S. Carpenter, Dent. 1924, p. 143.

20. Berdyaev, *The Destiny of Man*, p. 216.

Chapter III   Transcendence

1. A. A. Kee, *The Way of Transcendence*, Penguin Books 1971, p. xxvii.

2. See Roger Hazelton, 'Relocating Transcendence,' in *Union Seminary Quarterly Review*, XXX, 1975, pp. 101ff.

3. J. Moltmann, *The Future of Creation*, ET SCM Press 1979, p. 1.

4. Sartre, *Being and Nothingness*, p. 566.

5. F. W. Nietzsche, *Thus Spake Zarathustra*, ET Dent 1933, p. 5.

6. Nietzsche, op. cit., p. 7.

7. Karl Löwith, *From Hegel to Nietzsche*, ET Constable 1965, p. 185.

8. Sartre, op. cit., p. 89.

9. Sartre, op. cit., p. 90.

10. Marcel, *The Mystery of Being*, I, p. 49.

11. Ibid., p. 60.

12. S. Keen, *Gabriel Marcel*, Lutterworth Press 1966, p. 35.

13. Karl Marx, *Economic and Philosophical Manuscripts of 1844*, quoted by L. Kolakowski, *Main Currents of Marxism*, Oxford University Press 1978, Vol. I, p. 137.

14. Marx, *A Contribution to the Critique of Political Economy*, quoted by Kolakowski, op. cit., Vol. I, p. 335.

15. J. Plamenatz, *Karl Marx's Philosophy of Man*, Oxford University Press 1975, p. 119.

16. H. Marcuse, *One-Dimensional Man*, Sphere Books 1972, p. 11 n. 1.

17. Ibid., p. 24.

18. B. L. Lonergan, SJ, *Insight*, Darton, Longman and Todd 1970, p. 74.

19. Ibid., p. 348.

20. Ibid., p. 445.

21. Ibid., pp. 635–6.

22. Heidegger, *Being and Time*, p. 74.

23. Gen. 1. 26.

24. Irenaeus, *Against Heresies* IV, 38, 1–3.

25. G. Wainwright, *Doxology*, Epworth Press 1980, pp. 16–17.

26. II Cor. 3. 18.

27. I John 3. 2.

28. II Peter 1. 4.

29. J. R. Illingworth, *Divine Immanence*, Macmillan 1898, chapters iii and iv.

30. Karl Jaspers, *Philosophical Faith and Revelation*, ET Collins 1967, passim.

31. Nietzsche, op. cit., p. 77.

32. Charles Hartshorne, 'Divine Absoluteness and Divine Relativity', in *Transcendence*, ed. H. W. Richardson and D. R. Cutler, Beacon Press, Boston 1969, p. 169.

Chapter IV   Egoity

1. See above, p. 14.
2. See above, p. 6.
3. John Macmurray, *The Self as Agent*, Faber 1957, p. 84.
4. Gilbert Ryle, *The Concept of Mind*, Hutchinson 1949, p. 15.
5. Ibid., p. 81.
6. David Hume, *A Treatise of Human Nature*, ed. A. D. Lindsay, Dent. 1911, I, pp. 238–9.
7. Ryle, op. cit., p. 191.
8. Ibid., p. 195.
9. I. T. Ramsey, *Christian Empiricism*, ed. J. H. Gill, Sheldon Press 1974, p. 23.
10. See above, p. 16.
11. Sartre, *Being and Nothingness*, p. 74.
12. Macmurray, op. cit., pp. 32ff.
13. See above, p. 8.
14. John S. Dunne, *A Search for God in Time and Memory*, Sheldon Press 1975, p. 2.
15. Marcel, *The Mystery of Being*, I, p. 224.
16. See above, p. 19.
17. R. D. Laing, *The Divided Self*, Tavistock Publications 1965, p. 94.
18. See above, pp. 14, 38.
19. Gen. 3. 5.
20. W. Temple, *Christianity and the Social Order*, Penguin Books 1942, p. 38.
21. See above, p. 20.
22. Hans-Martin Barth, *Fulfilment*, ET SCM Press 1980, p. 55.

Chapter V   Embodiedness

1. Søren Kierkegaard, *The Concept of Anxiety*, ET Princeton University Press 1957, p. 39.
2. See above, pp. 7–8.
3. William Barrett, *The Illusion of Technique*, William Kimber 1978, p. 71.
4. Macmurray, *The Self as Agent*, p. 37.
5. Ryle, *The Concept of Mind*, p. 328.
6. Gen. 2. 7.
7. Wisdom 3. 1.
8. P. F. Strawson, *Individuals*, Methuen 1963, p. 113.
9. I. Cor. 15. 12–19.
10. Gen. 1. 28.
11. Strawson, op. cit., p. 99.
12. Sartre, *Being and Nothingness*, p. 305.
13. Arthur Schopenhauer, *The World as Will and Idea*, ET Kegan Paul 1883, I, pp. 425–6.
14. Jean-Paul Sartre, *The Emotions*, ET Philosophical Library, New York 1948, p. 52.
15. Ibid., p. 93.
16. John Macmurray, *Reason and Emotion*, Faber 1935, p. 25.
17. Blaise Pascal, *Pensées*, ed. L. Lafuma, Garnier-Flammavion, Paris 1973, (my own translation).
18. Ibid., p. 21.
19. Paul Tillich, *The Courage to Be*, Nisbet 1952.
20. See above, p. 21.
21. Paul Ricoeur, *Fallible Man*, Regnery, Chicago 1965, p. 161.

Chapter VI Cognition

1. See above, p. 6.
2. In a letter to Jacobi. See Ronald Gregor Smith, *J. G. Hamann: A Study in Christian Existence, with Selections from His Writings*, Collins 1960, p. 252.
3. See above, p. 3.
4. See above, p. 17.
5. E. Husserl, *Ideas*, ET Allen & Unwin 1931, p. 227.
6. Karl R. Popper, *Objective Knowledge*, Oxford University Press 1972, p. 7.
7. Bryan Magee, *Popper*, Fontana Books 1973, p. 38.
8. K. Popper, *The Logic of Scientific Discovery*, Hutchinson 1960, p. 41.
9. A. Flew and A. MacIntyre, eds., *New Essays in Philosophical Theology*, SCM Press 1955, p. 96ff.
10. John Rodwell, 'Myth and Truth in Scientific Inquiry,' in M. Goulder, ed., *Incarnation and Myth*, SCM Press 1979, p. 66ff.
11. Popper, *Objective Knowledge*, p. 106.
12. See above, p. 4.
13. Michael Polanyi, *Personal Knowledge*, Routledge 1964, p. xiii.
14. Ibid.
15. Ibid., p. xiv.
16. Ibid., p. 53.
17. Ibid., p. 206.
18. Ibid., p. 53.
19. Martin Buber, *I and Thou*, ET T. & T. Clark 1958, pp. 7–8.
20. Thomas Aquinas, *Summa Theologiae*, I, 12, 4.
21. Gen. 4. 1.
22. Hans-Georg Gadamer, *Truth and Method*, ET Sheed & Ward 1975, p. 244.
23. J. Calvin, *Institutes of the Christian Religion*, ET James Clarke 1953, I, p. 234.
24. K. Marx and F. Engels, *On Religion*, ed. Reinhold Niebuhr, Schocken Books, New York 1964, pp. 73–4.
25. J. Habermas, *Erkenntnis und Interesse*, Suhrkamp, Frankfurt 1973, p. 242.

Chapter VII Having

1. See above, p. 58.
2. Arthur Gibson, *The Faith of the Atheist*, Harper & Row, New York 1968, p. 102.
3. See above, p. 30.
4. John Salmond, *Jurisprudence*, Sweet & Maxwell 1930, p. 443.
5. Locke, *Of Civil Government*, II, vii, 87.
6. F. Benham, *Economics*, Pitman 1953, p. 11.
7. See W. S. Hudson, *Religion in America*, Scribner's, New York 1965, pp. 304–5.
8. Kolakowski, *Main Currents of Marxism*, I, p. 284.
9. See below, p. 109.
10. Plamenatz, *Karl Marx's Philosophy of Man*, p. 4.
11. E. R. Hughes, ed., *Chinese Philosophy in Classical Times*, Dent 1942, p. 106.
12. G. FitzGerald, 'Political Structures and Personal Development', in Dermot A. Lane, ed., *Liberation Theology: An Irish Dialogue*, Gill & Macmillan 1977, p. 69.
13. Thomas Aquinas, *Summa Theologiae*, IIa IIae, q. 66, a. 2.
14. Ibid., a. 7.
15. See above, p. 28.
16. G. Marcel, *Being and Having*, Dacre Press 1949, p. 148.
17. Ibid.

18. See above, p. 30.
19. See below, p. 112.
20. Acts 2. 44–45.
21. A. M. Ramsey, *Sacred and Secular*, Longmans 1965, p. 8.
22. Ibid., p. 18.
23. See below, pp. 83 and 172.

Chapter VIII   Sociality

1. Bernard Bosanquet, *The Principle of Individuality and Value*, Macmillan 1912, p. 68.
2. S. Kierkegaard, *Training in Christianity*, ET Princeton University Press 1941, p. 218.
3. See above, p. 38.
4. Thomas Aquinas, *Summa Theologiae*, Ia q. 50, a. 4.
5. Gen. 1. 26–27.
6. See above, p. 7.
7. Gen. 2. 18.
8. See above, p. 68.
9. See above, p. 64.
10. See above, p. 66.
11. See below, p. 137.
12. See above, p. 72.
13. K. Marx and F. Engels, *The German Ideology*, quoted by Plamenatz, *Karl Marx's Philosophy of Man*, p. 155.
14. Ludwig Feuerbach, *The Essence of Christianity*, ET Harper & Row, New York 1957, p. 92.
15. Martin Buber, *The Knowledge of Man*, ET Allen & Unwin 1965, pp. 59ff.
16. Martin Buber, *Between Man and Man*, ET Collins 1955, pp. 1ff.
17. Ibid., p. 203.
18. G. W. F. Hegel, *Phenomenology of Mind*, ET Allen & Unwin 1931, pp. 229ff.
19. E. R. Moberly, *Suffering, Innocent and Guilt*, SPCK 1978, p. 126.
20. Sartre, *Being and Nothingness*, pp. 364ff.
21. Buber, *I and Thou*, p. 75.
22. H. G. Cox, *The Secular City*, SCM Press 1965, pp. 44–5.
23. Julian of Norwich, *Showings*, ET SPCK 1979, pp. 236, etc.
24. Reinhold Niebuhr, *The Nature and Destiny of Man*, Nisbet 1941–3, Vol. II, p. 320.
25. Gene Outka, *Agape, an Ethical Analysis*, Yale University Press 1972, pp. 42–3.
26. Aloys Grillmeier, *Christ in Christian Tradition*, ET Mowbrays[2] 1975, p. 251.
27. John Macquarrie, *Three Issues in Ethics*, SCM Press 1970, p. 62.
28. See Eph. 2. 11ff. E. Schillebeeckx claims that 'if any book lays the foundations for a political theology in the New Testament, it is Ephesians, though the author himself does not see through its historical consequences or implications'. See *Christ: The Christian Experience in the Modern World*, ET SCM Press 1980, p. 196. Further on in the book Schillebeeckx returns to the 'political theology' of Ephesians. It has, he claims, as its specific perspective 'the gospel of peace', understood as nothing less than world peace. We shall see ourselves later that peace is the great social virtue, corresponding to love in the life of individuals and small groups (see below, Chapter XIV). 'Ephesians,' writes Schillebeeckx, 'provides a biblical basis for a political theology and a theology of liberation.' It does not simply duplicate human efforts towards a just society or a liberated existence but refers these to a source in God.

'The *religious* element – with its particular *liberating* and *critical* force – is the essential nucleus of the liberating theology of peace which we find in Ephesians' (italics in the original). Schillebeeckx concludes: 'In the last resort, the most striking feature of Ephesians seems to me to be its great courage in the face of the future. At a time when Christian communities were invisible cells in the world of their time, minority groups in the great cities of the ancient world, without any prospect of influencing the wider world or the society in which they were set, a *quantité négligeable*, the author of Ephesians dared to call the "community of God" the great *universal instrument of peace* in this world' (ibid. pp. 216–7).

Chapter IX   Language

1. See above, p. 6.
2. Gadamer, *Truth and Method*, pp. 432–3.
3. See above, p. 66.
4. E. V. McKnight *Meaning in Texts*, Fortress Press, Philadelphia 1978, p. 233.
5. Kant, *Critique of Pure Reason*, p. 93.
6. McKnight, op. cit., p. 248.
7. Heidegger, *Being and Time*, pp. 203ff.
8. M. Heidegger, *Introduction to Metaphysics*, Yale University Press 1959, p. 68.
9. M. Heidegger, *Über den Humanismus*, Klostermann, Frankfurt 1947, p. 10.
10. Gadamer, op. cit., p. 264.
11. George Berkeley, *Alciphron*, Fourth Dialogue.
12. F. W. Nietzsche, *Twilight of the Idols*, ET Penguin Books 1968, p. 38.
13. See above, p. 99.
14. See below, p. 199.
15. See above, p. 6.
16. In an earlier writing, I discussed three fundamental functions – expressing, referring and communication: see my *God-Talk*, SCM Press 1967, pp. 68ff. In the present discussion, I have added two more functions, articulation and creativity.
17. J. L. Austin, *How to Do Things with Words*, Oxford University Press 1962, p. 4.
18. See above, p. 65.
19. Peacocke, *Creation and the World of Science*, p. 67.
20. Barrett, *The Illusion of Technique*, p. 57.
21. See above, p. 61.
22. See above, p. 87.
23. See above, p. 38.
24. Heidegger, *Being and Time*, p. 211.
25. M. Heidegger, *The Piety of Thinking*, ET Indiana University Press 1976, p. 29.
26. Ibid.

Chapter X   Alienation

1. F. Johnson, ed., *Alienation*, Seminar Press 1973, p. 3.
2. Barrett, *The Illusion of Technique*, p. 133.
3. Hegel, *Phenomenology of the Mind*, p. 86.
4. Ibid., p. 758.
5. Ibid., p. 251.
6. Ibid., p. 753.
7. See above, p. 36.
8. Feuerbach, *The Essence of Christianity*, p. 30.

9. L. Feuerbach, *The Essence of Faith according to Luther*, ET Harper & Row, New York 1967, p. 41.

10. L. Feuerbach, *Lectures on the Essence of Religion*, ET Harper & Row, New York 1967, p. 17.

11. Ibid., p. 23.

12. Marx, 'Contribution to the Critique of Hegel's Philosophy of Right,' in *Marx and Engels on Religion*, p. 42.

13. See above, p. 77.

14. See above, p. 80.

15. F. W. Nietzsche, *The Joyful Wisdom*, ET Allen & Unwin 1910, p. 125.

16. H. Küng, *Does God Exist?*, ET Collins 1980, p. 415.

17. P. Masterson, *Atheism and Alienation*, University of Notre Dame Press 1971, p. 152.

18. See above, p. 40.

19. Gen. 2. 7.

20. Kierkegaard, *The Concept of Anxiety*, p. 38.

21. See above, p. 19.

22. Ricoeur, *Fallible Man*, p. 3.

23. See above, p. 32.

24. Ps. 51. 3.

25. P. Tillich, *Systematic Theology*, Nisbet 1953, I, p. 49.

26. F. Schleiermacher, *The Christian Faith*, ET T. & T. Clark 1928, p. 288.

27. Küng, *Does God Exist?*, p. 303.

28. H. Jonas, *The Gnostic Religion*, Beacon Press, Boston 1963, p. 52.

29. Hughes, *Chinese Philosophy in Classical Times*, pp. 1, 3.

30. F. Nietzsche, quoted by Jonas, op. cit., p. 324.

31. B. Pascal, *Pensées*, No. 391.

32. M. Arnold, 'Dover Beach,' in Helen Gardiner, ed., *The New Oxford Book of English Verse*, Oxford University Press 1972, no. 650.

33. P. Berger, *A Rumour of Angels*, Allen Lane 1969, pp. 67–8.

34. Ibid., p. 69.

35. J. Macquarrie, *Principles of Christian Theology*, SCM Press ²1977, p. 80.

36. Berger, op. cit., p. 69.

37. Küng, op. cit., p. 444.

38. K. S. Latourette, *A History of Christianity*, Eyre and Spottiswoode 1953, p. 241.

39. Eusebius of Caesares, *The Ecclesiastical History*, V, 1.

40. Ibid., X, 9.

41. Athanasius, *On the Incarnation*, 51–53.

42. See John Macquarrie, *God and Secularity*, Lutterworth Press 1967.

43. See above, p. 112.

44. Martin E. Marty, *The Modern Schism*, SCM Press 1969, p. 9.

45. J. Ridley, *Thomas Cranmer*, Oxford University Press 1962, p. 257.

46. See above, p. 76.

Chapter XI   Conscience

1. See above, p. 115.

2. Aristotle, *Ethica Nicomachea*, ET Oxford University Press 1925, II, 1.

3. See above, p. 90.

4. Rom. 2. 14–15.

5. Chu Hsi, in A. C. Bouquet, ed., *Sacred Books of the World*, Penguin Books 1954, p. 180.

6. Joseph Butler, *Works*, ed., W. E. Gladstone, Oxford University Press 1896, II, pp. 41–2.

7. J. S. Mill, *Utilitarianism*, ed. A. D. Lindsay Dent 1910, p. 26.

8. Butler, *Works*, I, p. 399.

9. Mill, op. cit., p. 26.

10. Sigmund Freud, *New Introductory Lectures on Psychoanalysis*, ET Hogarth Press 1933, p. 42.

11. Ibid., p. 88.

12. See above, p. 26.

13. Freud, op. cit., p. 88.

14. Benjamin Nelson in his introduction to S. Freud, *On Creativity and the Unconscious*, Harper Torchbooks, New York 1958, p. vii.

15. Freud, op. cit., p. 37.

16. See Gregory Zilboorg, 'Conscience and Superego,' in C. E. Nelson, ed., *Conscience*, Newman Press, New York 1973, pp. 210–23.

17. Heidegger, *Being and Time*, p. 316.

18. Nietzsche, *Thus Spake Zarathustra*, p. 54.

19. Ibid., p. 176.

20. S. Kierkegaard, *Fear and Trembling*, ET Princeton University Press 1954, p. 75.

21. Matt. 5. 21ff.

22. See above, p. 92.

23. F. H. Bradley, *Ethical Studies*, Oxford University Press 1876, p. 227.

24. Niebuhr, *The Nature and Destiny of Man*, I, pp. 221–2.

25. Heidegger, op. cit., pp. 313–4.

26. See above, p. 19.

27. See above, p. 44.

28. See below, p. 153.

29. Kierkegaard, *Either/Or*, II, pp. 270–1.

30. See above, pp. 46.

31. See above, p. 75.

32. See above, p. 58.

33. See above, p. 92.

34. See above, p. 117.

35. Peter Baelz, *Ethics and Belief*, Sheldon Press 1977, p. 47.

36. See above, p. 32.

37. M. F. Wiles, *Faith and the Mystery of God*, SCM Press 1982, pp. 109–10.

38. Col. 1. 15.

Chapter XII   Commitment

1. See above, p. 19.

2. Josef Goldbrunner, *Individuation*, ET Hollis 1955, p. 94.

3. Laing, *The Divided Self*, p. 44.

4. Rollo May, *Love and Will*, Norton, New York 1972, p. 285.

5. Heidegger, *Being and Time*, p. 343.

6. G. Marcel, *Homo Viator*, ET Gollancz 1951, pp. 135ff.

7. Sartre, *Being and Nothingness*, pp. 553ff.

8. Maurice Blondel, *L'action*, Paris 1893, p. ix.

9. J. M. Somerville, *Total Commitment*, Corpus Books, Washington 1968, pp. 17–18.

10. William James, *Selected Papers on Philosophy*, Dent 1917, p. 99ff.

11. Josiah Royce, *The Problem of Christianity*, Macmillan, New York 1913, II, p. 252.

12. Polanyi, *Personal Knowledge*, pp. 299ff.

13. R. Bultmann, *Theology of the New Testament*, ET SCM Press 1952, I, p. 316.

14. Royce, op. cit., I, p. 68.

15. Stanley Hauerwas, *Character and the Christian Life*, Trinity University Press, San Antonio, Texas 1975, p. 17.

16. William Temple, *Nature, Man and God*, Macmillan 1934, p. 390.

17. Hegel, *The Phenomenology of Mind*, p. 666.

18. See above, p. 138.

19. Reinhold Niebuhr, *Man's Nature and His Communities*, Scribner's, New York 1965, pp. 106–7.

20. Friedrich Schleiermacher, *On Religion*, ET Harper & Row, New York 1958, p. 39.

21. Mark 8. 34.

22. Küng, *On Being a Christian*, pp. 410–11.

23. See above, pp. 32f.

24. M. E. Zimmerman, *Eclipse of the Self*, Ohio University Press 1981, p. 80.

25. John Eckhart, in *Meister Eckhart: A New Translation*, by R. B. Blakney, Harper Torchbooks, New York 1941, p. 35.

26. Matt. 13. 44–46.

27. Luke 9. 59–60.

28. Luke 14. 26.

29. Hauerwas, op. cit., p. 119.

30. See above, pp. 131, 133.

31. See below, p. 187.

32. Rom. 9–11.

33. Luke 14. 28–30.

34. See above, p. 25.

35. I John 4. 19.

36. Jer. 2. 2, etc: Rev. 21. 1.

37. See above, p. 36.

38. John 1. 14.

39. I Cor. 15. 10.

40. S. Kierkegaard, *Either/Or*, ET Princeton University Press, 1944, II, pp. 3–157, 296ff., 321ff. See also George Price, *The Narrow Pass: A Study of Kierkegaard's Concept of Man*, Hutchinson 1963, pp. 171–4.

Chapter XIII   Belief

1. See above, p. 141.

2. Heb. 11. 6.

3. Joseph Butler, *Works*, I, p. 5.

4. See above, pp. 26, 34.

5. Kant, *Critique of Pure Reason*, p. 7.

6. Ibid., p. 29.

7. William James, 'The Will to Believe', in *Selected Papers in Philosophy*, p. 120.

8. Bertrand Russell, *Autobiography*, Allen and Unwin, Vol. I, p. 41.

9. Kierkegaard, *The Concept of Anxiety*, p. 125.

10. Pascal, *Pensées*, No. 381.

11. See above, p. 27.

12. Søren Kierkegaard, *Concluding Unscientific Postscript*, ET Princeton University Press 1941, p. 504.

13. L. P. Pojman, *Kierkegaard as Philosopher*, Waterleaf Press 1978, p. 34.

14. Kierkegaard, *Postcript*, p. 310.

15. S. Kierkegaard, *Philosophical Fragments*, ET Princeton University Press 1936, p. 29.

16. Ibid.

17. See above, pp. 61ff.

18. Basil Mitchell, *The Justification of Religious Belief*, Macmillan 1973, pp. 133f.

19. A. Flew, 'Theology and Falsification', in *New Essays in Philosophical Theology*, p. 97.

20. Anselm, *Proslogion*, I.

21. See above, p. 62.

22. Plamenatz, *Karl Marx's Philosophy of Man*, p. 177.

23. Berger, *A Rumour of Angels*, p. 50.

24. H. H. Price, *Essays in the Philosophy of Religion*, Oxford University Press 1972, p. 98.

25. Heidegger, *Introduction to Metaphysics*, p. 1.

26. Russell, *Autobiography*, Vol. III, p. 124.

27. P. R. Baelz, *The Forgotten Dream*, Mowbrays 1975, p. 2.

28. Mark 9. 24.

29. H. H. Price, *Belief*, Allen & Unwin 1969, p. 484.

30. Kant, *Critique of Pure Reason*, pp. 531–2.

Chapter XIV Love

1. See above, p. 144.

2. I Cor. 13. 13.

3. See above, p. 131.

4. D. D. Williams, *The Spirit and Forms of Love*, Harper and Row, New York 1969, p. 121.

5. Mark 8. 34–5.

6. John 12. 25.

7. Mark 12. 31.

8. Matt. 7. 12.

9. R. Bultmann, *The History of the Synoptic Tradition*, ET Blackwall 1963, p. 103.

10. Augustine, *On Christian Doctrine*, xxv, 26.

11. Butler, *Works*, II, p. 206.

12. See above, p. 148.

13. A. Ritschl, *Justification and Reconciliation*, ET T. & T. Clark 1900, p. 442.

14. Mark 3. 31–3.

15. Mark 7. 24–30.

16. Matt. 23.

17. Butler, *Works*, II, p. 219.

18. Matt. 25. 14–30.

19. See above, p. 88.

20. A. Nygren, *Agape and Eros*, ET SPCK 1953, p. 52.

21. Hosea 3. 1. I am indebted for this reference to the Very Revd E. W. Heaton, Dean of Christ Church, Oxford.

22. O. O'Donovan, *The Problem of Self-Love in St Augustine*, Yale University Press 1980, p. 11.

23. Luke 2. 41–51.

24. Macquarrie, *Principles of Christian Theology*, p. 350.

25. Luke 2. 41–51.

26. John 13. 23.
27. John 19. 26–27.
28. See above, p. 89.
29. Paul van Buren, *The Secular Meaning of the Gospel*, SCM Press 1963, p. 134.
30. I Cor. 13. 5, 7.
31. Matt. 5. 46–47.
32. Matt. 5. 44.
33. Luke 23. 34.
34. Lev. 19. 18; Matt. 19. 19.
35. G. B. Caird, *The Gospel of St Luke*, Penguin Books 1963, p. 148.
36. Luke 10. 25–37.
37. H. Thielicke, *Menschsein-Menschwerden*, R. Piper, Munich 1976, pp. 289–90.
38. See above, p. 92.
39. Augustine, *The City of God*, xix, 13.
40. I John 4. 19.
41. I John 4. 16.
42. See above, p. 37.
43. Mark 12. 30.
44. I John 4. 20.
45. Matt. 35. 35–40.
46. S. Kierkegaard, *Works of Love*, ET Princeton University Press 1962, p. 124.

Chapter XV Art

1. See above, p. 146.
2. I have to thank the Revd Dr Francis Vadakethala of Dharmaram College, Bangalore, for introducing me to this concept.
3. Klaus Klostermaier, *Hindu and Christian in Vrindaban*, ET SCM Press 1969, pp. 81–2.
4. Kierkegaard, *Either/Or*, II, p. 277.
5. A. N. Whitehead, *Process and Reality*, Cambridge University Press 1929, pp. 410–1.
6. A. N. Whitehead, *Science and the Modern World*, Cambridge University Press 1925, p. 130.
7. See above, p. 110.
8. R. E. Neale, *In Praise of Play*, Harper & Row, New York 1969, p. 13.
9. Kierkegaard, op. cit., II, p. 161.
10. Ibid., I, pp. 95, 97.
11. Ibid., I, p. 363.
12. Ibid., II, p. 10.
13. L. Wittgenstein, *Philosophical Investigations*, ET Blackwell 1968, p. 32.
14. E. Brunner, *Christianity and Civilization*, Nisbet 1948–9, Vol. II, p. 72.
15. M. Heidegger, 'The Origin of the Work of Art,' in *Basic Writings*, ed. D. F. Krell, Harper & Row 1978, pp. 169–71.
16. See above, pp. 105.
17. W. Shakespeare, *A Midsummer Night's Dream*, V, i.
18. See above, p. 36.
19. Jaspers, *Philosophical Faith and Revelation*, pp. 265–6.
20. Immanuel Kant, *The Critique of Judgment*, ET Oxford University Press 1952, pp. 94, 97.
21. Anselm of Canterbury, *Proslogion*, ET SCM Press 1974, p. 93.

Chapter XVI Religion

1. See above, p. 160.
2. L. Wittgenstein, *Tractatus Logico-Philosophicus*, ET Kegan Paul 1933, p. 185.
3. See above, p. 55.
4. Schleiermacher, *On Religion*, p. 18.
5. Ibid., p. 39.
6. Ibid., p. 61.
7. Ibid., p. 226.
8. Schleiermacher, *The Christian Faith*, p. 12.
9. Ibid., p. 126.
10. Ibid., p. 133.
11. R. Otto, 'How Schleiermacher Recovered the Sensus Numinis', in *Religious Essays*, ET Oxford University Press 1931, p. 75.
12. R. Otto, *The Idea of the Holy*, ET Oxford University Press, 1931, p. 75.
13. See above, p. 13.
14. Otto, op. cit., p. 8.
15. Gen. 18. 27.
16. Isa. 6. 5.
17. Mark 13. 32–42, with parallels.
18. Otto, op. cit., p. 88.
19. Ibid., p. 31.
20. Ibid., pp. 140ff.
21. See above, p. 36.
22. William James, *The Varieties of Religious Experience*, Longmans 1952, p. 269.
23. Ibid., p. 186ff.
24. Ibid., p. 502ff.
25. See J. A. Martin, Jr, *Empirical Philosophies of Religion*, King's Crown Press, New York 1945.
26. Martin Thornton, *My God: A Reappraisal of Normal Religious Experience*, Hodder 1974.
27. Peter Rohde, *Søren Kierkegaard*, ET Allen and Unwin 1963, p. 65.
28. Simone Weil, *Waiting on God*, ET Fontana Books 1959, p. 48.
29. See above, p. 33.
30. D. Bonhoeffer, *Letters and Papers from Prison*, ET SCM Press 1971, p. 341.
31. K. Rahner, *Spirit in the World*, ET Sheed & Ward 1968, pp. 280, 283.
32. J. Moltmann, *Theology of Hope*, ET SCM Press 1967.
33. Alister Hardy, *The Spiritual Nature of Man*, Oxford University Press 1979, p. 1.
34. Berger, *A Rumour of Angels*, p. 66.
35. Langdon Gilkey, *Naming the Whirlwind*, Bobbs-Merrill, Indianapolis 1969, p. 296.
36. J. G. Davies, *Every Day God*, SCM Press 1973, passim.
37. Feuerbach, *The Essence of Christianity*, p. 14.
38. John Baillie, *Our Knowledge of God*, Oxford University Press 1939, p. 226.
39. Tillich, *Systematic Theology*, I, p. 106.
40. See above, p. 70.
41. See above, p. 56.
42. Nietzsche, *The Twilight of the Idols*, p. 69. He says elsewhere in the book: 'I mistrust all systematizers and avoid them. The will to a system is a lack of integrity.'
43. R. Bultmann, *Jesus Christ and Mythology*, ET SCM Press 1958, p. 53.
44. Ninian Smart, *The Phenomenon of Religion*, Macmillan 1973, p. 52.

Chapter XVII   Suffering

1. J. A. Baker, *The Foolishness of God*, Darton, Longman and Todd 1970, pp. 54–5.
2. See above, p. 20.
3. Camus, *The Rebel*, p. 25.
4. Ritschl, *The Christian Doctrine of Justification and Reconciliation*, p. 444.
5. See above, p. 28.
6. See above, p. 126.
7. Basil Mitchell, *Morality: Religious and Secular*, Oxford University Press 1980, p. 130.
8. Sartre, *Being and Nothingness*, p. 556.
9. S. Freud, *New Introductory Lectures on Psychoanalysis*, ET Hogarth Press 1957, pp. 138–9.
10. U. Simon, *A Theology of Auschwitz*, Gollancz 1967, p. 81.
11. J. Hick, *Evil and the God of Love*, Macmillan 1966, pp. 370–1.
12. Whitehead, *Process and Reality*, p. 497.

Chapter XVIII   Death

1. See above, p. 8.
2. See above, p. 8.
3. John Donne, *Complete Poetry and Selected Prose*, ed. John Hayward, Nonesuch Press 1929, pp. 536, 538.
4. Wittgenstein, *Tractatus Logico-Philosophicus*, p. 185.
5. Sartre, *Being and Nothingness*, p. 539.
6. Heidegger, *Being and Time*, pp. 279ff.
7. Martin Heidegger, *Über den Humanismus*, Klostermann, Frankfurt 1947, p. 36.
8. Schleiermacher, *On Religion*, p. 39.
9. Ps. 90. 4.
10. Gen. 3. 5.
11. See above, p. 25.
12. Gen. 2. 17.
13. Karl Rahner, *On the Theology of Death*, ET Herder & Herder, New York 1965, p. 34.
14. Karl Jaspers, *Philosophie*, Springer Verlag, Berlin 1932, II, p. 220.

Chapter XIX   Hope

1. I have given a fuller treatment of hope in my book, *Christian Hope*, Mowbrays 1978.
2. 'Introduction to a Metaphysic of Hope' was the subtitle of his *Homo Viator*.
3. See above, p. 28.
4. Marcel, op. cit., p. 29.
5. E. Bloch, *Prinzip der Hoffnung*, Suhrkamp, Frankfurt 1959, pp. 284–5.
6. E. Bloch, *Man on His Own*, ET Herder & Herder, New York 1970, p. 152.
7. See above, p. 134.
8. See above, p. 183.
9. I have discussed some of these questions more fully in my book, *The Concept of Peace*, SCM Press 1973.
10. L. Kolakowski, *Main Currents of Marxism*, ET Oxford University Press 1978, III, p. 426.
11. See above, p. 184.
12. Rev. 21. 1.

13. E. O. James, *Prehistoric Religion*, Thames & Hudson 1957, p. 18.

14. H. Frankfort, *Ancient Egyptian Religion*, Harper & Row, New York, p. 88ff.

15. *Phaedo*, 106.

16. See above, p. 51.

17. I Cor. 15. 44, 50.

18. See above, p. 239.

Chapter XX Being

1. F. Nietzsche, *The Will to Power*, ET Allen & Unwin 1910, II, p. 107.

2. Ibid., p. 82.

3. A. H. Armstrong, *The Architecture of the Intelligible Universe in the Philosophy of Plotinus*, Cambridge University Press 1940, p. 4.

4. Augustine of Hippo, *On the Trinity*, X, 12.

5. G. W. Leibniz, *The Monadology and Other Philosophical Writings*, ET Oxford University Press 1898, p. 253.

6. K. Barth, *Church Dogmatics*, II/1, ET T. & T. Clark 1957, p. 204.

7. K. Barth, *The Humanity of God*, ET Collins 1961, pp. 33ff.

8. See above, p. 109.

9. W. Hamilton, *The New Essence of Christianity*, Darton, Longman & Todd 1966, p. 55.

10. See above, p. 6.

11. See above, pp. 5–6.

12. See above, p. 6.

13. Quoted by F. H. Bradley, *Appearance and Reality*, Oxford University Press 1893, p. 396. He does not state the source.

14. P. Teilhard de Chardin, *Hymn of the Universe*, ET Fontana Books 1970, p. 64.

15. Leibniz, op. cit., p. 235.

16. K. Jaspers, *The Perennial Scope of Philosophy*, ET Routledge 1950, pp. 17–18.

17. Matt. 17. 20.

18. Küng, *Does God Exist?*, p. 445.

19. Brand Blanshard, *Reason and Belief*, Allen and Unwin 1974, p. 9.

20. Charles Hartshorne and William L. Reese, eds., *Philosophers Speak of God*, University of Chicago Press 1953, p. 137.

Index